The Meaning of Race

The Meaning of Race

Race, History and Culture in Western Society

Kenan Malik

MACMILLAN

First published 1996 by
MACMILLAN PRESS LTD
Houndmills, Basingstoke, Hampshire RG21 6XS
and London
Companies and representatives
throughout the world

ISBN 0–333–62857–8 hardcover
ISBN 0–333–62858–6 paperback

A catalogue record for this book is available
from the British Library.

10 9 8 7 6 5 4 3 2 1
05 04 03 02 01 00 99 98 97 96

Printed in Great Britain
by T. J. Press Ltd., Padstow, Cornwall

Contents

Acknowledgements   vii

Introduction   1

1 Beyond the Liberal Hour   9

The Unmaking of Consensus   11
The Making of Consensus   13
The Meaning of the 'Liberal Hour' in Britain   19
Immigration and Assimilation in French Political Debate   26
Race and the Collapse of Consensus   29

2 The Social Limits to Equality   38

Race and the Enlightenment   39
Human Nature and Human Difference in Enlightenment
Discourse   43
Equality and Social Conflict   55
Equality, Slavery and Private Property   61
The Social Limits to Equality   68

3 The Making of a Discourse of Race   71

Romanticism, Particularism and Race   73
Race in the Post-Enlightenment World   79
From Romantic Reaction to Scientific Racism   84
Race and Class in Victorian England   91

4 Race in the Age of Democracy   101

The Fear of the Masses   104
Degeneration and Racial Planning   109
Race, Imperialism and Democracy   114
Race, Science and Politics   119
Race and the Nazi Experience   123

5 Race, Culture and Nationhood   128

'What is a Nation?'   130
Race, Culture and Nation   133

Culture as a Homologue of Race   140
From 'Many Men' to 'Many Worlds'   144

6 From Biological Hierarchy to Cultural Diversity   **149**

Franz Boas and the Remaking of the Culture Concept   150
The Ambiguity of the Culture Concept   156
Antihumanism and the Culture Concept   160
Lévi-Strauss and the Celebration of Inequality   163
The Meaning of Multiculturalism   169

7 Cultural Wars   **178**

Immigration, Assimilation and National History   183
Islam, Enlightenment and Citizenship   193
Élitism and the Underclass   198
The Bifurcated World   209

8 Universalism, Humanism and the Discourse of Race   **217**

The West and its 'Others'   220
Orientalism and Ahistoricism   227
Discourse, Power and Knowledge   230
Humanism, Colonialism and the Holocaust   236
Appearance, Essence and Equality   247

9 Equality and Emancipation   **260**

From the 'Right to be Equal' to the 'Right to be Different'   261
Transcending 'Race'   265

Notes and References   270

Bibliography   292

Index   304

Acknowledgements

All books are, to some extent at least, collective efforts. This is probably more true of this book than of most. *The Meaning of Race* is the product of almost a decade of discussion and debate with friends and colleagues, most of whom it would be impossibe to name in an acknowledgement such as this. I would like to thank in particular Frank Furedi, James Heartfield and Naseema Khan for their generosity with both their time and their ideas. Marek Kohn read early drafts of this book even as he was working on his own, *The Race Gallery*. Steve Jones, Robin Cohen and Farekh Ahmed all provided valuable comments on various chapters. Richard Ings was of great assistance with the French material. My thanks to them all.

Throughout the book I have borrowed freely from the work of various authors–Robert Miles' critique of the race relations paradigm, Maxim Silverman's analysis of race in French political discourse, Robin Blackburn's study of slavery, Eric Hobsbawm's history of nineteenth-century nationalism, Douglas Lorrimer's examination of race and class in Victorian England, Daniel Pick's investigation of the idea of degeneration, George Stocking's unearthing of the history of anthropology, Tzvetan Todorov's discussion of the relationship between universalism and particularism, Aijaz Ahmad's dissection of poststructuralism. Few of these authors — perhaps none of them–will agree with all my arguments in this book. I hope, however, that they will find in *The Meaning of Race* a useful addition to the discussion and debate around many of these themes.

Frances Arnold and Catherine Gray, my editors at the publishers, provided support and encouragement throughout the project.

Finally my thanks go to Kate Lowe, without whose loving companionship the writing of this book would have seemed so much more of a burden.

KENAN MALIK

Introduction

'All is race. There is no other truth.' So claimed Benjamin Disraeli in his novel *Tancred or The New Crusade*. In the late Victorian era race indeed did seem to be all. 'Scientific racism' claimed to have an explanation for everything from the cause of criminality to the nature of Britain's special destiny, from the origins of 'savage' people in Africa and Asia to the temper of class relations in Europe. Race explained the character of individuals, the structure of social communities and the fate of human societies.

Nearly a century later, the American historian Oscar Handlin, in his book *Race and Nationality in American Life*, was moved to ask 'What happened to race?'. Well might he have been perplexed. For more than a hundred years the racial make-up of the American nation had seemed of cardinal importance. Scientists, politicians, journalists – all had fiercely debated the impact of immigration on American 'racial stock', disputed the 'inferiority' or 'superiority' of different 'ethnic' groups and argued over the possibility of different 'races' being able to assimilate into a single nation. Yet in the 1950s, when Handlin was writing, historians, sociologists, biologists, even anthropologists seemed to have abandoned the concept of race. The experience of fascism and the Holocaust had drawn a dark veil over the once all-important debate. The term 'racism' entered the popular language for the first time in the interwar years; its increasingly widespread usage in the postwar period reflected the general moral distaste for defining, and discriminating between, people according to their biological attributes. In the postwar years, in intellectual and political discussion, the issue of race seemed to be taboo.

Today, both Disraeli and Handlin might find evidence for their respective views. Race seems to be both everywhere and nowhere. On the one hand there still exists a general abhorrence about discriminating between people according to their race. From the near-universal condemnation of 'ethnic cleansing' to the widespread support for legislation against racial discrimination, 'racism' is still regarded as a dirty word. Certainly only those on the fringes of society hold that one race is superior or inferior to another. And yet race seems to shape so much of our lives today. We continually categorise people according to their 'race' – Afro-Caribbean, white, Jewish. Discussions of culture, history or art often seem to centre around race – 'Asian culture', 'black history', 'African art'. Everything from criminality to the entrepreneurial spirit is given a racial connotation – witness the stereotypes of 'black muggers' or 'Asian shopkeepers'. Social policy on issues from adoption to education is discussed in relation to its impact on race. And race has become the central feature of contemporary political debate: from immigration panics to controversies over multicultural education, from debates about affirmative action to fears about the rise of fascism.

Western society seems to be repelled by the consequence of racial thinking yet forced to accept its importance. It is like someone who goes to watch a horror film. They know they will have to cover their eyes half way through, yet are drawn regardless to the cinema. The aim of this book is to explore the ambiguous and ambivalent relationship of Western society to the idea of 'race' both by examining its social meaning and by reconstructing its historical development.

One of the striking aspects of the study of race is that everyone 'knows' what a 'race' is, but no one can quite define it. Walter Bagehot's observation about a nation – 'We know what it is when you do not ask us, but we cannot very quickly explain or define it'[1] – applies equally to race. This is true even of those who consider themselves specialists in the field. 'Geneticists believe that anthropologists have decided what a race is. Ethnologists assume that their classifications embody principles which genetic science has proved to be correct. Politicians believe their prejudices have the sanction of genetic laws and the findings of physical anthropology to sustain them.[2] So wrote Lancelot Hogben, a leading opponent of scientific racism in the years before the Second World War. Hogben's sardonic observation seems equally apposite half a century later.

In popular language, 'race' is usually synonymous with 'colour'. We casually speak of Africans (or Afro-Caribbeans) as one race, Asians as another, Europeans or 'whites' as a third. Virtually everyone can distinguish between the physical characteristics of the major racial groups. Many even believe they can tell the difference between a Jew and a Gentile, or an Englishman and an Italian by physical appearance alone. This universal ability to distinguish between different human groups has given credence to the idea that races possess an objective reality.

This popular idea of race is buttressed by academic and political arguments. Much academic study continues to use the concept of race as both an analytical tool and an explanatory determinant. The paradigm of 'race relations' has been central to the academic study of race, particularly in Britain and the USA. When sociologists explain certain conflicts in society in terms of 'race relations' they suggest that it is the existence of different races in society that give rise to those conflicts. Even those who reject the race relations paradigm, from a radical or Marxist point of view, persist in using the idea of race in a manner that imputes to it an objective existence. In recent years the arguments of writers such as Robert Miles, who reject entirely the use of race as a sociological category, have gained ground. Nevertheless, traditional arguments about race dominate academic discourse.[3]

Despite this widespread usage of the term race, however, there has been precious little attempt to define the concept. In the absence of a clear definition, the concept of race in academic discourse has acquired by default the everyday meaning of the word. As Robert Miles has pointed out, while most academic writers 'deny that they are using the idea of "race" as if it referred to a biological hierarchy of fundamentally different groups of people', nevertheless 'the manner of their use of the notion commonly implies an acceptance of the existence of biological differences between human beings, differences which express the existence of distinct, self-reproducing groups'.[4]

The concept of 'race relations' is also a central feature of politics and law in many Western countries. British law, for instance, defines a 'race' or 'racial group' as 'a group of persons defined by reference to colour, race, nationality or ethnic or national origins'. Further, as Michael Banton notes, Britain's three Race Relations Acts suggest that 'each individual could be assigned to a race, and that relations between persons of different race were necessarily different from relations between persons of the same race.'[5] But this, as Miles points out, is a tautological argument: 'The definition is (necessarily) circular: a "race" is a group of people defined by "their race": this formulation assumes and legitimates as a reality that each human being "belongs" to a "race"'.[6]

In fact the legal definition of 'colour, race, nationality or ethnic or national origins', as accepted by both the House of Lords and the Court of Appeal in Britain, is based on the public definitions of these terms. In other words in legal and political, as in academic, discourse the concept of race is borrowed from everyday perceptions of differences and subsequently acts to legitimate as true the very definition on which it was based in the first place. This collapsing of perception and understanding can be seriously misleading. The sun appears to set and the moon appears to rise at night; we know that in reality neither actually happens. In the same way, the appearance that all human beings can be categorised by 'race' might seem seductively tangible but has no objective basis. Humanity is not like a Dulux colour chart with everyone falling into discrete categories, each with a unique name and character. Human beings are composed of a constellation of characteristics, physical and mental, which shade into each other. This point was recognised nearly

200 years ago by the naturalist Johann Friederich Blumenbach, the founder of modern anthropology:

> Although there seems to be so great a difference between widely separate nations, that you might easily take the inhabitants of the Cape of Good Hope, the Greenlanders and the Circassians for so many different species of man, yet when the matter is thoroughly considered, you see that all do so run into one another, and that one variety of mankind does so sensibly pass into another, that you cannot mark out the limits between them.[7]

This difficulty in defining a race was apparent even to those who, like Disraeli, considered that race was 'all'. William Ripley was a leading American anthropologist in the late nineteenth century whose division of Europeans into three distinct races was a cornerstone of Victorian racial theory. He was forced to admit, however, that there was no such thing as a pure race:

> No sooner have environmental influences, peculiar habits of life, and artificial selection commenced to generate distinct varieties of men from the common clay; no sooner has heredity set itself to perpetuate these; than chance, variation, migration, intermixture, and changing environments, with a host of minor dispersive factors, begin to efface this constructive work. Racial upbuilding and demolition, as we have said, have ever proceeded side by side. Never is the perfect type in view, while yet it is always possible.[8]

In recent years scientific research has demonstrated why anthropologists like Blumenbach and Ripley found it so difficult to define a 'race'. Geneticists have shown that 85 per cent of all genetic variation is between individuals within the same local population. A further 8 per cent is between local populations or groups within what is considered to be a major race. Just 7 per cent of genetic variation is between major races.[9]

What this means is that genetic variation between one Englishman and another, or between one Jamaican and another, can be nearly as great as the differences between a 'typical' Englishman and a 'typical' Jamaican. Every population is highly variable and whatever external physical signs there may be – such as skin colour – genetic features do not absolutely define one population and distinguish it from another. As geneticist Steve Jones has observed, 'modern genetics does in fact show that there are no separate groups within humanity (although there are noticeable differences among the peoples of the world)'.[10] Race exists only as a statistical correlation, not as an objective fact. The distinction we make between different races is not naturally given but is socially defined. As Blumenbach noted in his great work *The Varieties of Mankind*, 'very arbitrary indeed both in number and definition have been the varieties of mankind accepted by eminent men.' Nevertheless, he added, 'it will be found serviceable to the memory to have constituted certain classes into which the men of our planet may be divided'.[11] In other words, the division of humankind into discrete groups is entirely man-made. What is important is, as Robert Miles has noted, the process of *signification*, whereby certain features, and only certain ones, are chosen to convey meaning:

> In Europe, North America, and Australasia, the idea of 'race' is now usually (although not exclusively) employed to differentiate collectivities distinguished by skin colour, so that 'races' are either 'black' or 'white' but never 'big-eared' or 'small-eared'. The fact that only certain physical characteristics are signified to define 'races' in specific circumstances indicates that we are investigating not a given, natural division of the world's population, but the application of historically and culturally specific meanings to the totality of human physiological variation.[12]

There is nothing in human biology which suggests that skin colour should be the basis on which we divide humanity. '[C]lassification of mankind in geographical units defined by skin colour or headform', observed Lancelot Hogben more than half a century ago, 'would lead to a very different system from that based on hair texture or nasal index'.[13] The pattern of variation in one set of genes – say skin colour – is independent of that in another – blood group, enzyme or headform. The fact that we use certain physical characteristics – such as skin colour – to define a race but ignore others – such as hair texture – shows that the creation of a race is the product of social need, not biological fact.

We do not define races because biological data compels us so to do. Rather society begins with an a priori division of humanity into different races for which it subsequently finds a rationale in certain physical characteristics. As a result what constitutes a 'race' has changed quite dramatically over the past two hundred years, according to the particular needs of society at the time. If a Martian were to land on Earth it is unlikely that he would be able to distinguish between races in the fashion that we do. If he thought it necessary to divide human beings into discrete groups, it is quite possible that the boundaries of his divisions would be very different from ours.

The clue to the importance of race in Western thought, therefore, lies not in biology but in society. Racial theories are an expression of the way that a particular society views humanity, and in particular views the relationship between humanity, nature and society. When we meet a fellow human being there are a variety of ways we can respond. 'One could marvel at his fundamental likeness to oneself', George Stocking, an eminent historian of anthropology, has observed, 'or one could gasp at his immediately striking differences. One could regard these differences as of degree or of kind, as products of changing environment or of immutable heredity, as dynamic or static, as relative or absolute, as inconsequential or hierarchical.'[14] At different times Western society has regarded fellow human beings from other societies in each of these ways. The fact that in modern Western society the differences are paramount – and that these differences are codified as 'racial' – tells more about the society in which we live than it does about human nature.

To understand race, then, requires us to investigate how the understanding of that relationship between humanity, society and nature is socially and historically constructed: how, for example, a society or an age understands the relationship between human differences and human similarities; what meaning it imputes to concepts such as equality, humanity or culture; and how, and why, such concepts and meanings evolve over time. That is what *The Meaning of Race* sets out to do.

There are three main themes in the book. The first is that the social meaning of race in modern society emerges from the contradiction between an ideological commitment to equality and the persistence of inequality as a practical reality. The modern world grew out of the dissolution of feudalism and the emergence of capitalism. Capitalist ideology, as embodied in the Enlightenment, expressed hostility to the parochial, irrational nature of feudalism and proclaimed a belief in human equality and a universal society. In practice, however, the particular forms of capitalist society placed limits on the expression of equality. Capitalism destroyed the parochialism of feudal society, but it created divisions anew; divisions, moreover, which seemed as permanent as the old feudal ones. As social divisions persisted and acquired the status of permanence, so these differences presented themselves as if they were natural. The conviction grew that inequality, whether within Western society or between the West and the non-Western world, was in the natural order of things.

The tendency to view social differences as natural became rationalised through the discourse of race. The concept of race emerged, therefore, as a means of reconciling the conflict between the ideology of equality and the reality of the persistence of inequality. Race accounted for social inequalities by attributing them to nature. Through this process the universalism of Enlightenment discourse became degraded into a particularist vision of the world. *The Meaning of Race* examines the social constraints on equality that led to the development of racial ideology, and follows the development of that ideology over the past two hundred years.

The second theme in the book is an examination of the different forms that racial ideology can take. In classical nineteenth-century racial theory ('scientific racism'), racial differences were seen exclusively in biological terms. The impact of Nazism discredited biological theories of race. But it did not destroy the underlying belief that humanity is divided into discrete groups, each defined in some manner by immutable and ahistoric characteristics, and that human interaction is determined by the nature of these immutable differences. Rather, the idea of difference was transposed on to the concept of culture. A key aspect of this book is an examination of the relationship between race and culture. I argue that both have common roots in the degradation of Enlightenment universalism, and that both are expressions of a particularist, relativist, antihumanist philosophy.

The third theme is an examination of the impact of the breakup of the postwar order and the end of the Cold War on racial ideology. What we are witnessing in contemporary society is not a 'rise' in racism – this, I argue, is an irrational concept – but the repoliticisation of the notion of racial difference. The pluralist, liberal outlook of the postwar years was predicated on the experience of Nazism and the *realpolitik* of the Cold War. The consequence was the depoliticisation of the issue of race. The breakdown of the postwar consensus and the end of the Cold War has made it both possible and necessary for race to reemerge as a political issue.

The structure of this book is designed to explore these themes in both a logical and a historical fashion. Chapter 1 probes the main contours of contemporary racial ideology and shows how the disintegration of the postwar order is leading to the racialisation of social discourse. By reexamining the nature of the postwar consensus on race, I show that even at the height of the 'liberal hour', attitudes to race remained ambiguous.

In Chapter 2, I explore the historical roots of that ambiguity by examining the nature of the social constraints on equality in capitalist society as it emerged out of feudalism. The chapter considers the conflict between the ideology of the Enlightenment and the forms of capitalist society. My key argument is that inequality is not the product of racial differences, but rather that the perception of racial difference arises out of the persistence of social inequality.

Chapters 3 and 4 look at the development of classical racial theory. Chapter 3 describes how the contradiction between the ideology of equality and the reality of an unequal society slowly degraded Enlightenment optimism and belief in universalism and gave rise to the discourse of race. Central to the argument here is the idea that race developed initially as a response to class differences within European society, and was only later applied to differences between Europeans and non-Europeans, and hence became marked by colour differences. Chapter 4 examines the impact on the concept of race of mass democracy, on the one hand, and of imperialism, on the other. It also examines how classical racial theory was discredited, largely through the political impact of Nazism. It was at this point that the concept 'racism' entered the modern vocabulary. I argue that moral condemnation of Nazism and racism did not destroy the belief in race but simply recast it in a different form.

The remainder of the book examines the new forms acquired by racial discourse, largely by considering the relationship between 'race' and 'culture'. Chapter 5 returns to the contradiction between the ideology of equality and the reality of an unequal society, this time to examine how the development of the nation state in the nineteenth century helped to degrade the Enlightenment belief in the 'universal rights of Man' and to recast the concept of culture as a homologue for race. In Chapter 6, I examine the role of anthropology in popularising a particularist, antihumanist conception of culture and show how such a concept of culture underlies contemporary visions of 'multiculturalism'. Having explored the historical development of the concept of race, and having established its social meaning in Western society, I return in Chapter 7 to contemporary forms of racial discourse. I re-examine many of the issues first raised in Chapter 1 to show how culture, not biology, now mediates racial ideology.

The final two chapters provide a critique of poststructuralist and postmodern theories of difference which have become the backbone of contemporary antiracist discourse. I argue that such theories of difference, just like Romantic concepts of race, inevitably preclude the possibility of an equal society. They are the product of disenchantment with the prospects for social change and symbolise the acceptance of inequality as an inevitable fact of society. The final section of Chapter 9 looks at the possibility of transcending the discourse of race. It may be an unpopular claim to make in these postmodern times, but the argument here, and one that is central to the whole conception of the book, is that only a universalist conception of humanity can provide the political and philosophical basis on which to build a struggle for equality.

1

Beyond the Liberal Hour

War is raging across Europe. Bombers are screaming down on ancient cities. The Balkans are again a powder keg to the world. Unemployment is soaring and hatred of minorities is being stirred up not only by Nazi thugs in Bremen and Cottbus but all over Europe. In France everyone from the Socialist prime minister to the neo-liberal opposition is talking about chartered planes to repatriate immigrants. The scene should be set in the past, in grainy black and white. Instead it is all in glorious technicolour on the evening news. The 1930s – never a favourite decade – are back to haunt us.[1]

So wrote commentator Geoff Mulgan in November 1991, exactly two years after the fall of the Berlin Wall. Back in November 1989, the television pictures of young East Berliners atop the Wall with pickaxes, hacking away at the tyranny that had imprisoned them for thirty years, seemed to capture the new spirit of freedom spreading through Europe. After a century during which the continent had been first ravaged by two world wars and then torn apart by the Cold War, the crumbling of the Wall suggested too a crumbling away of the past. It was, many wanted to believe, the birth of a new era of peace and prosperity in European affairs.

It has not turned out so. Far from ushering in an epoch of democracy and progress, the end of the Cold War seems to have paved the way for the resurrection of 'The Dark Side of Europe', to quote the title of a recent book about European fascism. On both sides of the old Iron Curtain, nationalism, ethnic rivalry and hostility to foreigners have become characteristic features of domestic politics. 'There are old hatreds with their roots long lost in the mists of nationalism and crudely drawn boundaries', one newspaper has sadly observed. 'There are newer and cruder hatreds of those drawn to the richer parts of Europe from the former Communist states and North Africa.'[2]

In Western Europe, race and immigration have become two of the most explosive issues on the political agenda. Far-right groups have made spectacular advances at the polls by playing on people's fears of an 'invasion' by refugees and immigrants. Every West European country has raised the drawbridge to asylum-seekers. Racial violence has become woven into the fabric of society. From firebombings of mosques in

Britain to desecration of Jewish cemeteries in France, from assaults on refugee hostels in Germany to harassment of African street traders in Italy, no part of Europe – and no section of the immigrant or black community – has escaped the ferment. The spectacle of Nazi skinheads on the march in Germany led *The Economist* to suggest that, 'One might get the impression that Germany, particularly its eastern half, is fast returning to the 1930s.'[3]

Events in Eastern Europe appear to confirm the view of a Europe trapped in the half-nelson of history. Violent conflict between Muslims and Serbs, Armenians and Azeris, Chechens and Russians are all suggestive of the revival of 'old hatreds'. Anti-Semitism has resurfaced, sometimes in a virulent form. Hostility to Gypsies is overt. For many the conflict in the former Yugoslavia has given expression to their worst fears. 'I grew up in the Europe that had defeated the Third Reich and I believed that the bullets need not always triumph', observed journalist Ed Vulliamy in a BBC documentary on the Bosnian conflict. 'The war in Bosnia has changed all that.'[4] The emotive imagery of 'concentration camps', 'cattle trucks' and 'ethnic cleansing' seems to suggest that the spirit of the Third Reich, far from having been defeated, still stalks the Continent. After half a century of peace, war in the Balkans has indeed revealed the dark side of Europe.

How can we explain Europe's seeming headlong plunge into the past? The answer that emerges from this book is that the ideals of equality, pluralism and mutual tolerance which are taken to be the hallmarks of the postwar consensus were in many ways a peculiarity of the period. A unique combination of political, social and economic factors – the repercussions of the Nazi experience, the *realpolitik* of the Cold War, and the impact of the postwar economic revival among them – helped produce an age in which darker trends were kept at bay. In the postwar era both the perceptions of racial issues and the reality of 'race relations' were transformed. There was a conscious effort on the part of all Western governments to depoliticise the issue of race and to remove it from the political agenda. The result was to give rise to half a century of seeming racial harmony.

Postwar liberalism was, however, less an indelible transformation in social consciousness than a temporary gap in history. Whatever the changes in the public discussion and treatment of the issue of race, the centrality of racial themes to Western social discourse was left untouched. It could not be otherwise because, as I shall argue in this book, the discourse of race lies at the very heart of modern society. The postwar era was an age of impermanence sustained by a number of developments that have over the past two decades slowly ebbed away. As the postwar order has crumbled, so race has been pushed firmly back on to the political agenda. The aim of this chapter is to sketch out the relationship between the discourse of race and broader political and social trends which have transformed the contemporary meaning of race.

THE UNMAKING OF CONSENSUS

Western society is undergoing a profound political, social and intellectual crisis, a crisis that has caused people to question many of the consensual values that characterised the postwar era. This crisis has raised serious doubts about traditional political arrangements and values. The major political developments of the past few years have exacerbated these trends. The end of the Cold War, the collapse of communism, the onset of recession, the disintegration of Third World states – all have helped to shatter the old world order and usher in a new era of uncertainty and doubt. It is in this context that we need to understand the meaning of contemporary racism.

The end of the Cold War which divided Europe has led to significant political and social changes in the West as well as in the East. It has undermined the mechanisms through which Western powers enforced co-operation internationally and maintained social stability at home. Postwar institutions, both international and domestic, were predicated on the Cold War. Organisations such as Nato, the World Bank and the International Monetary Fund were the creation of Cold War politics and were organised around East–West rivalry.

The Cold War was equally important in domestic politics. Anticommunism was the ideological glue that bound together society. The crusade against the 'Evil Empire' gave a sense of mission to Western societies and a coherence to their political institutions. Political parties from the Italian Christian Democrats to the Republicans in the USA defined themselves to a great extent through their opposition to communism.

The ending of the Cold War has created a moral and political vacuum in Western countries. The crumbling of the postwar order has acted as a catalyst bringing to the surface many of the political and social insecurities facing Western societies. The political certainties of the past no longer seem valid and, as a result, the traditional parties of left, right and centre have been badly disorientated.

Most spectacular has been the collapse of the left. The demise of Stalinism in the East has helped to discredit leftwing ideas in the West and has brought into sharp focus long-standing disenchantment with policies of state intervention, welfarism and Keynesian economics. The validity of leftwing prescriptions to society's ills has been called into question, as has the possibility of creating any alternative to capitalism. This, together with the defeat of many trade union and working class

struggles, has undermined people's belief in collective action and social
change. Electorally, both Communist and socialist parties throughout the West have collapsed, and organisationally many have disintegrated.

This demise of the left has, until recently, camouflaged an equally
dramatic development – the collapse of the postwar right. The end of the
Cold War has had as corrosive an effect on the institutions of the governing classes as it has had on those of the labour movement. Most élite
institutions and rightwing parties are as much the product of the postwar consensus as Keynesianism and welfarism. The Second World War
destroyed most of the prewar conservative movements because of their
association with the Nazis. After 1945 conservative parties had to be
rebuilt from scratch – most notably the Christian Democratic Parties in
Germany and Italy. These postwar parties were not of the same mould as
the prewar right, and were shaped very much by the prevailing liberal
ethos of the time. The erosion of the postwar consensus has therefore
been as destructive on the right as on the left. From the disintegration of
the Christian Democrats in Italy to the discord and dissent that wracks
the British Conservative Party to the humiliation of the Republicans in
the American presidential election of 1992 – the first to take place after
the fall of the Berlin Wall – the established right appears to be as crisis-
ridden as the left.

Western society feels ill at ease with its politicians, its institutions, its
governmental policies, its social values. There is in society a lack of
vision, an absence of purpose, a failure of will. We live in an age in which
there is, to borrow a phrase from a Robert Frost poem, 'nothing to look
back to with pride/And nothing to look forward to with hope'. The
liberalism that permeated postwar society has all but ebbed away.

The most pervasive mood today is that of disenchantment. This sense
of disenchantment has been exacerbated by the economic crisis which
seems to suggest that politicians have no answer to the problems which
most people face. The ideologies that bound together or gave a sense of
purpose to society have either collapsed or lost their credibility. Alternative ideologies have been discredited. The old bonds that held society
together are dissolving. New ones have yet to be forged. The manner in
which the political and social changes of the past period have undermined the legitimacy of traditional political values without replacing
them with a cogent alternative has, as the *Financial Times* noted, fuelled
the growth of reaction:

> The most significant common factor behind the rightward swing has
> been the growing belief that the mainstream parties are impotent, out
> of touch and in at least some cases corrupt as well. In France, Germany,
> the Netherlands, Belgium and Austria – the principal countries where

the ultra-right has made the headlines – disenchantment with the parties in power has been combined with the feeling that the mainline opposition offers few genuine alternatives.

The breakdown of the postwar consensus has swept away the rules which governed social discourse over the past half-century. Like an orchestra without a conductor, society is becoming more discordant. At the same time themes and attitudes that had previously been considered unacceptable are no longer seen as illegitimate. This is most noticeable on the issue of race, where the discrediting of postwar liberalism has removed many of the taboos against racism that had existed in the postwar world.

The crumbling of the postwar consensus has dislocated the political centre to the right and weakened the purchase of liberal sentiments in Western societies. The weakening of liberalism has in turn allowed right-wing politics to take a much more assertive and reactionary form. Less constrained by the consensual arguments that held sway through the postwar years, rightwing politicians feel more confident about being openly racist and chauvinist.

The key feature of contemporary racism, then, is the erosion of the constraints that characterised the postwar era, at a time when wide-spread disenchantment with traditional political arrangements is combined with the lack of any alternative. To understand this better we need to look more closely at the nature of the postwar consensus and at the reasons for its demise.

THE MAKING OF CONSENSUS

The politics of the postwar era was shaped very much by the experience of the interwar years. Two world wars, Depression, fascism and the Holocaust made very poor advertisements for the capitalist system. It may be difficult to comprehend now, but in the thirties and forties the idea that the free market system was responsible for the ills of the world was widespread. Not simply radicals, but wide swathes of society, including virtually the whole of the intelligentsia, blamed capitalism, at least in part, for economic crisis, genocide and war.

The experience of the interwar years created profound disillusionment with the tenets of unrestrained capitalism. By the late 1930s, observes one study of the intellectual crisis in the West, 'there was an intellectual consensus, which had the support of virtually the entire ideological spectrum, that the notion of a free market capitalism was not sustainable'.[5]

Traditional capitalist ideas were so discredited that the ruling élite in the West was forced to abandon its attachment to free market policies and effect a compromise with the ideas of social democracy – state intervention, Keynesian economics, welfare reform. Such a programme was advocated not simply by liberals and radicals, but by conservatives too. Future British Conservative prime minister Harold Macmillan observed that 'planning is forced upon us . . . not for idealistic reasons but because the old mechanism which served us when markets were expanding naturally and spontaneously is no longer adequate when the tendency is in the opposite direction'.[6]

The experience of fascism and the Holocaust also discredited many of the ideological beliefs of the right. As Frank Furedi has observed, 'Nationalism, race, Western superiority, imperialism: virtually the entire political vocabulary of the right was put under scrutiny'.[7] The collaboration of so many conservative parties with the fascists discredited the whole conservative project. In the postwar period, American sociologist Daniel Bell notes, conservative thinkers were exiled to the margins:

> Since World War Two had the character of a 'just war' against fascism, rightwing ideologies and the intellectual and cultural figures associated with those causes, were inevitably discredited. After the preponderant reactionary influence in prewar European culture, no single rightwing figure retained any political credibility or influence.[8]

The marginalisation of conservative thought as a result of the experience of fascism established liberalism as the dominant viewpoint in the postwar years. The general perception of the postwar liberal consensus is that it was the product of the positive features of those years – economic prosperity, full employment, strong American leadership. Certainly these factors were important in establishing the conditions in which postwar liberalism could flourish. The overriding causes giving rise to the liberal consensus were, however, negative ones – the experience of mass unemployment, fascism, the Holocaust and war. Postwar social consciousness was shaped largely by the need not to be tainted by the political culture of prewar Europe.

We can see the importance of the negative experience of the thirties and forties when we consider postwar attitudes to racial matters. Prior to the Second World War, ideas of racial inferiority and superiority had been accepted as common-sense. When British eugenicist Karl Pearson wrote that, 'History shows me one way, and one way only, in which a state of civilisation has been produced, namely the struggle of race with race and the survival of the physically and mentally fitter race',[9] he was voicing a commonly accepted view. American president Theodore Roosevelt echoed Pearson's prejudices in justifying imperial expansion from a racial point of view:

The most ultimately righteous of all wars is a war with savages though it is apt to be also the most terrible and inhuman. The rude, fierce settler who drives the savage from the land lays all civilised mankind under a debt to him. American and Indian, Boer and Zulu, Cossack and Tartar, New Zealander and Maori – in each case the victor, horrible though many of his deeds are, has laid deep the foundations for the future greatness of a mighty people. The consequences of struggles for territory between civilised nations seem small by comparison.[10]

After the death camps and the Final Solution, the consequences no longer seemed so small by comparison. The Second World War helped rip away from racial conflict the cover of righteousness. 'The great and terrible war' acknowledged an international conference in 1945, 'was a war made possible by the denial of democratic principles of the dignity, equality and mutual respect for men, and by the propagation in their place, through ignorance and prejudice, of the doctrine of inequality of men and races.'[11]

It is instructive to compare the responses of the Western powers to the idea of racial equality in 1918 and in 1945. When, after the First World War, Japan attempted to include in the founding charter of the League of Nations a statement in support of racial equality, its efforts were brusquely dismissed by Western delegations. Western diplomats, wrote one contemporary observer, 'had neither time nor thought' for such matters.[12] It was a very different story after the Second World War. The ideas of racial equality, national sovereignty and self-determination were at the heart of the project of the United Nations. Not only did the UN promote these ideals through its charter, but Unesco sponsored a huge international scientific project to disprove the claims of racial science. Social scientists and biologists met on four occasions (1949, 1951, 1964 and 1967) to pool available knowledge on the idea of race. They concluded: 'For all practical social purposes "race" is not so much a biological phenomenon as a social myth. The myth of "race" has created an enormous amount of human and social damage.'[13] The experience of the Holocaust had transformed racial discourse. The very idea of race, which had been central to Western society for a century and more, was now officially consigned to being a 'myth'.

It was not simply the horrors of Nazi Germany that induced a change of heart on the part of the Western powers. The impact of the Cold War was equally potent in forcing the Western élite to reassess its ideas about race. For the Soviet Union race was a powerful weapon in its struggle with the West. 'The ideas of racial and national inequality', *Pravda* declared, 'find concrete expression in the policy which capitalistic governments adopt in connection with colonial and dependent peoples and

with minorities within parent countries.' *Pravda* singled out America for
particular censure:

> [T]he constitution of the USA guarantees to all citizens equal rights
> before the law; however, the Negro population, consisting of 13 000 000
> people, actually does not have these rights. Racial discrimination con-
> tinues to exist in all its forms and in all branches of the economy and
> culture of the country.

In contrast, claimed *Pravda*, the Soviet Union was free from racism:

> Only the Soviet Socialist government has constantly fought for real
> freedom, independence and equality of all peoples – large and small.
> Only in the USSR has real equality of free peoples, real friendship of
> peoples, free from all forms of exploitation, of national subjugation
> and racial discrimination been established.[14]

There was, of course, no truth to the claims for the Soviet Union's racial
policy. But that the West should take such claims seriously was itself an
indication of Western sensitivity on this issue. Soviet criticism was effective because race was the West's Achilles' heel. 'The foreign policy of a
nation, particularly a nation that does not rely upon possible military
aggression as a dominant influence', warned US Secretary of State
George C. Marshall, 'depends for most of its effectiveness on the moral
influence which that nation exerts throughout the world. The moral
influence of the United States is weakened to the extent that the civil
rights proclaimed by our Constitution are not fully confirmed in actual
practice.'[15]

Racism was a problem because it undermined the West's moral authority in the world. Many feared that Soviet propaganda in support of
equal rights and self-determination would allow Moscow to increase its
influence in the Third World. 'Ever since Lenin', warned the British
Spectator in 1957, 'Communists have recognised that the easiest way to
attack capitalist states was through their colonies – first by supporting
nationalist movements and then by organising a take-over of the local
party. The greatest successes of Communism since the war have been
gained among people susceptible to the rallying call against colonialism.'[16]

Western governments became obsessed with the potential that existed
for the Soviet Union to exploit the race issue. To forestall the extension of
communist influence, Western politicians recognised that they too
would have to clean up their image. In Britain the transformation of
Empire to Commonwealth was seen as the key in establishing harmonious relations with the Third World, a view staunchly promoted by the
conservative *Spectator*:

What makes the importance of the Commonwealth is its moral status in the world, and that moral status is very largely due to its being the only Western political organisation to throw a bridge between the European people and their ex-subjects of Africa and Asia. The Commonwealth is the only Western answer so far produced to the Soviet 'nationalities' policy, that masterstroke of Lenin's which gave Russia a flying start in dealing with peoples emerging from colonialism.[17]

'One consequence of this' the *Spectator* observed, 'is that we must strive at all costs to keep the multiracial character of the Commonwealth.' Meanwhile in America there were strenuous attempts to overturn Jim Crow laws in the South, end segregation and introduce civil rights legislation. 'The external pressure from the Cold War', one historian has observed, 'now began to play a monumental role in creating a new beginning for human equality in US politics. Just as the Nazi experience had turned the mirror toward US racial discrimination, so now the Soviet campaign held up a magnifying glass and invited the rest of the world to look through and see the United States at its worst.'[18]

President Harry Truman set up a Committee on Civil Rights which reported in 1947. 'Throughout the Pacific, Latin America, Africa, the Near, Middle and Far East', the report warned, 'the treatment which our Negroes receive is taken as a reflection of our attitude toward all dark-skinned peoples' and played 'into the hands of Communist propagandists'. To restore America to the moral high ground the report called for the prohibition of state restrictions on the black electoral franchise, a federal law against lynching, an end to segregation in housing and education, a fair employment act prohibiting discrimination and a denial of federal aid to those states that refused to comply. The ultimate goal, argued the report, must be 'the elimination of segregation based upon race, colour, creed, or national origin from American life.'[19]

The combination of the Nazi legacy and the *realpolitik* of the Cold War established a consensus across the ideological spectrum which espoused support for decolonisation and self-determination for Third World countries, opposition to colour bars and racial discrimination and a belief in equality and a pluralist political system. Virtually every Western nation condemned South African apartheid. Many introduced legislation to outlaw racial discrimination. Some, like Britain and the USA, established a whole official infrastructure to ease the problems created by the race question.

To what extent did these postwar changes transform the perception of race and the nature of race relations in Western society? The answer to that question is crucial to an understanding of contemporary racism. It is not, however, a straightforward answer. The legacy of the postwar period is an ambiguous one, an ambiguity which expresses some of the contradictions inherent in the relationship of modern Western society to the issue of race.

We can understand these contradictions better if we examine the impact of Britain's postwar race relations policy. Britain's approach is often cited as a model of liberal race relations. The passage of Britain's three Race Relations Acts in 1965, 1968 and 1976 respectively is widely seen as presaging the 'liberal hour' in British politics.[20] Michael Banton has written of the race relations laws that they 'were a recognition that racial harmony is a public good', while Ira Katznelson has described the legislation as the high-water mark of the two-party consensus to depoliticise the issue of race.[21] It was the moment, so the traditional account goes, when the British élite took a moral stand in favour of racial equality by enacting legislation to promote it in a positive fashion.

The three Race Relations Acts, however, were not enacted in isolation. They were part of a package of measures to deal with the 'problem' of race in the postwar period. Legislation outlawing racial discrimination went hand-in-hand with legislation restricting immigration, the aim of which was specifically to control the influx of black immigrants from the Commonwealth. These restrictions included the 1962 Commonwealth Immigrants Act (Britain's first postwar immigration law), the 1968 Commonwealth Immigrants Act, the 1969 Immigration Appeals Act and the 1971 Immigration Act. If the Race Relations Acts signified an ambition to promote racial harmony, equality and tolerance, immigration controls seemed to symbolise a continuing desire to assert racial difference. Roy Hattersley's famous aphorism, that 'Without limitation integration is impossible, without integration limitation is inexcusable', pithily summed up the interwoven nature of immigration law and race relations legislation.

The link between immigration control and race relations legislation expressed the contradictions of postwar liberalism. The acceptance of a liberal consensus on race did not mean that the ruling élite was any less racist than previously. Just as Harold Macmillan had noted that support for planning did not arise for 'idealistic reasons' but was simply a pragmatic response to the problems facing society, so belief in equality and pluralism did not evince an ideological conversion but was simply a survival strategy. The élite recognised that the experience of fascism and the consequences of the Cold War meant that the overt expression of racism was not politically acceptable.

In private, however, views had changed little. 'Prison for the strikers,/ Bring back the cat,/Kick out the niggers,/How about that?' That little piece of doggerel was penned in 1970 by Philip Larkin, one of Britain's most respected and acclaimed poets of the postwar generation. The publication of Larkin's letters in 1992 created outrage as they opened the door into a private world of racism, misogyny and bigotry.[22] The man described as 'the best loved poet of his generation', whose work struck 'a chord of sympathetic response in every English reader' and who had the 'capacity to create a recognisable and democratic vision of contemporary society'[23] was revealed to have instead nothing but contempt and hatred for what he considered the 'lower orders'.

The contrast between the civility of Larkin's poetry and the bigotry of his private letters sums up the contradictions of the postwar outlook. It revealed a ruling élite seemingly sanguine about the granting of equality but privately seething about the compromises it had been forced to make. We can see this more clearly if we follow the debate on immigration that took place in Britain in the years following the Second World War.

THE MEANING OF THE 'LIBERAL HOUR' IN BRITAIN

On 22 June 1948 the SS *Empire Windrush*, with 492 Jamaicans on board, docked at Tilbury, in east London. It was the first large-scale arrival in Britain of West Indians in the postwar period.

Eleven Labour MPs immediately wrote to the prime minister, Clement Attlee, bringing to his notice 'the fact that several hundred West Indians have arrived in this country trusting that our government will provide them with food, shelter and employment'. The MPs feared that 'their success might encourage other British subjects to follow their example', turning Britain into 'an open reception centre for immigration not selected in relation to health, education and training and above all regardless of whether assimilation was possible or not.' As far as they were concerned, assimilation was not possible, because 'An influx of coloured people domiciled here is likely to impair the harmony, strength and cohesion of our public and social life and cause discord and unhappiness among all concerned.'[24] Attlee responded that 'if our policy [of unrestricted immigration] were to result in a great influx of undesirables we might, however unwillingly, have to consider modifying it.'[25]

In this exchange are contained many of the assumptions that have shaped both official and popular attitudes to postwar immigration from the colonies. There are two kinds of British citizens: white people and 'undesirables'. Britain is in danger of being swamped by immigrants taking advantage of the nation's generosity. Immigrant standards of 'health, education and training' are lower than those of British people. Black people are incapable of assimilating British culture. A large black presence in Britain would create social tensions.

These arguments appeared again and again in official reports and confidential memos. As early as 1946, Labour Home Secretary Chuter Ede told a cabinet committee that he would be much happier if immigration 'could be limited to entrants from the Western countries, whose traditions and social backgrounds were more nearly equal to our own'.[26] In 1949 the Royal Commission on the British Population warned that, 'Immigration on a large scale to a fully established society like ours would only be welcomed without reserve if the immigrants were of good stock and not prevented by their religion and race from intermarrying with the host population and becoming merged with it.' It added that 'the sources of supply of suitable immigrants for Great Britain are limited, as is also the capacity of a fully established society like ours to absorb immigrants of an alien race and religion'.[27]

In 1950 the Labour cabinet set up a secret committee to review 'the further means which might be adopted to check the immigration into this country of coloured people from British Colonial Territories.'[28] Three years later the Conservative administration reconvened a civil service interdepartmental working group, first set up by the previous Labour government, to give consideration to the 'problem' of controlling colonial immigration. In 1955 prime minister Anthony Eden set up a committee of ministers

> to consider what form legislation should take, if it were to be decided that legislation to control entry into the United Kingdom of British subjects from overseas should be introduced; to consider also the intended effect of such legislation upon actual immigration, how any such control would be justified to Parliament and to the public, and the Commonwealth countries concerned.[29]

Why was the government so concerned to stem black immigration? A Cabinet minute from 1955 sums up the fears of the British élite: 'If immigration from the colonies and, for that matter, from India and Pakistan were allowed to continue unchecked, there was a real danger that over the years there would be a significant change in the racial character of the English people.'[30] And why was the government so concerned to maintain Britain's racial purity? Because, as the Colonial Office argued, 'a large coloured community as a noticeable feature of our social life would weaken . . . the concept of England or Britain to which people of British stock throughout the Commonwealth are attached.'[31]

For the British élite, its sense of self and identity was mediated through the concept of race. Britishness was a racial concept and large-scale migration from the colonies threatened to disrupt the racialised sense of national identity. Why it was necessary for the élite to conceive of its identity in racial terms we shall consider in the coming chapters. What is important here is to note the continuing central significance of race to élite discourse in the postwar period. Whatever transformation the Nazi experience may have wrought, it did not dislodge the absolute certainty within the élite that only through race could it understand itself and its relationship to the outside world.

But if the government feared the impact of black immigration upon the 'racial character' of the British people, it was equally fearful of taking any action to stem such immigration. There was a widespread recognition within ruling circles that while any controls on immigration had to be racial in form, the government could not be seen as openly espousing discriminatory controls. The 1950 secret Cabinet committee investigating the possibility of controls made clear the dilemma:

> Any solution depending on an apparent or concealed colour test would be so invidious as to make it impossible for adoption ... Nevertheless, the use of any powers taken to restrict the free entry of British subjects to this country would, as a general rule, be more or less confined to coloured persons.[32]

Four years later the Conservative secretary of state for Commonwealth relations made much the same point:

> I appreciate the force of the contention that, if we are to legislate for restrictions on the entry of British subjects and their employment here, the legislation should be non-discriminatory in form. This will not, however, conceal the fact that the problem with which we are in fact concerned is that of coloured immigration from colonial territories.[33]

The British government realised that to introduce discriminatory immigration controls would have caused moral outrage at home and abroad and undermined Britain's standing in the world. In the changed realities of the post-Nazi world, discriminatory immigration laws were as repellent as the existence of 'colour bars'. In particular discriminatory controls would have angered Britain's former colonies and existing colonies preparing for independence. At a time when the Commonwealth was still important as a symbol of Britain's global reach and as a bulwark against encroaching Soviet influence, such a policy seemed unthinkable.

The government therefore largely kept its racial fears private. In public ministers constantly reiterated their support for freedom of movement and for racial equality. In 1954 Henry Hopkinson, the minister of state for colonial affairs, praised Britain's open door policy:

> In a world in which restrictions on personal movement and immigration have increased we still take pride in the fact that a man can say *civis Britannicus sum* whatever his colour may be, and we can take pride in the fact that he wants and can come to the Mother country.[34]

Not only were government ministers careful to stress their commitment
to a non-discriminatory policy but they were determined to ensure
that their secret deliberations about controls were not publicly aired.
Prime minister Anthony Eden, at the same time as he set up a secret
Cabinet committee in November 1955 to investigate the possibility of
immigration controls, told parliament that no such controls were being
envisaged.[35]

The characteristic feature of the fifties was in fact the lack of any
discussion of domestic race relations. Compared to the following decades neither the press, nor indeed the public, appeared too concerned
with the question of immigration. True, certain politicians continually
raised the immigration question from a racial point of view and openly
called for racist controls. Prominent among them was the Conservative
MP Cyril Osborne, who claimed that 'Britain is a white man's country
and I want it to remain so'.[36] But such voices were isolated. They made
very little headway in changing public policy and were treated with
disdain by politicians on both sides of the House. By and large, Britain's
opinion formers tried to deal with the difficulties posed by the issue of
race by ignoring it.

The event that helped transform the domestic discussion on race issues
was the Notting Hill riots of August 1958.[37] Over a period of days large
mobs of white youths chased and attacked West Indian residents in
Notting Hill, west London. There were two immediate responses to the
riots. There was first a condemnation of the 'criminal minority' within
the white population who perpetrated the acts. 'You are a minute and
insignificant section of the population who have brought shame on the
district in which you live and have filled the whole nation with horror,
indignation and disgust', the judge, Justice Salmon, told the nine youths
convicted of assault during the disturbances. 'Everyone, irrespective of
the colour of their skin, is entitled to walk our streets erect and free from
fear.'[38]

Alongside such condemnation there were fears that uncontrolled immigration had created a volatile 'race relations' situation in Britain. Local
Labour MP George Rogers spoke for many when he claimed that West
Indians had 'made no attempt to adapt themselves to the way of life
here':

> The government must introduce legislation quickly to end the tremen-
> dous influx of coloured people from the Commonwealth ... Over-
> crowding has fostered vice, drugs, prostitution and the use of knives.
> For years white people have been tolerant. Now their tempers are up.[39]

For the first time, the government felt capable of openly admitting that
it had 'for some time been examining the result of this country's

time-honoured practice to allow free entry of immigrants from Commonwealth and colonial countries.' The statement added that 'while this study of major policy and its implications and effects on employment will continue, Her Majesty's Government do not think it right to take long-term decisions, except after careful consideration as a whole.'[40]

The Notting Hill riots helped make domestic race relations a political issue and allowed the government to speak openly of the possibility of immigration controls. But we should not overestimate its public impact. During the general election the following year, for example, the issue of race barely figured, while the anti-immigration candidate Oswald Mosley lost his deposit when he stood in Notting Hill. It would be another three years before the government felt compelled, and able, to introduce Britain's first postwar immigration law, the 1962 Commonwealth Immigrants Act.

The main impact of the riots was to embolden those within the élite, like Cyril Osborne, who had argued that the creation of a multiracial Britain was a grave mistake, and to tip the balance of argument towards the need for controls. A number of trends were already taking the government in that direction – the reduced importance of the Commonwealth, the forging of closer links with Europe and the desire to enter the European Economic Community, a more balanced assessment of the problem created by the Soviet Union and the reduced need for foreign labour. In the context of these developments, the debate around the Notting Hill riots helped push the élite towards the implementation of immigration controls.

The 1962 Act removed the automatic right of British citizens from the Commonwealth or the colonies to enter Britain. They could do so only if they possessed an employment voucher, were a dependant of someone already living in Britain, or were a student. The Act appeared to be non-racial. Not only did it apply to all British citizens with passports issued by Commonwealth or colonial governments, but it appeared to relate the rate of immigration to the availability of jobs in Britain.

In fact what impelled Britain to enact the 1962 Immigrants Act – and subsequent immigration legislation – were not economic factors but social and political ones. Britain had experienced an economic slowdown at the end of the fifties, but the economy still required extra labour. As Labour's Richard Crossman wrote in his diaries in 1966 'We have become illiberal and lowered quotas at a time when we have an acute shortage of labour'.[41] The future Labour home secretary Roy Jenkins admitted that 'the social factor' was 'more restrictive than the economic' in forcing the government to contain immigration.[42] That immigration controls were introduced for social, not economic, reasons is underlined by the fact that, while there was constant clamour for a stop to black immigration, there was no attempt to staunch the much larger flow of immigrants from Ireland.

But if social factors drove the government to impose controls, it was politically important to present such controls as a rational response to economic problems. Britain could not be seen openly advocating, or implementing, discriminatory laws. Tying immigration to job availability was a means of camouflaging the political and social needs driving the government to introduce controls.

The sensitivity of the élite to the race question became apparent every time the racial arguments for immigration control appeared too close to the surface. A good illustration is the 1968 Immigration Act. The 1968 Act is probably the most openly racist piece of legislation in Britain's post-war history. Rushed through parliament in three days by a Labour government, its sole aim was to prevent Kenyan Asians with British passports, expelled from Kenya, from entering Britain. It drew widespread criticism. Auberon Waugh, writing in the *Spectator*, described the Act as 'one of the most immoral pieces of legislation to have emerged from any British parliament,[43] while *The Times* commented: 'The Labour Party has a new ideology. It does not any longer profess to believe in the equality of man. It does not even believe in the equality of British citizens. It believes in the equality of white British citizens.'[44]

These attacks were partly motivated by party political reasons, Conservative sympathisers seeing the Act as a useful stick with which to beat a beleaguered Labour administration. But the criticisms were more than just that. The vehemence of the attack from the right on the 1968 Act illustrates the strength of the desire to be seen as champions of equality. Such critics had no objections to the idea of immigration controls: most were fierce advocates of the need for tighter controls; few would have quarrelled with the idea that it was black immigration that above all needed limiting. But all fervently believed that Britain could not afford to lose the moral high ground on the issue of racial equality.

It is in this context that we have to understand the 'liberal hour'. Shaken by the experience of fascism, postwar Western society adopted a pluralistic outlook and hoped to keep the issue of race off the political agenda. But a powerful undertow ensured that race, and immigration in particular, resurfaced as a political issue. The race relations legislation of the sixties was a response to the politicisation of race, and in particular to the imposition of immigration controls. The race relations laws aimed to bolster Britain's moral authority at a time when immigrations laws threatened to undermine it. They successfully promoted the idea of a tolerant, 'multicultural', pluralistic nation which was determined to stamp out any trace of discriminatory practice based on racial or ethnic difference.

At the same time the linking of controls and integration helped separate the economic and social arguments about immigration. On the one hand, it suggested that immigration controls had to be introduced for economic reasons; on the other, it implied that the presence of immigrants created social problems which required government intervention to ensure integration. In this way immigration controls were saved from the taint of racism while the problem of inequality was transformed from one of a racist society to one of the inability of immigrants to integrate. This reposing of the problem would play an important role in helping to recast the idea of race in the seventies and eighties. The race relations legislation was therefore not simply a product of the postwar liberal consensus on race, but was at the same time a product of the unravelling of that consensus.

The liberal hour was ambiguous in a further sense too. Not only was the race relations legislation of the sixties a response to the politicisation of race, it was itself a factor in racialising political discourse. As Robert Miles and Annie Phizacklea have observed, by framing the problem as one of 'race relations', policy-makers ensured that immigration was seen in racial terms: 'By legislating for race relations instead of against racism, the government was giving further substance to the idea of "race", ensuring that the problem was seen in terms of "colour", in terms of "them".'[45]

Because the problem was presented as one of relations between 'races', the legislation helped give credence to the idea that the difficulties arose from the presence of an 'alien wedge' in British society. The problem stemmed from the 'difference' of immigrants. Time and again politicians and official reports stressed the need for immigrants to integrate, and the dangers that existed if they failed to do so:

A separate racial community in our midst would be contrary to the English way of life and the only satisfactory longterm solution must be that immigrant pupils, many of whom are drawn from the Commonwealth, should be merged in the general community.[46]

The presence in this country of nearly a million immigrants from the Commonwealth with different social and cultural backgrounds raises a number of problems and creates various social tensions.[47]

The problem arises quite simply from the arrival in this country of many people of wholly alien cultures, habits and outlooks.[48]

By presenting the problem of equality as one of integration, the liberals recast the issue of race in a fashion that, as we shall see, was very important for racial discourse in the period to come. It helped transform the issue of race from a question of biology to one of culture and it provided a new language of race untainted by association with prewar biological racism.

IMMIGRATION AND ASSIMILATION IN FRENCH POLITICAL DEBATE

My interpretation of the genesis and underlying themes of postwar race relations policy in Britain is given substance if we compare the discussion in Britain with the parallel debate in France. It is a widely held view that there exists a sharp contrast between French and British approaches to race relations. On the one hand, there is a prevailing belief among British social scientists and policy-makers that France, along with other Continental countries, has failed to follow the British lead in legislating against racial discrimination and that this has played an important part in the growth of racial tensions in Europe in recent years. On the other hand, there is an equally staunch belief in France that British race relations policy has led to the creation of ghettos and ethnic conflicts. Marceau Long, president of the Haut Conseil a l'Intégration, spelled out what he regarded as the difference between the two approaches:

> One conception is based on the right of ethnic minorities, of communities; this is the concept which has been adopted in the Anglo-Saxon countries . . . The other concept is ours, French, and is based on individual rights . . . [The Anglo-Saxon approach] is another way of imprisoning people within ghettos, rather than affirming their opinions as individuals.[49]

Clearly there are major differences between the way the two countries have tackled the issues of race and immigration in the postwar period. The legacy of the French Revolution and of the republican tradition have influenced French policy. The historic particularities of the relationship between Britain and its empire shaped British policies on race. But underlying these differences, there is a commonality of approach which is rarely granted in the literature, a commonality conditioned by the fact that policy-makers in both countries were grappling with the same problem: the contradiction between the tendency to racialise social discourse and the desire to promote a belief in equality. Hence French race relations policy is based, as much as is British policy, on the idea of a link between control and integration:

> We must ensure a better control of immigrants entering the country, for without this action all attempts to improve immigrants' working and living conditions are likely to fail.[50]

> A policy of integration is only effective if the flow of immigration can be controlled.[51]

France's first postwar immigration controls were introduced in 1974 when President Valéry Giscard d'Estaing announced a temporary suspension of immigration followed by a suspension of family reunification. Although the right to family reunification was restored in 1975 (after the Conseil d'État had ruled it to be unconstitutional) the ban on primary immigration became permanent. Even before 1974, however, France had cut back on immigration. On 1 July 1968 the French government unilaterally limited Algerian immigration to 1000 a month; this was subsequently fixed at an annual rate of 35 000 by a Franco-Algerian accord signed later that year. Also in 1968 the government suppressed the process of regularisation for unqualified workers and made allocations of residence permits conditional on applicants having a job. In 1972 new measures required that immigrants have proof of work and decent housing; without such proof they faced deportation.

These measures linked immigration to employment and established the idea that economic factors underlay the implementation of control. As the 1977 report *Immigration et 7e Plan* put it, 'At a time of crisis, the simultaneous presence of a high level of unemployed French workers and large numbers of foreign workers in factories is bound to raise questions.'[52]

But, as in Britain, immigration controls were not primarily the product of economic crisis. Well after restrictions were introduced employers continued to welcome the influx of foreign workers:

> The presence of immigration gives our economy more flexibility, since immigrants are people who are extremely mobile, are willing to change firms and regions and, if needs be, become unemployed. Immigration is therefore beneficial in that it allows the country to save on the cost of education (which is incurred by the country of origin) and to help balance the nation's budget. As they are young, immigrants often pay more in taxes than they receive in allowances.[53]

After the permanent ban on primary immigration was imposed in 1974 certain sections of French industry, such as construction, which were dependant on immigrant labour, complained bitterly to the government.[54]

Social, not economic, concerns underlay restrictions on immigration. 'Our immigration policy', wrote Maurice Massenet, head of the Population and Migration section in the Ministry of Labour, 'must be oriented towards a new notion: that of the immigrant's capacity to adapt in our country.'

The Calvez report of 1969 on 'The problem of foreign workers' set out the themes of the new debate. The report, which Corentin Calvez produced for the Economic and Social Council, introduced into French

policy-making the link between limitation and integration. It also institutionalised the idea that there existed social limits to the tolerance of
immigrants.

Calvez argued that there was an economic case against immigration.
But her principle concern was its social impact. She recommended that

> precise studies be carried out on the threshold of tolerance which
> should not be exceeded in the areas of housing, schools and the work-
> place; that is, thresholds necessary to maintain a suitable social bal-
> ance, founded on the proportionate levels of foreigners, and variable
> according to the ethnic group.[55]

In order to further integration, she recommended that the government
take positive steps to improve the trade union rights, housing conditions
and education of immigrants already in the country. At the same time
she advised that immigration be reorientated towards those who would
be more assimilable into French society – in other words Europeans –
whereas North Africans should be regarded as temporary guestworkers:
'It seems desirable, therefore, more and more to give to the influx of
non-European origin, and particularly that from the Maghreb, the character of a temporary immigration for work.'[56]

The Calvez report became the cornerstone of French immigration and
race relations policy in the following decades. Successive administrations
curtailed immigration and shifted the balance towards Europeans – the
Franco-Portuguese accord of 1971, for example, allowed for an annual
influx of Portuguese workers nearly double that of Algerians. At the
same time the French government asserted its antiracist credentials and
its belief in equal rights. In July 1972, France enacted legislation outlawing incitement to racial hatred and racial discrimination. In 1974, at the
same time as the government put a halt to primary immigration, it
introduced a number of measures to improve the rights of foreigners and
to bring them into line with those of French nationals. This link between
control and integration was maintained by successive administrations,
both conservative and socialist, through the seventies and eighties. The
real impact of the Calvez report, however, was less practical than ideological. It reposed the 'race problem' from one of discriminatory policy
to one of the inability of certain immigrants to integrate. The issue of
immigration came to be defined in terms of citizenship, nationality and
identity. The new immigration policy helped racialise political discourse
in the seventies.

Even more than in Britain, French policy on race showed the contradictory demands of postwar race relations policy. As Maxim Silverman has
observed, 'At the same time [as racialising immigration] official discourse (in exemplary fashion) had to attempt to defuse and depoliticise

the very racialised categories which it had been deeply implicated in producing in the first place.'[57] But this proved much more difficult in France than in Britain.

In Britain both the imposition of immigration control and the enactment of race relations legislation took place relatively early. This allowed the British to establish the twin-track approach to race and to balance the imposition of control against the implementation of anti-discrimination laws. As a result Britain has been much more effective in dealing with the problems created by the politicisation of the race issue. Even in the seventies, with the country reeling from economic and social crises, the impact of Powellism and the growth of the far-right, Britain was far more successful than its Continental neighbours have been in minimising the social impact of the race question.

In France, on the other hand, immigration controls and race relations legislation came into being at a time when the postwar consensus was beginning to come apart. By the end of the sixties France was undergoing a major crisis of identity and self-belief. The social impact of the *trente glorieuses* – the postwar economic boom – the pace of industrialisation and depopulation of the countryside, growing unemployment, conflict over the degree of state intervention and uncertainty about France's role in Europe and on the wider world stage, all gave rise to sense of crisis and self-doubt. In this context, the contradictions within the race relations policy were much more difficult to resolve. The underlying trend towards a racialised discourse proved much stronger than the ability to depoliticise the race issue. From the seventies onwards race became a central theme in political debate and became inextricably bound with the disintegration of the postwar liberal consensus.

RACE AND THE COLLAPSE OF CONSENSUS

The postwar consensus embodied, as we have seen, the solution of the Western élite to the problems it had faced as a result of the horrors of the interwar years. By the seventies, however, what had once been the solution was now seen as symbolic of the problem itself. State intervention, welfarism, the 'nanny state', the trade unions, the multicultural society – these were now seen as the causes of the manifold difficulties which beset the Western world. Governments throughout Europe and in America increasingly viewed the postwar consensus as an obstacle which had to be cleared away before they could deal with the consequences of national decline, economic dislocation and social fragmentation.

From the late seventies, therefore, there began a concerted assault on the various elements of consensus. The policies of Ronald Reagan in America and of Margaret Thatcher in Britain symbolised the new mood.

But the backlash against consensus was not confined to Britain and America. Every Western government – even socialist administrations such as those in France, Spain and Greece – adopted similar strategies. At an ideological level it involved the discrediting of the ideas of collectivism and welfarism, of Keynesianism and social democracy. In their stead came an aggressive market-orientated economic doctrine and a highly individualistic social philosophy. At a practical level governments began reining in state expenditure, hacking away at welfare measures and rolling back civil rights legislation.

Race became an important part of this process for a number of reasons. First, immigration and the multicultural society were, as Tom Nairn has argued, the most visible symbols of social change in the postwar world:

> War was the great social experience of England in this century – yet war served only to confirm and revalidate the values of the past, to affirm the essential continuity of the national tradition. The only *new* experience, going sharply counter to tradition, has been that of the coloured immigration of the 1950s and 1960s.[58]

This is not to say that immigration *was* the most important change in postwar Britain, just that it has been *perceived* as such. Why this should be so – why, for example, in Nairn's terms, war should validate values of the past whereas immigration should seem to undermine them – is an important theme of this book and one which I shall examine in greater detail later.

The perception of immigration and the multicultural society as the most distinct facets of the changes brought about by the postwar world also made them the most potent metaphors for the rottenness of the postwar liberal legacy. Compared to other aspects of the postwar consensus, immigration could most easily be portrayed as alien to the national tradition, as responsible for creating an 'alien wedge' in our midst. Whereas welfare programmes or consensual trade union policies touched and improved the lives of millions, immigration and the multicultural society could more obviously be presented as problems that needed resolving. Whether the discussion was about immigrants in Europe or the inner city ghettos in the USA, the new social discourse sought to portray blacks as responsible for crime, unemployment, sexual immorality and the general undermining of the moral code.

Race became a useful battering ram against the postwar consensus. The very sensitivity of postwar liberals to the race question made the issue ideal for the new breed of conservatives. The postwar political class was unwilling to politicise racial issues; this made race a more powerful weapon in the hands of the right. Increasingly conservatives have pointed an accusing finger at liberals for refusing to bite the bullet over the immigration issue. Liberals, they say, have allowed all manner of illegal immigrants and bogus refugees to flood into Europe. These immigrants win liberal support by exploiting 'our sympathy and misplaced guilt':

> We fully sympathise with the needs of those who wish to settle in Western Europe. But we must also face the fact that they will lie, cheat, flout the law and pay criminal organisations thousands of pounds to smuggle them into our countries not to mention abusing and exploiting the tradition of Western liberalism . . . Illegal immigrants treat our laws with contempt because they observe that our governments do not have the will to uphold them . . . One of the most important root causes of this *laissez-faire* limpness is that a great many European politicians and intellectuals, particularly on the left, are still wallowing in guilt of one sort or other – guilt about our colonial past, guilt about our present economic success.[59]

Motivated by guilt about the past, liberals are unable to deal with the problems of the present. This is a very powerful argument because consensus was indeed built out of the need to deal with the social repercussions of the horrors of the past. 'We have no need to feel guilty any more', is the subtext of the message, 'therefore we have no need of the old consensus.' Through wallowing in their guilt, liberals are endangering our society; they lack the moral fibre to undertake the measures necessary to protect our nation. Indeed they are too limp even to protect 'the tradition of Western liberalism'.

In a similar vein, British journalist Paul Johnson argued after neo-Nazis attacked a refugee hostel in the German town of Rostock that the violence was the result 'not of fascism but of liberal immigration laws':

> In Germany, as in Britain, high-minded upper-middle-class progressives, who live in salubrious areas, are all in favour of the rights of asylum and compassion for refugees. Ordinary workers, at the bottom end of the housing market, and whose jobs are already at risk or have gone, take a different view; they have to pay the price of the radical consciences of the rich.[60]

Racism, continued Johnson, was not morally abhorrent, but simply 'self-preservation'. But liberals are too high-minded and guilt-ridden to understand the concerns of ordinary people.

The use of racial arguments to attack the values of postwar liberalism is not confined to Europe. The 'underclass' debate serves to illustrate how in the USA too race has become a stalking horse for a broader attack on consensual values. The underclass is defined in American social policy debate in an exclusively racial fashion as the black inhabitants of inner city ghettos. What marks out the underclass, according to conservatives, is its alien values and deviant behaviour:

> Behind the ghetto's crumbling walls, lives a large group of people who are more intractable, more socially alien and more hostile than almost anybody has imagined. They are the unreachables: the American underclass . . . Their bleak environment nurtures values that are often at odds with those of the majority – even the majority of the poor. Thus the underclass produces a highly disproportionate number of the nation's juvenile delinquents, school dropouts, drug addicts and welfare mothers, and much of the adult crime, family disruption, urban decay and demand for social expenditure.[61]

This seething mass of urban malevolence, say the conservatives, has been created by liberal policies. The gains of the civil rights movement, runs the argument, have removed institutionalised racism and ensured full equality of opportunity in the USA. But if the cancer of racism has been excised, the social and welfare policies of the sixties have created a new enemy – the black underclass:

> As a result of the liberal preoccupation with race, to the neglect of other social priorities, a black underclass has been created, an envious and ungovernable sector of urban society for whom the prospect of upward mobility has been overcast by recession and by the enervating effects of welfare dependency.[62]

Since society was not responsible for black disadvantage, so social intervention could not alleviate, and indeed could only exacerbate, the problem:

> How is it possible that anyone in good conscience should claim that too little money has been spent in, or on, the cities, when more than a trillion dollars has in one way or other been allocated to them by Washington since the 60s? How is it possible to go on declaring that what will save the young men of South Central LA, and the young girls they impregnate, and the illegitimate babies they sire, is jobs? How is it possible for anyone to look at these boys of the underclass – to look at them literally, with one's own eyes, and actually *see* them – and imagine that they either want or could hold on to jobs? . . . In short, how is it possible to persist in refusing to recognise that the condition of those young men is beyond the reach of government – that, indeed, the efforts of the government have done much to undermine their capacity to take charge of their own lives. Yet, taking charge of their own lives is the *only* thing that will save them.[63]

The association of blacks and welfare has proved a very potent weapon. In the imaginations of mainstream, middle America, tucked away safe in its suburban enclaves, the underclass has become symbolic of everything that is unAmerican and the inner city ghetto the repository of the enemy within, a menacing threat to the lifestyles and mores of white America. By associating the ghetto with the government programmes of the sixties, those policies themselves appear menacing. Raising the spectre of the underclass has become an effective way of challenging the liberal policies of the postwar years.

If the issue of race has proved a useful weapon against consensus, equally the erosion of consensus has helped legitimise racist attitudes. The discrediting of postwar liberalism has removed many of the taboos against racism that had existed in the postwar period. As a recent survey of anti-Semitism in France noted, 'the boundaries of the sayable have been pushed back' because of 'the erosion of a once strong taboo which, after the Second World War, was imposed by the sense of collective responsibility and guilt which French society felt towards its Jewish community'.[64]

Politicians feel less constrained by the niceties of the postwar liberal conventions. When Jacques Chirac, who was later to be president of France, claimed that France was suffering from an 'overdose of foreigners', what was shocking was less the sentiment he expressed than the manner in which he expressed it:

> The French working man who lives in la Goutte d'Or [a Paris suburb] sees on the landing of his council flat an immigrant father with four wives and a score of children, making 50 000 francs on welfare, without a job of course. If you add to that the noise and smell, no wonder the French worker goes crazy . . . We don't reject foreigners but there is an overdose in France.[65]

The liberal consensus had forced politicians to treat racial issues, in public at least, through a form of coded language, which cleansed the racist sentiments and recast them in polite, liberal terms. Chirac's outburst, and many similar ones by other respectable figures, show that politicians do not feel so constrained any more. The language of private discourse is becoming public.

I am not simply saying here that respectable politicians have in some way become more 'racist'. Such an assertion makes little sense, as I have argued that there has always existed a racialised private discourse. Rather I am arguing that the issue of race has become *politicised*. A private discourse has become public, less restrained by the conventions of postwar liberalism.

At the same time social discourse has become *racialised*. Social and political issues are increasingly perceived in racial terms. Race has become the medium through which public debate is conducted. Discussions about welfare policy, crime, education or the family are all framed around a debate about race. A recent review of American politics observed that 'raising issues involving race can no longer be described as simply an attempt to appeal to racism. Issues of crime, illegitimacy, quotas and the urban underclass are seen by voters, black and white, as affecting their security, their values, their rights, and their livelihoods and the competitive prospects of their children.'[66] Much the same can be said for Europe. Race has become the lens through which is refracted all of society's problems.

Not only has the erosion of consensus legitimised racism, but the politicisation of race has also provided the élite with a means with which to deal with the consequences of the erosion of consensus. The conservative backlash of the eighties, far from resolving the problems of Western society, has heightened them. In undermining the edifice of liberalism, conservatives have discovered to their horror that they have also mined under the very foundations of postwar society.

Society today is more fragmented and dispirited than it was a decade ago. The end of the Cold War, which finally signalled the demise of the postwar era, has catalysed and exacerbated all the corrosive trends that the conservatives had sought to combat. In undermining the postwar legacy, conservatives have undermined the means by which society was held together.

Politicians have responded to the corrosive effects of the new period by trying to use race to establish an element of social cohesion. Throughout Western Europe politicians have attempted to recreate national identity in a more exclusive form to give a sense of 'belonging' at a time of widespread disillusionment and despair. But that disillusionment and despair is itself the result of the lack of any positive vision in society that can inspire people to want to 'belong'. Identity, therefore, has to be recast in opposition to whom we are not, rather than in relation to who we are. And we, say the politicians, are not immigrants, refugees or the underclass.

The new discourse of immigration presents contemporary immigrants as different from previous inflows. Writing in a feature in *The Field*, former Conservative Cabinet minister Norman Tebbit bemoaned the impact of postwar migration on what he called 'our gentle nationalism':

Sadly what has been almost an age of innocence is ending. Our gentle nationalism, more a sense of nationality, was never built on any sense of racial purity. After all, the early history of these islands was of successive waves of immigrants mixing Celts, Britons, Angles, Saxons, Romans, Norse and Norman French. Later Flemish, Huguenot and Jewish immigrants were integrated to such an extent that only the

Jewish community remained identifiable and that only by a religion on which the culture of the whole nation is based. But in recent years our sense of insularity and nationality has been bruised by large waves of immigrants resistant to absorption, some defiantly claiming a right to superimpose their culture, even their law, upon the host community.[67]

In the past, says Tebbit, we never had to define 'Britishness' in too exclusive a fashion because the 'old immigrants' accepted that they were part of this identity. The 'new immigrants' however reject 'assimilation' and insist on proclaiming their separateness. This has not only disrupted a unitary sense of Britishness but, implies Tebbit, forced us to be more exclusive in how we define national identity.

In fact it is to rewrite history to argue that previous waves of immigration were easily assimilated into British society. Much recent research has shown how nineteenth-century Jews, East European and other immigrants faced hostility and discrimination in their struggle to become accepted as British.[68] All were treated as racially distinct. Many of the themes in the contemporary discourse of immigration were previously applied to European immigrants: their propensity for violence and criminal activity, their unhygienic habits, their sexual perversions, their inability to assimilate. The distinction now being drawn between new and old immigrants is simply a means of racialising current immigration, by writing out of history the racialisation of past immigrants.

A similar process can be seen in France where, as Maxim Silverman has observed, the 'new' immigration policy has been based around the distinction between immigrants who are easily assimilable and those who are not:

> Its fundamental message is to establish a dichotomy between the easy assimilation of previous (European) immigrants and the inassimilability of the new (African) immigrants. This dichotomy is at the heart of the contemporary racialisation of immigration. The 'newness' of the 'new policy' therefore lies not so much in the measures themselves but in the reformulation of the past history of immigration which it implies. It is the retrospective reconstruction of the idea of assimilation which is most significant here.[69]

In France too, however, as Silverman notes, 'the notion of the easy assimilation of past [European] immigrants is a myth'. As in Britain, much recent research has unearthed the history of the racialisation of previous immigrants.[70]

That the new discourse of immigration is an attempt to rewrite history is evident from the fact that commentators even draw a contrast between current immigration from Islamic countries and previous black immigration from non-Islamic states:

> Whereas many West Indian immigrants were disappointed to find that their desire to be seen as British was not requited when they came to the United Kingdom in the 1950s and 1960s, they did not bring with them an outlook on life which challenged the legitimacy of the British system. It is one thing to deal with immigrants, even great masses of them, who see the new host society as admirable and the place of their future prosperity ... it is quite another to come to terms with newcomers who reject many of the basic tenets of the society into which they are entering ... Whether European states or a united Europe can accept Islamic cantons in their midst remains to be seen.[71]

Immigrants who forty years ago were seen as 'likely to impair the harmony, strength and cohesion of our public and social life and to cause discord and unhappiness among all concerned' and who would cause 'a significant change in the racial character of the English people' have now been transformed into model citizens so that the next generation of immigrants can be presented as alien to the British (and European) way of life. The importance of such revisionism is that it helps stamp the mark of difference on current immigrants and hence creates the idea of a homogenous nation now being rent asunder by newcomers who do not understand 'our way of life'. Racialising contemporary immigration by rewriting the history of past immigration helps recast national identity through establishing the myth of a national homogeneity now being destroyed by the new immigrants.

Western identity is not simply being recast against the 'difference' of the new immigrants. It is also being recast in opposition to the 'menace' of the Third World. Increasingly the Third World is portrayed in the West as a threat to Western traditions of democracy and freedom. Islam, in particular, is presented as a pre-Enlightenment force threatening the civilised standards of Western liberal democracy. As one recent study of the New World Order has observed, the Cold War between East and West is being replaced by a 'civilisational cold war' between the West and the Third World, and in particular between the West and Islam. Such a 'societal cold war', the author argues, 'would serve to strengthen European identity.'[72]

The demonisation of the Third World is rarely racially explicit: commentaries on the Third World pose the problem in terms of cultural or civilisational differences, not racial ones. But the subtext is always a discussion of race. The distinction between the West and the Third World is premised on ideas of racial difference. The portrayal of the Third World as ignorant, incapable and uncivilised helps endow the West with a certain moral superiority. It revives notions of 'The White Man's Burden' – that the West has a moral obligation, by virtue of its innate superiority, to bring civilisation to the rest of the globe:

> [M]ost African states are not fit to govern themselves. Their continued existence, and the violence and human degradation they breed, are a threat to stability and peace as well as an affront to our consciences . . . [T]he civilised world must . . . go to Africa and govern.[73]

The racial theme here is barely concealed. The contempt for African states and their people is expressive of desire to voice a sense of racial superiority. As we shall see in Chapter 7, the new discourse of the Third World plays an important part in the remaking of race.

The erosion of the postwar consensus, then, has revealed the centrality of race in Western society. As the glacis of postwar liberalism has shattered, so it has made acute the sense of crisis, a crisis that has increasingly been articulated in racial terms. Race is becoming the lens through which is refracted our understanding of society.

Yet the racialisation of society is an ambiguous process. Western society remains formally committed to equality, and ideologies of racial superiority and the practice of overt discrimination remain a source of embarrassment. The experience of fascism and the Holocaust cannot simply be erased from the memory; they remain powerful factors that shape our response to the issue of race.

The very ambiguity of society about this issue, however, reveals the centrality of race in the Western tradition. Despite powerful forces compelling society towards equality, the powerful undertow of race has asserted itself ever more forcefully over the past two decades. What is it about the Western world that makes race such a central social motif? That is the question to which I now want to turn.

2

The Social Limits to Equality

On 28 July 1993 three officers from Britain's Aliens Deportation Group (ADG) arrived at the north London flat of Joy Gardner to deport her. Gardner had been born in Jamaica, but had come to Britain six years earlier. Her mother, Myrna Simpson, had lived in Britain for more than 33 years. Her half-brother, three uncles, and two aunts also lived in Britain. She was married to a British citizen and her son, Graeme, was born in Britain. Under Britain's immigration laws, however, Gardner was considered to be an 'illegal immigrant'. The immigration authorities declared her marriage to be fraudulent and imposed a deportation order on her. The officers from the ADG manacled her with leg, arm and body belts, cuffed her hands and bound 13 feet of sticky tape around her body, including seven times around her face. Gardner died from asphyxiation. When the three officers involved were tried for unlawful killing, they were found not guilty. The *Daily Mail* declared the verdict to be correct because 'Gardner had no right to be in Britain in the first place'.[1]

The Gardner case is interesting because it demonstrates well the contingent nature of equality. Joy Gardner was denied the rights that most people in Britain take for granted because she was not a British citizen, and, moreover, she was a black non-citizen. No British citizen would expect to have their marriage questioned, no British citizen would expect to be deported and no British citizen, not even a criminal, would have been bound and gagged like Joy Gardner was. And had a British citizen died in these circumstances, it is highly unlikely that those responsible for his or her death would have escaped a guilty verdict.

'We hold these truths to be self-evident' wrote the authors of the American Declaration of Independence: that 'all men are created equal' and that all possess certain 'inalienable rights' which include 'life, liberty and the pursuit of happiness'. But, as the Gardner case illustrates, the idea of equality and the notion of inalienable rights is anything but 'self-evident', and some men (and women) are clearly less equal, and have less of a right to 'life, liberty and the pursuit of happiness', than others. Such a seemingly disingenuous approach to equality has always been so. At the time when the founding fathers of the American Republic were declaring all men to be equal, they denied that same equality to millions of black slaves. Since then equality has been a fiercely contested term. Most Western democracies denied the majority of their citizens

38

equal voting rights until well into this century. Today, immigrants in general, and black people in particular, have restricted political and legal rights in many Western nations. Even where they formally possess such rights, in practice few are treated as if 'all men are created equal'.

Why has the implementation of such a seemingly self-evident concept as equality created such practical problems? The answer lies in the fact that equality is not an 'inalienable' or 'natural' right, but a social one, created through human endeavour. Its meaning and scope is therefore determined by the nature of particular societies. It is the social nature of equality, and the dilemmas this often creates, that lies at the heart of the ambiguous attitude of Western society towards the notion of 'race'.

The common-sense view of racial inequality is that the denial of equal rights to different racial groups arises from the very existence of races. Certain people are denied equal rights, or are treated differently, because they belong to, or are perceived to belong to, a different 'race'. According to this argument, our tendency to categorise people by race and to infer different qualities in different races has allowed society to restrict the scope of equality along racial lines.

This, however, is a tautological argument. As we have seen race, like equality, is a social, not biological concept. If there is nothing natural about 'races', the question arises as to why society feels it necessary to categorise people according to race. Attributing inequality to race does not solve the conundrum of equality because races themselves are social constructions, the creation of which has to be explained.

I want to argue here the opposite to the common-sense view: that it is not racial differentiation that has led to the denial of equality, but the social constraints placed on the scope of equality that has led to the racial categorisation of humanity. In other words, it is not 'race' that gives rise to inequality but inequality that gives rise to 'race.' The nature of modern society has created inequalities between different social groups and these have come to be perceived in racial terms. The ambiguous attitude to race that I noted in the last chapter arises from an ambivalent attitude to equality. My aim in this chapter is to examine the relationship between race and equality in modern society by looking at why equality poses a dilemma for us.

RACE AND THE ENLIGHTENMENT

To grasp the meaning of race we need to investigate how the understanding of the relationship between humanity, society and nature is socially and historically constructed: how, for example, a society or an age understands the relationship between human differences and human similarities; what meaning it imputes to concepts such as equality, humanity or culture; and how, and why, such concepts and meanings evolve over time. The modern meaning of such concepts has been framed to a large extent by the philosophical revolution unleashed by the Enlightenment, the intellectual wind of change that swept through Europe in the eighteenth century. I want to show that the Enlightenment, and the emerging capitalist society that accompanied it, established for the first time in history the possibility of human equality but did so in social circumstances that constrained its expression. The tension between a profound belief in equality and the social limits on its articulation, I will argue, has been central to the creation of the modern discourse of race.

Many recent contributions to the debate on the origins of racism similarly highlight the importance of the Enlightenment in establishing the modern discourse of race, but they have done so for very different reasons from mine, suggesting that racial ideology can be traced back to the categories of thought invented by the Enlightenment.[2] These authors argue that the concepts of reason and universalism and the scientific methods of observation and categorisation bear the imprint of racial thought, for it is through such categories that a racial typology has become manifest.

George Mosse, for instance, argues that 'Eighteenth century Europe was the cradle of modern racism' because 'racism has its foundations' in the Enlightenment 'preoccupation with a rational universe, nature and aesthetics'.[3] Similarly, David Goldberg argues that 'The emergence of independent scientific domains of anthropology and biology defined a classificatory order of racial groupings – subspecies of Homo sapiens – along correlated physical and cultural matrixes':

> Empiricism encouraged the tabulation of perceivable differences between peoples and from this it deduced their natural differences. Rationalism proposed initial innate distinctions (especially mental ones) to explain the perceived behavioural disparities.[4]

The very means that the Enlightenment *philosophes* developed for understanding the world caused them to divide the humanity on racial lines. 'If premodernity lacked any conceiving of the differences between human beings as racial differences', argues Goldberg, 'modernity comes increasingly to be defined by and through race.' This is because 'the shift from medieval premodernity to modernity is in part the shift from a religiously defined to a racially defined discourse of human identity and personhood.'[5]

I have considerable sympathy with Goldberg's approach and I agree in particular with his contention that in premodern society 'there was no explicit category of race or of racial differentiation'. But I reject the argument that the epistemological categories of modernity necessarily give rise to a racial division of humanity. Belief in reason, espousal of the scientific method and a universalist conviction do not of themselves imply a racial viewpoint. That in the nineteenth century science, reason and universalism came to be harnessed to a discourse of race is a development that has to be explained through historical analysis; it is not logically given by the nature of scientific or rational thought.

The argument that the categories of modernity necessarily give rise to a racial division of humanity conflates two different meanings of 'modernity'. On the one hand there is modernity in the sense of an intellectual or philosophical outlook which holds that it is possible to apprehend the world through reason and science – an outlook that came to be associated primarily with the Enlightenment. On the other hand modernity has also come to mean the particular society in which these ideas found expression – in other words, capitalism. 'By *modernity*', writes Goldberg,

I will mean throughout that general period emerging from the sixteenth century in the historical formation of what only relatively recently has come to be called 'the West'. This self-understanding becomes self-conscious in the seventeenth century, reaching intellectual and material maturity in the Enlightenment, and solidifies as Western hegemony the following century.[6]

We can see here how Goldberg uses the term to mean at one and the same time a historical period, a specific form of society and a particular intellectual outlook. He goes on to make clear this conceptual conflation:

The modern project . . . emerges as and in terms of the broad sweep of sociointellectual conditions. These include the commodification and capital accumulation of market-based society, the legal formation of private property and systems of contract, the moral and political conception of rational self-interested subjects, and the increasing replacement of God and religious doctrine by Reason and Nature as the final arbiters of a justificatory appeal in epistemology, metaphysics and science, as well as in morality, legality and politics.[7]

Intellectual movements and socioeconomic developments are without doubt related. The economic and social changes in Europe from the sixteenth century onwards laid the ground for the transformation of its intellectual outlook. This new outlook in turn acted as an intellectual weapon in the hands of the nascent capitalist class as it sought to overthrow feudal society. But is there any justification in regarding the period from the sixteenth century on as a unitary 'sociointellectual' project?

I think not. Particularly in the context of the discussion of the emergence of ideas of race, such a generalisation serves more to confuse than to clarify.

It is true, as Goldberg argues, that many of the concepts of Enlightenment discourse became reified through the development of bourgeois philosophy. The idea of reason, for instance, was transformed into a transcendental category (Reason with a capital R) existing independently of human consciousness and acting to make intelligible the social and natural world. The notion of 'rights' similarly acquired a metaphysical aspect and came to be seen as rooted not in human endeavour but in nature. Social subjects were transformed into an abstract, atomistic Subject that was divorced both from the contingencies of history and from the particularities of social and political relations. It is true also that such reification and naturalisation played an important role in the creation of a discourse of race. This, indeed, is one of the significant arguments of this book. But we should not assume from this that the racialisation of social discourse was implicit in the categories of Enlightenment thought. Rather this argument should impress on us the need to investigate, on the one hand, how and why the reification of Enlightenment categories took place and, on the other, the relation between this process and the creation of a discourse of race.

I take the Enlightenment as the starting point for my discussion of race, not because Enlightenment discourse was imbricated with the concept of race, but because through Enlightenment philosophy humanity had for the first time a concept of a human universality that could transcend perceived differences. Before the modern concept of race could develop, the modern concepts of equality and humanity had to develop too. Racial difference and inequality can only have meaning in a world which has accepted the possibility of social equality and a common humanity. The achievement of the Enlightenment was that it helped to produce just such a world. This is why the modern discourse of race is necessarily different from pre-Enlightenment views of human differences.

In theory, the object of the Enlightenment was to set all human beings free. As Eric Hobsbawm has rightly observed, 'All progressive, rationalist and humanist ideologies are implicit in it, and indeed come out of it'.[8] How was a discourse whose aim was the emancipation of all humanity transformed into one which helped enslave half the world? To understand that we need to examine the relationship between ideological and social development over the past 200 years, not assume it to be a unitary 'sociointellectual' movement. I begin therefore by laying out the broad outlines of the Enlightenment view of human nature and of race. Having established the essence of the Enlightenment outlook, I will then look at how these ideas and concepts expressed themselves through the development of modern capitalist society. I can then move on in the next chapter to consider how these forms gave rise to the modern discourse of race.

HUMAN NATURE AND HUMAN DIFFERENCE IN ENLIGHTENMENT DISCOURSE

The pre-Enlightenment view of the world was characterised by its irrational premises, static nature and parochial scope. Man's relation was fixed to God and to nature. The world was ordered according to God's will and true knowledge was available only to the Supreme Being.

Difference and inequality were an integral part of the medieval consciousness of the social and natural world. In a society that found itself constantly subordinate to the whims of nature, social divisions were inevitably seen as natural. To the medieval mind differences between individuals and groups were the result of God's will. The serf, the slave, the peasant, the artisan, the lord, the king – all were allotted their place in the world by divine sanction. Not just human office but natural order was preordained. The Great Chain of Being linked the cosmos from the most miserable mollusc to the Supreme Being. Near the apex of this chain stood Man, himself graded by social rank. In this great chain, the humblest as well as the greatest played their part in preserving order and carrying out God's bidding. As Alexander Pope remarked in his *Essay on Man*,

> Without this just gradation, could they be
> Subjected, these to those, or all to thee?

In this world of fixed relations and limited experiences, irrational prejudices attached themselves to anything and everything out of the ordinary. In communities that were ethnically homogeneous, geographically isolated, technologically backward, and socially conservative, prejudice and superstition were the natural responses to the strange and the unknown. What we would today call racial prejudices were certainly common. In the isolated, ignorant world of feudal Europe, Africans were often portrayed as devils, monsters or apes. The seventeenth-century traveller and writer Sir Thomas Herbert summed up the general premodern view of Africans:

> Their language is rather apishly rather than articulately founded, with whom 'tis thought they have unnatural mixture . . . Having a voice 'twixt humane and beast, makes that supposition to be of more credit, that they have a beastly copulation or conjuncture. So as considering the resemblance they bear with Baboons, which I could observe kept

frequent company with the Women, their speech . . . rather agreeing
with beasts than men . . . these may be said to be the descendants of
Satyrs, if any such ever were.[9]

Views such as Herbert's were common. But we should not confuse them
with modern racism. To do so would be to view medieval Europe with
twentieth-century eyes. Worse, it would be to impose the values of
modern industrial society on a world that still believed that the sun
revolved around the earth. Reason, equality, humanity – these were
unknown concepts in Herbert's world. In an age when witches were
burnt because they were 'different', fear of the unknown led to irrational
suspicions about people who spoke a different dialect or language, worshipped a different God or had a different colour skin.

In his book *European Encounters with the New World*, Anthony Pagden
relates the tale of Bemoin, a Wolof prince from West Africa who, in 1488,
came to Portugal to ask for assistance in a war in which he was engaged.
'Because the Portuguese accepted that *mutatis mutandis* all forms of
government were identical throughout the world', notes Pagden, 'John
II, self-proclaimed Lord of Guinea, received him as he would any visiting
prince'.

While in Portugal Bemoin converted to Christianity. He was baptised,
with the King and Queen of Portugal acting as his godparents. Four days
later he was made a knight. 'In Portugal then', observes Pagden, 'he had
become a noble, a member of the Royal Household and a Christian
Vassal of the "Lord of Guinea". He had, that is become, European in
everything but his skin colour.'

Bemoin returned to West Africa with a fleet of ships, men and military
equipment to help him prosecute his war. When the fleet had almost
reached its destination, however, the Portuguese commander, Pero Vaz,
killed Bemoin and then turned his ships around and set sail for home.
'Once poor Bemoin had slipped away from the mouth of the Tagus',
Pagden concludes, 'he had, for all those in Portugal, already lost his
identity as the king's *afilhado*':

> He had become part of another world. In the African Atlantic, far from
> the reaches of the network of kinship and culture which enlaced all
> men and made them what they were, Bemoin had become nothing but
> a 'black', a thing, like any other slave who could be tossed overboard
> to shorten a tedious journey.[10]

Bemoin's story is of interest because it shows how in premodern times
the physical limits of Europe placed constraints on social perceptions of
'difference'. The same individual could be treated in very distinct
fashion according to his physical relationship to Europe. Despite Be-

moin's strangeness in colour, religion, habits and garb he was nevertheless accepted as 'one of us' so long as he was in Portugal. In the course of
travelling to Africa, however, he became a stranger and was treated as
such. The medieval view of social difference is clearly dissimilar to the
modern concept of race.

The Enlightenment was the harbinger of intellectual modernity. The
philosophes of the Enlightenment strained to sweep aside the ignorance
and prejudice that characterised the medieval world. For men like Montesquieu, Voltaire, Rousseau, Linnaeus, Buffon, Diderot and Condillac
reason and observation were the key to apprehending the world. Irving
Zeitlin is very much to the point when he claims that, for the intellectuals
of the Enlightenment, 'philosophising became something different from
what it was before':

> The eighteenth-century thinkers had lost faith in the closed self-con-
> tained, metaphysical systems of the preceding century; they had lost
> patience with the philosophy confined to definite immutable axioms
> and deductions from them . . . [The Enlightenment] attributed to
> thought a creative and critical function, 'the power and task of shaping
> life itself'. Philosophy was no longer merely a matter of abstract think-
> ing; it acquired the practical function of criticising existing institutions
> to show that they were unreasonable and unnatural. It demanded that
> such institutions and the entire old order be replaced by a new one that
> was more reasonable, natural and hence necessary . . . Enlightenment
> thinking, then, had a *negative* and *critical* as well as a positive side. It
> was not so much the particular doctrines, axioms and theorems that
> lent it a new and original quality; rather it was the process of criticis-
> ing, doubting and tearing down – as well as building up.[11]

For the Enlightenment thinkers all aspects of human life and works were
subject to critical examination. They rejected the authority of tradition in
all branches of knowledge. Truth became the central goal of the intellectuals of this age, but not truth founded on revelation, tradition or authority. Rather it was reason and observation that were to be the twin
pillars of truth. As the Marquis of Halifax sourly observed, 'The world
has grown saucy and expecteth reasons, and good ones too, before they
give up their own opinions to other men's dictates.'[12]

The *philosophes* believed that the world – both natural and social – was
ordered according to laws which could be discovered through a combination of empirical study and inductive reasoning. To the Enlightenment
mind, facts were not just a chaotic, haphazard jumble of random elements. They fell, rather, into finite patterns and exhibited definite forms,
regularities and relationships. In the opening to his *Spirit of the Laws*,
Montesquieu laid out clearly the new belief that natural or social

phenomena were not arbitrary or random but were governed by specific laws which could be apprehended by humanity:

> Laws in their most general signification are the necessary relations derived from the nature of things. In this sense all beings have their laws, the Deity has his law, the material World had its law, the intelligences superior to man have their laws, the beasts their laws, man his laws.[13]

Such laws were comprehended not through deductive reasoning, as seventeenth-century rationalists had believed, but through a combination of empirical data and inductive logic. Hence, as Zeitlin rightly observes, the Enlightenment *philosophes* helped establish the modern scientific method through their synthesis of two previously separate philosophical traditions – rationalism and empiricism. The *philosophes* understood that 'Reason itself will not yield a knowledge of reality, neither will observation and experimentation alone yield such knowledge. Knowledge of reality, whether natural or social, depends on the unity of reason and observation in the scientific method.'[14]

The *philosophes* drew on the scientific method of Isaac Newton and the philosophical approach of John Locke. The beautiful simplicity of Newton's law of gravity which seemed to explain the operation of every kind of earthly and celestial movement, and which appeared to have been induced from observation, was the model of reasoning for the Enlightenment.

Locke accomplished for human thought that which Newton had achieved for celestial motion. In his *Essay Concerning Human Understanding* Locke rejected the view developed by Descartes that ideas were innate. He argued instead that ideas were either the direct products of sense impressions – that the human brain responds to stimuli as a photographic film responds to light – or else they were reflections of the mind on sensory impressions. This view of human thought not as intuitive but as learned was a major breakthrough.

Locke, like Newton, worked within a pre-Enlightenment framework. But, the implications of his thinking were to dominate Enlightenment belief. Locke's philosophical outlook helped create an intellectual milieu which, as historian Norman Hampson has noted, believed in

> toleration (since beliefs were largely a product of the environment); acceptance of the potential equality of man, except as regards natural intelligence (since human differences were not due to hereditary distinctions of 'blood', but to differences of environment); the assumption that society, by the regulation of material conditions, could promote the moral improvement of its members; a new psychology and a new

attitude to education, based on the belief that human irrationality was the product of erroneous association of ideas, which had become fixed in childhood.[15]

Locke's political views too had a major impact on Enlightenment thinkers. Locke's belief in 'inalienable rights' rooted in nature proved very appealing to Enlightenment political philosophy and has indeed become part of the foundation of modern liberalism. The American writer Nathan Tarcov has claimed, for instance, that 'Locke is *our* philosopher', because his political arguments are codified in the American Declaration of Independence:

> [I]t can be safely assumed that every one of us, before we ever heard of Locke, had heard that all men are created equal, that they are endowed with certain inalienable rights, that among them are life, liberty and the pursuit of happiness, that to secure these rights governments are instituted among men, deriving their just powers from the consent of the governed, and that, whenever any form of government becomes destructive of these ends, it is the right of the people to alter or abolish it.[16]

The acceptance of these social and political ideas transformed the understanding of humanity's relation to nature and society and established what the *philosophes* considered to be a science of human nature. Through such a science they hoped to reform society rationally. There were often sharp differences between individuals and schools of thought. British thinkers tended towards empiricism, the French towards materialism. The early Enlightenment thinkers were still influenced by seventeenth-century rationalism; the later ones, especially Rousseau and Kant, prefigured the Romantic, idealist and socialist traditions of the following century. Diderot believed that human nature belonged entirely to the realm of biology; Rousseau violently disagreed. Hume, unlike Condorcet, denied the possibility of access to objective knowledge. Voltaire was a Deist; many of his contemporaries were atheists. Hume believed that the sense of obligation was an empirically examinable sentiment; Kant founded his moral philosophy on the refutation of this thesis.

Beneath these differences, however, there were a number of beliefs that all held in common and which marked out a revolution in the understanding of humanity. All the *philosophes* believed, to a lesser or greater degree, that humans were by nature rational and sociable, and hence different from other animals. 'Man is a reasonable being', wrote Buffon. 'The animal is totally deprived of that noble faculty. And as there is no intermediate point between a positive and a negative, between a rational and an irrational animal, it is evident that man's nature is entirely different from that of the animal.' Further, this rationality expressed itself through human sociability:

> Man augmented his own powers and his knowledge by uniting them with those of his fellow creatures ... Man commands the universe solely because he has learned to govern himself and to submit to the laws to society.

Finally, argued Buffon, the capacity to form societies is inherent in all human beings:

> Thus man in every situation and under every climate tends equally towards society. It is uniform effect of a necessary cause; for without this natural tendency, the propagation of the species, and of course, the existence of mankind would soon cease.[17]

The *philosophes* did not just hold that all humanity was rational and sociable. They also believed, as David Hume observed, that there existed a static human nature, common to all:

> It is universally acknowledged that there is a great uniformity among the acts of men, in all nations and ages, and that human nature remains the same in its principles and operations ... Mankind are so much made the same, in all times and places, that history informs us of nothing new or strange in this particular. Its chief use is only to discover the constant and universal principles of human nature.[18]

The belief in a universal human nature led logically to the notion that the divisions among humanity were either artificial or to a large extent irrelevant in comparison to its elements of commonality. Wilhelm von Humboldt passionately expressed the belief that in the concept of the unity of humankind lay the Enlightenment's most valuable possession:

> If we would indicate an idea which throughout the whole course of history has ever more and more widely extended its empire – or which more than any other testifies to the much contested and still more decidedly misunderstood perfectibility of the whole human race – it is that of establishing our common humanity – of striving to remove the barriers which prejudice and limited views of every kind have erected amongst men, and to treat all mankind without reference to religion, nation or colour, as one fraternity, one great community, fitted for the attainment of one object, the unrestrained development of the psychical powers.[19]

Not only did Enlightenment philosophers declare the unity of human-kind, but they believed that all were potentially equal. 'Whilst we maintain the unity of the human species', wrote von Humboldt's brother, the naturalist and explorer Alexander, 'we at the same time must repel the depressing assumption of the superior and inferior races of men.'[20] The French traveller Baron Lahontan concurred. 'Since men are all made of the same clay', he argued, 'there should be no distinction or superiority among them.[21]

This belief in the unity of humanity and the equality of Man was held by virtually all Enlightenment thinkers. Human beings were naturally equal; inequality was created by society. 'Man was born free', noted Jean-Jacques Rousseau in his famous opening to *The Social Contract*, 'but he is everywhere in chains.'[22] The certainty that there existed a universal human nature and a common human psyche led to a greater willingness to accept unfamiliar values and to a more tolerant and humanistic attitude to non-European peoples. Different cultures and mores were regarded as different outward manifestations of the same inner nature. Leibniz went so far as calling on the Chinese (whose achievements were widely admired within the Enlightenment) to send missionaries to civilise Europeans.

The Enlightenment was marked by an embrace of cosmopolitanism and a distaste for particularist outlooks. It is necessary, argued Rousseau, 'to shake off the yoke of national prejudices, to learn to study men by their resemblances and their differences, and to acquire a universal knowledge which was not that of one century or one country exclusively, but being that of all times and of all places, was, so as to speak, the universal science of the wise'.[23] He claimed that 'there is no longer a France, a Germany, a Spain, not even an England, there are only Europeans. All have the same tastes, the same passions, the same way of life.' Montesquieu's view that he was 'human by necessity' but 'French by accident' was endorsed by many.

For the Enlightenment *philosophes* human differences, whether physical or cultural, were not differences in kind but in degree. In his *Discourse on Inequality*, Rousseau derided the views of travellers who believed that differences between peoples showed that some were closer to beasts, and argued that human diversity could be understood in a rational fashion. It is worth quoting the passage at length for its elegant prose, cool logic and egalitarian assumptions sum up the best features of Enlightenment thinking:

> Among the men we know, either through our own acquaintance, or through historians or travellers, some are black, others white, others red; some have long hair, others have only woolly curls, some are almost covered in hair, others have not even a beard. There have been,

and perhaps still are, peoples of gigantic height, and leaving aside the
fable of the pygmies, which may well be only an exaggeration, we
know that the Laplanders and especially the Greenlanders, are very
much below the average height of man . . . All these facts, of which it
is easy to supply incontestable proofs, can only surprise those who are
accustomed to looking simply at the objects which surround them,
and who are ignorant of the powerful effects of the diversity of envi-
ronments, of the air, of foods, of the style of living, of habits in general,
and above all, the astonishing effects of the same causes when they act
continually over a long series of generations. Today when trade, travel
and conquests bring various peoples closer together, and when their
ways of living become constantly more alike as a result of frequent
communication, one notices that certain national differences have
diminished and everyone can see, for example, that the French of
today have no longer those tall, blond pale bodies described by the
Latin historians . . . All these observations on the variety which a thousand causes can produce and in fact have produced in the human
species, prompt me to doubt whether those every different animals
resembling men and taken by travellers without much scrutiny to be
beasts, either because of a few differences they observed in external
conformation, or simply because the animal did not speak, were not in
fact real savage men, whose race, dispersed since antiquity in the
forests, with no opportunity to develop any of its potential faculties,
had not acquired any measure of perfection.[24]

How modern the passage sounds, and how different from either the
views of medieval travellers or of nineteenth-century racial scientists.
There are a number of aspects of this passage that are worth noting. First,
Rousseau does not elevate the importance of one physical characteristic
–such as colour – above another. He is largely indifferent to the social or
moral meaning of physical differences. Second, he believes that physical
differences are plastic – that they are caused by environmental factors
and change over time. Third, he argues that all humans have the potential for perfectibility – by which he means not aspiring to a perfect type,
but the possibility for self-improvement – but this potential can only be
released under certain environmental or social circumstances. Finally, he
believes that technological and social progress helps diminish differences between peoples. Taken together, these arguments embody the progressive nature of Enlightenment universalism.

For Rousseau, as for many of his contemporaries, there was a dialectical relationship between the unity of humanity and its diversity. It
was necessary to study and understand strange and different cultures, Rousseau argued, if one was to understand the commonality of
'man':

When one wants to study men, one must consider those around one. But to study man, one must expand the range of one's vision. One must first observe the differences in order to discover the properties.[25]

Indeed Rousseau chides European travellers for failing to do just that:

In the two or three centuries since the inhabitants of Europe have been flooding into other parts of the world, endlessly publishing new collections of voyages and travel, I am persuaded that we have come to know no other men except Europeans; moreover it appears from the ridiculous prejudices, which have not died out even among men of letters, that every author produces under the pompous name of the study of man nothing much more than the study of men of his own country.[26]

Rousseau's criticisms of what we would today call 'ethnocentric' attitudes are well merited. What is striking about Enlightenment discourse, however, is the lack of any discussion of race. Enlightenment thinkers may have thought of other cultures solely in terms of their own, but they rarely categorised humanity in racial terms. Compared to writings both before and after, eighteenth-century works show a remarkable disdain for racial arguments.

In 1800 the French anthropologist Joseph-Marie Degerando wrote his *Considerations on the diverse methods to follow in the observation of savage peoples* as a methodological memoir for the Société des Observateurs de l'Homme in Paris. Though it comes at the very end of the century of light, Degerando's work is infused with the spirit of the Enlightenment. His aim in the memoir was to establish a scientific basis for the study of non-European peoples. Like Rousseau, Degerando regarded most travellers' accounts of foreign cultures as simply a transposition of their understanding of European life:

[T]hey habitually judge the customs of Savages by analogies drawn from our own customs, when in fact they are so little related to each other ... They make the Savage reason as we do when the Savage does not himself explain his reasoning. So it is that they often pronounce such severe sentences on a nation, that they have accused them of cruelty, of theft, of debauchery, of atheism.[27]

Instead Degerando set out a strict methodology that scientists should follow to obtain the information. His point of departure was a universalist and rationalist framework established by the Enlightenment. We know what humanity in general is like, he argued, but we need to use scientific methods to determine where particular human beings fitted in with respect to the ideal type.

Scientists, he said, must begin by learning the language of the people under study. They can then investigate the kind of ideas these people possess, beginning with the simplest forms (knowledge of qualities such as colour) before moving on to more complex abstract ideas of which 'even savages cannot be utterly deprived', though Degerando did believe that 'the ideas with which the Savages would be least occupied are those belonging to reflection'. The observer would then examine the savages' moral ideas, again beginning with those closest to sensory experience, such as joy or fear, before moving on to such moral categories as judgement and will. Degerando insists that the observer must not take anything for granted, but must begin from first principles in trying to understand the modes of reasoning and kinds of beliefs of his subjects. This is clear from the questions Degerando poses about the subject:

> Does he go back from the knowledge of effects to the supposition of certain causes, and how does he imagine these causes? Does he allow a first cause? Does he attribute it to intelligence, power, wisdom, and goodness? Does he believe it to be immaterial?[28]

After studying the individual, the scientist must investigate the 'savage in society'. Like Buffon, Degerando was convinced that 'there is no species of savages among whom is not to be found at least the beginnings of society.' The study of society must include observation of domestic, political, civil, economic and religious life. The scientist must also study the 'traditions' of savage peoples.

What is striking in all this, as George Stocking observes, is that in a methodological memoir on anthropological research Degerando did not think it necessary to deal with the question of racial differences:

> What is utterly lacking in Degerando's *Considerations* is any concept of 'race', any notion of permanent hereditary differences between groups of the human family . . . [T]he different savage groups were always 'peoples' or 'nations' – never 'races'; and their differences were environmental rather than hereditary.[29]

Degerando considered it essential to establish a scientific understanding of the differences between 'civilised' and 'savage' man. But he did not for a moment doubt that there existed a commonality that bound both together. Science, for Degerando, was a means of establishing our common humanity, not – as it was to be in the following century – a means of demonstrating the natural inferiority of certain groups of people, and superiority of others.

Like most of his contemporaries, Degerando believed that the highest form of civilisation was European culture. But civilisation, for Degerando, did not belong to Europeans; all humanity could aspire to reach the summit of social development. What more 'touching purpose' could there be, asked Degerando, than 'to reestablish the holy knots of universal society, than to meet again these ancient parents separated by a long exile from the rest of the common family, than to extend the hand by which they raise themselves to a more happy state?'[30]

The Enlightenment belief in a common, universal human nature tended to undermine any proclivity for a racial categorisation of humanity. There were of course exceptions. Voltaire, for instance, claimed that 'Only a blind man could doubt that the whites, Negroes, albinos, Hottentots, Laplanders, Chinese are entirely different races.'[31] David Hume, even though he argued that 'it is universally acknowledged that there is great uniformity among the acts of men, in all nations and ages, and human nature remains still the same in its principles and operations', nevertheless also wrote that 'I am apt to suspect the negroes to be naturally inferior to the whites':

> There scarcely ever was a civilised nation of that complexion, nor even any individual, eminent either in action or speculation. No ingenious manufactures amongst them, no arts, no sciences. On the other, the most rude and barbarous of the whites, such as the ancient Germans, the present Tartars, have still something eminent about them, in their valour, form of government, or some other particular. Such a uniform and constant difference could not happen, in so many countries and ages, if nature had not made an initial distinction between these breeds of men.[32]

We should remember, however, that Hume's comment came but in footnote and is out of sympathy with his usual line of reasoning. Indeed in his essay *Of Commerce*, he argues the very opposite to the above. Hume asks, 'What is the reason why no people living between the tropics could ever yet attain to any art of civility, or even reach any police in their government, and any military discipline, while few nations in the temperate climates have been altogether deprived of these advantages?' His answer was not that the people of the tropics were naturally inferior but that the tropical environment rendered it unnecessary for them to develop European forms of civilisation:

> It is probable that one cause of this phenomenon is the warmth and equality of the weather in the torrid zone, which renders clothes and houses less requisite for the inhabitants and thereby remove, in part, that necessity which is the great spur to industry and invention . . .

Not to mention, that the fewer goods or possessions of this kind any people enjoy, the fewer quarrels are likely to arise amongst them, and the less necessity will there be for a settled police or regular authority, to protect and defend them from foreign enemies, or from each other.[33]

Rousseau would not have disagreed with that. We should remember too that neither Hume nor Voltaire was an enthusiastic supporter of the Enlightenment belief in equality. Voltaire was a strong believer in 'enlightened absolutism', while, as we shall, see, Hume's thought was to play a major part in the conservative reaction to the Enlightenment.

  In general, differences between human groups were inevitably seen as environmental, not natural. Even those eighteenth-century writers whose work is sometimes considered to have prefigured nineteenth-century scientific racism held strongly to their environmentalist belief. Buffon, for instance, is often portrayed as the founder of scientific racism. Tzvetan Todorov has said of him that 'the racialist theory in its entirety is found in Buffon's writings'.[34] It is true that Buffon accepted the existence of races and, unlike virtually all his contemporaries, even accepted slavery. His views, however, were a long way from nineteenth-century racism. Human differences, including physical differences, were, he asserted, the product of environmental or cultural factors: '[T]he differences of colour depend much, though not entirely upon the climates. There are many other causes . . . The nature of food is one of the principle causes . . . Manners, or the mode of living, may also have considerable effects.'[35]

  Enlightenment thinkers clearly held prejudiced and racist views and looked down on less enlightened souls as inferiors. It would have been astonishing if it had been otherwise. But what was absent was any sustained discourse of race. Michael Banton, Robert Miles and Anthony Barker, in their various surveys of racial thinking, have all argued that, in Banton's words, 'though there was a substantial literature in the seventeenth and eighteenth centuries about Africans and other non-Europeans, the word "race" was rarely used either to describe peoples or in accounts of differences between them'.[36] Contrast eighteenth-century views on human differences with those of the following century and the special qualities of Enlightenment discourse becomes clear. How very dissimilar are the views of men like Degerando or Rousseau to those of British naturalist Thomas Huxley a century later. Huxley was a liberal, a humanitarian and one of the most progressive men of his age. He no doubt considered himself as standing in the Enlightenment tradition. Yet his concept of race was diametrically opposed to that of the *philosophes*:

  It is simply incredible that, when all his disabilities are removed, and our prognathous relative has a fair field and no favour, as well as no oppressor, he will be able to compete successfully with his bigger-brained and smaller-jawed rival, in a contest that is to be carried out by thoughts and not by bites. The highest places in the hierarchy of civilisation will assuredly not be within the reach of our dusky cousins, though it is by no means necessary that they should be restricted to the lowest.[37]

Any history of the development of the modern concept of race, then, will have to account for how the view of a common humanity held by men such as Blumenbach, Degerando and Rousseau was overturned. The modern concept of race is not simply a continuation of age-old prejudices. It could only have risen in opposition to the Enlightenment view. How and why did that happen?

EQUALITY AND SOCIAL CONFLICT

The tolerance, egalitarianism and optimism that characterised the Enlightenment derived, at least in part, from the relative stability of Europe in the first part of the eighteenth century. Economically, there had been steady development through the early part of the eighteenth century. But, with the exception of England, this barely touched the lives of the vast majority of the population. The Continent was overwhelmingly rural and life for the majority remained parochial, fragmented and inward-looking. Of the new, growing entrepreneurial class, the key figures were the merchant, the financier, and the colonial planter, not the 'industrialist' who, in any case, was more likely to be an artisan selling his own goods than a factory owner. The 'Industrial Revolution' did not begin until the 1780s, and then only in England. In the rest of Europe, the repercussions of industrialisation were not felt until the following century.

Politically, again with the exception of Britain, most of Europe was under the rule of feudal absolutism throughout the century of light. At the top of the absolutist order were hereditary monarchs, enthroned by divine right. Below them were hierarchies of landed nobles. Buttressing the whole system was an orthodoxy of churches and a clutter of institutions whose power seemed to derive from their very obsolescence. Even in England, which was seen by most of Europe as a bastion of individual rights, Parliament derived its power from traditional rights and privileges, not from its role as a democratic institution.

Enlightenment discourse aimed to free humanity from the grip of tradition and unreason, to abolish archaic institutions based on prescription and to establish society on a more rational foundation. As such it appealed to the nascent bourgeoisie, whose aspirations to economic, political and social power required the undermining of feudal institutions. But those who led the 'middle way' in society, as David Hume put it, lacked the social means to effect change. There developed therefore a relationship between the educated classes who formed the backbone of the Enlightenment and the feudal rulers of Europe.

Enlightenment rationality appealed to feudal monarchs who wanted to modernise their kingdoms without upsetting the old social order. As the ramshackle feudal bureaucracy grew in size and importance, so monarchs were obliged to curb the more anarchic tendencies of the nobility and to introduce non-aristocratic civil servants into their government ministries in an effort to run their system more efficiently. 'In those days', observes Hobsbawm,

> princes adopted the slogan of enlightenment as governments in our time, and for analogous reasons, adopt those of planning; and as in our day some who adopted them in theory did very little about them in practice, and most who did so were less interested in the ideal which lay behind the enlightened (or the planned) society, than in the practical advantage of adopting the most up-to-date methods of multiplying their revenue, wealth and power.[38]

Hence the feudal rulers of Europe drew on the new learning of the Enlightenment to buttress their decaying regimes.

At the same time the emerging class of entrepreneurs and professionals began to look to the powerful central apparatus of an 'enlightened' monarchy to further their own social aims. For such individuals the main obstacle to progress seemed to be the nobility. The aspiring middle classes of Europe hoped therefore to use the monarchy to reform society in the way that England had reformed itself in the previous century. They desired not social revolution but the removal of the impediments to individual self-advancement. The best means to achieve this appeared to be through the power and privilege of the monarchy.

The Enlightenment, then, developed not so much as the handmaiden of capitalism but more as an ideology that could appeal to different social forces. In the first part of the eighteenth century it helped cement a symbiotic relationship between the rising middle classes and decaying feudal absolutism. 'A prince needed the middle class and its ideas to modernise his state', observes Hobsbawm. 'A weak middle class needed a prince to batter down the resistance of entrenched aristocratic and clerical reaction to progress.'[39] In England the Settlement of 1688 had effected a reconciliation between the interests of the nascent bourgeoisie and those of the old order which helped create a political oligarchy within which market forces could develop. But in Continental Europe, and particularly in France, the attempt to manage economic, political and social change within the framework of the old feudal society created increasing conflict from the mid-eighteenth century onwards, conflict that would undermine the Enlightenment project even as the middle classes who championed the philosophy achieved power.

On the one hand, it was clear that the aspirations of the capitalist class could not be met within the bounds of a feudal, absolutist society. Absolute monarchy could not break loose from the hierarchy of landed nobles to which it belonged, whose values it symbolised and incorporated and on whose support it largely depended. It could not achieve the root-and-branch social transformation which the progress of the economy required and which the rising social groups called for.

On the other hand, the increasing power possessed by the middle classes led them to re-examine the philosophical tenets of the Enlightenment. The concepts which had been useful to batter down the old order became dangerous in maintaining the new. In the volatile social and political climate that the breakdown of feudal society created, it became clear that the philosophy of the Enlightenment equally appealed to those who sought a much more fundamental transformation of society than that to which many sections of the middle classes aspired. Bourgeois radicals such as the American patriots sought to break free from the claims of political oligarchy and fashioned a new discourse of rights to justify their arguments. The poor, the propertyless and the dispossessed, such as the Parisian masses who provided the social support for the revolutionary Jacobin regime of 1793–4, challenged the sanctity of property in the name of social equality. Toussaint L'Ouverture and the black masses of Saint-Domingue in the French West Indies emancipated themselves from slavery and declared national independence in the name of the Universal Rights of Man.

For the rising bourgeoisie the idea of a natural equality and of a common human nature had been an important argument in opposition to the notion of a divinely sanctioned social order. The concepts of reason and progress appealed to a class whose strength lay in its ability to revolutionise the productive process. To create a workforce for their enterprises, the capitalists had to undermine the idea of social obligation inherent in the feudal system and declare all men to be 'free'. The universalistic, optimistic outlook of the Enlightenment helped the nascent bourgeoisie rally opinion against the old order. The fusion of capitalist aspiration and Enlightenment philosophy reached its apogee in the French Revolution.

But the French Revolution was also to demonstrate the social limits to Enlightenment ideas of equality. Unlike in England, where the old order was able to come to a compromise with the new social classes, no such compromise was possible in France. This had two consequences. First, the middle classes could not achieve power by harnessing history and tradition as in Britain, but only through a rejection of tradition and in the name of an abstract principle – that of universal rights. The appeal to principle imbued the Revolution with historical importance as it became universally seen as the social embodiment of Enlightenment reason. Secondly, as a result of the intransigence of the old order, the bourgeoisie had to mobilise the masses – the peasantry, the Parisian *sans-culottes*, the Saint-Domingue slaves – to prevent the restoration of the *ancien régime*. The combination of an appeal to abstract principle and the mobilisation of the masses pushed the Revolution much further along the road to equality than any social movement had gone before. It is no coincidence that English and American radicals who migrated to France because of their sympathy with the revolutionary cause found themselves to be moderates there. Tom Paine, for instance, regarded as an extremist in England and America, lined up in France with the more conservative Girondins, not with the revolutionary Jacobins.

The French Revolution became the practical embodiment of the Enlightenment belief in equality, and one that inspired radicals throughout Europe and indeed the world. But it also became, for many, an illustration of the darker side of reason. The social and political upheaval caused by the Revolution created a backlash against the Enlightenment within sections of the bourgeoisie. Isaiah Berlin has summed up the new doubts about reason and equality raised by the social turmoil of Revolutionary France:

> The French Revolution was founded on the notion of timeless truths given to the faculty of reason with which all men were endowed. It was dedicated to the creation or restoration of a static and harmonious society, founded on unaltering principles, a dream of classical perfection, or, at least, the closest approximation to it feasible on earth. It preached a peaceful universalism and a rational humanitarianism. But its consequence threw into relief the precariousness of human institutions; the disturbing phenomenon of apparently irresistible change; the clash of irreconcilable values and ideas; the insufficiency of simple formulas; the complexity of men and societies; the poetry of action, disruption, heroism and war; the effectiveness of mobs and of great men; the crucial role played by chance; the feebleness of reason before the power of fanatically believed doctrines; the unpredictability of events.[40]

The Revolution demonstrated that the self-confidence of the educated classes, their readiness to engage in radical political and philosophical speculation and their willingness to mock religion and embrace the principles of the natural equality of man all rested on the almost universal conviction that the social order was static, or at least that change would be orderly and contained. It brought into sharp focus the already contradictory attitudes of the bourgeoisie towards the idea of equality. On the one hand the belief in equality was at the heart of the bourgeois political programme. On the other the defence of private property seemed to require a defence of inequality. 'Wherever there is great property', wrote Adam Smith in *The Wealth of Nations,* 'there is great inequality. For every one rich man there must be at least five hundred poor, and the affluence of the few supposes the indigence of the many.'[41] In an early draft of *The Wealth of Nations,*[42] Smith accepted that such inequality was the product not of nature, but of society:

> In reality, the difference of natural talents in different men is perhaps much less than we are aware of, and the very different genius which appears to distinguish men of different professions when grown up to maturity, is not, perhaps, so much the cause as the effect of the division of labour.[43]

Such inequality, however, was the price to be paid for economic progress and capitalist utility. At the same time, since the poor would be unwilling to accept such inequality, society needed to ensure that the rights of the propertied were protected:

> The affluence of the rich excites the indignation of the poor, who are both driven by want and prompted by envy, to invade his possessions. It is only under the shelter of the civil magistrate that the owner of that valuable property, which is acquired by the labour of many years, or perhaps of many successive generations, can sleep a single night in security . . . The acquisition of valuable and extensive property, there-fore, necessarily requires the establishment of civil government.[44]

Smith accepted the concept of equality in the abstract. The needs of property-owning democracy, however, induced him to accept that there had to be limits to this equality, that the propertyless classes had to be denied certain rights to protect the rights of the propertied classes. For Rousseau, on the other hand, the inequality established by private property ran contrary to natural law. Rousseau opened his *Discourse on Inequality* by observing that there are 'two sorts of inequality in the human species':

> [T]he first I call natural or physical because it is established by nature, and consists of differences in age, health, strength of body and qualities of the mind and soul; the second we might call moral or political inequality because it derives from a sort of convention, and is established, or at least authorised, by the consent of men. This latter

inequality consists of the different privileges which some enjoy to the prejudice of others – such as their being richer, more honoured, more powerful than others, and even getting themselves obeyed by others.[45]

The inequality decreed by private property ran contrary to the dictates of nature:

[I]nequality, being almost non-existent in the state of nature, derives its force and its growth from the development of our faculties and the progress of the human mind, and finally becomes fixed and legitimate through the institution of property and laws. It follows . . . that moral inequality, authorised by positive law alone, is contrary to natural right, whenever it is not matched in exact proportion with physical inequality . . . for it is manifestly contrary to the law of nature, however defined, that a child should govern an old man, that an imbecile should lead a wise man, and that a handful of people should gorge themselves with superfluities while a hungry multitude goes in want of necessities.[46]

The distinction that Rousseau draws between natural and artificial inequality is important in our narrative of race. For, as I shall argue in the next chapter, the modern concept of race arises from the attempt to attribute to nature the inequality that Rousseau rightly regards as the product of the moral or political domain. But that is to run ahead of the argument. For now, I want to examine the limitations on the Enlightenment concept of equality placed by the social needs of the new society.

Smith and Rousseau were both leading figures of the Enlightenment. In the abstract they both accepted the ideas of equality and human unity that were woven into the thread of Enlightenment thought. But by the eve of the French Revolution the meaning of a term such as equality could no longer be a matter simply of abstract debate. Its significance was a social, not simply an intellectual, matter. In the early part of the eighteenth century, it had seemed to many that science and reason alone could settle social disputes and help promote reform and change. By the end of the century, contending social forces disputed the very meaning of such terms. The interests of different strands of bourgeois opinion, of various fractions of the capitalist class, of defenders of the dying feudal order and of the growing dispossessed and propertyless classes all seemed irreconcilable.

In this context, the debate between Smith and Rousseau could not be settled intellectually. Each represented not simply a different strand of Enlightenment thought but a different social force. Smith articulated the interests of the capitalist class, Rousseau was the voice of the dispossessed. For Smith, the needs of property seemed to imply a social restriction on equality. For Rousseau, the needs of equality seemed to require restrictions on property rights. The conflict between the different meanings of equality which their arguments embodied could only be reconciled through social struggle.

EQUALITY, SLAVERY AND PRIVATE PROPERTY

One of the clearest illustrations of both the conflict between the defence of equality and the defence of property relations, and its social resolution, can be seen in the debate about slavery that took place through the eighteenth and nineteenth centuries. Reviewing the debate on slavery allows us to understand better both the relationship between equality and race and the origins of racial discourse.

In 1839 Alexis de Tocqueville helped prepare a report on slavery for the French Chamber of Deputies. 'Man has never had the right to possess man', claimed the report, 'and the fact of possession always has been and still is illegitimate.' De Tocqueville's philosophical opposition to slavery could not have been clearer. Yet from a practical point of view de Tocqueville claimed rights for slaveholders that his philosophical position would have seemed to deny. 'If the Negroes have the right to become free', he was to write, 'it is undeniable that the colonials have the right not to be ruined by the Negroes' freedom.' The right of slaveholders included the receipt of 'an indemnity representing the venal value of freed slaves' and a 'temporary' ban on 'the right [of Negroes] to become property owners.' It was as if the right of possession of man by man was illegitimate but the fact of such possession – the actually existing property relations – endowed it with legitimacy.

De Tocqueville's attempt to reconcile the rights of slaves with those of slaveholders shows the difficulty which the Euro-American political tradition has faced in dealing with the concept of equality. De Tocqueville was a liberal and a democrat. That even he should demand that restrictions be placed upon the abolition of slavery demonstrates the degree of ambivalence towards equality.

Many have seen in the vacillating attitude to slavery – and in the fact that the institution should remain legal for almost a century after the Declaration of the Rights of Man – evidence for the deep-seated nature of racism in Western culture.[47] Racism, such authors suggest, was responsible for slavery, or at least for the ambivalence of the opposition to it. In fact racism played little role in creating or justifying modern slavery. Rather the difficulties raised by slavery came from the fact that it was seen as a form of property. Reposing the question of slavery in this fashion helps us reconsider the origins of racial discourse.

Slavery was rarely rationalised on the grounds that Africans were biologically inferior or non-human. As Anthony Barker notes, 'the debate over slavery never developed into a debate over the nature of the Negro.'[48] Nor did the treatment of African slaves as merchandise mean that all Africans were regarded in this fashion, or that they were always regarded so. In 1765 William Blackstone published his *Commentaries on the Laws of England*, an attempt to codify England's legal and constitutional doctrine. In it he argued that the 'spirit of liberty is so implanted in our constitution, and rooted in our very soil, that a slave or a negro, the moment he lands in England falls under the protection of the laws and becomes *eo instanto* a freeman.'[49] Such arguments fit ill with the idea that a belief in the inherent inferiority of Africans fuelled the transatlantic slave trade.

Seymour Drescher notes that at the start of the campaign for abolition of slavery, the defenders of the system attempted to use both racial and biblical arguments to defend traffic in human cargo. 'Quite significantly, however', he writes, 'neither line of argument was sustained in either polemical or Parliamentary debate.'[50] The political mood of eighteenth-century England simply did not allow for such arguments. Historians such as Peter Fryer have pointed to the work of authors such as Jamaican planter Edward Long to argue the case for a racial basis for slavery.[51] Certainly Long's *History of Jamaica*, written in part as a response to the gains of the abolitionist movement, is a sustained polemic on 'the dissimilarity [of Africans] to the rest of mankind', an insistence that they 'are a different species' and a comparison of their intellect with that of orang-utangs. But, as David Brion Davis points out, Long's affirmation of black inferiority was 'totally unrepresentative of his time'.[52] In Drescher's words, 'Racial, biblical and classical Aristotelian proslavery arguments occupied a very subordinate place in British political discourse during the eighteenth and early nineteenth centuries.'[53]

The principal arguments for slavery were not racial but centred around the practicality or economic utility of the use of slaves. According to Barker there was a general lack of interest in racial differences beyond the rationalisation of cheap tropical labour. Black slaves were regarded as the only available labour to work New World plantations and as best suited to work in the tropics. Even Montesquieu, for all his abhorrence of slavery, conceded that enslavement might sometimes be a necessary evil:

There are countries where the excess of heat enervates the body, and renders a man so slothful and dispirited, that nothing but the fear of chastisement can oblige them to perform any laborious duty: slavery is there more reconcilable to reason; and the master being as lazy with respect to his sovereign, as is his slave to him, this adds a political, to a civil slavery.[54]

We might today find such claims distasteful. But we should be careful not to attribute such sentiments to 'racism'. It was economic utility, not racial ideology, that underpinned the arguments for slavery.

Precisely because slavery was defended for its practical utility, the main debate was that between the rights of property-owners and the right to liberty. In Britain, it was, as Drescher observes, the 'transfer of social relationships from the slave colonies of the New World to the metropolis which first converted the latent social contradiction between slavery and freedom in Britain into a public issue.'[55] Slavery in the West Indies was far enough away not to be too troubling to the conscience. It was when slaves came to Britain that conflict between a philosophical outlook and a social institution came to the fore.

In 1771 Granville Sharpe, the Quaker anti-slavery campaigner, secured a warrant for the arrest of a master who had attempted to drag an unwilling slave to a waiting boat on the Thames, so as to return him to the West Indies. At the trial, the judge, Lord Mansfield, who a year later was to preside over the famous Somerset case, opened proceedings by noting that he himself had always respected the right of property in slaves. This made no impression on the jury. Mansfield insisted that the only issue for the jury to consider was whether or not the evidence of ownership was conclusive. The jury ignored Mansfield's pronouncements. When the foreman announced that they did not find the servant to be the defendant's property, the jury collectively shouted 'No property! No property!'[56]

The trial provided a little vignette of the whole slavery debate. How one perceived slavery depended largely on how one perceived private property. The most conservative commentators argued that slavery should be reformed but not necessarily abolished. 'The property of the West Indians is at stake', one pro-slavery MP remarked during a parliamentary debate in 1790 (meaning by 'West Indian' white colonists). 'And though men may be generous with their own property they should not be so with the property of others.'[57] Edmund Burke, writing in the wake of the French Revolution, felt that 'the cause of humanity would be far more benefited by the continuance of the trade and servitude, regulated and reformed, than the total destruction of both or either.'[58]

More liberal commentators tended to support the abolition of the slave trade on humanitarian grounds, but were anxious about the real motives of abolitionists. Lord Gibbon wrote to Lord Sheffield on the eve of a House of Commons vote in 1792 on a motion to abolish the slave trade:

If it proceeded only from an impulse of humanity, I cannot be displeased . . . But in this rage against slavery, in the numerous petitions against the slave trade, was there no leaven of democratic principles? No wild ideas of the rights and natural equality of man?[59]

Gibbon's paternalistic 'impulse of humanity' clearly did not extend as far as equal rights or democratic ideas. Others were more radical in their opposition to slavery but tended to stress the rights of both slaves and of slaveholders. The Scottish philosopher Francis Hutcheson, for instance, believed that slavery was a violation of 'all sense of natural justice': 'No damage done or crime committed can change a rational creature into a piece of goods void of all right, and incapable of acquiring any, or of receiving any injury from the proprietor.'[60] The conclusion that Hutcheson drew from this was not, however, that slavery should be abolished forthwith. It was rather that slaves had a right to be free once they had paid off through their unfree labour that which it had cost their master to procure them:

> Thus suppose that a merchant buys a hundred such slaves; so that his whole charges on the voyage, and prime cost of the captives, adding also a reasonable merchant's profit upon the stock employed, amount to a thousand pounds. These captives are his debtors jointly for this sum; and as soon as the value of their labours beyond maintenance amounts to this sum, and the legal interest from the time it was advanced, they have a right to be free.[61]

As Robin Blackburn notes, Hutcheson's difficulty arose from his 'wish to attack slavery but not to infringe legally acquired property rights or to question long-term indenture or even service for life, such as still survived in the coal mines of eighteenth-century Scotland.'[62] The ambivalence of such liberals often led them to compromise by attacking the slave trade, but not slavery itself. Attacking a branch of commerce was easier than attacking a form of property.

Liberal anti-slavery impulses were strengthened by the fact they could find support in the new theories of political economy. Both Adam Smith in *The Wealth of Nations* and John Millar in *The Origin of the Distinction of Ranks*, penned strong polemics against slavery on the grounds that it was an unprofitable and unproductive form of labour, compared to free labour. The importance of slavery to mercantile capital and the desire to defend property rights, however, generally ensured that in practice liberals adopted a more pusillanimous position.

Those who were hostile to property rights, on the other hand, tended to take an unequivocal view of the iniquities of slavery. A good illustration is George Wallace, whose arguments on slavery had a major impact on Rousseau, the Encyclopedists and other Enlightenment thinkers. In his *System of the Principles of the Law of Scotland*, Wallace declared that every slave 'has a right to be free, for he never lost his liberty' since 'his prince had no power to dispose of him'. The right to liberty every slave 'carries about with him and is entitled everywhere to get it declared':

As soon, therefore, as he comes into a country, in which the judges are not forgetful of their own humanity, it is their duty to remember that he is a man and to declare him to be free.[63]

Wallace's anti-slavery radicalism came more easily to him because of his unusual lack of respect for private property:

Property, that bane of human felicity, is too deeply rooted in society, and is thought too essential to the subsistence of it, easily to be abolished. But it must necessarily be banished out of the world before an Utopia can be established.[64]

Such radicals often defended the use of violence to overthrow colonial slavery, as they did to overthrow 'wage slavery' at home, and called on whites to join the struggle. An anti-slavery pamphlet published in London in 1760 attacked the institution in most uncompromising terms:

And so all the black men in our plantations, who are by unjust force deprived of their liberty, and held in slavery, as they have none upon the earth to appeal to, may lawfully repel that force with force, and to recover their liberty, destroy their oppressors; and not only so but it is the duty of others, white as well as blacks, to assist those miserable creatures, if they can, in their attempts to deliver them out of slavery, and to rescue them out of the hands of cruel tyrants.[65]

Just as attitudes to slavery were largely shaped by attitudes to property, so the fortunes of the abolition movement fluctuated according to the ebb and flow of the broader social currents. When radicals were on the march, the cause of anti-slavery prospered. When radicals were on the defensive it faltered.

The breakdown of the old order and the radicalisation of society at the end of the 1780s helped put slavery at the centre of the political agenda. 'In the midst of Britain's great interwar boom and the French Revolution', writes Seymour Drescher, 'abolitionism became entwined with more general assertions of human rights and with the diffuse movements to make England a more equal society.' Thomas Hardy, who with Tom Paine and others founded the London Corresponding Society in January 1792, declared that the Rights of Man 'are not confined to this small island but are extended to the whole human race, black or white, high or low, rich or poor.'[66] Of course, abolitionism was more than simply a variant of radical politics. It drew support from all sections of society. But, in England, its impetus in this period came from the crisis of the Hanoverian regime and the space this opened up for more progressive politics.

The impact of the Jacobin regime in France, on the other hand, the growing anti-French chauvinism in Britain and Britain's declaration of war with France divided the abolitionists, provoked a counter-revolutionary mobilisation and put the radical forces on the defensive. Abolitionism slipped out of British politics for more than a decade. It was not until the early 1800s, for reasons too complex to consider here, that abolitionism was to return to British political debate.[67]

The case of France shows even more clearly how the fate of abolitionism rested to a large degree on the fortunes of wider social movements. The *philosophes*, as we have already seen, were fiercely opposed to slavery. 'The tenor of French writing on slavery', Robin Blackburn observes, 'had often been more radical, if also more rhetorical, than that to be found in Britain or the United States, and less inclined to take the form of a systematic moral tract.'[68] In 1770 the Abbé Raynal penned a remarkable polemic against unfree labour in his *Histoire des Deux Indes*, which went through 55 editions in five languages in the following 30 years. Arguing that 'natural liberty is the right which nature has given to everyone to dispose of himself according to his will', Raynal both prophesied and defended the revolutionary overthrow of slavery: 'These enterprises are so many indicators of the impending storm, and the negroes only want a chief, sufficiently courageous to lead them to vengeance and slaughter . . . Where is the new Spartacus?'[69]

Even more than in England, however, the middle classes in France were resistant to the claims of the abolitionists. The strength of the old order in France and the weakness of the bourgeoisie meant that it was dependent largely on colonial trade. Colonial wealth played a major part in the growth of bourgeois power in ports such as Bordeaux and Nantes. One in five members of the National Assembly owned colonial property, and a much larger number were linked to the colonies through trade or administration. The narrow base of the French capitalist class meant that it was even more important that slavery be protected as private property. The radical Jacobins, as much as the moderate Girondins, drew their power from colonial trade. The result, as historian Michael Kennedy notes, is that despite the Jacobin Revolutionary clubs' 'oft-expressed devotion for liberty and equality', they 'long remained indifferent to the horrors of slavery and the slave trade.'[70]

The radicals in the Assembly took their stand, not on the abolition of slavery, but on civic rights for 'free men of colour'. The Assembly agreed that qualified blacks – that is, those with property – should have the vote. But the delegates refused to oppose, indeed barely considered the issue of, slavery. On 4 March 1790 the Committee on Colonies declared that 'the National Assembly does not intend to make any innovations in any of the branches of commerce between France and the colonies, whether direct or indirect.' As a warning to abolitionists it put 'colonists and their property under the special safeguard of the nation and declares guilty of treason whoever seeks to foment risings against them.'[71]

As in England the justification for slavery was economic, not racial. Indeed, given the granting of the vote to qualified men of colour – something denied to many *petit blancs,* or poor whites, because of the property qualification – racial arguments in favour of slavery would not have been credible. Moderate republican leaders maintained that inequality was an evil, but a lesser evil than the chaos, disorder and economic ruin that would spring from the abolition of slavery. 'This regime is absurd', Girondist leader Antoine Barnave said of the slave colony on Saint Domingue, 'but one cannot handle it roughly without unleashing the greatest disorder. This regime is oppressive, but it gives livelihood to several million Frenchmen. This regime is barbarous but a still greater barbarity will result if you interfere with it without the necessary knowledge.'[72] More radical delegates challenged such arguments. 'You urge without ceasing the Rights of Man', claimed Robespierre. 'But you believe in them so little yourself that you have sanctified slavery constitutionally.'[73] But such critics did little in practice to challenge slavery.

What transformed the situation was the social power of the masses. In August 1791 Saint-Domingue slaves rose in rebellion. Initially anti-Republican, the rebels, and in particular their foremost leader, Toussaint L'Ouverture, came to realise that the emancipatory logic of the French Revolution could provide the ideological fuel for the rebellion. On the other side, Légér Félicité Sonthonax, the Jacobin commissioner sent to Saint-Domingue in July 1792, recognised that he needed black allies in his struggle against moderate and racist Republicans on the one hand and the encroaching Spanish and English forces on the other. He announced a local decree of general emancipation in August 1793.

Meanwhile, in metropolitan France, the Parisian masses – faced with royalist plots, intervention from abroad and a vacillating Girondin government – armed themselves, stormed the Tuilleries, imprisoned the royal family, dissolved the legislative, elected a new parliament, the National Convention, and helped put the Jacobins in power. In this new political climate private property was no longer sacred. Indeed the rich were now held to be suspect in their patriotism. The issue of slavery became of central importance, as C. L. R. James wonderfully describes in *The Black Jacobins,* his magnificent narrative of the Haitian revolution:

> The workers and peasants of France could not have been expected to take any interest in the colonial question in normal times, any more than one can expect similar interest from British or French workers today. But now they were roused. They were striking at royalty, tyranny, reaction and oppression of all types and with these they

included slavery. The prejudice of race is superficially the most irrational of all prejudices and by a perfectly comprehensible reaction the
Paris workers, from indifference in 1789, had come by this time to
detest no section of the aristocracy so much as those whom they called
'the aristocrats of the skin'.[74]

On 3 February 1794, in the presence of delegates from Saint-Domingue,
the Convention abolished slavery in the name of the Universal Rights of
Man. 'In consequence', it declared, 'all men, without distinction of colour, domiciled in the colonies, are French citizens, and enjoy all the rights
enjoyed under the Constitution.' Property, as C. L. R. James was memor-
ably to put it, had listened to reason but only because it had been cowed
by violence.[75]

THE SOCIAL LIMITS TO EQUALITY

I have dealt with the relationship between slavery and property at some
length for two reasons. First, it illustrates my argument that the logic of
Enlightenment universalism was at heart emancipatory, but that the
particular form adopted by Enlightenment universalism depended on
the balance of social forces. Robin Blackburn has summed up well the
relationship between Enlightenment ideology and contending social
forces in the abolition of slavery during the momentous days of the
French Revolution:

> There was a universalistic emancipatory element in the French Revol-
> ution, but those who issued the Declaration of the Rights of Man were
> by no means always aware of it, or willing to follow through its logic.
> Here we may see the limitations as well as the achievements of a
> formal, abstract mode of reasoning characteristic of increasingly mar-
> ketised social relations. For the emancipatory promise to be fulfilled
> there was needed the independent action of formerly excluded, op-
> pressed and exploited social layers – radicalised *sans culottes* and slave
> rebels who understood that there could be no peace with slavery or
> slaveholders.[76]

Despite the arguments of Goldberg and others that I mentioned at the
beginning of this chapter, what the discussion of slavery helps establish
is that the categories of Enlightenment discourse were not imbricated
with racial ideology. On the contrary, the Enlightenment helped establish
for the first time, in theory at least, the possibility of human emancipation. But it did so in social circumstances that limited the expression of
its emancipatory potential. Where social forces drawing on the logic of

Enlightenment discourse had sufficient strength, they could pursue the goal of equality beyond that envisaged by those who drew up the Declaration of the Rights of Man, or the American Declaration of Independence. But where such forces were weak, the contradictory attitude of the capitalist class towards equality ensured that increasing limits were placed on its expression.

The second reason for examining the relationship between slavery and property is that it helps us understand the relationship between the concept of race and social restrictions on equality. The traditional, indeed common-sense, understanding is that a racial view of humanity has led to a restriction on the rights of certain groups in society, whether formally or informally. People are denied equality, or treated differently, because they are, or are perceived to be, racially different.

As I suggested at the start of the chapter, this is a tautological argument, amounting to the assertion that racial differences give rise to racial inequality. The discussion of slavery allows us to view this process in a different way. It is not racial categorisation but the social needs of modern society that impel it to restrict the concept of equal rights. Economic utility and the desire not to challenge property rights, not racial ideology, gave rise to Western ambivalence about slavery. The particular forms that capitalist society adopted ensured that Enlightenment universalism became degraded in practice. It was through this process that the discourse of race developed.

Ambivalence towards slavery is not the only illustration of the contradiction between Enlightenment discourse and capitalist social relations. The conflict between nationalism and universalism provides another illustration of the degradation of the Enlightenment outlook. The Declaration of the Rights of Man seemed to imply that all humanity should be accorded those rights. Yet, in practice, those rights were enforced and defended through the mechanism of a nation state. In other words in order to be able to exercise universal rights, one had to belong to a nation, to be a citizen. But guaranteeing rights through national citizenship by definition excluded those rights from all who were not citizens. Through the development of capitalist society, the nation-state became the mechanism for protecting rights, but in so doing denied those very rights to others. The rights of 'man' and the rights of a citizen seemed necessarily contradictory. As Rousseau wrote, 'Forced to combat nature or the social institutions, one must choose between making a man or a citizen, for one cannot make both at the same time.'[77]

The particular forms of modern society, then, undermined the emancipatory potential of Enlightenment ideology. In destroying the old divisions of feudal society, capitalism nevertheless created divisions anew. And these new divisions seemed to be as permanent as the old ones of feudalism. Increasingly many began to regard social hierarchy as naturally given, the result of biological differences within humankind. As Tom Paine was to write, 'The great mass of the poor in all countries are become an hereditary race, and it is next to impossible for them to get out of that state of themselves.'[78] Paine's aim in this pamphlet was in fact to criticise the creation of social divisions which seemed so permanent as to be natural. But this perception of social differences as natural, and indeed as 'racial', increasingly became an accepted outlook of Victorian writers. As the Dean observes in Jane Austen's *Pride and Prejudice*, 'the poor are born to serve the rich' and the rich are born 'to be served by the poor'.

The process through which Enlightenment universalism was degraded to a naturalistic vision of society was a long and complex one. At the time when Austen was writing, the Dean's view would have been treated with derision. Indeed Austen's intention was to satirise such arguments. In the early nineteenth century the bourgeoisie still exuded the confidence of a rising class and felt that whatever the problems within the new society, these would undoubtedly be overcome. But increasingly through the nineteenth century, as social problems were not overcome, so the conviction grew that inequality was in the natural order of things. That which Rousseau had regarded as 'political' or 'moral' inequalities, and that which even Adam Smith had viewed as socially created divisions, increasingly began to be seen as natural phenomena. By the end of the Victorian era such a view had acquired both the stamp of scientific truth and the status of common sense.

It was out of this conviction that inequality was natural that the modern concept of race arose. The idea of 'race' developed as a way of explaining the persistence of social divisions in a society that proclaimed its belief in equality. Racial theories accounted for social inequalities by ascribing them to nature. As Condorcet put it, racial theories made 'nature herself an accomplice in the crime of political inequality'.

I am arguing here neither a simplistic 'conspiracy' theory nor that the *function* of racial ideology was to explain social inequality. The concept of race was not created or invented to meet a particular social need. Rather, as social divisions persisted and acquired the status of permanence, so differences presented themselves as if they were natural, not social. The social constraints on equality began to appear as natural ones. In this process the ideas of natural difference which held sway in the pre-Enlightenment world were recast into a discourse of race. Racial ideology was the inevitable product of the persistence of differences of rank, class and peoples in a society that had accepted the concept of equality.

3

The Making of a Discourse
of Race

'I discern two sorts of inequality in the human species', wrote Rousseau in his *Discourse on Inequality*. The first was 'natural or physical' which pertained to biological differences between individuals – 'differences in age, health, strength of body and qualities of the mind and soul'. The second type of inequality was that between social groups. This, Rousseau argued, was 'moral or political inequality' which was 'established, or at least authorised, by the consent of men.' 'Such inequality', he wrote, 'consists of the different privileges that some enjoy to the prejudice of others – such as their being richer, more honoured, more powerful than others, and even getting themselves obeyed by others.'[1] One way to understand the narrative of race is as the story of how the second type of inequality became reduced to the first – in other words, how social inequalities became regarded as natural ones. It is through the conflation of social and natural inequality that the contradiction between the universalist ideology of capitalist society and the particularist reality of capitalist social relations becomes grasped in the discourse of race.

The aim of this chapter is to investigate how this came about by fleshing out the mediations between the contradictions within capitalist society and the making of a racial discourse. My aim is not to provide a simple 'definition' of 'race'. The concept of race is too complex and multi-faceted to be reduced to single, straightforward definitions. Different social groups and different historical periods have understood race in radically different ways. The concept of race arose from the contradictions of equality in modern society but it is not an expression of a single phenomenon or relationship. Rather it is a medium through which the changing relationship between humanity, society and nature has been understood in a variety of ways. What is important to understand are the ways in which this changing relationship has been, and still is, expressed through the discourse of race.

Central to this was the complex interplay between the embrace of progress and the fear of it that shaped much of social discourse in the nineteenth century. It was largely through this interplay that the ideas and concepts of the Enlightenment were recast, that social inequalities

71

were naturalised and that the conundrum of equality was reforged as the concept of race. I aim in this chapter to weave these broader debates into the discussion of the development of the discourse of race, so as to understand better the meaning of race in the Western intellectual tradition.

In overthrowing the static world of absolutist Europe, capitalism had brought into being a society that seemed forever in flux. Industrialisation, urbanisation, new forms of agriculture, the coming of the railways – socially and technologically the world seemed to be changing at a dizzying pace. In a famous passage in *The Communist Manifesto* Marx and Engels described the transformative nature of capitalism:

> Constant revolutionising of production, uninterrupted disturbance of all social conditions, everlasting uncertainty and agitation distinguish the bourgeois epoch from all earlier ones. All fixed, fast-frozen relations, with their train of ancient and venerable prejudices and opinions, are swept away, all new-formed ones becoming antiquated before they can ossify. All that is solid melts into air, all that is holy is profaned, and man is at last compelled to face with sober senses the real conditions of life, and his relations with his kind.[2]

Scientific and technological transformation was enthusiastically welcomed by most sections of society through the nineteenth century. The meaning of progress, however, began subtly to change. Eighteenth-century *philosophes* had regarded progress as inevitable, but had also seen it as the product of human endeavour. Increasingly through the nineteenth century the inevitability of progress was stripped of its human aspects and became simply the working out of the laws of nature. Moreover, at the same time as the acclamation of scientific progress there developed growing anxieties about the pace and nature of social change.

Through the eighteenth century social change had seemed both welcome and inevitable. But in the aftermath of the French Revolution, many within the new ruling élite began to fear such change. This fear of change became particularly acute once a new force emerged in society – the working class – which was not only potentially a new agent of change, but one for which change was fuelled by a vision of an entirely different sort of society. The reaction against social upheaval that was initially articulated by the conservative and Romantic movements became, as the nineteenth century progressed, a central theme of all discourse.

The sense of foreboding about change, and the strain of pessimism about social developments, found expression in the idea of *degeneration*. The notion of degeneration expressed a sense both of inevitable progress and of inevitable regression: 'Evolution ever climbing after some ideal good / And reversion ever dragging Evolution in the mud', as Tennyson put it in *Locksley Hall Sixty Years After*. As the nineteenth century wore on, so degeneration became increasingly viewed not simply as a failure to advance but as a social pathology infecting the very soul of the nation, a transcendental malady for which society had no cure.

It was against this background that the discourse of race developed. The sense of society trapped by both inevitable advance and natural regression helped shape a racial outlook on the world. The notion of race expressed both the idea of superiority given by certain evolution and the sense of pessimism given by inescapable regression. It expressed the perception that these processes were natural, and indeed that social differences, fixed as they were against this background of progress and regression controlled by objective laws, were themselves natural. It expressed too the sense of crisis engendered by the breakdown of Enlightenment optimism, and fear of social change. In all these ways the discourse of race developed as a way of understanding the changing relationship between humanity, society and nature.

ROMANTICISM, PARTICULARISM AND RACE

It is in the Romantic reaction against the Enlightenment that we find the initial backlash against the egalitarian and universalistic assumptions of the *philosophes*. 'Romanticism', however, can be a misleading term. Although it has become a well-established historical and literary category, it is difficult to define either as a philosophy or as a movement. As Roy Porter and Mikulas Teich observe, Romanticism, unlike previous historical periods, was not a coherent or stable phenomenon:

> For all its local differences, the Reformation had possessed a substantial unity, grounded upon a common core of beliefs . . . and is readily enough identified with social forces which overall can be called historically 'progressive'. The same is true of the Enlightenment. The aspirations and programmes of *philosophes* in London and Paris, Turin and Berlin espoused common criticism of the ignorance, superstition, bigotry and injustice of the *ancien régime*, a shared confidence in the powers of reason to build a better world . . . Romanticism presents a much more confused and contradictory picture . . . [I]n the maelstrom of [the French] Revolution and its aftermath, there were no longer the easy targets and the ready solutions which had united the *philosophes* – indeed the Revolution itself had proved the nemesis of such optimism. What was to be done appeared ambiguously different to European Romantics operating from within diverse national, social and cultural climates.[3]

What we now consider to be Romanticism was a number of different strands of thought all of which simultaneously both drew upon and opposed the categories of Enlightenment discourse. The very nature of Romanticism, with its celebration of particularist values, ensured its fragmentary character.

The early Romantics were repelled by the social consequences of capitalist society and moved by the misery caused by industrialisation. William Blake, himself a London artisan and a radical enemy of the established order, captured this sentiment when he invoked the 'dark satanic mills' in a call to arms to rid the world of these forces of corruption and degradation.

This rebellious strand of Romantic thought tended to be anti-capitalist and supportive of the 'common man'. It applauded the French Revolution and in general supported radical movements against social injustice and hierarchical institutions. The brand of Utopian anti-capitalism represented by Blake, Rousseau and Shelley is in many ways better seen as a precursor to the nineteenth-century socialist tradition than as part of the Romantic reaction against the Enlightenment. Certainly, such writers upheld the universalistic outlook of the Enlightenment and deprecated the particularist philosophy that lay at the heart of Romanticism.

There were, however, more conservative threads to the Romantic tradition. Many attributed the conflict and disharmony of the late eighteenth and early nineteenth centuries to the uncritical acceptance of Enlightenment assumptions and the attempt to reorder society according to rational principles. English philosopher Edmund Burke, the founder of modern conservatism, English Romantics such as William Wordsworth and Samuel Coleridge in their later years, French Catholic reactionaries such as Louis de Bonald and Joseph-Marie de Maistre and German Romantics such as Friederich Schelling, all helped create a fusion of conservatism and Romanticism.

The disorder, anarchy and radical changes which these men observed after the French Revolution led them to stress order and stability, tradition and authority, status and hierarchy. Society for Burke, Bonald or Schelling was akin to an organism, and as in an organism all the parts needed to operate in harmony with each other. Burke rejected the abstract rational conception of 'natural rights'. On the contrary, he argued, an individual only has those rights and privileges which prevail in a given community and which allow that community to progress in a harmonic fashion. For Burke, status and hierarchy was essential to society. He feared that equality would destroy the natural and time-honoured agencies through which social stability was maintained.

Burke also insisted on the positive value of irrational sentiment, such as ritual, ceremony and worship. Enlightenment philosophers, in their merciless criticism of prejudice, had, he believed, weakened the sacred supports of society. Tradition and instinct were necessary to maintain authority. 'The bulk of mankind', argued Burke, 'have neither leisure nor knowledge sufficient to reason right; why should they be taught to reason at all? Will not honest instinct prompt and wholesome prejudices guide them, much better than half reasoning?'[4] It is in this conserva-tive/Romantic reaction to the Enlightenment, with its renewed stress on tradition, hierarchy, inequality and unreason, that we shall find the genesis of the modern discourse of race.

At the root of both the radical and conservative strands of Romanticism lay the breakdown of the utilitarian view of society. In the classical liberal outlook, drawn from Locke, human beings were seen as self-con-tained atoms with certain built-in passions and drives, each seeking above all to maximise his satisfactions and minimise his dissatisfactions. In the course of pursuing this self-interest, each individual finds it ad-vantageous to enter into certain relations with other individuals. Society is born out of a multitude of such individual contracts. Social aims were the arithmetic sum of individual aims. For the early Enlightenment thinkers individual aspiration inevitably corresponded with social need. As Pope wrote in his *Essay on Man:*

> Thus God and Nature linked the general frame,
> And bade Self-love and Social be the same.

Half a century later, Adam Smith was to put the same argument in more secular, and less poetic, terms in *The Wealth of Nations:*

> Every individual exerts himself to find out the most advantageous employment for whatever his capital can command. The study of his own advantage necessarily leads him to prefer that which is most advantageous to society.[5]

But even as Smith was writing, other Enlightenment philosophers, troubled by increasing social conflict, were challenging this notion of the inevitable correspondence of individual and social needs. In Rousseau's novel *La Nouvelle Héloïse,* Julie wonders, '[W]hich concerns me more, that I should achieve happiness at the expense of the rest of mankind or that the rest of mankind should achieve its happiness at my expense?'. In the newly emerging society individual desire and moral duty seemed to point in opposite directions.

The late Enlightenment thinkers attempted to reconcile the dishar-mony between the individual and the social through two seemingly contradictory arguments. On the one hand they placed stress on the idea of an 'inner voice', that spoke uniquely to every individual and guided their moral actions, and on the other they emphasised the concept of community and nation, stressing the importance of the collective over the individual. Both these concepts became central motifs of the Romantic tradition, and key ideas in the development of a racial discourse.

Philosophically, the idea of the inner voice finds its genesis in the challenge that philosophers like David Hume and, in particular, Immanuel Kant made to the early Enlightenment elision of knowledge and ethics, and to the belief that reason was sufficient to comprehend the world. Faith and intuition, they believed, were also required to order and understand external reality. In his *Critique of Pure Reason* Kant insisted that one cannot know the world as it actually is. Empirical knowledge could convey information, not about things as they really existed *(noumena)*, but only as they were perceived as *phenomena* by a human observer, who imposed upon them the dimensions of time and space, which belonged to the observer, not the object.

In the subsequent *Critique of Practical Reason* Kant placed the responsibility for moral actions within an inner faculty, the mind's intuitive awareness of itself as *noumenon*, and of its obligations. Moral duty arose from the nature of the mind itself and appeared as a 'categorical imperative'. Rejecting the associationist psychology of Locke, Kant tried to free the mind from its dependence on solely external sources for knowledge and to give a renewed validity to truth derived from the spiritual realm. Moral judgement depended not on an appreciation of the identity of self-interest and the common welfare but on an 'inner voice' that was independent and could never be alienated to an external authority.

This idea of the 'inner voice' led to a preoccupation with individual conscience and to a new stress on the importance and uniqueness of the individual. In Locke's associationist psychology, minds were seen as computers, processing sense-data according to universal laws. A given environment, physical or social, would therefore produce relatively homogenous values. Following Rousseau and Kant, the new view introduced the idea of the unique subject consciously interacting with the external world.

The idea of the inner voice also helped downgrade the previous stress placed on reason and elevated the emphasis on emotion and imagination. As Marianne put it in Marivaux's *La Vie de Marianne*, 'I believe that only feeling can give us reliable information about ourselves and we must not put too much trust on what our minds twist to their own convenience.' In reaction to the eighteenth-century exaltation of reason, the new outlook extolled instead emotion and imagination, leading to the great revival of literature, poetry and art with which we associate the Romantic movement.

At the same time as this elevation of the individual, the Romantic tradition also placed great stress on collective order. In contrast to the Enlightenment concept of society as the product of a multitude of individual contracts, a more organic sense of society developed. This sense of collective being was encouraged by the breakdown of Enlightenment cosmopolitanism and the unfolding of new national rivalries. In the post-Enlightenment world, as Irving Zeitlin observes, 'the group, the community and the nation ... became important concepts':

> Historic memories and loyalties were viewed as binding the individual to his nation, a category now elevated to a position of supreme importance. Gone was the cosmopolitanism of the Enlightenment. Increasingly, the nineteenth century turned to the investigations of the origins of existing institutions rather than their transformation according to rational principles.[6]

In *The Social Contract*, Rousseau had argued for a political concept of a nation in which 'the total alienation of each member, with all his rights, to the community as a whole' was guaranteed by conscious decision. The conservative/Romantic tradition, however, posited a more transcendental sense of the collective. 'A nation', Burke wrote, 'is not an idea of only local extent and individual momentary aggregation':

> It is an idea of continuity, which extends in time as well as in numbers and in space. And this is the choice, not of one day, or one set of people, not a tumultuary and giddy choice; it is the deliberate election of the ages and of generations; it is a constitution made by what is ten thousand times better than choice, it is made by peculiar circumstances, occasions, tempers, dispositions and moral, civil and social habitudes of the people, which disclose themselves only in a long space of time.[7]

For Burke, then, the nation was a collective expression of the intuitive spirit that bound a particular people together. It was created not through conscious contract but through the disclosure of tradition through time.

The Kantian stress on the idea of an intuitive, non-rational form of thought, and the new regard for group loyalty, allowed the Romantics to posit the notion of an unchanging inner essence within human beings, an essence beyond the reach of history or society. This common essence provided the means of binding together communities by providing a sense of 'belonging' that could overcome the fragmentary effects of capitalist society, and furthermore a sense of belonging that transcended history. This essence found expression through the sense of 'race'.

The conservative/Romantic stress on social cohesion and solidarity led, paradoxically, to an emphasis on social divisions. A 'community' was defined as much by its *exclusion* of those who did not belong as by its *inclusion* of those who did. Thus what came to define racial essence within the Romantic tradition was that it was not universally

constituted – the whole of humanity did not possess a common innate
nature. This particularism lies at the heart of all racial thinking. We can
see this clearly in the work of Johann Gottfried von Herder, the German
philosopher who was a seminal figure in transforming the Enlightenment understanding of universalism and in developing (albeit unwit-
tingly) the Romantic notion of race.

Herder rejected the eighteenth-century idea that reality was ordered in
terms of universal, timeless, objective, unalterable laws which rational
investigation could discover. He maintained, rather, that every activity,
situation, historical period or civilisation possessed a unique character of
its own. Any attempt to reduce such phenomena to a regular pattern of
uniform elements, and to describe or analyse them in terms of universal
rules, tended to obscure precisely those crucial differences which constituted the specific quality of the object under study.

Herder believed in the incommensurability of the values of different
cultures and societies. Each people, he argued, was unique, the uniqueness given by its particular culture, language, history and modes of
living. 'Let us follow our own path', he wrote, 'let men speak well or ill
of our nation, our literature, our language: they are ours, they are ourselves and let that be enough.'[8]Artificial, polyglot entities like the Haps-
burg Empire were, Herder argued, absurd monsters contrary to nature –
'a lion's head with a dragon's tail, an eagle's wing, a bear's paw, [sewn
together] in one unpatriotic symbol of a state'.[9]

Like Rousseau, Herder believed that the individual could not realise
himself in isolation since his values arose from a relationship with society. Unlike Rousseau, he posited an organic relationship between an
individual and the culture and people to which he belonged, a relationship which shaped his very being. For Herder, the people or *volk* was
both a contract between contemporaries and a continuing dialogue between the generations. Although Herder was politically and philosophically very dissimilar to Burke, nevertheless he believed with Burke that
the nation was 'a partnership between those who are living, those who
are dead and those who are to be born'.[10]

The nature of a people was expressed through its *volksgeist* – the unchanging spirit of a people refined through history. What gave unity to
the life and culture of a people was the continuity of this original spirit.
The *volksgeist* was expressed through myths, songs and sagas which, for
Herder, carried the eternal heritage of a people, far removed from the
ephemera of science and modernity. Myths and legends represented,
wrote Herder, a cultural heritage that reached back to the origins of a
people and, if conserved, could rejuvenate its spirit.

Language was particularly crucial to the delineation of a people. 'Has
a nation anything more precious than the language of its fathers?' Herder asked rhetorically. 'In it dwell its entire world of tradition, history,

religion, principles of existence; its whole heart and soul.'[11] Language provided the mode of living and the means of thinking. 'Each nation speaks in the manner it thinks', Herder believed, 'and thinks in the manner it speaks.'[12] A foreign language was for Herder something foreign to the soul: 'I am able to stammer with intense effort in the words of a foreign language; its spirit will evade me.'[13]

Herder himself was a child of the Enlightenment and rejected racial arguments, protesting for instance that 'a monkey is not your brother, but a negro is and you should not rob and oppress him.'[14] He was particularly harsh on the degradation brought about by colonial ventures:

'Can you name a land where Europeans have entered without defiling themselves forever before defenceless, trusting mankind, by the unjust word, greedy deceit, crushing oppression, diseases, fatal gifts they have brought? Our part of the earth should be called not the wisest but the most arrogant, aggressive, money-minded: what it has given these peoples is not civilisation but the destruction of the rudiments of their own cultures wherever they could achieve this.[15]

The consequence of Herder's belief in difference as the motivating force in history was, however, to undermine the idea of human equality and unity. Herder's stress on the specificity of societies or cultures provided an important antidote to the tendency of Enlightenment *philosophes* to eternalise historical phenomena under the guise of universal law. But in arguing for the incommensurability of different societies, Herder discarded the common yardstick by which to gauge humanity. Difference was inevitable, and universalism contrary to the dictates of nature. 'Whom nature separated by language, customs, character', Herder argued, 'let no man artificially join together by chemistry.'

However much he might have regarded himself as within the tradition of tolerant universalism encouraged by Enlightenment values, the consequence of his particularist outlook was to encourage a racial viewpoint. Once it was accepted that different peoples were motivated by particular sentiments, unique to themselves, it was but a short step to view these differences as racial. Herder's *volksgeist* became transformed into racial make-up, an unchanging substance, the foundation of all physical appearance and mental potential and the basis for division and difference within humankind.

RACE IN THE POST-ENLIGHTENMENT WORLD

In pre-Enlightenment usage, the term 'race' had designated a family line, its biological continuity through the course of generations sustaining the integrity of noble lineages and the social order. Race provided a natural foundation for the hierarchy of virtues, aptitudes, temperaments that culminated in the values and habits of the nobility and justified aristocratic prerogatives. In the immediate post-Enlightenment world, social commentators recast this idea of race to describe the breakdown of the universalistic outlook and the increasing sense of the permanence of social divisions. Race now was not given by divine sanction as previously, but nor was it as yet based on natural law. Rather it arose from the sense that social differences were important and less amenable to eradication than the eighteenth-century thinkers had believed.

The notion of race in the immediate post-Enlightenment world was most imprecise. The idea of 'peoples', 'nations', 'classes' and 'races' all merged together. Race often expressed a vague sense of difference and the characterisation of that difference was based variously on physical traits, languages, the aptitude for civilisation and the peculiarities of customs and behaviours. Many naturalists and anthropologists, still influenced by Enlightenment thinking, suggested that race was a passing, even reversible, phenomenon. The French physician Julien-Joseph Virey, for instance, a disciple of Buffon and Montesquieu, maintained that the distinction between the idea of 'species' and that of 'race' lay in the permanence of one and the emphemeral nature of the other:

> That which distinguishes a species from a race in natural history is the permanence of characteristic traits in spite of adverse influence of climate, nutrition and other external factors, whereas races are no more than fluctuating modifications of a single primordial species.[16]

Virey has clearly moved away from the kind of ideas that were central to men like Degerando, accepting as he does the notion of racial divisions as a valid distinction in nature. Nevertheless he rejects the idea that these are permanent differences, believing instead that they are but 'fluctuating modifications' of a single type.

New voices, however, were already beginning to challenge the idea that social distinctions were created by environmental differences and were temporary or changeable. According to the French naturalist and anti-Royalist, Augustin Thierry,

> New physiological investigations, together with a deeper look at the great events which have changed the social conditions of various nations, prove that the physical and moral constitution of various peoples depends much more on their heritage and the primitive race to which they belong than on the climactic influence under which they have fallen by chance.[17]

The essence of humanity, in this new outlook, was less its aspirations to reasoned change than its blind submission to history.

A crucial aspect of the emerging notion of race was that it referred not so much to differences between territorially distinct populations, as to differences *within* a particular society. What we would now consider to be class or social distinctions were seen as racial ones. Thus Augustin Thierry was to describe the division of France into classes in racial terms:

> We imagine that we are one nation, but we are two nations on the same land, two nations hostile in their memories and irreconcilable in their projects: one has conquered the other ... Whatever miscegenation went on between these primitive races, their perpetually contradictory spirits have survived until today in two ever-distinct parts of a mixed population.[18]

I want to stress the importance of understanding the genesis of the modern discourse of race as part of the attempt to articulate differences *within* European society. There exists an almost axiomatic belief among historians, anthropologists and sociologists that the concept of race arose out of colonialism and the European conquest of the rest of the world. The anthropologist Johannes Fabian, for instance, argues that racial anthropology is 'in the end about the relationship between the West and the Rest'.[19] Edward Said claims that 'Western knowledge or representation of the non-European world' is the key to understanding racial ideology.[20] Peter Fryer, in *Staying Power*, his wonderful history of black people in Britain, considers that racial ideology grew out of three beliefs: 'the idea that Africans were, in one way or another, closely connected with apes; the idea that people with differently coloured skins had different origins; and the idea that human beings could be graded hierarchically according to skin colour.'[21]

It is certainly true that racial theory came eventually to be underpinned by its insistence on the inferiority of non-Western peoples. But imputing the idea of racial difference simply to the distinction between 'the West and the rest' is, as Daniel Pick observes, to 'flatten out historical differences, shifts within Europe and the West'. The idea of racial difference, Pick notes, 'evolved not only in relation to a colonial "other"'. Rather, '[t]he object of the racial anthropology which emerged in the period was not only Africa or the Orient, but also the "primitive" areas and groups within the home country'.[22]

The very process by which nationhood was constructed in Europe was also the process through which was revealed the internal divisions within the nation. Eugen Weber, for example, has shown the extraordinary modernising effort which was required to unify France and her rural populations, and the traumatic and lengthy process of cultural,

educational, political and economic 'self-colonisation' that this en-
tailed.[23] This process created the modern French nation, and allowed for
ideas of French (and European) superiority over non-European cultures.
But it also reinforced a sense of how socially and anthropologically alien
was the mass of the rural, and indeed urban, population in the nation, so
alien indeed that such groups were considered to be of different races.

There was a dialectical process through which capitalist modernisation, which allowed European élites to proclaim their superiority over
non-European peoples, also revealed the inferiority of the masses within
their own nation. In an address to the Medico-Psychological Society of
Paris in 1857, Philippe Buchez considered the meaning of social differentiation within France:

> [Consider] a population like ours, placed in the most favourable cir-
> cumstances; possessed of a powerful civilisation; amongst the highest
> ranking nations in science, the arts and industry. Our task now, I
> maintain, is to find out how it can happen that within a population
> such as ours, races may form – not merely one but several races – so
> miserable, inferior and bastardised that they may be classed below the
> most inferior savage races, for their inferiority is sometimes beyond
> cure.[24]

The sense of racial superiority that European élite classes felt over non-
European society cannot be understood outside of the sense of the inferiority imposed upon the masses at home. As Pick notes, 'the appeals to
superiority over other races . . . was projected over perceptions of social
divisions at home'.[25] Indeed I would go further still and argue that the
discourse of race arose out of perceived differences within European
society and only later was it systematically applied to differences of skin
colour.

The initial impetus for seeing social divisions within Europe as racial
came from the antiegalitarian assumptions of the conservative/Roman-
tic movement. On the one hand, the conservative/Romantics considered
the claim to equality as fatally undermining social cohesion and believed
that social hierarchy was necessary for the maintenance of order. On the
other hand, they hoped that resurrecting the historical roots and evolution of different peoples could help re-establish a feeling of belonging
destroyed by the abstract rationalism of Enlightenment cosmopolitanism. The French naturalist Eusebé de Salles, for example, believed that
the sense of historical continuity denoted by race could provide the
social cohesion and order that hereditary distinctions had established in
the feudal world. 'There is no more significant symptom', he wrote, 'than
the tendency of European peoples to reconstitute themselves as nationalities no longer based on religious beliefs or the hereditary rights of their

princes, but on their origins and traditions as distinctive races of a greater family.' He added that 'the eternal need for faith seeks a solid base when the faith of other times and other interests have been shaken. The history of human races, if it finds this solid base, must be classed high in the public esteem.'[26]

In arguing for the necessity of permanent distinctions in society, and for the return of some form of aristocratic élite, the Romantics reforged the old idea of race. The work of Count Arthur Gobineau, whose *Essays on the Inequality of Races* is often considered the seminal tract of modern racism, provides a good illustration of the concept of race within the tradition of Romantic aristocratic reaction. Gobineau was a minor French aristocrat who regarded the 1789 Revolution as an unmitigated disaster, the product of racial degeneration. His starting point was the need to struggle against democracy, against what he considered to be the 'unnatural' idea of equality. In 'normal times', he asserted, inequality was accepted as axiomatic. Racial miscegenation, however, had created dangerous illusions: 'The majority of the citizens of a state once that mixed blood is flowing in their veins, feel prompted by their large numbers to proclaim as a generally valid truth something which only holds good for themselves: that all men are equal.'[27] For Gobineau, all history was the history of racial struggle. 'The basic organisation and strength of all civilisations', he asserted, 'are equal to the traits and spirit of the dominant race.' Gobineau divided the world into three races. These races did not simply people different parts of the world; they constituted different social strata in every country:

> It has already been established that every social order is founded upon three original classes, each of which represents a racial variety: the nobility, a more or less accurate reflection of the conquering race; the bourgeoisie composed of mixed stock coming close to the chief race; and the common people who live in servitude or at least in a very depressed position. These last belong to a lower race which came about in the south through miscegenation with the negroes and in the north with Finns.[28]

Though history consisted of racial struggle, only the white race, for Gobineau, could be considered as part of history:

> In the oriental world, the unremitting struggle of racial forces was only enacted between the aryan element on the one hand, and the black and yellow principle on the other. It is superfluous to mention that where only the black races were in contest or the yellow races were moving within their own circle, or even where mixtures of black and yellow-skinned peoples were at odds with each other, no history is

possible. They did not create anything, and no memory of them has survived . . . History results only from the mutual contact of the white races.[29]

The main elements of Gobineau's theory – history as racial struggle; a racial typology that incorporated class distinctions; civilisation as the preserve of whites; an unremitting hostility toward the idea of equality – recur within the tradition of scientific racism that dominated Western thinking at the end of the nineteenth century. But Gobineau was to the mid-nineteenth century an anachronism. He was a champion of the feudal aristocracy in a society which held contempt for such backward-looking views, a defender of mysticism and unreason in an age that worshipped technology and progress. 'A theory of race that is useful and can be taken seriously', Houston Stewart Chamberlain, the English racist and adviser to Adolf Hitler, was later to observe, 'cannot be constructed on the tale of Sem, Cham and Japhet and such ingenious intuitions, mixed with hair-raising hypotheses, but only on a thorough and comprehensive knowledge of natural science.'[30] For racial theory to become more embedded in society it had to shed its feudal trappings and put on the mask of science.

FROM ROMANTIC REACTION TO SCIENTIFIC RACISM

The Victorian age was predominantly liberal and forward-looking. The intelligentsia in most European nations, certainly until the last decades of the century, remained steadfast in its support for political democracy and individual rights. It was an age, too, of science and invention, and one that worshipped the notion of progress no less than had the previous century. The French *Larousse Dictionary* believed that 'Humanity is perfectible and it moves incessantly from less good to better, from ignorance to science, from barbarism to civilisation':

The idea that humanity becomes day by day better and happier is particularly dear to our century. Faith in the law of progress is the true faith of our century.[31]

This extravagant belief in science was even more true of Britain. In the 'workshop of the world' industrial progress and technical advance as exemplified by the great exhibition of 1851 engendered a positive spirit. In 1836 G. R. Porter opened the first volume of his *Progress of the Nation* by announcing that the present generation had witnessed the 'greatest advances in civilisation that can be found recorded in the annals of mankind'.[32] Tennyson's response to his first train journey ('let the great world spin, forever down the grooves of change') summed up the exuberant confidence in progress that infused Victorian England.

But the Victorian age was also a period in which the liberal intelligentsia grew increasingly fearful for social stability and cohesion. The emergence of the working class and the growth of social conflicts cast a dark shadow over what had hitherto seemed a lustrous age. If the French Revolution had catalysed the conservative/Romantic reaction against the Enlightenment, the revolutions of 1848 had a similar impact on liberal opinion. The social upheavals which swept through Europe that year warned many liberals of the problem of social stability. In the response of English liberal Walter Bagehot to the revolutions of 1848 one finds an echo of Burke's fears in the wake of the French Revolution: 'The first duty of society is the preservation of society . . . To keep up this system we must sacrifice everything. Parliaments, liberty, leading articles, essays, eloquence, all are good but they are secondary.'[33] The events of 1848, writes Daniel Pick, 'seemed to demonstrate the radical unpredictability of change, the irreducibility of new social phenomena to earlier models':

> In the wake of 1848 there was an extraordinary flurry of historical interpretation and re-orientation. Certainly to many contemporaries, the vicissitudes of revolution seemed to call into question the very terms of liberal progressivism. Pessimism began to colonise liberalism in increasingly powerful and sustained ways. 'Pessimism', wrote Charles de Remusat in 1860, 'has made great progress in recent times.' Many Frenchmen, he added, who thirty or forty years earlier had been full of hope and enthusiasm for the principles of the Revolution had now come to the conclusion that modern democracy was no more than 'turbulent decadence'.[34]

The move away from the universalist, humanist tradition of the eighteenth century was hastened by further developments in the second half of the nineteenth century. The Franco-Prussian war of 1870 strengthened nationalism, particularly in France, where defeat came as a profound shock and humiliation. The age of imperialist expansion, exemplified by the 'Scramble for Africa' in the 1880s and 1890s, promoted both nationalist and racist sentiment.

Liberal attitudes towards the working class also underwent considerable transformation. The 'fear of the masses' which the revolutions of 1848 aroused was strengthened by the Paris Commune of 1871 when the *sans-culottes* – the poor and the dispossessed – took control of the city. The link between class, criminality, heredity and social revolt came to the fore of social discussion. Radicals and democrats, the French historian Hippolyte Taine argued, found their audience among 'the human cast-offs who infest the capitals, amongst the epileptic and scrofulous rabble, heirs of a vicious blood, who . . . bring *dégénérescence* into civilisation, imbecility, the distraction of an enfeebled temperament, retrograde instincts and an ill-constructed brain.'[35] In the last third of the nineteenth century the understanding of the nature of 'the mob' was a major preoccupation in science, literature and political discourse.

How could society reconcile its belief in social progress with its desire for social stability and fear of social anarchy? This was the question that the liberal intelligentsia began to ask itself. Increasingly the answer seemed to be to look to science to legitimise social order. Science replaced God as the guarantor of social relations. To tame science in this fashion, nineteenth-century thinkers stripped Enlightenment thought of its 'negative', 'critical' aspects. 'Positivism' became the credo of Victorian liberalism.

For Auguste Comte, the founder of positivism, 'true science has no other aim than the establishment of intellectual order which is the basis of every other order.'[36] He was contemptuous of both the 'metaphysicians' of the Enlightenment and the conservatives who reacted against them, the former for believing that progress and order were opposing principles, the latter for wishing to return to a pre-Enlightenment order. Instead, he argued, order and progress could be united in a science which sought to make society as rational as possible. 'True liberty', wrote Comte, 'is nothing else than a rational submission to the preponderance of the laws of nature.'[37]

Positivism united order and progress by subsuming society to the laws of nature. This naturalisation of social relations sought to impose harmony upon a social world where no such harmony existed, rent as it was by conflict and division. Since society was governed by natural laws, claimed the positivists, it could not be any other way. Society – divisions and all – was the inevitable product of natural development. This approach made positivism attractive to the intelligentsia throughout Europe. In England Benjamin Kidd claimed that 'history and politics are merely the last chapters of biology – the last and greatest – up to which all that has gone before leads in an orderly sequence.'[38] German sociologist Ludwig Gumplowicz argued that the task of natural science was 'to explain the process of history through the governance of unalterable natural laws.'[39]

The reorientation of the scientific outlook towards the positivist vision of the world transformed the way that scientists looked at the relationship between humanity, society and nature and opened the way for racial science. The emergence of the positivist outlook catalysed a shift from a view of human beings as primarily social creatures, governed by social laws, to a view of human beings as primarily biological entities governed by natural laws. This scientific reorientation, argues historian

Nancy Stepan, brought about a change 'from an emphasis on the fundamental physical and moral homogeneity of man, despite superficial differences, to an emphasis on the essential heterogeneity of mankind, despite superficial similarities'.[40]

The new 'science of Man' incorporated a number of ideas that were to be central to the scientific racism of the second half of the nineteenth century. The first was a teleological view of history. Human development was seen as purposive, leading ever forward to the triumph of civilisation, which was defined as contemporary European society. This social evolutionism had its roots in the one-sided Enlightenment view of reason and progress. Enlightenment thinkers professed a mechanical view of progress, seeing it as the unfolding of an already existing blueprint. As the critical aspects of Enlightenment thought were stripped away, so the determinist aspects contained within the idea of an inexorable march of progress became the dominant feature of social thinking. The English essayist William Greg expressed the racial implications of teleological thinking when he insisted that, 'the negroes are made on purpose to serve the whites, just as the black ants are made on purpose to serve the red.'[41]

The second aspect of the new science was the belief in the continuity of the human and the animal world. The naturalists of the eighteenth century had combined their view that human beings were part of the natural world with the belief that a great gulf existed between humans and animals. In his *On the Natural Varieties of Man* Blumenbach insisted that the gap between humans and other animals was not merely a function of rationality and speech but the result of a whole catalogue of physical and mental differences. Blumenbach's approach pointed to the importance of seeing *homo sapiens* as the only truly social, cultural animal.

Nineteenth-century science, however, drawn to the notion of human society constrained by natural laws, saw the origins of all human faculties in animal life. The germ of even the most complex ideas – reasoning, imagination, curiosity, inventiveness, aesthetic sense, morality – were to be found within animals. Human nature was not different in kind from that of animals, but only in degree or quantity. Moreover, instinct and imitative behaviour, which had previously been consigned to the animal world, were now seen as human qualities too.

The third key feature of the new science was the belief that mental abilities were related to physical characteristics. Austrian anatomist Johann Franz Gall believed that there existed a correlation between people's mental abilities and the shape of their heads. Phrenology, as the investigation of this correlation came to be known, laid the basis for future racial science by insisting that external signs could provide a true indication of innate ability and that this correlation demonstrated not simply individual differences but differences between various groups of human beings. As Johann Spurzheim argued,

> It is of great importance to consider the heads of different nations . . . The foreheads of negroes, for instance, are very narrow, their talents of music and mathematics are also in general very limited. The Chinese, who are fond of colours, have the arch of the eyebrows much vaulted, and we shall see that this is the sign of a greater development of the organ of colour. According to Blumenbach, the heads of the Kalmucks are depressed from above, and very large sideward above the organ, which gives the disposition to covet. It is also admitted that this nation is inclined to steal, etc.[42]

Phrenology itself had waned in popularity by the 1840s as its assertions were disproved. But while the conclusions drawn by phrenology were discredited, its influence was nevertheless long-lasting because its fundamental principle, that individual function must correspond with different parts of the brain, was accepted by most biologists. It was this principle that gave weight to repeated assertions that *some* technique – whether the measurement of cranial capacity, facial angle, cephalic index, brain volume, or brain weight – would provide a true indication of innate ability, and that by such a measure the races of humankind would be found to form a scale of being.

The consequence of these three concepts taken in unity was to validate the idea of a hierarchy generated outside of society and governed by natural rather than social laws. 'Independently of all political institutions', claimed the naturalist William Smellie, 'nature herself has formed the human species into castes and ranks. How many gradations may be traced between a stupid Huron, or a Hottentot, and a profound philosopher! Here the distance is immense, but nature has occupied the whole by almost infinite shades of discrimination.'[43]

The new science established the idea of an evolutionary ladder, running from inanimate matter through lowly forms of life to humanity itself. Nature had evolved by gradual means from the most backward types to the highest forms. 'Primitive' people were seen as the link between European civilisation and primates. This outlook was encouraged by the anthropological view that contemporary backward societies represented human beings arrested at an earlier stage of evolution.

Victorian social evolutionism thus rejected the Enlightenment idea that there was a unilinear sequence of social or intellectual stages and that all humanity could reach the highest stage. For the Victorians, different groups had diverged, stopped or regressed along the evolutionary path, according to their racial capacities. While the general level of civilisation always advanced, thanks to the progressive nature of the superior races, inferior races would never be able to keep up or catch up.

The pivotal figure in promoting determinist racial science in Britain was Scottish anatomist Robert Knox (probably best known for his role in the Burke and Hare grave-robbing scandal). *The Races of Men*, published in 1850 largely in response to the social upheavals of 1848, introduced the idea of 'transcendental anatomy', the belief that there was a unifying plan which brought together and explained all phenomena of the living world. The history of life forms, from invertebrates up to living humans, was simply the result of the unfolding of this plan. The unity was revealed by uncommon deformations of the plan. Webbed hands, for example, would occasionally appear in humans, indicating man's links to aquatic animals. For Knox different races were created through the arrest of embryonic development at different stages, a process parallel-ing the differential development of humanity along the evolutionary ladder. The Saxon race stood at the most highly developed stage of the organic plan.

The conviction of scientists such as Knox that inequality was the pro-duct of natural selection was little different from Gobineau's racial the-ories. Indeed Knox's *The Races of Men* was close in spirit to Gobineau's *The Inequality of the Races*. But *The Races of Men* was far more influential because of its invocation of science. Racial science secularised the ideas contained in Gobineau, and indeed in the Great Chain of Being, substi-tuting natural, scientific processes for God as the guarantor of social equilibrium.

Although there was a reorientation in the scientific outlook during the first half of the nineteenth century, and though the ideas of men like Robert Knox became more prominent, we should be careful not to over-state their influence. Most prominent scientists found distasteful the theories propounded by Knox or by James Hunt, an anthropologist who stressed polygenism – the idea that different races have different evolu-tionary origins. Thomas Huxley wrote scathingly about Hunt's compari-son between the negro and the ape. British anthropology at this stage was influenced more by the humanist outlook of men such as Huxley and James Prichard, the leading ethnologist of the day, than by the racial determinism of Hunt and Knox. Indeed Hunt left the leading anthropo-logical society of the day, the Ethnological Society, in disgust, influenced as it was by Prichard's humanist views, and founded the Anthropologi-cal Society of London to pursue more vigorously his racial theories.

This is not say that scientists like Huxley and Prichard were propo-nents of equality in the way that the Enlightenment thinkers had been. Huxley, as we have already seen, believed in the innate inferiority of the negro to the European. However, this belief in natural inequality coex-isted with a more humanist, universalist tradition drawn from the En-

lightenment. Huxley and Prichard, for example, were both lifelong opponents of slavery. The conflicting demands of racial science and Enlightenment humanism led to heated disputes on issues such as the
compatibility of ideas of racial determinism with notions of freedom of
will and moral choice.

It was only in the latter part of the century that the more determinist
forms of racial thought became acceptable. This shift was to a large
extent a reflection of the political and social changes we have already
considered – the concern for social stability, the fear of working-class
unrest, the growth of national rivalries, the emergence of imperialism.
But it was also underpinned by a major scientific development – Charles
Darwin's theory of evolution by natural selection. Social Darwinism, the
application of Darwinian theory to society, validated the biological outlook of positivism and formed the crucial link between racial thought as
part of aristocratic reaction and racial thought as part of mainstream
discourse.

Charles Darwin's *The Origin of Species,* published in 1859, was a mile-
stone of modern biology. The theory of evolution by natural selection is
one of the greatest scientific breakthroughs of the past 200 years and has
played an immense role in shaping the modern view of the world. At the
time Darwin's theory was welcomed by liberal and radical commentators. Huxley immediately espoused it for its challenge to theological
dogma. Marx hailed it for breaking with teleological conceptions of
development.

Darwin's theory emerged, however, in an intellectual and political
milieu that, as we have seen, was already open to biological ideas of
society and to the concept of social evolution. Even the phrase 'the
survival of the fittest', which many have attributed to Charles Darwin,
was in fact coined by Herbert Spencer, some eight years prior to the
publication of *The Origin of Species.* It was the intellectual and political
climate of mid to late Victorian England, and not the theory of evolution
itself, that shaped the way that Darwinism was applied to society.

In applying the theory of evolution to society, social Darwinists rejected the core of Darwin's theory. Evolution by natural selection was a
theory of change; random variation within populations provided the
basis for adaptation to changing circumstances. Racial theory, on the
other hand, required the fixity of characteristics – race only had meaning
if characters which defined a racial group remained constant over time.
For a social Darwinist such as Spencer, struggle eliminated the impure
specimens of the race and helped perpetuate the ideal type. In contrast
Darwin dismissed the idea of an ideal type of a species as nonsense.

Similarly, social Darwinists differed considerably from Darwin on the
impact of population pressure on evolutionary change. Social Darwinists saw the impact of population growth as a conservative force, leading

to the preservation of society in its present form. Darwin, on the other hand, treated it as a force for change. For Darwin, population pressure was not only one of the strongest impulses towards evolutionary change, but was also the result of the selective process. Again, social Darwinists diverged from Darwinian theory in their understanding of the concept of 'fitness'. For Darwin fitness was gauged by the number of progeny an individual left behind. For social Darwinists, and in particular for eugenicists, the problem was that the 'unfit' – most notably the working class – seemed to be more fertile than the 'fit'.

In the context of racial science, however, these differences mattered little. Darwinism was not necessary to prove racial differences. The starting point of racial science was the reality of 'race'. Victorian society simply adapted Darwin's theory to suit its preformed conceptions. The impact of social Darwinism paradoxically was to reassert many of the traditional ways in which the concepts of the 'survival of the fittest' and population pressure had been used prior to Darwin. The struggle for existence was used as a mechanism through which a social and natural hierarchy was preserved by allowing organisms to be distributed within the hierarchy according to their fitness. The idea of fitness tended to be imbued with conventional notions of the desirable and the valuable. Change and evolution became the means by which ultimate order and realisation of these ideal faculties and types was achieved.

What Darwinism did was to allow racial science to create a dynamic concept of hierarchy. The pre-Enlightenment Great Chain of Being was static – the result of divine ordination. Indeed it was antievolutionist. In appropriating the concept of evolution by natural selection racial science married the idea of a fixed hierarchy with that of progress – those at the top of the hierarchy arrived there on merit, because of their natural superiority in the struggle for existence. Racial scientists were now able to establish the idea of social hierarchy and explain it by scientific means.

RACE AND CLASS IN VICTORIAN ENGLAND

Today, the concept of race is so intertwined with the idea of 'colour' that it is often difficult to comprehend the Victorian notion of race. For the Victorians race was a description of social distinctions, not of colour differences. Indeed, as I have already argued, the view of non-Europeans as an inferior race was but an extension of the already existing view of the working class at home and took considerable time to become established as the normative view. Douglas Lorimer's study of race and class in the Victorian age has provided considerable evidence that until the middle of the century black people were treated according to their social status rather than the colour of their skin:

Like their eighteenth-century forefathers, the mid-Victorians accepted an individual black according to his ability to conform to English social conventions. A dark complexion did not inevitably signify lowly social status . . . In spite of theories claiming the Negro was inferior, the variable conduct of the English at this time showed that these racist assumptions had not sufficient support to influence patterns of behaviour. In the absence of any consensus over the significance of racial differences, mid-Victorians simply treated each individual black according to their evaluation of his social standing.[44]

As the idea of the permanence of social hierarchy took hold within liberal circles, however, commentators became increasingly sceptical about the idea of negroes aspiring to high social status. As a result, observes Lorimer, 'the conventional norms about the correct bearing towards one's social inferiors, whether black or white, were extended to include all blacks regardless of an individual's character or background.'

Lorimer's comments should alert us to a problem in assessing the importance of race in the mid-nineteenth century. Much of the discussion on race was led either by writers working in the colonies or by anthropologists studying 'savage people'. This gave such writing on the one hand a more determinist, less humanist aspect than much of political discussion at the time, and on the other led to a concentration on the issue of colour. But taken in the context of the broader debate in society, the issue of colour only became important as a more determinist social typology developed in the latter part of the century.

Mid-Victorian perceptions of colour and class are well illustrated by the debate on the relationship between American slavery and the English factory system. When it was published in 1852, Harriet Beecher Stowe's anti-slavery novel *Uncle Tom's Cabin* (subtitled *Life among the Lowly*) created a considerable furore in Britain, because of the comparison it drew between American slaves and English workers. In the novel, slave-owner Augustine St Clare justifies slavery on the grounds that the condition of his slaves is no worse than that of factory operatives in England:

> Look at the high and the low, all the world over, and it is the same story; the lower classes used up, body, soul and spirit, for the good of the upper. It is so in England; it is so everywhere; and yet all Christendom stands aghast, with virtuous indignation, because we do the thing in a slightly different shape from what they do it.

English commentators angrily rejected the comparison at the time, arguing that slavery was a denial of human rights and morally reprehensible whereas the exploitation of workers through the factory system was an unexceptional fact of life. An article in the *British Mother's Magazine* argued that though both American slaves and English paupers lived in a state of degradation, the slave's condition was an enforced one, whereas the condition of the English poor was 'to a large extent their own fault'.[45] Another writer argued that if American slaves truly lived in the same condition as English workers, then slavery would be defensible.[46] Few thought that blacks should be treated differently from white labourers:

> [T]here is no natural disqualification of the black population, which should deprive them of the right to enjoy equal political and social privileges with ourselves; or in the words of Uncle Tom, . . . 'As far as our coloured brethren have had the advantages of education and civilisation, they have been as peaceful, as orderly, as devout as those of a fairer skin'.[47]

This hostility to slavery on the part of English liberals demonstrated their unwillingness to forgo entirely the universalistic ideas that had been forged in the eighteenth century and their sensitivity to the notion that inequality at home was not natural but socially enforced like the enslavement of African-Americans. An underlying belief in equality remained a central feature of the liberal outlook. Yet, if most British writers rejected the comparison between slavery and the factory system as a justification for the treatment of American negroes, most were equally willing to use the same analogy to justify class distinctions in England. A vignette in the *Saturday Review* of working-class life is typical of English middle-class attitudes of this era:

> The Bethnal Green poor . . . are a caste apart, a race of whom we know nothing, whose lives are of quite different complexion from ours, persons with whom we have no point of contact. And although there is not quite the same separation of classes or castes in the country, yet the great mass of the agricultural poor are divided from the educated and comfortable, from squires, and parsons and tradespeople, by a barrier which custom has forged through long centuries, and which only very exceptional circumstances ever beat down, and then only for an instant. The slaves are separated from the whites by more glaring . . . marks of distinction; but still distinctions and separations, like those of English classes which always endure, which last from the cradle to the grave, which prevent anything like association or companionship, produce a general effect on the life of the extreme poor, and subject them to isolation, which offer a very fair parallel to the separation of the slaves from the whites.

This separation of the classes was important because each had to keep to their allotted place in the social ladder:

> The English poor man or child is expected always to remember the condition in which God has placed him, exactly as the negro is expected to remember the skin which God has given him. The relation in both instances is that of perpetual superior to perpetual inferior, of chief to dependent, and no amount of kindness or goodness is suffered to alter this relation.[48]

Class division denoted the relation of 'perpetual superior to perpetual inferior' a distinction that to the Victorians was every bit as visible as that between black and white, or slave and master. We can see here clearly how the gap between an abstract belief in equality and a society built on social distinction created the space for a racial view of the world. Social rank, for the Victorians, was the consequence of individual achievement and aptitude. Yet it was clear that individuals largely occupied the same rank as their parents. The son or daughter of a factory hand or of a farm labourer rarely became a philosopher or factory-owner. This seemed to suggest that differences of class expressed hereditary distinctions. As John Stuart Mill was to complain, social commentators 'revolved in their eternal circle of landlords, capitalists and labourers, until they seemed to think of the distinction of society into these three classes as though it were one of God's ordinances.'[49]

The idea of the permanence of social divisions was strengthened by the belief that social fluidity would undermine national cohesion. The fact that the rank order in society appeared to be 'one of God's ordinances' combined with a feeling that the social structure *needed* to be static to create a racialised view of social difference. Hence while most English commentators were opposed to forced enslavement, they nevertheless considered the class system to be as permanent as any racial distinction. For Victorian liberals it was the only way to understand social inequality in their society.

Journalist Henry Mayhew, the discoverer of urban poverty in mid-Victorian England, set the tone for the discussion of social divisions. In his study of *London Labour and the London Poor* Mayhew divided humanity into two sorts:

> Of the thousand millions of human beings that are said to constitute the population of the entire globe, there are – socially, morally and perhaps even physically considered – but two distinct and broadly marked races, viz., the wanderers and the settlers – the vagabond and the citizen – the nomadic and the civilised tribes.[50]

Every society, wrote Mayhew, had its citizens and its vagabonds. London 'street-folk' were the vagabonds of England, and were in every way a 'race apart':

> The nomad then is distinguished from the civilised man by his repugnance to regular and continuous labour – by his want of providence in laying up store for the future – by his inability to perceive consequences ever so slightly removed from immediate apprehension – by his passion for stupefying herbs and roots, and, when possible, for intoxicating fermented liquors – by his extraordinary powers of enduring privation – by his comparative insensibility to pain – by his immoderate love of gaming, frequently risking his own personal liberty upon a single cast – by his love of libidinous dances – by the pleasure he experiences in witnessing the suffering of sentient creatures – by his delight in warfare and all perilous sports – by the looseness of his notions as to property – by the absence of chastity among his women and his disregard of female honour – and, lastly, by his vague sense of religion – his rude idea of a Creator, and utter absence of all appreciation of the mercy of the divine spirit.[51]

Mayhew's 'vagabonds' did not encompass the working class as a whole but were studies of the outcasts of society – what one London magistrate called a 'race lower than any yet known.'[52] Mayhew provided a description not of the 'respectable working class' but, in the words of the subtitles of his various volumes, of 'street sellers, street buyers, street finders, street performers, street artisans, street labourers, prostitutes, thieves, swindlers and beggars'. Nevertheless, in dissecting the life of the 'street-folk', Mayhew pointed the way to establishing, a scientific understanding of the whole of society. The relationship between 'outcast London' and 'respectable society' provided the model for understanding social stratification in the rest of society.

Mayhew's writings (which have since become a major source for historians and sociologists) demonstrate clearly the Victorian view of race as signifying social as opposed to colour distinctions. Racial divisions existed not so much between different societies as within each society. Mayhew's work also shows the nineteenth-century tendency to elide social, moral and physical distinctions into a single racial hierarchy. This elision allowed Victorian writers to view social and natural problems in the same terms. Gertrude Himmelfarb, in a discussion of an official report on *The Sanitary Condition of the Labouring Population of Great Britain*, notes that 'the same words – "residuum", "refuse", "offal" – were used to denote the sewage waste that constituted the sanitary problem and the human waste that constituted the social problem.'[53] In the positivist outlook that defined mid-century society, natural waste and human waste were thought susceptible to similar treatment.

The naturalisation of social or moral attributes was underscored by the insistence that physical distinctions were outward manifestations of inherent moral differences. Mayhew himself considered that the nomadic race was distinguished by a 'greater relative development of the jaws and cheekbones' and 'broad lozenge-shaped faces', indicating an enlargement of 'the organs subservient to sensation and the animal faculties' and giving rise to 'distinctive moral and intellectual features'.

Other racial scientists attempted to be more precise in their delineation of the racial hierarchy. Otto Ammon devised 'Ammon's law', which stated that urban populations were more highly dolichocephalic, or long-headed, because this racial type showed 'a stronger inclination to city life and a greater aptitude for success there' than brachycephalic, or broad-headed, people. Further, added Ammon, 'the upper classes in the cities are the most dolichocephalic of all'. William Ripley concurred that 'there is some characteristic of the long headed race or types, either their energy, ambition or hardiness, which makes them peculiarly prone to migrate from the country to the city.' English psychologists W. E. D. and C. D. Whetham, on the other hand, thought that those who migrated to the cities were inferior to those who remained in the country:

> Taking the population of England as a whole, in a general sense the upper classes and the country folk seem, on the whole, to be fairer and taller than the industrial sections of the population; a disposition which may indicate a natural drift of the northern race towards modes of life giving openings for their directive and organising powers and to their love of a free life in the open air.[54]

The difference between the views of Ammon and Ripley on the one hand, and of the Whethams on the other, demonstrates different political needs. Ammon and Ripley wanted to show that immigrants to the USA at the end of the nineteenth century, who were largely from the Mediterranean countries, were of inferior stock to those already settled in America. The Whethams wanted to prove the inferiority of the urban working class in Britain. The contrasting theories show that what was important to Victorian society were not the facts of racial difference but merely the existence of a hierarchy.

It is in the context of such a hierarchy that arguments for the inferiority of the non-white races became part of mainstream scientific and social thinking. The Prichardian Ethnological Society, which had championed a more humanist outlook, went into decline in the 1850s and James Hunt's Anthropological Society, the institutional cutting edge of the new racial science in England, gained support. The theory of polygenesis – the idea that different races evolved by different means – grew in influence. Liberals such as Huxley adopted a more determinist stance. In

1862, Huxley observed of the white race, that 'with them has originated everything that is original in science, in art, in law, in politics and in mechanical inventions. In their hands, at the moment, lies the order of the social world, and to them its progress is committed.'[55]

The social élite in England now measured non-white races by the same yardstick that it had previously used to demarcate itself from the 'lower orders' at home. 'The English governing classes in the 1860s', Bernard Semmel has observed,

> regarded the Irish and the non-European native just as they had, quite openly, regarded their own labouring classes for many centuries: as thoroughly undisciplined, with a tendency to revert to bestial behaviour, consequently requiring to be kept in order by force, and by occasional but severe flashes of violence; vicious and sly, incapable of telling the truth, naturally lazy and unwilling to work unless under compulsion.[56]

The descriptions of Africans and negroes were strikingly similar to those of the 'residuum' at home. This was how one colonial administrator described the typical black African:

> [A] happy, thriftless, excitable person, lacking in self-control, discipline and foresight . . . His thoughts are concentrated on the events and feelings of the moment, and he suffers little from apprehension for the future, or grief for the past . . . [H]is own insensitivity to pain, and his disregard for life – whether his own or another's—cause him to appear callous to suffering . . . He lacks power of organisation, and is conspicuously deficient in the management and control alike of men or of business . . . He is prone to imitate anything new in dress or custom.[57]

It might have been Henry Mayhew describing the London streetfolk.

The so-called 'Governor Eyre' controversy of 1865 brought out well the commonality of outlook towards blacks and the working class. In October 1865 a local rising by peasantry in Jamaica was put down by the island's governor, Edward John Eyre, with the utmost ferocity. Eyre's actions created much debate in England. Many of those who defended him did so, interestingly, by comparing the negro to the English worker. 'The negro', observed Edwin Hood, 'is in Jamaica as the costermonger is in Whitechapel; he is very likely often nearly a savage with the mind of a child.'[58] The *Saturday Review* suggested that the negro 'is neither ferociously cruel nor habitually malignant. He often does cruel and barbarous things; but then so do our draymen and hackney-coachmen and grooms and farm servants through want of either thought or power of thinking.'[59]

Sometimes commentators went as far as to refer to English workers as 'negroes'. The *Daily Telegraph*, on hearing reports that the pro-independence Jamaica Committee planned a counter-rally to a banquet in Eyre's honour in Southampton, was moved to comment that 'there are a good many negroes in Southampton, who have the taste of their tribe for any disturbance that appears safe, and who are probably imbued with the conviction that it is a proper thing to hoot and yell at a number of gentlemen going to a dinner party.'[60] In fact, as Douglas Lorimer observes,

> the *Daily Telegraph's* 'negroes' were . . . the very English and very white Southampton mob who thronged the streets outside the banquet hall, while their more respectable working class colleagues attended the largest popular meeting in the city's history to protest against the official reception given to Governor Eyre.[61]

The Southampton incident reveals both the élite view of blacks and English workers as being part of the same 'tribe', and the fact that, even as late as the 1860s, there remained considerable working-class sympathy and identification with the plight of blacks in the colonies. This caused immense concern at home and the élite view of the inferiority of non-white races was to a large extent driven by domestic considerations. 'We do not admit of equality even amongst our own race', observed Commander Bedford Pym in a speech to the Anthropological Society in the wake of the Governor Eyre affair. 'To suppose that two alien races can compose a political unity is simply ridiculous. One section *must* govern the other.'[62] To admit to black equality would be to undermine the idea of inequality at home. As V. G. Kiernan observes, 'discontented native in the colonies, labour agitator in the mills, were the same serpent in alternate disguises. Much of the talk about the barbarism or darkness of the outer world, which it was Europe's mission to rout, was a transmuted fear of the masses at home.'[63] At the same time, many in the colonies watched labour unrest in the metropolitan countries with horror and argued that only a rigid racial divide saved them from a similar fate. As Cecil Rhodes told the Cape Colony parliament, the strength of the colony lay in the depth of the racial divide:

> When I see the labour troubles that are occurring in the United States and when I see the troubles that are going to occur with the English people in their own country on the social question and the labour question, I feel rather glad that the labour question here is connected with the native question . . . At any rate, if the whites maintain their position as the supreme race, the day may come when we shall all be thankful that we have the natives with us in their proper position. We

shall be thankful that we have escaped those difficulties which are going on amongst all of the old nations of the world.[64]

Racial science agreed on a common social typology that included both the 'lower orders' in European society and non-European peoples, and justified the inferiority of both. 'The lowest strata of the European societies', wrote French psychologist Gustav LeBon, 'is homologous with the primitive men.' He added that, given sufficient time, 'the superior grades of a population [would be] separated from the inferior grades by a distance as great as that which separates the white man from the negro, or even the negro from the monkey.'[65]

The primitives of other cultures, and those within Britain, Henrika Kuklick observes, 'were all represented as examples of incomplete realization of human potential':

All of these relationships were analogous: primitives to Europeans; children to adults; women to men; the poor to the élite. When children grew to maturity, their development recapitulated both the moral and material history of the race; while negotiating the moral stages of past ages, they played with the tools of their ancestors – the bow and arrow used by the hunter, and the rattle of the witch-doctor.[66]

When they viewed other cultures in the aggregate, Victorians considered that non-Western peoples were like the children of European societies. But, Kuklick notes, Victorian anthropology recognised the same distinctions within primitive cultures that it recognised within its own society. Hence, nineteenth-century anthropologists believed that 'non-Western ruling classes were closer to British gentlemen in manners and attitudes than were their subordinate folk'. Similarly, '[c]hildren of advanced societies resembled primitive peoples, with flat noses, forward-opening nostrils, wideset eyes, large mouths and undeveloped frontal sinuses.' At the same time 'the lower orders in Britain displayed physical capabilities of strength and endurance' that showed similarities with primitive people, but which 'their social superiors had lost during the course of their maturation into rational beings'.[67]

Francis Galton, the founder of eugenics, believed that 'beside . . . three points of difference – endurance of steady labour, tameness of disposition and prolonged development – I know of none that very markedly distinguishes the nature of the lower classes of civilised man from that of barbarians.'[68] Galton divided both black and white populations into 24 grades, from A at the bottom to X at the top, and believed that 'classes E to F of the negro may roughly be considered as the equivalent of our C and D.'[69]

Racial theories, then, as they unfolded in the nineteenth century were part of a broader development – the use of natural explanations for social phenomena. As the critical outlook of the Enlightenment gave way to the positivist vision of the Victorian age, so the belief in social transformation was replaced by the doctrine of a naturally-sanctioned social order. Racial theory provided legitimacy for inequality. 'Racial science', claimed the phrenologist Johann Spurzheim, 'will exercise a great influence on the welfare of nations, in indicating clearly the difference between natural and arbitrary nobility, and in fanning the relations between individuals to each other in general, and between those who govern and those who are governed in particular.'[70]

Scientific racism helped generate a hierarchy, underpinned by forces beyond the reach of humanity, that justified the superiority of the ruling class, both at home and abroad. It proclaimed the fitness of the capitalist class to rule over the working class and of the white race to rule over the black. And it did so not in the name of divine will or aristocratic reaction but of science and progress.

4
Race in the Age of Democracy

Scientific racism presents us with a paradox. It provided the justification for some of the most barbarous acts committed by humankind. Read by a generation which knows of the horrors of Auschwitz, Robert Knox's assessment of 'the dark races' still chills the heart:

> What signify these dark races to us? Who cares particularly for the Negro, or the Hottentot or the Kaffir? These latter have proved a very troublesome race, and the sooner they are put out of the way the better ... Destined by the nature of their race to run, like all other animals, a certain limited course of existence, it matters little how their extinction is brought about.[1]

Yet scientific racism was not simply the product of conservative, backward-looking reactionaries but, as we have seen, was espoused by men who were by and large politically liberal, scientifically minded and believed in progress and modernity. Indeed so great was the identification between science and progress, on the one hand, and racial thinking, on the other, that opponents of racial theories were forced to turn their backs on science. Alfred Russel Wallace, co-discoverer of evolutionary theory with Darwin, and a lifelong socialist, eventually rejected rational explanations for human development. To overcome the trap of social Darwinism, Wallace was forced to deny that human evolution could be understood in scientific terms. Rather, he posited the existence of a non-natural, spiritual agent, which he called a 'will-force', as responsible for human development.

Advocates of scientific racism were not only among the foremost thinkers of their age, many were also fervent advocates of social reform. Phrenologists claimed that from a knowledge of one's inborn faculties, as determined from the shape of the head, an individual programme of education could be drawn up whereby one's abilities could be strengthened and one's weaknesses overcome. Phrenologists were involved in a number of reform movements in the 1830s and 1840s, from prison reform to women's education, the reform of lunatic asylums, the popular health movement and opposition to slavery and colonialism.

Social Darwinism was used initially to attack areas of special social and political privilege in British society. Liberals looked to Darwinism to attack intuitionism – the notion of innate ideas – and the belief in the immutability of human nature and the divine origin of human thought. Liberal writers such as Leslie Stephen and Walter Bagehot appropriated social Darwinism to develop a liberal version of organicist theory which, unlike conservative organicist theory, stressed the possibility of evolution and change. Eugenics was seen as a reforming movement and won the support of Fabians such as the Webbs and socialists like Harold Laski, who were attracted by the arguments for the necessity for state intervention and planning to improve the quality of working-class life. The pioneering sexologist Havelock Ellis argued that 'negative eugenics' – preventing the lower orders from breeding – was the most progressive and radical way of dealing with poverty:

> The superficially sympathetic man flings a coin to the beggar; the more deeply sympathetic man builds an almhouse for him so he need no longer beg; but perhaps most radically sympathetic of all is the man who arranges that the beggar should not be born.[2]

For nineteenth- and early twentieth-century progressives, social change and racial improvement went hand in hand. Greta Jones has summed up well the contradictory nature of much of racial science. Liberal social Darwinists, she notes, represented the two sides of liberal politics:

> On the one hand they provided reasons for intellectual and political freedom and argued the dysgenic character of many of the social and political constraints existing in mid-century Britain. They defended the possibility of an ethics without religion. They used naturalistic explanations of the origins of man's faculties against the protagonists of the notion of an unchanging and preordained human nature. On the other hand they justified hierarchy, moral superiority and social order.[3]

For conservatives, belief in hierarchy and innate superiority lay at the core of their view of the world. For liberals matters were not so simple. Though they fervently believed that social change and racial improvement went hand in hand they were often unable to reconcile the two. There was frequently a tension between their belief in political freedom and their desire for social order, between their attachment to the Enlightenment concept of universalism and their particularist defence of white middle-class superiority.

This tension arose from the very nature of the discourse of race, emerging as it did out of the paradox of equality in modern society. The limits placed on equality by capitalist social relations led to a racialised view of social difference, but equally the discourse of race made acute the political and philosophical problems created by the contradictory nature of equality. I want in this chapter to examine how social and political developments at the end of the nineteenth and beginning of the twentieth centuries – the coming of mass democracy, the age of imperialist expansion, and the impact of Nazism – brought these liberal ambiguities to the surface and transformed the discourse of race.

In a sense, the emergence of racial theory in the early part of the nineteenth century can be seen as a response to a crisis of social theory that was barely recognised as such. The breakdown of Enlightenment universalism, the difficulties which social disharmony posed to the utilitarian outlook, and the conflict between the desire for social progress and the fear of social anarchy all questioned the assumptions of the liberal social theory of the early nineteenth century. But the seemingly inexorable economic and technical advance, the continuing strand of humanist thought and the certainties of the positivist viewpoint all helped to camouflage the extent to which the classical liberal outlook had been undermined.

Evolutionary social theory and racial anthropology emerged, to paraphrase Weber, in debate with the ghosts of Rousseau and Kant. The discourse of race embodied principles clearly at variance with Enlightenment humanism. But racial theory's attachment to objective laws and scientific principles, and the possibility it raised for the rational reform of society, seemed to many to encapsulate a continuation of eighteenth-century ideas. Racial theory provided a way of understanding the antinomies of the post-Enlightenment world through a discourse that could still claim affinity with Enlightenment rationality.

With the breakdown of the positivist outlook in the latter part of the century, however, the crisis of social theory became much more explicit and the ambiguities in the liberal response to ideas such as progress and reason crystallised out. The ambiguities in the liberal response to racial theory also became much more transparent. Political and social changes, in particular the arrival of mass democracy and the expansion of imperialist power, added to the crisis of liberal ideology. They also forced a reformulation of the discourse of race.

But the experience which, more than any other, catalysed the transformation of the whole discussion of race was the nightmare of Nazi rule in Germany. The practical exposition of racial theory in the Third Reich, culminating in the Final Solution, created a popular moral revulsion against racism. The impact of Nazism was to throw into disrepute the biological arguments for racial superiority and to discredit the overt expressions of racism. The assumptions of racial thinking – in particular the idea that humanity can be divided into discrete groups and that these

divisions have a social consequence – went unchallenged. Though the
political use of racial science was discredited, its conceptual framework
was never destroyed. The discourse of race was reformulated, but the
concept of race never disappeared. The aim of this chapter is to trace out
how this came about.

THE FEAR OF THE MASSES

In the latter decades of the nineteenth century the vote was gradually
extended to sections of society beyond the hitherto magic circle of white,
propertied males. Sections of the working class, and then women too,
were drawn into the electoral process. By the early part of the twentieth
century most Western countries had something close to universal suffrage.

This extension of suffrage took place at a time when the major Western
nations were beset by economic crisis – exemplified by the Great Depression of the 1880s – and increasing social and class conflict. These
changes introduced a spirit of pessimism into what had been up until
then an optimistic era. Slowly, and almost surreptitiously, the first
doubts crept in about the ability of science to solve society's ills. Philosophers such as Nietzsche, sociologists such as Pareto, scientists such as
Freud began challenging the rationalism which had until then informed
intellectual and political discussion. The growing revolt against positivism expressed the new unease within society.

The unease revealed itself through anxiety about the lower orders. It
was in this context that nineteenth-century society – and particularly
Victorian England – 'rediscovered' the poor. The *fin de siécle* concern with
the urban poor was a reflection not of growing poverty – in reality the
standard of living even for the most wretched sections of society was
rising – but of fears for social progress. There is, wrote George Sims in
How the Poor Live, 'a dark continent that is within easy walking distance
of the General Post Office'.[4] It was the darkness within that most concerned observers. As Gertrude Himmelfarb has observed in her out-
standing study on *The Idea of Poverty*, the poor were 'important not so
much in themselves, nor even in relation to the rest of society, as in
revealing the limits of progress, the precariousness of civilisation':

> There evidently existed, not in 'darkest Africa' but in the most ad-
> vanced city of the most advanced country in the world, at the very
> apex of civilisation, the equivalent of Bushmen and Fingoes, tribes
> which resisted amelioration and acculturation, refused to be drawn
> into the mainstream of culture, perversely persisted in a way of life
> and work that was an affront to civilised society. It was as if some

primitive spirit, some vestige of primeval nature, were mocking the proud presumptions of modernity.[5]

Liberals welcomed the social advancement that was embodied in the extension of political suffrage. Yet the persistence of poverty seemed to question the very idea of progress. It seemed to imply a sense of degeneration rather than evolutionary advancement and it brought to the fore anxieties about the ability of the élite to govern. If progress was not inevitable, many were forced to ask themselves, what was the basis on which the ruling class ruled? Encapsulated in the 'rediscovery of poverty' in the late nineteenth century were the ambiguities in the liberal attitudes to social progress and social power. These developments led to a debate in *fin de siècle* Britain about democracy and the masses. Fabian Beatrice Webb summed up in her autobiography the two major topics of discussion in her circle:

> [O]n the one hand the meaning of the poverty of masses of men; and on the other the practicability or desirability of political and industrial democracy as a means of redressing the grievances of the majority of people. Was the poverty of the many a necessary condition of the wealth of the nation and of its progress in civilisation? And if the bulk of the people were to remain poor and uneducated, was it desirable, was it even safe, to entrust them with the weapon of trade unionism, and, through the ballot box, with making and controlling the government of Great Britain with its enormous wealth and far-flung dominions?[6]

The outcome of these debates was to strengthen racist sentiment, but in a contradictory fashion. Elite theories became even more important in sustaining the self-belief of the governing classes. The idea of race became central in establishing within the élite the sense of its being and mission. As Houston Stewart Chamberlain observed, 'Nothing is so convincing as the consciousness of the possession of race':

> Race lifts a man above himself, it endows him with extraordinary – I might almost say supernatural – powers, so entirely does it distinguish him from the individual who springs from the chaotic jumble of peoples drawn from all parts of the world.[7]

The concept of race provided a sense of superiority when social reality might suggest otherwise. But the coming of mass democracy made it more difficult to pursue such discussion in public. Racial ideas thus became more important but the nature of racial theories was transformed and many aspects of what had hitherto been an open discussion now became more internal to the ruling élite.

For conservative thinkers, the extension of the suffrage confirmed their traditional opposition to democracy. Now, however, many hitherto liberals joined them in warning of the menace of the masses. 'The crowd' was an important motif in *fin de siècle* discussion. In the eyes of an increasingly fearful intelligentsia, the 'sodden mass of unskilled labour', to use C. F. Masterman's phrase, were 'reared in a Crowd, labour in a Crowd, in a Crowd take their enjoyment, die in a Crowd and in a Crowd are buried'.[8]

John Carey, in *The Intellectuals and the Masses*, his entertaining study of the relationship between élitism and modernism, demonstrates well how deep-seated was this élite fear of the masses.[9] Writers, poets, scientists, philosophers – all betrayed their concern about the new developments. In his significantly titled *The Revolt of the Masses*, Spanish philosopher José Ortega y Gasset claimed that society had created 'a gigantic mass of humanity which, launched like a torrent over the historic area, has inundated it'.[10] Such a mixture of contempt and fear was typical. 'I believe', wrote Gustav Flaubert, 'that the mob, the mass, the herd will always be despicable'.[11] Flaubert's fellow countryman Émile Zola – who, we should remember, was an ardent socialist – drew on the work of racial science in his cycle of Rougon-Macquart novels to show not only that physical characteristics determined mental and moral attributes but also that the crowd was the medium through which degenerate racial traits expressed themselves. T. S. Eliot's famous lines from *The Waste Land*, which echo Dante's *Inferno*, capture the belief within the élite that the masses were dead to humanity:

> A crowd flowed over London Bridge, so many,
> I had not thought death had undone so many.

The fear of the masses found its scientific expression in the new discipline of crowd psychology. Its pioneer was Frenchman Gustav LeBon, who applied to the study of crowd behaviour the growing fashion to ascribe human behaviour to instinct. LeBon regarded humanity as torn between the primal elements of instinct and reason. The élite was capable of suppressing the former and making use of reason. The mass, however, could not reason and was controlled wholly by instinct, which, for LeBon, was an expression in modern society of an atavistic characteristic perpetuated by heredity beyond the stage of social evolution where it served a real adaptive function.

Crowds, argued LeBon, are moved entirely by suggestion, impulse and emotion. They are by nature violent and destructive. In a crowd the individual loses his individuality and becomes simply part of an animal herd. The crowd manifests a single mind and acts as one through pure instinct. Further, argued LeBon, the masses behave in a similar way even when not in a crowd. What LeBon termed a 'psychological crowd' – such as the democratic electorate – was also moved by atavistic impulses, not reason. The notion of liberty, LeBon wrote, 'is merely ignorance of the causes of which man is slave'. 'To be slaves', he added, 'is the natural condition of all living beings'.[12]

Sigmund Freud, who considered LeBon's 'character sketch of the group mind' to be 'brilliant', appropriated many of his ideas. Mass man, wrote Freud, threw off the mechanisms which repressed his unconscious instinct. 'The apparently new characteristics he then displays', Freud believed, 'are in fact the manifestations of this unconscious, in which all that is evil in the human mind is contained as a predisposition'. For Freud the relationship between the ego and the id was akin to the relationship between the élite and the masses. The mind, wrote Freud, is like 'the modern State in which a mob, eager for enjoyment and destruction, has to be held down forcibly by a prudent superior class'. The superior class was superior because it could suppress the promptings of the unconscious within its own psyche, unlike the masses who were 'lazy and unintelligent' and 'have no love for instinctual renunciation'.[13]

Vilfredo Pareto translated these ideas into a sociological theory. For Pareto all societies were divided into a minority governing élite and the masses, distinguished biologically. The élite acted primarily on the basis of enlightened self-interest, whereas the lower, subject classes were moved largely by sentiment. To further its interests the élite found it expedient to appeal for support to the sentiments of the lower classes. The mass was impelled into action by blind forces, whereas the élite conducted itself according to a rational understanding of its situation.

The lesson many drew from the work of psychologists such as Freud and LeBon, and of sociologists such as Pareto, was that liberty was too precious to entrust to democracy. When Beatrice Webb asked 'are men to be governed by emotions or by reason . . . in harmony with the desires of the bulk of citizens or according to the fervent aspirations of a militant minority, in defiance of the will of the majority?',[14] she summed up one of the key debates in intellectual circles. For many, the answer was that liberty was irreconcilable with democracy. '[I]ntellectual freedom and social equality', claimed W. B. Yeats, 'are incompatible'.[15]

The laws of biology, many argued, were inimical to the tenets of democracy. Since the masses were incapable of rational behaviour, they should not be allowed to participate in the governance of society. Such a view was not confined to conservatives. Many socialists too believed that the lower orders simply were not intelligent or rational enough to be able to know their own interests. Parliamentary democracy, Aldous Huxley believed, was a system in which 'confidence tricksters, rich men, quacks may be given power by the votes of an electorate composed in great part of mental Peter Pans, whose childishness renders them

peculiarly susceptible to the blandishments of demagogues and the tire-
lessly repeated suggestion of the rich men's papers'.[16] The vast majority
of people, Huxley believed were imbeciles:

> About 99.5% of the entire population of the planet are as stupid and
> philistine ('tho in different ways) as the great masses of the English.
> The important thing, it seems to me, is not to attack the 99.5% – except
> for exercise – but to try to see that the 0.5% survives, keeps its quality
> up to the highest possible level and, if possible, dominates the rest. The
> imbecility of 99.5% is appalling – but, after all, what else can you
> expect?[17]

Given the imbecility of the masses, the 'ideal state' would be one 'controlled by an aristocracy of intellect'.[18] The attempt to provide mass
education was widely decried because inculcating the masses with the
false belief that they could reason would weaken, in the words of T. S.
Eliot, 'our ancient edifices to make ready the ground upon which the
barbarian nomads of the future will encamp in their mechanised ca-
ravans'.[19] Until now, the argument ran, the masses had known their
station in society. The extension of suffrage and education facilities would
break down the natural hierarchy in society. That is why it was necessary
to follow the dictates of biology rather than those of democracy:

> The essential difference between the ideals of democracy and those
> which biological observation teaches us to be sound, is this: democ-
> racy regards class distinctions as evil; we perceive them to be essential.
> It is the heterogeneity of modern man which has given him his control
> of the forces of nature. The maintenance of that heterogeneity, that
> differentiation of members, is a condition of progress. The aim of social
> reform must not be to abolish class, but to provide that each individual
> shall so far as is possible get into the right class, stay there and usually
> his children after him.[20]

Even those who held that democracy was useful often did so because it
helped to further biological aims. Sociologist Gaetano Mosca, for instance, believed that if democracy was used conservatively, it could help
replenish the élite:

> When the democratic tendency does not exert too great an influence,
> to the exclusion of other tendencies, it represents a conservative force.
> It enables ruling classes to be continually replenished through the
> admission of new elements who have inborn talents for leadership and
> a will to lead, and so prevents that exhaustion of aristocracies of birth
> which usually paves the way for great social cataclysms.[21]

Society was naturally divided into 'the ruling classes' and the masses. Unfortunately, the ruling classes had a tendency to degenerate and to become exhausted. They had to be continually replenished by the best elements of the lower orders. Within limits, democracy could help humanity overcome the limitations of biology. But, wrote Mosca, 'the dogma of equality' propounded by Rousseau and Marx inevitably undermined social order, for it replaced moderation with fanaticism. Even for Mosca, then, democracy always had to be subservient to biology.

DEGENERATION AND RACIAL PLANNING

The arguments of men such as Mosca and Pareto suggest that behind the fear of the masses lay doubts about the ability of the governing classes to govern. Many intellectuals interpreted the social and economic crises of the latter years of the nineteenth century as a crisis of ruling-class legitimacy. 'History', wrote Pareto, 'is a graveyard of aristocracies.' This new sense of the precariousness of social order asserted itself through the discussion of degeneration. In the political and scientific discourse of the late nineteenth century the concept of degeneration expressed, at one and the same time, the physical and moral depravity of the lower orders, the decadence of the governing classes and the racial impoverishment of society as a whole. It explained the nature of criminality, the crisis of legitimacy and the growing sense of social anarchy.

We have already seen how the ideas of evolution and degeneration combined to shape post-Enlightenment discourse. Degeneration expressed the growing social pessimism of the nineteenth century. In the first half of the nineteenth century, however, this pessimism, and hence the attraction of degenerationist theories, was kept in check by economic advance and the strength of the positivist outlook. But as the century progressed, degeneration, in the words of Daniel Pick, 'moved from its place as occasional sub-current of wider philosophies and political or economic theories, or homilies about the horrors of the French and the Industrial Revolutions, to become the centre of a scientific and medical investigation'. Increasingly, the 'potential degeneration of European society' was discussed not as a 'religious, philosophical or ethical problem, but as an empirically demonstrable medical, biological or physical anthropological fact'.[22]

The discourse of degeneration imputed to heredity the cause of criminality, poverty, imbecility and moral depravity. '[P]auperism', the Eugenics Education Society claimed in its submission to the Poor Law Commission, 'is due to inherent defects which are hereditarily transmitted' including 'drunkenness, theft, persistent laziness, a tubercule diathesis, mental deficiency, deliberate moral obliquity, or general weakness of character manifested by want of initiative or energy or stamina and an inclination to attribute their misfortune to their own too great generosity or too great goodness, and generally to bad luck'.[23]

The afflictions of the lower orders – crime, suicide, alcoholism, prostitution – were understood to be social pathologies, endangering the race as a whole by constituting a degenerative process within. The degenerate were thus seen both as racially distinct and as causing the degeneration of the race as a whole. Degeneration was not so much the social condition of the poor as a self-reproducing pathological process, a causal agent in the blood, in the body and in the race which engendered a cycle of historical and social decline.

In France defeat by the Prussians in 1870 and the horrors of the Paris Commune the following year brought the issue of national degeneracy to the fore. For more progressive and liberal thinkers, the question was of how the glories of the French Revolution and of the Napoleonic era had been dissipated in defeat at the hands of the Prussians. In his novel *The Débâcle* Zola takes a scalpel to the social and racial decline of France as revealed by the Franco-Prussian war. For the novel's central character, Maurice, '[t]he degeneration of his race, which explained how France, victorious with the grandfathers, could be beaten in the time of their grandsons, weighed down on his heart like a hereditary disease getting steadily worse and leading to inevitable destruction when the appointed hour came.' For others, such as Taine, the French Revolution itself had bequeathed a process of degeneration which reached its apotheosis in defeat in the Franco-Prussian war and the madness of the Commune. Defeat confirmed their belief that equality and democracy were themselves symptoms of degeneracy. In Britain the initial defeats in the Boer War had a similar impact. The conditions of the urban slums, and the physical and mental state of the working class, which particularly came to notice through the state of army recruits during the Boer War, led to a firm belief that the British stock as a whole had declined.

Unlike previous racial theories, the new arguments held that degeneration could not be recognised by external features alone. '[T]he typical character of the head in degenerate beings will not be the sole element of our classifications', wrote Augustin Benedict Morel, the French founder of the science of degeneracy. 'The distinctions do not rest only upon external differences, but upon internal differences too'.[24] Degeneration intimated, then, both universality and invisibility. It suggested that traditional methods of racial science were inadequate to the new tasks which now presented themselves. Differences were more fluid, more internal than suggested by traditional racial science. Degeneration was a process which, as Pick suggests, 'could usurp all boundaries of discernable identity, threatening the very overthrow of civilisation and progress'. While the dangerous classes were visibly different and racially alien, they were simultaneously invisible and within. It was as though the dangerous classes had entered the very physiology of the nation.

This tension between the *degenerate,* as visible, racially different stock, and *degeneracy,* as an invisible essence which threatened all society, expressed both the fear of the lower orders and the fear that all classes and races had been afflicted by the malady. In Emile Zola's *Nana,* the eponymous anti-heroine embodies both the hereditary defects of the lower classes and the destructive power of *dégénérescence* which she could visit on the rest of society:

> It was the story of a girl descended from four or five generations of drunkards, her blood tainted by an accumulated inheritance of poverty and drink, which in her case had taken the form of a nervous derangement of the sexual instinct. She had grown up in the slums, in the gutters of Paris; and now tall and beautiful, and as well made as a plant nurtured in the dungheap, she was avenging the paupers and outcasts of whom she was the product. With her the rottenness that was allowed to ferment among the lower classes was rising to the surface and rotting the aristocracy. She had become a force of nature, a ferment of destruction, unwittingly corrupting and disorganising Paris between her snow-white thighs.[25]

Nana was damned by her heredity, her blood tainted by the criminality of her forebears. But the degeneration she carried within her was not visible from the outside. This invisibility of her racial malady made her an instrument of revenge for the lower classes upon the aristocracy.

For many, degeneration within European nations was a far greater problem than the racial inferiority of non-European peoples. 'Between the intellectual state of the wildest Bosjeman and that of the most civilised European', wrote Morel, 'there is less difference than between the intellectual state of the same European and that of the degenerate being':

> The first, in fact, is susceptible of racial modification, and his descendants can revert to a more perfect type. The second is susceptible only of a relative amelioration, and hereditary influences will weigh heavily upon his posterity. He will remain all his life what he is in reality—a specimen of degeneration in the human species, an example of the morbid deviation from the normal type of man.[26]

Given the widespread belief among contemporary scholars that the discourse of race developed exclusively in relation to non-European peoples, it is interesting not only that Morel compares the racial inferiority of European lower orders to that of non-Europeans but that he should see the first as absolute inferiority and the second as relative.

The discourse of degeneration expressed the sense of the precariousness of civilisation and of the disenchantment with the idea of human beings as thinking, rational subjects. But this disillusionment with the Enlightenment belief in rationality did not express itself, as it later would in the twentieth century, as a rejection of the scientific method. Rather science was seen as the prerogative of the few. The bulk of humanity was regarded as naturally irrational and prone to degenerative tendencies. Therefore it seemed to many that it was not sufficient to leave society to the sway of natural laws as the positivists had believed. What was required was intervention and planning, for the 'intellectual aristocracy' to use science and reason to overcome the defects of human nature. The discourse of degeneration underpinned, therefore, a critique of *laissez-faire* policies. It was at the heart of new social movements for a planned society and a welfare state. At the same time planning was seen by many to apply not simply to the social and economic arenas, but to the racial arena too. As Aldous Huxley noted, eugenic methods acted not as a 'substitute for the improvement of the environment, but as a supplement to it'.[27]

The view that racial degeneration was the product of overbreeding by the lower orders gave new support to the eugenics movement. Geneticist Ronald Fisher believed that 'the biologically successful members of our society are to be found principally among its social failures'. On the other hand, 'classes of persons who are prosperous and socially successful are on the whole biological failures'.[28] As a result of this imbalance, socialist and eugenicist Harold Laski contended, Britain was 'fostering the weaker part of mankind until its numbers have become a positive danger to mankind'.[29] Economist Alfred Marshall linked the fear of the overbreeding lower orders to that of the overbreeding non-European races:

A check to the growth of the population would do great harm if it affected only the more intelligent races and in particular the more intelligent classes of these races. There does indeed appear to be some danger of this evil. For instance, if the lower classes of Englishmen multiply more rapidly than those which are morally and physically superior, not only will the population of England deteriorate, but also that part of the population of America and Australia which descends from Englishmen will be less intelligent than it otherwise would be. Again if Englishmen multiply less rapidly than the Chinese, this spiritless race will overrun portions of the earth that otherwise would have been peopled by English vigour.[30]

The answer to the racial problems created by the lopsided rise in population was a breeding programme that could, in the words of

Françis Galton, 'improve the racial qualities of future generations'. This would include the forcible sterilisation of the 'unfit' elements in society and inducements to persuade the middle class to breed more. Aldous Huxley, in common with many of his contemporaries, believed in a universal child benefit system so as to make it more financially viable for middle-class families to have children. For Huxley eugenics would be at the heart of a programme for a rationally planned society:

> In the future we envisage eugenics will be practised in order to improve the human breed and the instincts will not be ruthlessly repressed, but, as far as possible, sublimated so as to express themselves in socially harmless ways. Education will not be the same for all individuals. Children of different types will receive different training. Society will be organised as a hierarchy of mental quality and the form of government will be aristocratic in the literal sense of the world – that is to say, the best will rule . . . Our children will look forward to a new caste system based on differences in natural ability, to a Machiavellian system of education designed to give members of the lower castes only that which it is profitable for the members of the upper castes that they should know.[31]

In private, many subscribed to more drastic measures. Nietzsche's despairing wail – 'I wish a storm would come and shake all this rottenness and wormeatenness from the tree!' – was echoed by much of the intelligentsia. In a letter to Blanche Jennings, D. H. Lawrence chillingly describes how he would dispose of society's outcasts:

> If I had my way, I would build a lethal chamber as big as the Crystal Palace, with a military band playing softly, and a Cinematograph working brightly; then I'd go out in the back streets and main streets and bring them in, all the sick, the halt and the maimed; I would lead them gently, and they would smile me a weary thanks; and the band would softly bubble out the 'Hallelujah Chorus'.[32]

'What else would softly bubble out in order to make his lethal chamber lethal Lawrence even here does not specify', John Carey, who cites the letter, dryly observes, 'but maybe his later interest in poison gas gives us a clue to the direction of his imaginings.'[33]

Eugenics, by definition, could not be a mass movement. Nevertheless it won the support of wide swathes of the middle class and the intelligentsia. In Britain, the eugenics movement commanded the support of many of the most eminent figures of the time including, at different times, Charles Sherrington, Ronald Fisher, J. B. S. Haldane, Julian

Huxley, Patrick Geddes, William MacDougal, Cyril Burt, Charles Spearman, John Maynard Keynes, Havelock Ellis and Arthur Balfour.

In America support for eugenicist ideas went to the very top. 'It is
obvious that if in the future racial qualities are to be improved', claimed
president Theodore Roosevelt in 1913,

> that improvement must be wrought mainly by favouring the fecundity
> of the worthy types and frowning on the fecundity of the unworthy
> types. At present we do just the reverse. There is no check to the
> fecundity of those who are subnormal, both intellectually and morally,
> while the provident and the thrifty tend to develop a cold selfishness,
> which makes them refuse to breed at all.[34]

Between 1907, when Indiana became the first state to approve 'an act to
prevent the procreation of confined criminals, idiots, imbeciles and
rapists', and the Second World War, thirty states passed laws sanctioning
the forcible sterilisation of the 'intellectually and morally subnormal'.

In Germany the Nazi government promulgated in 1933 eugenics legislation based on American eugenicist Harry Laughlin's 'Model Eugenical
Sterilisation Law'. This model law called for the sterilisation of 'the
socially inadequate classes' including the 'feebleminded', the 'insane',
the 'criminalistic', the 'epileptic', the 'inebriate', the 'diseased', the
'blind', the 'deaf' and the 'dependent', a category which included 'or-
phans, ne'er-do-wells, the homeless, tramps and paupers'.[35] The Nazis
set up special eugenics courts to rule on every case; it is estimated that
between 1933 and 1945 some two million people were ruled to be dys-
genic and were sterilised.

RACE, IMPERIALISM AND DEMOCRACY

If the extension of the suffrage encouraged certain sections of the intelligentsia to stress the anti-democratic aspects of racial theory, other more
liberal commentators felt that the problem with mass democracy lay in
the impact of imperialism. Liberals such as Leonard Hobhouse, J. A.
Hobson and Graham Wallas were as fearful of the 'crowd' as were
Lawrence and Eliot, Marshall and Galton. But the problem, as they
perceived it, lay in the way that nationalism and imperialist fervour had
seduced the masses.

The coming of imperialism had a dramatic impact on both international relations and domestic politics. Between 1880 and the First World
War most of the world outside Europe and the Americas was parcelled
up into territories under the direct rule or indirect political control of a
handful of European states – Britain, France, Germany, Italy, Holland,

Belgium, Portugal and Spain – and the USA and Japan. Britain, long the world's leading economic power, gained 4m sq. miles of territory in these years to become the empire on which the sun never set. By the eve of the First World War the British Empire covered one-fifth of the world's land mass and included a quarter of its people.

For a nation like Britain, this unprecedented colonial expansion seemed to offer a way out of its manifold problems. By opening up new spheres of investments, new markets and new sources of raw materials imperialism held the promise of a solution to the nation's economic crisis. Further, the establishment of new colonies and spheres of influence helped curb the scope of emergent rivals, such as Germany and the USA, and safeguarded existing holdings, notably India, against such competitors.

Domestically, the possession of the Empire buttressed the self-esteem of the ruling class at a time when political and economic crises were beginning to sap its morale. The fact that Britain (and a handful of other largely white nations) now ruled the globe appeared to confirm a sense of inherent superiority:

> I believe that the British race is the greatest of governing races the world has ever seen. I say this not merely as an empty boast, but as proved and shown by the success which we have had in administering vast dominions.[36]

As Lord Rosebery observed, 'What *is* Empire but the predominance of race?'

The braggadocio that accompanied Queen Victoria's Diamond Jubilee celebration in 1897 summed up the importance of the Empire for ruling class self-assurance. 'How many millions of years has the sun stood in heaven?', asked the *Daily Mail* the day after the Jubilee procession through London. 'But the sun never looked down until yesterday upon the embodiment of so much energy and power.'[37]

The imperial ideal was not simply an evocation of racial superiority but expressed too the highest sense of moral duty. Late Victorian society saw itself as a benign, civilising influence, making sacrifices for the good of the sullen, slothful and ungrateful heathens in the darkest corners of the globe. The aim, in David Livingstone's words, were to bring the 'three Cs' – Commerce, Christianity and Civilisation – to the rest of the world. It was this concept of imperialism as a moral crusade which Rudyard Kipling captured in the idea of the 'White Man's Burden' – a notion which embodied the sense both of Western superiority and of a moral obligation placed upon the West to act for the good of humankind.

At the same time as encapsulating a sense of moral and racial superiority, the Empire also offered a new source of popular legitimacy for the

British ruling class. 'Imperialism', historian Eric Hobsbawm has observed, 'encouraged the masses, and especially the potentially discontented, to identify themselves with the imperial state and nation, and
thus unconsciously to endow the social and political system represented
by that state with justification and legitimacy'.[38] Or, as Cecil Rhodes put
it more pithily, 'If you want to avoid civil war you must become imper-
ialists.' The social conflicts that so worried the establishment in the latter
part of the nineteenth century could be subsumed to a sense of national
pride in the civilising mission of British imperialism and to a sense of
moral superiority over the rest of the world.

By the end of the nineteenth century, nationalism and racial thinking
had ceased to be an élite ideology and became part of popular culture.
'Imperialism in the air', Beatrice Webb recorded in her diary in June 1897.
'All classes drunk with sightseeing and hysterical loyalty.' The racial
superiority of the British people was celebrated in mass circulation
newspapers, in penny-dreadful novels and in popular entertainment. A
favourite music hall song of the time both captured the patriotic mood
and gave a new word to the English language:

> We don't want to fight, but, by Jingo if we do,
> We've got the ships, we've got the men, we've got the money too.

The political and social benefits of the infusion of imperialist passion
into popular culture was apparent. But it also highlighted the contradictory nature of racial thinking. Racial theory developed as an élite theory,
an ideology through which the governing classes could both understand
and explain a world of inequality and hierarchy. But in establishing
racism as a mass force, an élite theory was becoming the property of the
many. This was deeply troubling and disturbing for sections, particularly liberal sections, of the intelligentsia.

The appeal to racial feeling and to imperialist fervour, many liberals
feared, could only strengthen the 'herd mentality' of the masses. These
forebodings were strengthened by 'mafficking' – the mass xenophobic
jubilation at the relief of Mafeking during the Boer War. For men such as
Hobson, Hobhouse and Wallas the politics of racial or 'herd' feeling
forewarned of the undermining of the liberal ethos. Liberals had hoped
that the extension of democracy would strengthen the liberal sentiments
in British society. The impact of imperialism and of racial thinking,
however, had been to strengthen illiberal sentiments.

Many liberals were unsure about how to reconcile national and racial
sentiment with mass society. 'It is . . . pretty clear to anyone who marks
the influence of nationalism during the past fifty years', Alfred Dicey
wrote in a letter to Liberal elder statesman Lord Bryce, 'that a sentiment
which seemed to Mazzini and Cavour almost wholly good, contains

within it a good deal of possible evil.'[39] Certain sections of liberal opinion felt compelled to oppose imperialism as a way of defending political democracy in Britain. Such opposition to imperialism should not be confused with opposition to the idea of racial inequality. All were fervent believers in the superiority of the white race. Gilbert Murray, a liberal anti-imperialist, expressed the prevailing view of racial superiority:

> There is in the world a hierarchy of races . . . [T]hose nations which eat more, claim more, and get higher wages, will direct and rule the others, and the lower work of the world will tend in the long run to be done by the lower breeds of men. This much we of the ruling colour will no doubt accept as obvious.[40]

However, such liberals distinguished between the reality of a racial hierarchy and the deleterious impact of racial thinking on the working class. Élite theory, as far as they were concerned, should remain the property of the élite.

Opposition to democracy and opposition to imperialism both expressed attempts by different sections of the Western élite to recast racial thinking in the new age. Both views, however, were minority trends. The general impact of the developments at the turn of the century was to entrench the ideas of hierarchy, and hence of racial thinking, but to transform the concept of race more into an issue of colour.

The rise of political democracy modified the application of the language of racial inferiority to the working class. The idea of the inferiority of the lower orders did not disappear but was increasingly couched in social or cultural rather than biological terms. Unemployment, for example, was seen more and more as the product of the moral malaise of the unemployed. At the same time it became a discussion more internal to the ruling class. The élite's sense of superiority was essential in establishing its belief in its own right to rule; but such views increasingly became confined to private diaries and to dinner table talk.

The gradual admission of the working class into the system of political democracy helped refocus the language of race more exclusively upon black and white, West and the Third World. Imperialism provided the material basis with which to substantiate the thesis of white, Western superiority. Imperialist expansion seemed to confirm the belief that history was a racial struggle and that the white race would eventually eliminate the black and yellow races. All must appreciate the 'race importance', wrote Theodore Roosevelt, of the struggle between whites and the 'scattered savage tribes, whose life was but a few degrees less meaningless, squalid and ferocious than that of the wild beasts.' The elimination of the inferior races would be 'for the benefit of civilisation and in the interests of mankind.'[41]

The 'colour line' now became the chief way of understanding and dividing the world. In the colonies, colour demarcated social difference in a much more rigid way than previously, as James Morris observes of British India in the late Victorian era:

> The British had not always been so colour-conscious. In the early days of the East India Company social intercourse between white men and brown had been easy and respectful, and imperialists of the nineties must have viewed with mixed feelings a splendid picture that still hung prominently in Fort St. George at Madras: attributed to Chinnery, it showed the plump adventurer Stringer Lawrence, who went to India in 1748, amicably walking with the Nawab of the Carnatic like a pair of poets on a picnic – the Englishman florid and thick set, the Indian marvellously shining with jewels, and the two of them promenading side by side across the canvas in a kind of springy minuet. It was not the association of the two men that must have struck a jarring note – there were many friendships still between Britons and Indian princes. It was the picture's suggestion that here was a meeting between absolute equals, each representing a great and attractive civilisation, consorting to music in the sunshine.[42]

'Colour bars' and racial exclusion became a way of life both in the colonies and in the metropolitan countries. The 1890s and the first decades of the twentieth century were the age of immigration controls. In 1896 several Australian states passed Colored Races Restriction and Regulation Acts, excluding native inhabitants of Asia, Africa, and the Pacific Islands. 'If we want a homogenous Australia, we must have a white Australia', the *Sydney Daily Telegraph* declared. 'It is not much use . . . to shut out Chinamen, and leave the door open to millions of Hindoos, Arabs, Burmese, Angolese, and the other coloured races which swarm British Asia.'[43]

Canada similarly followed a 'White Canada' policy, the 1910 Immigration Act prohibiting the entry 'of immigrants belonging to any race deemed unsuitable to the climate or requirements of Canada.' When the newly created Union of South Africa established a series of discriminatory and exclusionary statutes, the London *Times* declared that 'the brown, black and yellow races of the world' had to realise that 'inequality is inevitable . . . not due to inferior status but to facts of race.'[44] As a result of such policies, one commentator sympathetic to racial policies wrote, 'the rising tide of colour finds itself walled in by white dikes debarring it from many a promised land which it would fain deluge with its dusky waves.'[45]

The rise of Japan as a world power emphasised the distinction between white and other races. The issue of the 'Yellow peril' dominated much of the discussion on international policy in Asia and the Pacific. 'In this struggle [between races]', the Australian C. H. Kirmess argued, 'the still larger issue is bound up with whether the White or Yellow race shall gain final supremacy. Christian civilisation cannot afford the loss of this continent. For Australia is the precious front buckle in the white girdle of power and progress encircling the globe.' The lyrics of 'White Canada forever' express this prevailing opinion: 'We welcome as brothers all white men still, but the shifty yellow race . . . must find another place.' US president Theodore Roosevelt, ever keen to promote America's role in defending the white race, thundered that Japan had to be taught a military lesson if it did not voluntarily limit the movements of its nationals:

> We have got to build up our Western country with our white civilisation and we must retain the power to say who shall and who shall not come to our country. Now, it may be that Japan will adopt a different attitude, will demand that her people be permitted to go where they think fit, so I thought it wise to send that fleet around the Pacific to be ready to maintain our rights . . . The fleet is there in the [racial] interests of the whole Pacific Coast, the interests of British Columbia, as well as those of California, and it is in the interests of Australia as well . . . [For] self preservation is the first law of nature.[46]

By the early decades of the twentieth century, then, the concept of race had taken on a very different meaning. Whereas in the past belief in the inferiority of non-European peoples was an extension of the already-existing belief in the inferiority of the lower orders at home, now it became a central part of racial discourse. The idea of 'backwardness', which had previously applied to the working class at home, became exclusively associated with the 'native' in the colonies. This reorientation of racial thought helped establish racism as a mass ideology and win popular support for élite ideas of hierarchy. It also helped promote the idea which is so strong today: that racial language was developed in order specifically to describe distinctions between black and white.

RACE, SCIENCE AND POLITICS

In the half century the followed the publication of *The Origin of Species* scientific racism reached its zenith. American anthropologist William Ripley estimated that by 1899 one and a half million adults and ten million children had been measured in Europe and America for their racial identity. 'In an atmosphere of growing nationalism, rivalry and anxiety when . . . theories of difference and exclusion, whether based on

class, nation or race, seemed almost necessary for social identification
and moral orientation', notes Nancy Stepan, 'scientific racism no longer
seemed an aberration of Western intellectual traditions, but its very
essence.'[47]

Yet, as George Stocking has put it, 'nothing failed like success.' 'The
more precise and extensive the observation and measurement of mankind', Stocking noted, 'the more tenuous was the "reality" of the races
they served to define.'[48] Leading German racial scientist Ludwig Gumplowicz summed up the state of anthropological research at the end of
the nineteenth century:

> The sorry role played by all anthropological measuring of skulls and
> the like can be appreciated by anyone who has ever tried to gain
> enlightenment through these studies of mankind's different types.
> Everything is higgledy-piggledy, and the 'mean' figures and measure-
> ments offer no palpable result. What one anthropologist describes as
> the Germanic type, another deems apposite to the slave type. We find
> Mongolian types among 'Aryans', and we constantly land in the posi-
> tion of taking 'Aryans' for Semites and vice versa if we abide by
> anthropological categories.[49]

Every measure of racial type used by racial science, from headform to
blood groups, was shown to be changeable and not exclusive to any one
race. As racial scientists searched desperately for more and more trivial
manifestations of race, one biologist noted, apparently without a hint of
irony, that 'it is on the degree of curliness or twist in the hair that the most
fundamental divisions in the human race are based.'[50] The lack of scientific validity forced racial scientists to adopt increasingly more metaphysical conceptions of race. 'Race in the present state of things is an
abstract conception', Paul Broca, the leading physical anthropologist of
his age, conceded. Race was, he continued, 'a conception of continuity in
discontinuity, of unity in diversity. It is the rehabilitation of a real but
directly unobtainable thing.'[51]

When Harvard anthropologist Richard Dixon set out in the early twenties to write a 'Racial history of man', he gave up entirely on scientific
categories. Faced with the sheer complexity of classification, the fact that
each study used a different criterion, and the lack of any agreement on
what were the important traits that defined racial difference, Dixon's
answer was to do away with objective measurement altogether. Instead,
as he himself notes, he 'set up arbitrary standards, and using these as our
measure, determine[d] the character and relationships of people in terms
of arbitrarily selected units.'[52] This truly was an Alice-in-Wonderland
science where the acceptance that something did not exist became the
starting point for proving that it did. As one historian dryly notes,

'Whether Dixon's original intention was to refute physical anthropology through sarcasm is difficult to say.'[53]

In the end it mattered little that the scientific basis of racial divisions was tenuous at best. Race was a social category, not a scientific one. What was important, as Gumplowicz pointed out, was not that races existed, but that society should be organised as if they did:

> In my home region I was ... already struck by the circumstances that the individual social classes represented quite heterogeneous races; there was the Polish nobility, which rightly always considered itself of different stock from the farmer; there was the German middle class and beside it the Jews – so many classes, so many races ... But my subsequent experience and knowledge, coupled with mature reflection, taught me that in the Western European countries, the individual classes of society have already long ceased to represent anthropological races ... and yet they behave to each other like races and carry on a social racial struggle ... In my *Racial Struggle*, the anthropological concept of race has been renounced, but the racial struggle has remained the same, although the races have not been anthropological ones for a very long time. But it is the *struggle* that counts; it provides an explanation for all phenomena in the State, the genesis of justice and State development.[54]

Races have no anthropological basis, acknowledges Gumplowicz. But yet, he argues, it is necessary to maintain the racial struggle, because it is on this that modern society is based. We therefore have to carry on regardless and insist that races are real phenomena because this is the only way we know how to organise and to understand society.

What the development of scientific racism reveals is the power of social forces over ideological ones. Scientific ideas were important to the Victorians because of their belief in progress. But scientific principles were to a large degree subordinate to social and political claims. The naturalisation of a social hierarchy was, as we have seen, the product of social developments in the nineteenth century. Science was to a large extent simply the legitimator of social or political arguments. As one historian of racial science has noted:

> So 'natural', deep and fixed did the differences between human races seem to scientists, and so distinct their moral, intellectual and physical value, that the scientists' view of human races served to structure the very reception they gave to novel scientific theories and to influence the very interpretation they put upon new empirical data about mankind ... The scientists' deepest commitment seems to have been to the notion that the social and cultural differences observed between

\people should be understood as realities of nature. To a large extent, the history of racial science is a history of a series of accommodations of the sciences to the demands of deeply held convictions about the 'naturalness' of the inequalities between human races.[55]

The relationship between race and science is well illustrated by the history of recapitulation theory. The theory of recapitulation held that embryonic and juvenile development of the individual recapitulates evolutionary development, the embryo and young child passing through higher and higher evolutionary stages until it is fully developed. Recapitulationists also argued that in individuals from 'inferior races', development was arrested at an earlier evolutionary stage. In other words the foetus is less developed and hence the adult is retarded. Recapitulationist theory was highly influential in the late Victorian era, leading in particular to the view that black adults were of the same developmental stage as white children. Racial scientists obtained much 'evidence' showing that black adults retained juvenile features and hence were inferior.[56]

By the 1920s, however, it was clear that in evolutionary development, contrary to the assertions of recapitulationist theory, the more advanced species maintained more juvenile characteristics. Humans, for example, have evolved by retaining juvenile features common to primates and even mammals in general. Logically, the collapse of the recapitulationist theory should have caused racial science to reconsider the thesis of white superiority and indeed to regard blacks as the superior race. In fact, as biologist Stephen Jay Gould shows, the opposite happened. The scientific evidence of the previous half century was discarded, and racial scientists suddenly discovered that whites, unlike blacks, retain juvenile features. The idea that black adults were like white children was dumped overnight for the belief that white adults were really like black children. 'The white race appears to be the most progressive', observed Louis Bolk, a leading racial scientist of the time, 'being the most retarded.'[57] What was important to racial science was not scientific facts but the ideology of race.

The debate among racial scientists at the turn of the century about the nature of their discipline reveals that there was no logical relationship between the discourse of science and that of race. The fact that racial theories had appropriated scientific arguments for self-validation was historically contingent. There was no dynamic within scientific discourse itself that lent itself to racial theories. Social and political factors determined the relationship. By the same token, there was nothing inevitable about the demise of scientific racism. As Elazar Barkan observes in his lucid study on *The Retreat of Scientific Racism*, 'science could lend itself as easily to either a racist or an antiracist interpretation, whether by biologists or social scientists.'[58] What finally undermined classical racial science was not scientific evidence but the social and political consequences of racial theory.

RACE AND THE NAZI EXPERIENCE

A complex set of factors merged in the early part of this century to weaken the power of racial theories. The rising power of Japan, dramatically illustrated by its military defeat of Russia in 1905, a defeat which all regarded as a white power being humiliated by a non-white one, helped undermine the idea of an inherent white superiority. The growing revolt in the colonies and the rise of Third World nationalism seemed to symbolise the weakening hold of Europe and America over the rest of the world. Growing rivalries between the major imperialist powers, and the horrors in particular of the First World War, led to the breakup of the so-called 'white consensus'. The increasing pessimism of the élite in the West led, as we have seen, to the breakdown of the social evolutionist and positivist outlook which had underpinned the biological theories of racial difference. Scientific advance helped interrogate many of the assumptions of racial theory, while the opening up of academia to what had up until then been marginal influences – Jewish and women scholars for instance – created a more tolerant climate which was less conducive to racial theories. But what finally catalysed the destruction of scientific racism was the implementation of racial theories in Nazi Germany.

When the Nazis seized power in Germany in 1933, they proceeded to execute in practice many of the theories of scientific racism. The eugenics movement in both Britain and the USA initially greeted the Nazis' sterilisation laws of 1933 with interest and even enthusiasm. But as the full horror of Nazi practices, from mass sterilisation to the concentration camps, became clear, so the clamour of opposition to racial thinking grew. Even so, as Elazar Barkan argues, the demise of racial science 'was not a foregone conclusion'. It required considerable struggle and political manoeuvring. Barkan notes that the scientists' response to the Nazis falls into three phases. During 1933 and 1934, 'the issue of race was faced only indirectly'. From 1934 to 1938 there was 'stalemate': 'while efforts to counter racism through institutionalised scientific channels were frustrated, anti-racist publications by individuals became popular'. From 1938 on, 'the scientific community declared itself against racism.'[59]

Though Barkan does not elaborate, what his timetable demonstrates is that the scientific response followed very closely the mainstream political response in Britain and the USA to the Nazis. Initially, there was little hostility to the Nazi regime, except from the left; indeed many leading figures – such as British newspaper baron Lord Rothermere – welcomed

Hitler's accession to power. There then followed a period of stand-off between the 'appeasers' and those who were becoming increasingly hostile to Hitler's intent. It was only on the eve of war itself that main-stream opinion shifted decisively against the Nazis.

It was at this point that racial science finally began to give way. The Allies fought the war in defence of democracy against fascism, racism and tyranny. They denounced the Nazis' unspeakable crimes against humanity. How, after this, could leading thinkers and scientists maintain their belief in the very racial theories that had fuelled the Nazi horrors? After the deathcamps and the Holocaust it became nigh on impossible openly to espouse belief in racial superiority.

The sheer depth of the horrors of Nazi Germany forced scientist and politician alike to react against the political use of racial ideology. But in associating racism with the Nazis, and in opposing the consequences of scientific racism on moral grounds, scientists ensured that the under-lying assumptions of racial thinking – that humanity can be divided into discrete groups which are 'different', if not inferior or superior – went unchallenged. This becomes clearer when we study more carefully what changed in racial science – and what remained the same.

In the early twenties the biologist Julian Huxley (grandson of the famous Thomas Huxley) wrote a series of articles in the British *Spectator* about American life. In these articles Huxley laid out his belief that 'the negro mind is as different from the white mind as the negro from the white body':

> You only have to go to a nigger camp-meeting to see the African mind in operation – the shrieks, the dancing and yelling and sweating, the surrender to the most violent emotion, the ecstatic blending of the soul of the Congo with the practice of the Salvation Army. So far, no very satisfactory psychological measure has been found for racial differen-ces: that will come, but meanwhile the differences are patent.

Huxley opposed miscegenation because this would give blacks ideas above their station in life:

> [B]y putting some of the white man's mind into the mulatto you not only make him more capable and more ambitious (there are no auth-enticated cases of pure blacks rising to any eminence), but you increase his discontent and create an obvious injustice if you continue to treat him like any full blooded African. The American negro is making trouble because of the American white blood that is in him.[60]

For Huxley what determined a person's mental capacity, moral probity and social behaviour was the colour of the 'blood' he had in him. 'Blood' also determined how society should treat individuals. It was acceptable to treat 'full blooded Africans' like chattels; put some white blood in him, however, and such treatment would amount to 'injustice'.

Huxley went on to advocate the partition of America, into a segregated North, where 'the negro should be kept out or at least allowed no privileges' and a racially mixed South. Southern European immigrants should be allowed to 'invade' the South because they 'appear to have no particular prejudice against intermarriage with coloured races'.[61]

Huxley was liberal, cosmopolitan and progressive. The fact that he should espouse some of the basest prejudices of the time showed how deep such ideas ran into the Western intellectual tradition. A decade later, however, Huxley's views on race seemed entirely different. 'The term [race]', he wrote in 1931, 'is often used as if "races" were definite biological entities, sharply marked off from each other. This is simply not true.'[62] By the mid-thirties Huxley was a leading antiracist who spent much of his considerable talents in publicising the fight against Nazism. In 1935 Huxley wrote, together with fellow biologist A. C. Haddon, a book that more than any other in this period popularised the struggle against racial science. *We Europeans* attacked the Nazis' use of science to promote their racial theories and became one of the most influential antiracist books of the time. Yet a closer scrutiny of *We Europeans* shows that while Huxley and Haddon were fierce in their condemnation of Nazi practices, they nevertheless retained their belief in many of the assumptions of racial science.

In *We Europeans* Huxley and Haddon attacked the idea of 'race' because it was being used to 'rationalise emotion'. Instead they proposed the use of the term 'ethnic group'. Huxley and Haddon proposed that the major divisions of man be referred to as 'subspecies', that these be divided into primary races called 'major subspecies' and that other geographical groups (for instance, the division of Europeans into 'Nordic, Euroasiatic and Mediterranean') be termed 'minor subspecies'. It was less a conceptual than a semantic debate with the proponents of racial science. As Barkan observes, 'The authors did not deny the biological and anthropological nature of race and were committed to traditional ethnology, but they opposed its use on the grounds of the political implications'.[63]

What Huxley and Haddon were concerned with was to refute the Nazi argument (which was the traditional belief in racial science) that Europeans could be disaggregated into distinct races. They argued in *We Europeans* that 'any biological arrangement of the types of European man is still largely a subjective process' – but apparently not sufficiently subjective to prevent them from terming the three main European groups 'minor subspecies'. Huxley and Haddon denied the Nazi claim that Jews were a separate race and should be treated as such. Yet they proceeded to divide humanity into three biological groups according to skin colour, hair and nose type:

We can thus distinguish three major groupings of mankind:

(1) Black woolly hair, dark brown or black skin, and a broad nose.
(2) Wavy or curly hair of any colour from black to flaxen, dark brown to white skin, and a typically medium or narrow nose with usually a high bridge.
(3) Straight lank dark hair, yellowish skin, nose with a tendency to be broad and low-bridged.[64]

In other words, while Huxley and Haddon rejected the political use of race classification in Nazi Germany, they nevertheless accepted the reality of natural divisions within humankind, though they preferred to term them 'ethnic groups' rather than 'races'. This was the crux of the antiracist case. As an editorial in *Nature* put it, scientists should relinquish the term 'race' because the politicians 'had appropriated it'.[65]

Most other opponents of racial theory adopted a similar stance. Anthropologist Ruth Benedict accepted that 'race is a classification based on traits which are hereditary' but distinguished the scientific study of race from 'the dogma that one ethnic group is condemned by nature to congenital inferiority and another group is destined to congenital superiority'.[66] Like Huxley and Haddon, Benedict rejected the political use of the concept of race while accepting the scientific validity of dividing humanity into discrete biological units.

Not only did Huxley and Haddon accept the reality of racial differences, they also accepted that such differences had social consequences. Hence they argued in *We Europeans* that genetic differences between different classes were functionally important in fitting them to do certain tasks in society. The working class was shorter because 'short types may be better suited to town life or factory conditions, and therefore be favoured in an urban-industrial civilisation.'[67] Huxley continued to believe too that it was 'wholly probable that true negroes have slightly lower average intelligence than the whites or the yellows'.[68]

Most importantly, Huxley and Haddon, like most of their peers, maintained a distinction between the scientific study of race and the social meaning of race. They were willing to accept that from a scientific point of view there was no such thing as a 'superior' or 'inferior' race. But they continued to believe that, from a social point of view, racial differences were important. As a result Huxley maintained his opposition to miscegenation and supported the restrictions on the immigration of Asian 'races' into America and Australia.

The impact of the Nazis, then, was to throw into disrepute the biological arguments for racial superiority and to discredit the overt expressions of racism, while maintaining intact all the assumptions of racial thinking – in particular that humanity can be divided into discrete groups, that these divisions are to some degree immutable and that they have social consequences. The political use of racial science was discredited; but its conceptual framework was never destroyed. This ambiguity to the concept of race was maintained into the postwar period.

Biological science is often considered to have been refounded in the postwar years to take into account the discrediting of racial theories. Yet at a fundamental level, there were continuities with prewar science. Classical racial theory had been underpinned by a number of ideas about society – the view that society is governed by natural laws; a belief in social evolutionism; a teleological conception of historical development; support for tradition and hierarchy as the mainstay of social stability. In the postwar world these underlying ideas remained but the forms they adopted altered. Discussions of human differences were dominated by the categories of 'culture' and 'history' rather than those of 'race' and 'biology'. In the next two chapters I want to investigate the evolution of cultural theories of human difference and their relation to biological theories of race.

5

Race, Culture and Nationhood

In a report on the 1993 conference of the International Air Transport Association, the aviation magazine *Flight International* quoted accident statistics for 1959–93. These showed that the number of crashes per million airline departures caused by the aircraft's crew varied widely across the world. Drawing on the work of behavioural scientist Geert Hofstede, the magazine linked such variations to national cultural differences.

According to *Flight International* two cultural factors identified in Hofstede's studies had a clear correlation with airline safety: 'individualism' and an index of 'power distance' which indicated the degree to which people were willing to defer to their superiors. Countries identified as showing a high degree of individualism and a short power-distance – such as Australia, Austria, Britain, Denmark, Ireland, Norway, Sweden and the USA – had good safety records. Countries whose cultures lacked an individualist outlook and with hierarchical attitudes characteristic of a long power-distance – such as China, Colombia, Ecuador, Indonesia, Korea, Pakistan, Venezuela and West Africa – had fared badly.

The most striking aspect of the two lists is their correlation with common definitions of 'race'. Those in the first list are all white European, American or Australasian countries. Those on the second list are all non-white Third World states. Yet the report made no attempt to define the two classes by race. Indeed had the authors claimed that white pilots were better at flying aircraft than non-white pilots, it would have been considered an unacceptable and racist conclusion. By presenting the same argument in cultural terms, however, they were deemed to have conducted an important scientific analysis. The inhabitants of China, Colombia, Ecuador, Indonesia, Korea, Pakistan, Venezuela and West Africa were 'culturally different' from those of Australia, Austria, Britain, Denmark, Ireland, Norway, Sweden and the USA. This cultural difference made them inferior pilots.

By transposing racial difference to cultural difference the notions of 'inferiority' and 'superiority' had become acceptable, even scientific. The study was subsequently cited as an authoritative work on the cause of air crashes. When in August 1994 a Moroccan pilot deliberately crashed his plane as an act of suicide, and caused the deaths of 43 people, the *Guardian* newspaper suggested that his female co-pilot might have been unable to stop him because of their 'cultural background', implying that her culture imbued in her a lack of individual initiative and sense of deference to her superiors even unto death.[1]

The notion of 'cultural difference' presented here has, however, no more validity than that of 'racial difference'. In what way, for instance, can countries as socially and historically disparate as China, Ecuador and West Africa (which is, in any case, not even a country) be considered culturally similar to one another but collectively distinct from Ireland, Austria and the USA? By what criteria can all inhabitants of the former states be considered to be 'lacking in individualism' and accepting of 'hierarchical attitudes'? And in what way could such traits be said to be the possession of nations such as Britain, Denmark or the USA?

If there is a factor common to all the countries on the first list that makes them distinct from those on the second, it is related more to social than to cultural factors. They are largely impoverished countries likely to be in possession of ageing aircraft fleets in a high state of disrepair and with inadequate training facilities for their pilots. Social, not cultural, factors were the most plausible causes of national differences in pilot error. Yet few commentators thought it necessary to investigate such social differences.

The discussion of the cultural backgrounds of pilots may seem somewhat obscure and irrelevant to the main subject of this book. Yet it provides a good illustration of a development that is crucial to my argument – the transposition of racial arguments into the sphere of culture. In the last chapter we saw how the Nazi experience had catalysed the revolt against racial theories without undermining the underlying assumptions of racial thinking – in particular the assumption that humanity can be divided into discrete groups and that these divisions have a social consequence. In the remainder of the book I want to investigate how these assumptions have been reformulated through the discourse of culture. In Chapters 7 and 8, I shall examine the role that the concept of culture plays in recasting contemporary meanings of difference and inequality. Before that, however, we need to understand what we mean by 'culture' and how historically the discourse of culture has developed. That is the aim of this chapter and Chapter 6.

In most people's minds the concepts of race and of culture would appear to be mutually exclusive. One refers to imputed biological differences which are regarded as permanent and which, within the discourse of race, give rise to theories of inferiority and superiority. The other refers to historically or socially constructed differences which would seem to contain no connotations of permanent hierarchical distinctions; indeed the discourse of culture would seem to provide a powerful tool with which to challenge the ideas of immutable hereditary differences.

I want to show, however, that the modern concept of culture, like that of race, is animated by a hostility to ideas of human universality, that both espouse a philosophical relativism and that at the core of both lies an antihumanist outlook. As the discussion of the cultural backgrounds of airline pilots reveals, the concept of culture can embody many of the same meanings as the idea of race. Cultural traits, such as 'individualism' or 'power-index', can be as powerful a marker of human groups as biological traits such as skin colour or headform.

In reconstructing the development of the discourse of culture I will begin by looking at the relationship between the concept of culture and ideas of nationhood. The changing nature of the nation-state in the nineteenth century allowed for an elision between Enlightenment and Romantic discourses, an elision through which the concept of culture as envisioned by the Enlightenment *philosophes* began to be transformed. In this remaking of the meaning of culture we can see many of the same themes that animated the discourse of race – a hostility to universalism, a pessimism about social progress, a fear of social disunity. By examining how the idea of cultural relativism differed from the notion of racial difference, I will in this chapter draw out the relationship, at both the social and the philosophical level, between the discourse of race and that of culture. I will then, in the next chapter, consider how the science of anthropology has transformed the idea of culture into one that fits the modern concept of 'multiculturalism'.

'WHAT IS A NATION?'

In 1882 the French philologist Ernest Renan delivered a lecture at the Sorbonne in Paris that was to prove immensely influential. Entitled 'What is a Nation?', the lecture sought to establish the difference between the Enlightenment and the Romantic traditions of nationhood.

Renan rejected racial concepts of nationhood: 'The primordial right of races is as narrow and as perilous for genuine progress as the national principle is just and right.'[2] He accepted that 'in the tribes and cities of antiquity, the fact of race was . . . of very real importance'. But, he argued, a combination of conquest, migration and modernisation had created nations that were so ethnically mixed as to be indecipherable according to racial categories:

France is Celtic, Iberic and Germanic. Germany is Germanic, Celtic and Slav. Italy is a country where the ethnographic argument is most confounded. Gauls, Etruscans, Pelasgians and Greeks, not to mention many other elements, intersect in an indecipherable mixture. The British Isles, considered as a whole, present a mixture of Celtic and Germanic blood, the proportions of which are singularly difficult to define.

Renan distinguished between anthropological and philological or historical interpretations of the notion of 'races'. For anthropologists, races were essentially zoological categories. Renan, however, objected to the reduction of human history to the level of biological function:

> Human history is essentially different from zoology, and race is not everything, as it is among the rodents or the felines, and one does not have the right to go through the world fingering people's skulls, and taking them by the throat saying, 'You are of our blood; you belong to us!'

The study of language and history, Renan observed, 'does not lead to the same divisions as does physiology'. Whereas for anthropologists 'race' is a fixed entity, for historians it is something 'that is made and unmade'. This is why there could be no such thing as a 'pure race' and 'to make politics depend upon ethnographic analysis is to surrender it to a chimera.'

In place of racial concepts, Renan posited a political definition of nationhood. A nation, he argued, was a voluntary contract between its members – 'a daily plebiscite' as he put it. What held a nation together was a conscious decision on the part of every member of a nation to affirm his or her acceptance of that nation's collective identity and cultural and historical heritage: 'More valuable by far than common customs posts and frontiers conforming to strategic ideas is the fact of sharing, in the past, a glorious heritage and regrets, and of having, in the future, [a shared] programme to put into effect.' Our sense of shared values and our collective affirmation of such values is what constitutes a nation.

'What is a nation?' is a useful starting point in a discussion of the modern concept of cultural difference. Renan's argument has come to be seen as a classic expression of the dichotomy between the French and the German conceptions of the nation, between the universalist ideas of the French Enlightenment and the particularist beliefs of German Romanticism. The first conceives of a nation as a voluntary association or contract, the second as a predetermined community bound by blood and heredity. In this understanding of the distinction between the Enlightenment and the Romantic traditions, the former is seen as positing human differences in terms of *culture*, the latter in terms of *race*.

Enlightenment discourse, as we have seen in previous chapters, was indeed by and large antithetical to racial classifications. The modern idea of race developed through the particularist categories of the Romantic reaction to Enlightenment rationalism. Yet the dichotomy between race and culture, and indeed between what are taken to be the Romantic and

Enlightenment traditions, is not as clearcut as it may at first seem. Renan's argument, like the distinction between the two traditions, is more blurred and confusing than many of his admirers will admit. Indeed 'What is a nation?' can be read not so much as a triumphant vindication of the Enlightenment tradition as a text that subverts the essence of Enlightenment discourse while maintaining in form an affinity to eighteenth-century rationalist ideas. In the interstice between the essence of Renan's argument and its form, we can begin to tease out the real meaning of the modern concept of culture.

It is true that Renan upheld in his lecture some of the best principles of the universalist tradition:

> Let us not abandon the fundamental principle that man is a reasonable and moral being, before he is cooped up in such and such a language, before he is a member of such and such a race, before he belongs to such and such a culture. Before French, German or Italian culture there is human culture.

Yet Renan conceived of his universalist aspirations in terms that would have made more sense to Coleridge and Schelling than they would have to Rousseau or Kant. 'A community of interest', he declared, did not 'suffice to make a nation' because, while it may be capable of establishing 'trade agreements', nation-building requires something more. Nationhood 'has a sentimental side to it; it is both soul and body at once'. For all his attachment to Enlightenment rationality, at heart Renan's concept of a nation fits snugly within the metaphysical poetics of the Romantic tradition. 'A nation', he writes, 'is a soul, a spiritual principle'. Two aspects ('which in truth are but one') constitute this spiritual principle:

> One is the possession in common of a rich legacy of memories; the other day is present-day consent, the desire to live together, the will to perpetuate the value of the heritage that one has received in an undivided form. Man, Gentlemen, does not improvise. The nation, like the individual, is the culmination of the long past of endeavours, sacrifice and devotion. Of all cults, that of the ancestors is the most legitimate, for the ancestors have made us what we are. A heroic past, great men, glory (by which I understand genuine glory), this is the social capital upon which one bases a national idea. To have common glories in the past and to have a common will in the present; to have performed great deeds together, to wish to perform still more – these are the essential conditions for being a people.

As Maxim Silverman observes, 'This is not the imagery of the rational Enlightenment; it is the imagery of romanticism'.[3] What appeared to be

a celebration of Enlightenment ideas of universalis~
transformed into a mystical, Romantic notion of nati~
sent' of a people to being citizens of a nation has here a v~
meaning from that of Enlightenment *philosophes*. For Rousseau, ~
consent meant the rational acceptance of certain duties premised upon
the granting of rights conferred by citizenship. For Renan it appeared to
mean the transcendental affirmation of a common heritage and values.
As Tzvetan Todorov asks,

> If man does not improvise himself, if he is determined by his past, if it
> is his ancestors who are expressing themselves through him, can one
> still speak of his entrance into the nation as a act of free adherence, an
> exercise of free will? If our ancestors have made us what we are, can
> we still hold the individual responsible for his acts, can we make him
> answer to moral requirements? And if I love my home not because it is
> a good one but because it is mine, can I still claim that patriotism is
> governed by universalism?[4]

Far from being an affirmation of Enlightenment values, 'What is a nation?' presents a subtle elision of Enlightenment and Romantic discourses. Renan appropriates the forms of Enlightenment discourse as an
aspect of French national culture. But his concept of a national culture or
history is transcendental in the Romantic sense ('the culmination of the
long past of endeavours, sacrifice and devotion'). Culture, for Renan,
was a transhistorical entity that shaped contemporary lives and in whose
power the contemporary nation was in thrall. Critical though Renan was
of the idea of a 'pure race', his concept of culture appears almost as
absolutist and as exclusive.

RACE, CULTURE AND NATION

The understanding of the relationship between 'race', 'culture' and 'nation' that informs Renan's text was predicated on a new concept of
nationhood that began developing towards the end of the nineteenth
century. I want therefore to look at how changing concepts of the nation
impacted on perceptions of the relationship between 'race' and 'culture'.

The idea of nationhood which developed towards the end of the eighteenth century was very different from that which existed in Renan's era,
and indeed from contemporary concepts of what constitutes a nation.
Fuelled by the universalist ideas of the Enlightenment, and by the practical consequences of the American, Dutch and French Revolutions, there
developed what we might call the 'revolutionary-democratic' idea of
a nation. The nation was seen as the expression of the collective

sovereignty of the people – the idea captured by Renan when he talked of the nation as a 'daily plebiscite'.

At the heart of this idea of nationhood was the concept of citizenship and of mass participation or choice. The nation was a voluntary, political association. Ethnicity or other elements of historic continuity were irrelevant to the nation in this sense; even language was only relevant on pragmatic grounds.[5] As Eric Hobsbawm has observed, 'What distinguished the American colonists from King George and his supporters was neither language nor ethnicity, and conversely, the French Republic saw no difficulty in electing the Anglo-American Tom Paine to its National Assembly'.[6]

What characterised the Enlightenment notion of the nation was that it represented the common interests against particular interests, the common good against privilege. To eighteenth-century radicals patriotism was seen not as an inward-looking chauvinist philosophy but as an outward-looking progressive ideal. The Tory Dr Johnson described nationalists (or, more strictly, patriots) as 'factious disturbers of government', and indeed they were.

Patriots, whether English, American or French, defined themselves through their desire to overthrow the old order of feudal privilege and to recreate society as a sovereign nation of citizens. The *patrie* to which they gave their loyalty was not a pre-existing community defined by blood and soil, but a nation created by the political choice of its members, who, in the process of nation-building, made subservient the more parochial and irrational loyalties to which they may previously have been attached. Condorcet, for instance, argued for the creation of a French nation-state on the grounds of universalism:

> As truth, reason, justice, the rights of man, the interests of property, of liberty, of security, are in all places the same; we cannot discover why all the provinces of a state, or even all states, should not have the same civil and criminal laws, and the same laws relative to commerce. A good law should be good for all men. A true proposition is true everywhere.[7]

In its initial phase the arguments for nation-building were very different from, indeed the very opposite of, contemporary nationalist arguments. Hence Hobsbawm cautions that 'We cannot therefore read into the revolutionary "nation" anything like the later nationalist programme of establishing nation-states for bodies defined in terms of criteria so hotly debated by the nineteenth-century theorists, such as ethnicity, common language, religion, territory and common historical memories.'[8]

In the revolutionary-democratic tradition, the creation of the nation was seen as necessary to overcome the parochialism of feudal life and to establish a mechanism through which to exercise the rights of Man. It was a stepping stone towards more universal forms of social organisation. This idea of the nation as a progressive, universalising force was common both to Enlightenment discourse and that of nineteenth-century liberals.

The theory of social evolution, which as we have seen dominated much of nineteenth-century liberal thinking, held that the scale of human life inevitably expanded, moving progressively from family to community, from the tribal to the national, eventually culminating in a global society. Nations were important not in and of themselves, not because they expressed the 'inner will' or 'soul' of a people, but only in so far as they extended the scale of human society. As Maurice Block argued when he wrote the entry for 'Nationalities, the principle of' in the *Cyclopedia of Political Science* in 1889, 'If our doctrine were to be summed up in the form of a proposition, we should perhaps say that, generally, the principle of nationalities is legitimate when it tends to unite, in a compact whole, scattered groups of populations, and illegitimate when it tends to divide a state.'[9]

The modern-day concern with separatism, and support for 'nations' created through the fragmentation of other states, would have been anathema to such thinkers. Few in the nineteenth century thought it strange that there should exist multinational, multilingual or multiethnic nation-states. After all, the oldest and most unquestioned nation-states, such as Britain, France and Spain, were all recognised at this time to be ethnically and linguistically heterogeneous, however much we may have since come to believe in the essential homogeneity of such nations.

It was widely accepted that the creation of heterogeneous nations could enable rather than obstruct the ability of smaller populations to contribute to the wider project of humanity. As John Stuart Mill put it,

Nobody can suppose that it is not more beneficial for a Breton or a Basque of French Navarre to be . . . a member of the French nationality, admitted on equal terms to all the privileges of French citizenship . . . than to sulk on his own rocks, the half-savage relic of past times, revolving in his own little mental orbit, without participation or interest in the general movement of the world.

'The same applies', he added, 'to the Welshman or the Scottish Highlander as members of the British nation.'[10] Such views were not simply an expression of chauvinism (though clearly a large element of this was involved) but also of the belief in the progressive nature of the struggle against parochialism and division.

But if the idea of the nation was as a stepping-stone towards a more universal society, in practice the construction of nation-states created a new barrier to such universal aspirations. The establishment of nation-

states generated a conflict between the universalism of the Enlightenment concept of Man and the particularist framework of the nation
within which Enlightenment Man was situated. As we have already seen
in Chapter 2, Rousseau's 'man' was in conflict with his 'citizen', since the
universality of the former was constrained by the nationality of the latter.
'By defining the common good within the exclusive framework of the
nation', Maxim Silverman has observed, 'the Revolution crystallised the
tension between universalism and particularism in the Enlightenment.'
He adds that 'The republican ideal – founded on the liberal conception
of the free individual inherited from the philosophers of the Enlightenment – was therefore hijacked by the nation and was quickly incorporated within a distinction between nationals (citizens) and non-nationals
(non-citizens)'.[11]

The early nation presented two faces. On the one hand there was what
Todorov calls the 'internal' nation and Silverman the 'open' nation. This
was the nation-state as destroyer of parochial divisions and ancient
privileges and as guarantor of the rights of citizenship. The nation in this
sense allowed people to identify with a collectivity beyond the narrow
confines of their immediate community and to understand themselves as
part of a more universal society; and at the same time helped established
both the ideologies and the institutions which were to be the harbingers
of democracy. On the other hand there was the 'external' or 'closed'
nation, the nation as the institutionalisation of the difference between
citizen and foreigner, between 'us' and 'them'. Here the nation presented
itself as exclusive, not inclusive, and became the source of chauvinist and
élitist ideologies. At one and the same time, the nation 'created a space of
equality for all citizens' and 'set one nation against another'.[12]

Yet if the Revolutionary model of the nation was the site of such
ambiguity, its consequences were not immediately apparent. The period
of the Revolution established the nation as the guarantor of the common
good but the distinction between the rights of the citizen and the denial
of such rights to foreigners remained blurred. As Silverman has observed, 'The discrepancy between nationals and foreigners established at
the time of the Revolution remained more conceptual than actual':

> The concept of the foreigner remained a very ill-defined one compared
> to subsequent representations, whilst access to citizenship for those of
> foreign origin was a fairly simple procedure. The word 'immigrant'
> hardly appeared at all in documents of the time. National frontiers
> remained as ill-defined as under the Ancien Regime, whilst social
> rights were scarce for nationals and foreigners alike.[13]

Though nationalism as an expression of chauvinist ideas towards foreigners became more evident in the early decades of the nineteenth

century, nevertheless the progressive, 'open' side of the nation remained to the fore in liberal discourse. It was not until the second half of the century that the nation began to be seen predominantly in 'closed' terms and that the distinction between citizen and foreigner became crystallised both in popular and in official language. It was now that the idea of a homogenous national culture and of a nation as the embodiment of an organic history and heritage began to take hold. The nation became less the product of a voluntary political association than the incarnation of a particular ethnic, linguistic or racial identity.

A number of factors helped produce this transformation in the concept of the nation. Perhaps the most important was the development of the modern state. The state as we know it today did not exist in the early decades of the last century. The institutions of state control and administration – the civil service, the police force, the education system, the welfare system – were either non-existent or present only in a primitive form.

Political and economic changes in the second half of the nineteenth century helped create national state institutions in forms that are recognisable today. The transformation of society wrought by industrialisation, the growth of the working class and the intensification of class conflict, the necessity for state support for the national economy and industries, the development of international rivalries – all compelled the nations of Western Europe to establish a new and intrusive framework of state institutions, including a civil service and agencies of law and order and of social welfare. It was a process through which domestic social relations were defined and institutionalised. The introduction of the census in the latter decades of the century, for instance, helped governments both to enumerate their populations and to define their citizens. The growth of a public education system helped establish national curricula and standardise examinations and awards. The establishment of a civil service helped create a national administrative framework. Even the physical boundaries of the nation-state were now established with new precision. The notion of natural frontiers had had little meaning in the previous century. Now borders were delineated, border posts and customs established, passports and immigration laws instituted.

The consequence of all this was the creation of a set of new institutions within which peoples' entire lives were framed. 'The state', Hobsbawm has pointed out, 'increasingly defined the largest stage on which the crucial activities determining human lives as subjects and citizens were played out. Indeed, it increasingly defined as well as registered their civil existence (*état civil*).'[14]

The institutionalisation of social relations through the state was paralleled by the institutionalisation of a national ideology. The development of the state as the central stage of social life raised new questions about how to establish and maintain the loyalty and co-operation of the mass of the people. As Hobsbawn notes, the very fact of the state's direct and increasingly intrusive relations with the subjects or citizens as individuals 'tended to weaken the older devices by means of which social subordination had largely been maintained'.[15]

Old social loyalties had been weakened; new ones had to be built. As the Italian nationalist leader Massimo d'Azelio observed in 1860, after Italian unification, 'We have made Italy; now we must make Italians.'[16] The problems of creating national loyalty was particularly acute in new nation-states such as Italy or the USA, where nationhood imposed a sense of collectivity upon disparate peoples who had not previously considered themselves to be part of the same collective. Older, and more established, nations such as Britain and France faced similar predicaments; here the problem was less one of establishing a sense of nationhood than of legitimising the emergent institutions of the nation-state as the true repositories of that nationhood. The questions of national loyalty and social cohesion became particularly acute as the establishment of mass democracy – itself a product of the development of the nation-state – drew the masses into the political arena.

The new national loyalties that men such as d'Azelio strained to establish were very different from the concept of patriotism held by eighteenth-century radicals. The nation was no longer seen as a stepping-stone to a more universal society but as the culmination of historical evolution. What became important about the nation was that it could act as an embodiment of difference. As the French socialist Jules Michelet observed, the old parochialism had been replaced by the new:

> Humanitarians are fools to believe that the walls, hedges, barriers which were between them of old are done away with. On the contrary, a few antiquated prejudices may have died out; but a growing personality separates more and more nations and individuals.[17]

The new nationalism was fearful of Enlightenment ideas. In the wake of events such as the revolutions of 1848, and the Paris Commune of 1871, universalist ideas were associated with revolutionary principles and social disorder. As we observed in Chapter 3, the impact of these events was to force the liberal intelligentsia to move rapidly away from their previously held humanist beliefs. The failure of society to overcome national and social divisions led many to see such divisions as natural. Cosmopolitanism gave way to a celebration of national and cultural particularism.

Michelet's work provides a good illustration, in this context, of the changing idea of nationhood. A lifelong socialist and humanitarian, and a great advocate of the principles of equality and justice, Michelet considered himself to be in the Revolutionary tradition. Yet he openly acknowledged that he no longer believed in the Enlightenment concept of universalism:

I have also sacrificed another religion – the humanitarian dream of a philosophy which believes that it can save the individual by destroying the citizens, denying the nations, and renouncing the fatherland. The fatherland, my fatherland can alone save the world.[18]

According to Michelet, nationalism was necessary to maintain social harmony: 'The most powerful means employed by God to create and develop distinctive originality is to maintain the world harmoniously divided into those grand and beautiful systems which we call nations.'[19] Drawing on the legacy of Herder, as well as of Rousseau, the new nationalists approved of the destruction of petty parochialism ('Our French provincialism is rapidly disappearing', Michelet noted approvingly in *The People*) but yet conceived of nations as self-contained, organic entities whose importance lay in their uniqueness and particularity.

So, as the physical, geographical limits of France (or Italy or the USA) as a nation-state was established, as the social institutions that represented France were created and as the distinctions between French citizens and foreigners were delineated, so France as a *history* and as a *culture* was constructed. The idea was established of the nation as a cultural community progressing through time, linking past, present and future. 'Everything we are', wrote the French nationalist Maurice Barrès, 'arises from the historical and geographical conditions of our country.' He added that 'Our national character will be the better maintained to the extent that the conditions in which we live continue to resemble the ones that formed our ancestors.'[20]

Retrospectively the nation was homogenised. Contemporary beliefs, values and mores were eternalised, depicted as having been ever-present in the nation's history. Michelet, for instance, considered that a peculiarly 'French genius' had helped it establish liberty, equality and fraternity through the Revolution, but that these values could be traced back to the Gauls, 'the most perfectible of human races'.[21]

Similarly, nationalists now looked to their particular national language as being the repository in a Herderian sense of the nation's soul. Yet, as Hobsbawm has reminded us, national language is the product of nationalism, not the other way round. In 1789, half the population of France did not speak French, and only 12 per cent spoke it 'correctly'. At the moment of Italian unification in 1860, only 2 per cent of the population used Italian for everyday purposes. Rather than being the embodiments of nationhood, national languages were by and large 'semi-artificial constructs' which were created to establish a sense of national cohesion:

> They are the opposite of what national mythologies supposes them to be, namely the primordial foundations of national culture and the matrices of the national mind. They are usually attempts to devise a standardised idiom out of a multiplicity of actually spoken idioms, which are thereafter downgraded to dialects, the main problem in their construction being usually which dialect to choose as the base of the standardised and homogenised language.[22]

As Renan himself admitted, 'forgetting, I would even go so far as to say historical error, is a crucial factor in the creation of a nation, which is why progress in historical studies often constitutes a danger for [the principle of] nationality'.[23] Nationalists rewrote the past to establish the idea of an organic nationhood stretching back through time. Such historical rewriting (or 'forgetting') was buttressed by the invention of national traditions. Public symbols – such as the national anthem and the flag – ceremonies and rituals – such as Bastille Day in France or royal rituals in Britain – all helped to cement the idea of a transhistorical nationhood.[24]

The process through which national culture, history and identity were created was also the process through which the relationship between citizen and foreigner was transformed. Not only did the delineation of the 'national' help establish more clearly the 'foreign' but the very meanings of 'citizen' and 'foreigner' were recast. Citizenship was increasingly defined not so much in terms of political affiliation but more in terms of a transcendental notion of belonging. Foreigners were no longer, in Daniel Lochak's words, 'those who are born outside the frontiers of the state but, in a much more profound way, those who do not belong to the body of the nation'.[25] The nation began to be seen in organic terms, in much the same way as the early conservatives had conceived of the community. Citizens were part of the living culture of the nation, whereas non-nationals were 'invaders' or 'parasites'.

CULTURE AS A HOMOLOGUE OF RACE

It is in this context of the changing nature of the nation-state that we need to understand Renan's essay 'What is a nation?'. The aim of Renan's text was to appropriate the universalist tradition of the Enlightenment as the particularist heritage of France. In so doing he created a concept of culture that was homologous to the idea of race.

Renan did not reject the idea that humanity was divided into races. He simply rejected the concept of biological races. When in 1890 Renan wrote a preface to *The Future of Science,* a book originally written in 1848, he stressed that at the time of its writing 'I had not a sufficiently clear perception of the inequalities of races'. The 'onward course of civilisation' had, however, 'made manifest its general laws' and half a century on 'the inferiority of certain races to others is proved'.[26] But such inferiority or differences could not be understood in biological or anthropological terms. The important distinctions in contemporary human society were those of culture and language. 'There are linguistic races', Renan believed, 'but they have nothing to do with the anthropological races.'[27] But if linguistic races had nothing to do with anthropological races, nevertheless one acted as a homologue to the other:

> Language is therefore almost completely substituted for race in the division of humanity into groups, or rather the word 'race' changes meaning. Language, religion, laws, mores brought the race into being much more than blood did.[28]

In a memorable phrase, Tzvetan Todorov describes Renan's use of the concept of the 'linguistic race' as 'the tourniquet that allows him to bring "race" into communication with language':

> Far from separating language (and culture) from 'race', Renan on the contrary legitimises the production of 'linguistic races' through the ambiguous use he makes of the term 'race' . . . Far from jettisoning the concept of 'race', Renan's work gives it a new footing, since it is with Renan (and certain of his contemporaries) that the terms 'Aryan' and 'Semite' cease to designate language families and begin to apply to races – that is human beings.[29]

In Renan's text the concept of 'nation' and of 'culture' is ambiguous, slipping almost imperceptibly from a political or voluntarist to an absolutist meaning. Others drew on Renan and were less ambiguous about their use of nation and culture in an absolutist fashion. Maurice Barrès saw himself as a disciple of Renan and indeed described a nation in almost the same words as Renan's: 'A nation is the shared possession of an ancient cemetery and the will to continue to maintain the prominence of that undivided heritage.'[30] But Barrès extinguished the ambiguity of Renan's concept by stripping nationhood of any voluntary impulse. The nation's past entirely determined the nation's present: 'There is not even freedom of thought. I can only live according to my dead.'[31] Charles Maurras, founder of the far-right *Action Français,* similarly believed that 'A fatherland is a union of families constituted by history and geography; its principle excludes the principle of the liberty of individuals, of individual equality.'[32]

The concept of 'nation' has here been plundered entirely of any universalist impulse and exists only in its particularist form. 'German truth and English truth have nothing to do with French truth', Barrès believed, 'and they can poison us'. Barrès repudiated the idea that the French people were a race: 'We are definitely not a race but a nation.' Yet his idea of a nation was as entombing as that of a race. Born into a particular nation or culture, one could not escape it. 'If I were to be naturalised as a Chinese and conform scrupulously to the prescriptions of Chinese law', believed Barrès, 'I would not stop forming French ideas and associating them in French.'[33]

The changing vision of nationhood through the nineteenth century, which was predicated on the changing nature of the nation-state, helped recreate the relationship between 'race' and 'culture'. Just as the degradation of Enlightenment universalism gave rise to the discourse of race, so the breakdown of the cosmopolitan outlook helped produce a particularist concept of culture.

We should recall that for the *philosophes* of the Enlightenment there was but a single culture or civilisation to which all humanity belonged. For men like Rousseau and Degerando different people might be at different levels of civilisation but there was no reason that all could not reach the peak. Different peoples and societies were simply different manifestations of the same common humanity.

The nineteenth-century English anthropologist E. B. Tylor, whose work drew heavily on the Enlightenment tradition, encapsulated this universalist principle when he observed that it was 'no more reasonable to suppose the laws of the mind [to be] differently constituted in Australia and in England, in the time of the cave dwellers and in the time of . . . sheet-iron houses, than to suppose that the laws of chemical combination' would vary from one age to another.[34] For Tylor, differences between human societies were neither permanent nor a consequence of unequal faculties. 'The wide differences in the civilisation and mental state of the various races of mankind', he wrote, 'are rather differences of development than of origin, rather of degree than of kind.' The 'mental uniformity' of humankind was revealed to him by the difficulty he had in finding 'among a list of twenty items of art or knowledge, custom or superstition, taken at random from a description of any uncivilised race, a single one to which something closely analogous may not be found elsewhere among some other race, unlike the first in physical characters and living thousands of miles off'.[35]

Contrast this with the argument of French writer Hippolyte Taine, a contemporary of Renan and Barrès, who mocked the Enlightenment belief that 'men of every race and century were all but identical: the Greek, the barbarian, the Hindoo, the man of the Renaissance, and the man of the eighteenth century as if they had been turned out of a common mould, and all in conformity to a certain abstract conception, which served for the whole human race.' Echoing de Maistre's jibe that 'I have seen Frenchmen, Italians, Russians, and so on . . . but I must say, as for *man*, I have never come across him anywhere', Taine believed that Enlightenment *philosophes* 'knew man, but not men': '[T]hey did not know that the moral constitution of a people or an age is as particular or as distinct as the physical structure of a family of plants or an order of animals.'[36]

The work of the French thinkers of the late nineteenth century was important in allowing the themes of racial discourse to be recast in a more acceptable form. Rejecting the idea of biological races, they nevertheless maintained the essence of a racial outlook while substituting culture for biology as the medium of human difference. The ever-perceptive Tzvetan Todorov observes that 'In the transformations that Renan and Taine, or even LeBon, bring to racialist doctrine, we can see a prefiguration of its contemporary outlines':

The term 'race', having already outlived its usefulness, will be replaced by the much more appropriate term 'culture'; declarations of superiority and inferiority, the residue of an attachment to the universalist framework, will be set aside in favour of a glorification of difference . . . What will remain unchanged, on the other hand, is the rigidity of determinism (cultural rather than physical now) and the discontinuity of humanity, compartmentalised into cultures that cannot and must not communicate with one another effectively. The period of classical racialism seems definitely behind us, in the wake of the widespread condemnation of Nazi Germany's policies towards Jews . . . Modern racialism, which is better known as 'culturalism' originates in the writings of Renan, Taine and LeBon; it replaces physical race with linguistic, historical or psychological race. It shares certain features with its ancestor, but not all; this has allowed it to abandon the compromised term 'race' . . . Nevertheless it can continue to play the role formerly assumed by racialism. In our day racist behaviours have clearly not disappeared, or even changed; but the discourse that legitimises them is no longer the same; rather than appealing to racialism, it appeals to nationalist or culturalist doctrine, or to the 'right to difference'.[37]

The idea of the absolute nature of cultural difference has indeed become a key theme of the contemporary discourse of racial difference. Listen to the words of rightwing British politician Enoch Powell, speaking in 1968, and the echoes of Barrès and LeBon are unmistakeable: 'A West Indian or an Asian does not by being born in England become an Englishman. In law he becomes a United Kingdom citizen by birth; in fact he is a West Indian or an Asian still'.[38] The British comedian Bernard

Manning, notorious for his racist jokes, has put the same idea much more pungently and offensively: 'They think they are English just because they were born here. That's like saying that just because a dog is born in a stable, it must be a horse.'

National belonging is given not by citizenship, nor even by birth, but by an undefinable quality of possessing the essence of 'Englishness' or 'Asianness'. What Todorov calls 'culturalism' we shall examine more closely in the next two chapters. I want for the moment, however, to investigate further the relationship between 'race' and 'culture', and in particular the connection between racial 'difference' and cultural 'relativism'.

FROM 'MANY MEN' TO 'MANY WORLDS'

At the heart of the cultural concept developed by Renan, Michelet and others is the idea that cultural values and norms are *relative*. 'The great progress of modern thought', Renan claimed, 'has been the substitution ... of the category of the relative for the conception of the absolute.'[39] LeBon similarly believed that 'the substitution of relative ideas for abstract notions' was 'the greatest conquest of science'.[40] Deriving from the Herderian idea of every people being animated by its own *volksgeist,* the idea of the 'relative' meant that different peoples had their own mutually incomprehensible laws, customs, mores and truths. 'Different people' LeBon wrote, 'cannot feel, think or act in the same manner'. The consequence, he argued, was that 'they cannot comprehend one another.'[41]

No law and no truth could apply to all peoples. According to Barrès, 'The assertion that a thing is good and true always needs to be backed up by an answer to the following question: With respect to what is that thing good or true?' And the answer had to be with respect to one's particular nation or culture. Hence, for French nationals, 'nationalism requires us to judge everything with respect to France'.[42]

A good illustration of Barrès' relativist outlook came with *l'affair Dreyfus*. In 1894 Captain Alfred Dreyfus, a French army officer, was court-martialled and sentenced to life imprisonment on the notorious Devil's Island for being a German spy. His main crime was that he was Jewish. As evidence mounted pointing to Dreyfus's innocence, and as to who was the real spy, the case split France. Novelist Émile Zola published his famous *J'Accuse*, an open letter to the president of the Republic in which he accused the Army and the government of a judicial crime. The anti-Dreyfusards, on the other hand, exemplified by Barrès, would not countenance the idea that Dreyfus might be innocent.

According to Barrès, whether or not Dreyfus was innocent or guilty according to an absolute sense of truth was immaterial. The affair could not be judged in the name of an abstract justice. It could only be judged according to the interests of France. If Dreyfus was proved guilty then the verdict would have strengthened the French army and hence France itself. If, on the other hand, Dreyfus was shown to be innocent, the army would have been discredited and the nation harmed. Hence, argued Barrès, whatever the absolute truth of the matter, French justice required that Dreyfus be condemned.

Barrès' relativism paradoxically made him sympathetic to Dreyfus's plight. Even though Dreyfus had to be condemned, he was not responsible for his actions. Dreyfus, Barrès believed, could not help acting as a Jew rather than as a Frenchman: 'Here are ways of thinking and speaking apt to shock the French, but they are most natural for him; they are sincere and we may call them innate.' Barrès was led to wonder whether it was right to judge an individual for actions dictated by his culture, nation or people. Rather than condemn him to Devil's Island, Barrès mused, perhaps it would be better 'to set him up near a chair of comparative ethnology'.[43]

For Barrès, then, cultural relativism led him to regard cultures as absolute entities, which governed the every action of those who were born into them and which were inaccessible to those who belonged to other cultures. In other words, cultural relativism carried the same qualities as racial difference. To modern-day readers this association of relativism with a racist outlook might seem strange. We have grown accustomed to seeing relativism as a progressive, antiracist viewpoint. Multiculturalism, pluralism, respect for other cultures, denial of racial hierarchy – all seem to depend upon the idea that every culture is equally valuable and that the protection, and indeed promotion, of cultural diversity is an essential aspect of a democratic and non-racist society.

How can we understand the relationship between racial difference and cultural relativity, given that the latter seems to embody both racist and antiracist perspectives? To arrive at the answer we need to pull together a number of different threads. First, at the heart of the discourse of cultural relativism, whether of the nineteenth century or, as we shall see in Chapter 8, of contemporary theory, there lies a hostility to Enlightenment universalism as implacable as that in the discourse of race. Second, the discourse of race and that of culture express two different forms of hostility to universalism. Third, the key to understanding the difference between the concept of race and that of culture lies in the different ideas of social progress embodied in each.

The philosophy of cultural relativism, like theories of racial difference, arose out of a disdain for a universalistic outlook. Barrès was fierce in his opposition to what he called 'the Kantianism of our classes' which 'claims to govern universal man, abstract man, without taking individual differences into account'.[44] Taking such differences into account required that, unlike the Enlightenment *philosophes*, we judge people differently according to their race, nationality or culture.

Hostility to universalism can, however, take different forms. Ernest Gellner has pointed out that there are two sets of questions that arise from the debate between universalism and relativism: '[I]s there but one kind of man, or are there many? Is there but one world, or are there many?'[45] Though the two questions are intimately related, they also represent different epistemological attitudes. Whereas the first questions the biological unity of humankind, the second questions the very idea of a single truth or objective understanding of the world. Belief in a single world assumes that common laws and values operate across all societies but that different people respond in different ways to them. Herbert Spencer expressed this idea well when he explained how his views differed from those of eighteenth-century *philosophes*: 'In early life we have been taught that human nature is everywhere the same . . . This error we must replace by the truth that the laws of thought are every-where the same.'[46] For Spencer, therefore, the same, objective social laws operated in every society and culture, but different peoples responded to these objective laws in different ways, the nature of the response being determined by the racial make-up of any given people. Belief in many worlds, on the other hand, denies a common objective understanding of the world and in its place posits a plurality of ways of understanding and evaluating the world around us. Since the social world is con-structed by the people who inhabit that society, and is not given in nature, so every world is specific to the people who inhabit it and incommensurate with the social worlds that other people inhabit.

Schematically, one may say that the discourse of race (or more specifi-cally the discourse of scientific racism) holds that there is one world but that it is inhabited by different types of humanity, whereas the discourse of culture holds that there is one type of humanity, but that it inhabits different worlds. Of course the distinction between the two is not a clear-cut or straightforward one. Many racial formalists have also denied the possibility of a single truth, whereas cultural relativists have often accepted the idea of biological differences within humankind. In the writings of Barrès and LeBon we can discern elements of both racial formalism and cultural relativism. Nevertheless we can perceive in the last decades of the nineteenth century and the first decades of the twen-tieth a shift from the discourse of race to the discourse of culture which is largely embodied in a shift from a belief in a single world inhabited by different types of humanity to a belief in a single type of humanity inhabiting different cultural or symbolic worlds.

The discourse of race and the discourse of culture both emerged out of the degradation of universalism, but they did so in different ways. Nine-teenth-century racial theorists, for all their disdain of universalist ideas, maintained nevertheless a belief in the idea of reason as a weapon of social transformation and of social progress as the companion of a teleological history. Given this belief in inevitable social progress, the growing gulf between 'civilised man' and the 'primitives' that was evident both within and without European society led many to see such differences in natural, and hence in racial, terms. Victorian social evolutionists were led to posit a hierarchical view of humanity, seeing different groups of peoples as arrested at different point along the evolutionary scale and believing that progress and reason were the prerogative only of certain races.

In the discourse of culture, on the other hand, even this residual attachment to Enlightenment discourse is expunged. The development of cultural relativist theories required more than the privileging of the idea of difference. It required a disenchantment with the notion of social evolution, a disbelief in the doctrine of inevitable social progress and a disillusionment with the values of one's own culture. '[A]s an historical development', George Stocking has observed, cultural relativism 'involved, if not disillusion, at least a rejection of contemporary values and an alienation from contemporary society.'[47]

It was the emergence of such trends in the early part of this century, and in particular in the wake of the First World War, which gave rise to relativist theories of culture. The First World War brought an end to what Eric Hobsbawm has called 'the long nineteenth century', the era of hope and progress, and ushered in the 'Age of Catastrophe'. It was an age in which, as Hobsbawm observes, there were times when even intelligent conservatives would not bet on the survival of their system.[48] In the context of a general pessimism about social progress, and indeed about social survival, the idea of difference was transformed from the notion of 'many men in a single world' to a 'single type of man inhabiting many worlds'. If social development has not overcome the vast gulfs that separate different peoples, many argued, then perhaps that was because such differences reflected the fact that different peoples inhabit different social worlds, each of which is as valid and as real as the other.

We have already seen how in the writings of Renan and his contemporaries the shape of contemporary cultural relativism was already visible. But such writings were marked by the stamp of nineteenth-century optimism. However much Renan, Barrès or Michelet were averse to Enlightenment discourse they were still sustained by its afterglow. The main force in the shift from a racial to a cultural view of human differences was not nineteenth-century history or philology but twentieth-century anthropology. Anthropology had always been the most particularist of the social sciences. In the context of Victorian positivism and social evolutionism, this had manifested itself through physical anthropology

and theories of biological differences. As the positivist outlook disintegrated along with the long nineteenth century, so anthropological
particularism re-expressed itself in cultural terms. It is to this that we
now turn.

6
From Biological Hierarchy to Cultural Diversity

A white South African, sitting down to breakfast at the end of the 1980s, might have come across an 'educational' comic strip entitled 'Did You Know?' on the back of his or her cornflakes packet which explained to a white audience the peculiarities of black behaviour. 'Kelloggs believe that "to know more is to understand more" – especially when it comes to other languages, cultures and customs', ran the explanatory tag. 'Hence the "Did you know?" series ... a lighthearted but hopefully helpful bridge of communication and understanding'. One cartoon strip shows a white man greeting his black servant. 'Why does she look away whenever I greet her?', he wonders. Kelloggs provides the explanation: 'Traditionally, the senior person greets first. And, in black cultures, it is often a sign of respect to avoid eye contact and not raise one's voice when talking to one's senior.'

Another cartoon strip depicts a white woman giving some milk to her black servant. Kelloggs again provides some helpful advice: 'It is customary to use two hands when giving or receiving things. Often gratitude is expressed with gestures – a slight curtsy, or clapping of the hands.' And so it goes on.

In the context of apartheid South Africa, it is easy to recognise that such 'explanations' of different cultural habits were little more than apologies for enforced codes of black inferiority and for the maintenance of racial barriers. Yet the preservation and explanation of cultural differences is a central aspect of pluralist and antiracist policies in Western nations. We live in a world which at one and the same time abhors the creation of apartheid racial barriers but applauds the maintenance of cultural diversity, a world in which the aim of much social and educational policy is to ensure cultural separation. Multicultural education, for instance, which is entrenched on both sides of the Atlantic, has been described as a means to 'provide such [cultural] enrichment by fostering understanding and acceptance of cultural differences'.[1] In Britain the policy of the Inner London Education Authority was to ensure that, 'within a society that is cohesive not uniform, cultures are respected, differences are recognised and individual identities are secure'.[2] Many social work departments in both Britain and the USA oppose 'transracial adoption' (the adoption of

149

black children by white families) on the grounds that it is necessary to maintain the specific cultural identity of the black child.

Understanding the richness of human cultural endeavour is a vital and fruitful quest. But contemporary visions of cultural difference seek to learn about other cultural forms not to create a more rich and universal culture, but to imprison us more effectively in a human zoo of differences. The aim of multiculturalist education policies is to preserve cultural differences as they present themselves in society, seemingly believing that these differences are static and immutable. The explicit link that opponents of transracial adoption make between 'race' and 'culture' – the 'race' of a child determines the 'culture' in which he or she should be brought up – reveals a view of culture as a predetermined, natural phenomenon.

One American collection of articles on multiculturalism argues that 'As we learn more about ecology and of ways to preserve nature, we should also learn the great value of diversity and seek to preserve a diverse cultural heritage'.[3] The analogy here between the preservation of nature and that of culture is telling. As we have already seen, the concept of race arises through the naturalisation of social differences. Regarding cultural diversity in natural terms can only ensure that culture acquires an immutable character, and hence becomes a homologue for race. Multiculturalists would no doubt abhor the racist policies of apartheid. But what links the two is a Romantic concept of human difference and the desire to understand better other cultures so as to preserve more effectively the differences.

In this chapter I want to examine the key role played by anthropologists in popularising the understanding of culture as an immutable, inflexible essence and to explain how the anthropological concept of culture came to be the cornerstone of antiracist discourse. I shall trace the development of the culture concept from Franz Boas, the German-American anthropologist who established the science of cultural anthropology, to Claude Lévi-Strauss, the French structuralist who became a key influence on postwar pluralist thinking. By following the development of the culture concept we can understand how it acquired its particularist, antihumanist form. In the final section of the chapter I shall unravel the real meaning of 'multiculturalism'.

FRANZ BOAS AND THE REMAKING OF THE CULTURE CONCEPT

The central figure in the story of the making of twentieth-century cultural anthropology is the German-American, Franz Boas.[4] It would be difficult to overestimate the impact of Boas, not simply on anthropology, but on our everyday perceptions of race, culture and difference. Contemporary ideas such as multiculturalism, pluralism, respect for other cultures, and belief in the importance of tradition and history are all significant themes in Boas' work. His major impact, however, was, as Carl Degler has suggested, in reorientating anthropological thinking and in establishing culture, not race, as the key object of anthropological study:

> Boas's influence upon American social scientists in matters of race can hardly be exaggerated. At the same time that racial segregation was being imposed by law in the states of the American South, and eugenics was emerging as a hereditarian solution to social problems, Boas was embarking upon a life-long assault on the idea that race was a primary source of the differences to be found in the mental or social capabilities of human groups. He accomplished this mission largely through his almost ceaseless articulation of the concept of culture.[5]

The legacy of Boas remains, however, an ambiguous one. Boas certainly played a prominent part in the replacement of racial theories of human difference with cultural theories, and in so doing helped undermine the power of scientific racism. Yet the concept of culture that he helped develop to a large extent rearticulated the themes of racial theory in a different guise. Influenced both by the German Romantic tradition and by a liberal, egalitarian outlook, the problem facing Boas, notes George Stocking, was how to define the Romantic notion of 'the genius of the people' in terms other than racial heredity. His answer, ultimately, was the anthropological idea of culture.[6]

Born in Germany, Boas emigrated to America in 1887 after completing his studies in physics at the universities of Heidelberg, Bonn, Kiel and Berlin. His shift from physics to anthropology coincided with his emigration from Germany. As a physicist Boas had made a field trip to the Arctic to study colour perception among the Eskimos. He related in a letter the impact of meeting 'savages':

> I often ask myself what advantages our 'good society' possesses over that of the 'savages'. The more I see of their customs, the more I realise that we have no right to look down on them. Where amongst our people would you find such hospitality? . . . We have no right to blame them for their forms and superstitions which may seem ridiculous to us. We 'highly educated people' are much worse, relatively speaking . . . As a thinking person, for me the most important result of this trip lies in the strengthening of my point of view that the idea of a 'cultured' person is merely relative and that a person's worth should be judged by his *Herzensbildung*.[7]

We can see here Boas's characteristic philosophical egalitarianism and cultural relativism. We can also see that these characteristics arise largely

from his disillusionment with the values of 'our "good society"'. It was
this disillusionment with the modes of modernity that fuelled Boas's
philosophy all his life. It was the root of the ambiguity in his treatment
of the idea of culture. The egalitarianism that arose out the Enlightenment was positive and forward-looking. The *philosophes* held that social
progress could overcome artificial divisions and differences and reveal
our essential commonality. Boas's egalitarianism arose, on the contrary,
from the belief that such progress was not possible. Humanity was equal
not because differences could be overcome but because every difference
was equally valid. For Boas, then, 'equality' meant the acceptance of the
actual inequalities of society but the regarding of these inequalities as
different manifestations of a common humanity.

Boas's first major contribution to anthropology was *The Mind of Primitive
Man*, published in 1911. There were two main theses in the book. The first
was that race, culture and language were independent variables and should
not be confused. The process of human migration and of historical changes
had caused the three categories to overlap, but it was necessary for scientists
to distinguish between them in discussing human difference.

It is important to recognise the significance of Boas's argument here.
Boas is not contesting the concept of race, nor the division of humanity
into different races. He is contesting, rather, the basis on which such
division occurs, arguing that biological races differ from linguistic and
cultural races and that the three categories should not be confused or
conflated. In essence Boas offers a sophisticated form of the argument
already articulated by Renan in 'What is a nation?'.

In his later work Boas would demonstrate that physical attributes which
were considered to be markers for racial difference, such as the shape of
the skull, were in fact plastic and hence unstable as racial markers. For
instance, in a famous study Boas conducted for the US Congress Immigration Commission, he showed that the differences between first and second generation Americans born of different ethnicities were smaller than
those between the respective European populations, and that Americans
born of immigrant stock had headforms closer to the American average
than their European forebears.[8] The conclusion that Boas, and his followers, were to draw from such results was that races had to be defined
according to linguistic or cultural criteria, not biological ones.

The second major theme in *The Mind of Primitive Man* was a critique of
hierarchical theories of race. The claims for the superiority of the white,
or Anglo-Saxon, race were, Boas argued, scientifically spurious. The
mental capacities of all human beings were fundamentally similar. Boas
believed that 'the organisation of mind is practically identical among all
races of man; that mental activity follows the same laws everywhere, but
that its manifestations depend upon the character of individual experience that is subjected to the action of these laws'.[9]

This sounds like the pure milk of Enlightenment universalism. But there was a fundamental difference between the argument put forward by Boas and that of an Enlightenment anthropologist such as Degerando. The Enlightenment *philosophes* (and later anthropologists influenced by this tradition, such as E. B. Tylor) posited the psychic unity of humankind on the grounds that all human beings were rational. Only in certain circumstances, however, was this rationality allowed to come to fruition. Tylor, for instance, argued that the customs and beliefs of 'primitive man', whether in the past or in contemporary society, were the products of conscious reasoning handicapped by an inadequate knowledge about nature:

> Had the experience of ancient man been larger, they would have seen their way to faster steps in culture. But we civilised moderns have just that wider knowledge which the rude ancients wanted. Acquainted with events and their consequences far and wide over the world, we are able to direct our own course with more confidence towards improvement. In a word, mankind is passing from the age of unconscious to that of conscious progress.[10]

In other words, for Tylor 'primitive man' reasoned soundly from false premises. As knowledge increased, premises became more sound and progress took place on a rational or scientific basis. For Boas, on the other hand, belief in the equality of 'primitive' and 'civilised' man rested to a large extent on his belief that 'civilised man' had a limited grasp of reason. Whereas Tylor regarded primitive folklore as originally rational in origin, but surviving as irrational custom, Boas, driven by a more pessimistic vision of humanity, saw the culture of advanced peoples as folklore, unconscious in origin but central to the maintenance of society through its rationalisation of traditional forms of behaviour. Even scientific thought, for Boas, was analogous to the thought processes of 'primitive man'.

Enlightenment thinkers had seen human beings as conscious, creative subjects constantly making and remaking the world around them. In the hands of nineteenth-century social evolutionists this argument had become a rationale for 'race'. The creativity of humankind, they argued, meant that all societies independently created their own customs and culture. The fact, then, that some societies were more advanced than others meant that some were naturally more creative than others, that less-advanced societies were retarded on the social evolutionary scale.

Boas tackled the racist logic of the social evolutionists by denying the creative aspects of humanity. Human beings were, for Boas, essentially uninventive. Their creativity was expressed not in independent invention but in the manipulation and reinterpretation of elements given to them by their cultural tradition, or borrowed from other cultural traditions.

Important consequences flowed from these differences in approach to human reason and creativity. In the Enlightenment tradition, the application of reason to social problems helped dissolve human differences and ensure that even those considered 'primitive' could enter the highest reaches of civilisation. This was the transformative content of Enlightenment universalism. This was taken furthest in the works of Marx, for whom the transformative nature of conscious activity acted as the link between the particular and the universal. For Marx human beings were conscious, active subjects making and remaking the world around them. The process of transforming society was also the process of overcoming parochialism and division and of revealing the commonality of humanity.

For Boas, however, customs, rituals and habits were of vital importance in the maintenance of societies. Culture was synonymous not so much with conscious activity as with unconscious tradition. He drew on the Romantic vision of culture as heritage and habit, the role of which was to allow the past to shape the present. Tradition and history moulded an individual's behaviour to such an extent that 'we cannot remodel, without serious emotional resistance, any of the fundamental lines of thought and action which are determined by our early education, and which form the subconscious basis of all our activities.' Learned 'less by instruction than imitation', cultural mores 'constitute the whole series of well-established habits according to which the necessary actions of every day life are performed'.[11] 'The idea of culture', observes Stocking, 'which once connoted all that freed men from the blind weight of tradition, was now identified with that very burden, and that burden was seen as functional to the continuing daily existence of individuals in any culture and at every level of civilisation.'[12]

For Boas, then, the particularity of cultures was essential in maintaining social stability. Every society had developed its own habits, rituals and cultural forms which helped integrate individuals and gave them a means to relate to each other and to the outside world. Boas suggests that culture has an adaptive function and that social change and progress could be harmful both to the individual and to society. It was an argument that harked back to Burke, Coleridge, de Maistre and other conservative critics of the French Revolution who believed that the social forces unleashed by the revolutionary change undermined the essential props of both the individual and society. This argument was given new shape in the early part of this century through the work of the French sociologist, Émile Durkheim.

Durkheim considered social facts to be objective phenomena which should be considered on their own terms. Social phenomena existed prior to any individual and exercised a constraint upon his behaviour. Cultural habits and customs existed before the birth of an individual and survived his death. Individuals did not freely choose a culture but were compelled to adopt one. Cultural traits were neither accidental nor incidental. Every custom and habit had a function in society and was necessary for its survival. Even crime was necessary to society, since, by dramatising deviance and retribution, it strengthened the sentiments which supported the moral order.[13] Central to this approach was the concept of 'collective representation', by which Durkheim meant the beliefs, values and symbols that were common to any particular society. Collective representations served as a means of picturing the world meaningfully to members of that particular social group. For Durkheim, individuals' modes of thinking and feeling were shaped by such collective representations imposed on them by their society.

Collective representations were rational by relative rather than absolute standards – they were appropriate in so far as they served to motivate individuals to play their proper social roles. There could not be any other way for individuals in a particular society to make sense of the world. For Durkheim different people inhabited different symbolic worlds of meaning, each as real and as true as any other. From the viewpoint of one culture, the ideas and mores of another may have seemed backward or irrational. But this was only because the collective representations of one culture – the means through which people in that culture make sense of the world – were necessarily different from those of another culture. In other words, the ways and beliefs of each culture were rational in their own terms, but necessarily irrational in terms of a differing culture. The logic of such an argument was that a particular culture could be comprehensible only to those who were an organic part of it.

Society, for Durkheim, was essentially a moral order. The preservation of this order depended upon the maintenance of sentiments of social solidarity, and the embedding into the individual of the values and norms of that society through collective representations – or culture. Cultural change could therefore lead to social breakdown. From a functionalist point of view it was necessary to maintain the particularities of any culture – from tribal customs to traditional food habits, from religious rituals to political procedures – if social anarchy was to be averted. This inevitably led to a static, and conservative, view of social development.

Durkheim's concept of the relationship between the individual and society, and of collective representations as the source of meaning and truth, has stood at the core of virtually every anthropological strand in the twentieth century. Durkheim's views were most visibly appropriated by British anthropologist Bronislaw Malinowski, who coined the term 'functional anthropology'. His British contemporary and rival Andrew Radcliffe Brown, while often critical of Malinowski's functionalism, was nevertheless equally indebted to Durkheim. There were often fierce disputes between British social anthropologists and American cultural anthropologists (mainly the students of Boas). Nevertheless, cultural anthropology also drew heavily on Durkheim's functionalism.

For functionalists of every variety, society was akin to an organism, a harmonious complex of integrated and mutually reinforcing institutions. 'Every custom and belief of primitive society', wrote Radcliffe Brown, 'plays some determinate part in the social life of the community, just as every organ of a living body plays some part in the general life of the organism.'[14] Cultures were integrated wholes, in which every custom existed to fulfil a purpose and therefore had to survive intact.

The conclusion to be drawn from the functionalist thesis was that differences between human societies must be retained to maintain a harmonious relationship between individual and society and between different societies. And herein lay the ambiguity of the new anthropological outlook, for this was a conclusion barely different from that drawn by Gobineau, Renan, LeBon or Barrès. Boas, Durkheim, Manilowski and others began from entirely different premises and most remained staunchly egalitarian in outlook, but in espousing a relativist viewpoint they could not but come to a conclusion that echoed the themes of racial thinking.

What Boas and the functionalists did was effectively to turn the evolutionary ladder of Victorian racial theory on to its side, and to conceive of humanity as horizontally rather than vertically segmented. Humanity was not arranged at different points along an ever-rising vertical axis, as the social evolutionists had believed, but at different points along a stationary horizontal axis. Humanity was composed of a multitude of peoples each inhabiting their own symbolic and social worlds.

Dispossessed of faith in evolutionary progress, functionalists envisioned society, and social difference, in static terms. But envisage it in terms of differences they did. In the discourse of culture, differences may not have been hierarchically ordered, but differences nevertheless governed human intercourse. In this way, like Banquo's ghost, the spectre of race continued to haunt the new concept of culture.

THE AMBIGUITY OF THE CULTURE CONCEPT

The ambiguity of the new concept of culture can be seen particularly in the work of Boas. For all his egalitarian principles Boas still maintained a belief in racial differences. Boas argued in an article in *Science*, for instance, that on average the size of the brain of the negroid races is less than the brain of the other races; and the difference in favour of the mongoloid and white races is so great, that we are justified in assuming a certain correlation between their mental ability and the increased size of their brain.[15]

Admittedly this article was written early in his anthropological career, but similar ideas stayed with him throughout his life. In *The Mind of Primitive Man*, for example, Boas argued that environmental influences 'are of quite secondary importance when compared to the far-reaching influence of heredity':

The descendants of a negro will always be negro; the descendants of whites, whites; and we may go considerably further, and may recognise that the essential detailed characters of a type will always be reproduced in the descendants, although they may be modified to a considerable degree by the influence of environment.[16]

Again, in a letter to Jeremiah Jenks in 1909, Boas discussed the policy implications of his study on the headforms of immigrants. He suggested that southern European immigrants should intermarry with Negroes, reproducing the standard prejudice of the time that the 'Mediterranean type' was more attracted to miscegenation than was the 'Nordic type' from northern Europe. 'Lightening up' Negroes through an 'influx of white blood' was, he suggested, the best way to deal with the problem of racism:

[T]he question before us is that of whether it is better to keep an industrially and socially inferior black population, or whether we should fare better by encouraging the gradual process of lightening up this large body of people by the influx of white blood?[17]

I do not introduce all this to suggest that Boas was racist. That he assuredly was not, though he was a man of his times, who articulated many contemporary ideas about race and heredity. What Boas's acceptance of racial ideas does reveal is the ambiguous relationship between the concept of culture that he articulated and the older forms of racial thinking.

There was considerable intercourse in the early part of this century between the cultural relativists and the racial formalists. As Elazar Barkan notes of American anthropological circles, 'the fact that professional interaction occurred between the Boasians and the members of the Galton Society [hardline eugenicists] suggests that, despite their confrontational substantive views, they were operating within a single discourse'.[18]

In the intellectual ambience of the time there was a certain fluidity in the use of biological and social categories. Even the most vociferous advocates of racial difference accepted the importance of social factors in determining human behaviour. The American eugenicist Charles Davenport was co-founder of the Galton Society and the most prominent racist among American scientists. Yet he accepted the importance of environmental factors in shaping an individual's behaviour. Referring to the nature – nurture controversy, he wrote:

> The truth does not exactly lie between the doctrines; it comprehends them both. What a child becomes is always the resultant of two sets of forces acting from the moment the fertilised egg starts development – one is the set of internal tendencies, the other is a set of external influences.[19]

The acceptance of environmental determinants of human behaviour was partly grounded in ideological beliefs. As Davenport ruefully noted, many of his academic colleagues were disbelieving of biological theories of racial difference 'on the grounds that it is a pessimistic and fatalistic doctrine'.[20] At the same time, belief in environmentalism was made easier by the strength of support for Lamarckian theory.

Jean-Baptiste Lamarck was an early nineteenth-century French naturalist and philosopher who, half a century before Darwin published *The Origin of Species*, propounded the principle of the inheritance of acquired characteristics. Darwin argued that evolution was fuelled by natural selection of spontaneous variation in heredity. A variety of genetical forms already existed in any given environment and, as that environment changed, those variations least suited to the changes died out while those variations that were best-adapted flourished. Central to this thesis was the denial of consciousness in selection. Lamarck, on the other hand, believed that evolutionary change occurred as a consequence of an organism's effort to adapt itself to changed conditions in the environment. According to Lamarck, an organism's needs brought about 'an inclination toward the actions appropriate to their satisfactions'. Further, 'actions becoming habitual have occasioned the development of the organs which execute them'. Such physical changes might be 'preserved by reproduction to the new individuals that arise'.[21] In other words, behaviour patterns of parents could be inherited by their offspring.

It is easy to see why Lamarck's theory should appeal to reform-minded social scientists. Lamarckism provided the bridge between the biological and the social, and afforded a mechanism for social and cultural factors to affect human evolution. Whereas Darwinian theory implied that evolutionary change occurred accidentally and spontaneously, Lamarckism allowed for consciousness and will in evolution. To an age, and an intellectual milieu, that still believed in the rational reform of society, Lamarck's ideas seemed to provide an argument both for the plasticity of human types and the possibility of willed change. G. J. Romanes, for instance, approved of Lamarckism because it ensured that 'natural selection is not left to wait, as it were, for the required variation to arise fortuitously; but is from the first furnished by the intelligence of the animal with the particular variations which are needed'.[22]

Through the mechanism of the inheritance of acquired characteristics the social behaviour of humans was potentially a major factor in the overall scheme of human physical evolution. Lamarckism provided both an explanation of how social and cultural factors could affect human behaviour and the confidence that social changes could transform humanity. In this intellectual climate Boas's arguments seemed eminently reasonable. Indeed once use-inheritance had been discredited as a biological phenomenon, cultural theories seemed to the only means of maintaining a continued belief in Lamarckian evolution. Culture seemed to provide a mechanism whereby the particularities of a people could be conveyed unchanged from generation to generation and one, moreover, which suggested an explanation for the seemingly immutable differences between different social groups.

The replacement of racial theories by cultural theories was not a case of a set of well-substantiated theories being unambiguously disproved and overturned by new and conclusive evidence. Rather it was the case that culture and history could account for human differences as well, if not better, than race and biology. As Carl Degler has perceptively observed, the shift from 'race' to 'culture' was largely painless and fuelled by ideological commitment rather than scientific knowledge:

> [R]ather than the biological or hereditarian point of view being tenaciously defended, it was rather easily and quickly overthrown and supplanted. That overturning was accomplished not because of highly persuasive empirical evidence, unknown before, but rather by a willingness to substitute a new assumption or alternative explanation, powered by an ideological commitment to open opportunity for the socially disadvantaged.[23]

Given the changing ideological, social and intellectual assumptions of the time, cultural theories triumphed. The new anthropological concept of culture, Stocking has noted, 'provided a functionally equivalent substitute for the older idea of "race temperament"':

> It explained all the same phenomena, but it did so in strictly nonbiological terms, and indeed its full efficacy as an explanatory concept depended on the rejection of the inheritance of acquired characteristics

... All that was necessary to make the adjustment ... was the substitution of a word. For 'race' read 'culture' or 'civilisation', for 'racial heredity' read 'cultural heritage', and the change had taken place. From the implicitly Lamarckian 'racial instincts' to an ambiguous 'centuries of racial experience' to a purely cultural 'centuries of tradition' was a fairly easy transition – especially when the notion of 'racial instincts' had in fact been largely based on centuries of experience and tradition.[24]

The discourse of culture, then, reconceived the concept of race in an egalitarian manner. It expunged the notion of a hierarchically-ordered humanity, but maintained nevertheless a belief in the classification of humanity according to its differences, a classification in which, as in classical racial theory, the fluidity and constant transmutation of distinctions between human groups was seen as so much mere 'noise' in contrast to the immutable differences that human intercourse supposedly revealed.

The discourse of culture emerged out of the same conundrum that had produced the discourse of race – the seeming irreconcilability between a belief in equality and the persistence of social differences. Both attempted to resolve the conundrum by accepting that different peoples were fundamentally different. The discourse of race conceived of this difference in terms of biological hierarchy, the discourse of culture in terms of cultural diversity. What united the two was their common rejection of a universalistic outlook.

ANTIHUMANISM AND THE CULTURE CONCEPT

By the 1920s physical anthropology and theories of racial formalism found themselves in disarray, partly because of internal methodological contradictions, partly because of the general decline in scientific naturalism and partly because of wider social and political trends. Anthropologists and sociologists now turned to a host of approaches to explain human differences: functionalism and structuralism, social anthropology and cultural anthropology, historicism and diffusionism. Despite the often bitter disputes between the different approaches all subscribed to certain common themes – a rejection of biological determinism, the separation of the biological and the social, an egalitarianism expressed through a relativistic outlook, and an antihumanist attitude. This latter came to be the defining feature of the modern culture concept and the means through which its anti-universalistic outlook was expressed.

Humanism, we should recall, is the philosophy which developed through the Renaissance and came to fruition in the Enlightenment, and which considers humanity to have an exceptional status in nature and which holds to the concept of the unity of humankind. Antihumanism denies such exceptional status, blurring the distinction between human and non-human by 'decentring' humanity, and questions the idea of human universality. I shall explore more fully the relationship between antihumanism and the discourse of race in Chapter 8. Here I want simply to look at how the development of the culture concept in the wake of Franz Boas's work denied the idea of humans as uniquely creative beings constantly remaking their world and posited instead a view of humanity as a prisoner of forces beyond its control – and at how such an anti-humanist view helped reconceive the concept of race.

In a series of articles in *American Anthropologist* between 1910 and 1917 Alfred Kroeber, a student of Boas's, set out the arguments for the divorce of the biological and the social. Social and biological evolution, he wrote, are 'fundamentally different, unconnected, and even in a sense opposite'.[25] In his most influential essay, 'The Superorganic', he separated the social context from the biological by placing human culture in a different category: the superorganic.

All racial differences, Kroeber argued, could be explained in social or cultural terms: '[A] complete and consistent explanation can be given for so-called racial differences, on the basis of purely civilisational and non-organic causes.'[26] By this he meant not that racial differences were arbitrary or illusory but that culture had the same explanatory force and determining qualities as race. If Kroeber's desire was to separate the social and the biological, his method was to transform culture into a homologue of race.

We can see this more clearly in Kroeber's critique of Gustav LeBon's racial conception of history. LeBon had claimed that it was 'not the 18th Brumaire but the soul of his race [which] established Napoleon.' Kroeber dismissed this formulation as nonsensical but argued that the statement would make perfect sense if 'race' was replaced by 'civilisation' and the idea of 'soul' taken metaphorically. Similarly LeBon's statement that 'crossbreeding' destroyed a civilisation because it destroyed 'the soul of the people that possessed it' could be made historically meaningful if for 'crossbreeding' one substituted 'sudden contact or conflict of ideals'. Kroeber agreed with LeBon's claim that 'a people is guided far more by its dead than by its living' but argued that the guiding force was not racial heredity but social heritage. Finally Kroeber argued that the 'theory of heredity by acquirement' – that is, Lamarckism – made sense only if was seen as a cultural, not a biological process.[27]

Kroeber preserved the essence of LeBon's argument but transposed it on to the cultural plane. Reversing Kroeber's argument, we could say that replacing culture or civilisation with race would make Kroeber's work perfectly meaningful for LeBon.

Culture, for Kroeber, was not the conscious creation of humanity but the unconscious product of human activity which stood above and beyond society. The very term Kroeber used to describe culture – the 'Superorganic' – gave a sense of this distance between humanity and its culture. As Claude Lévi-Strauss approvingly observed of Kroeber, 'In his eyes, culture is a specific category, as distinct from life itself as life is distinct from inanimate matter'.[28] Like race, culture appears as a transcendental category outside of our immediate consciousness but which is transmitted from generation to generation. Like race, it defines 'who we are' by 'where we have come from' so that the dead weigh heavily on the activities of the living. Cultural intercourse, like racial miscegenation, could be calamitous to the societies involved.

Subsequent anthropologists brought out more forcefully the idea of culture as an existence outside of human activity. Robert Lowie, a contemporary of Kroeber's and a fellow student of Boas's, argued that 'culture is a thing *sui generis*, which can be explained only in terms of itself'.[29] Culture, the product of human endeavour, is here reified, transformed into an object, estranged from humanity, and deemed inexplicable except in terms of itself. In a review of Lowie's *Culture and Ethnology*, Berthold Laufer went further still and dismissed the very idea that culture was amenable to human understanding. Repeating verbatim Lowie's claim that 'culture is a thing *sui generis*', Laufer argued that culture could not 'be forced into the straightjacket of any theory': 'As nature has no laws, so culture has none. It is as vast and as free as the ocean, throwing its waves and its currents in all directions . . . Our present and future lie in the past.'[30] Gobineau or LeBon would not have disagreed with this formulation (though they would surely have been dismayed at the depth of Laufer's irrationalism).

The antihumanist themes implicit in the work of Boas, Kroeber and Lowie were developed by the next generation of anthropologists, in particular Margaret Mead, Ruth Benedict and Leslie White. Benedict's *Patterns of Culture*, first published in 1934, was influential in popularising the idea that culture, not race, was responsible for explaining human behaviour and differences. Another student of Boas, Benedict wrote her book largely for ideological reasons – to expose 'nationalism and racial snobbery'. Her message was that culture, not biology, shaped human societies. In primitive man, she pointed out, 'not one item of his tribal social organisation, of his language, of his local religion is carried in his germ cell'. In contrast to Melville Hersvokits who argued that the mores of black America were rooted in traditional African culture,[31] Benedict argued that the social behaviour and customs of black people in America were not the product of their African heritage but 'closer to the forms that are current in white groups'.[32]

But if Benedict dismissed the idea that race determined human action, she did not do so on humanist grounds. Just as racial formalists thought that humans were malleable creatures dictated to by their race, so Benedict argued the same about culture. 'The vast proportion of all individuals who are born into any society', Benedict claimed, 'always ... [assume] the behaviour dictated by that society.' 'Most people', she added, 'are shaped to the form of their culture because of the malleability of their original endowment.' Hence 'the great mass of individuals take quite readily the form that is presented to them.' Those that do not conform are considered deviant or pathological.[33]

Human beings are uninventive, easily manipulated creatures whose very plasticity (the aspect of humanity that once connoted their ability to be creative and independent) allows their behaviour to be moulded along particular lines. The logic of this argument was brutally clarified by another anthropologist, Leslie White. In his *Science of Culture*, White argued that individual consciousness has little impact on social behaviour, because 'it is the individual who is explained in terms of his culture, not the other way round':

Instead of regarding the individual as the First Cause, as a prime mover, as the initiator and determinant of the culture process we now see him as a component part, and a tiny and relatively insignificant part at that, of a vast, socio-cultural system that embraces innumerable individuals at any one time and extends back into their remote past as well.[34]

Once more echoing Lowie, White concluded that 'For the purposes of scientific interpretation, the culture process may be regarded as a thing *sui generis;* culture is explainable in terms of culture.'[35] Humans do not make culture, culture makes humans. An individual cannot escape the force of destiny imposed by his culture and history. Culture, like race, governs our very being.

LÉVI-STRAUSS AND THE CELEBRATION OF INEQUALITY

We can draw together the different strands of the argument I have presented in this chapter by looking at the work of one influential, modern anthropologist – Claude Lévi-Strauss. Aside from Boas there has been no anthropologist this century whose stature has been greater than that of Lévi-Strauss, and certainly none who has been more influential in the postwar era. Like Boas, the influence of Lévi-Strauss has spread far beyond anthropology. The key force behind the development of the discipline of structural anthropology, Lévi-Strauss stands as a pivot between earlier functionalist theories and poststructuralist and post-modernist theories of difference.[36]

Lévi-Strauss expresses the same ambivalent attitude to human univer-sality that we have already seen in Boas, Kroeber and others. On the one hand, writing on 'The Scope of Anthropology', he seems to believe that 'Our ultimate goal is to arrive at certain universal forms of thought and morality.'[37] Yet he also seems to believe that 'because such general char-acteristics are universal, they pertain to biology and psychology'.[38] For anthropology, however, 'the ultimate goal is not to know what the so-cieties under study "are" ... but to discover how they differ from one another. As in linguistics, the study of *contrastive features* constitute the object of anthropology.'[39]

In other words, for Lévi-Strauss, as for Boas, human unity is expressed purely at a biological level, while culture expresses purely its differences. Biologically, humanity is singular, but culturally and socially it is many. Each culture is marked by certain features, these features are absent from other cultures, and possession of these features makes one different from another. Lévi-Strauss expressed this idea well when he compared cul-tures to 'trains moving each on its own track, at its own speed in its own direction':

> The trains rolling alongside ours are permanently present for us; through the windows of our compartments, we can observe at our leisure the various kinds of car, the faces and gestures of the passen-gers. But if, on an oblique or a parallel track, a train passes in the other direction, we perceive only a vague, fleeting, barely identifiable image, usually just a momentary blur in our visual field, supplying no infor-mation about the event itself and merely irritating us because it inter-rupts our placid contemplation of the landscape which serves as the backdrop to our daydreaming.
>
> Every member of a culture is as tightly bound up with it as this ideal traveller is with his own train. From birth and, as I have said, probably even before, the things and beings in our environment establish in each one of us an array of complex references forming a system – conduct, motivations, implicit judgements – which education then confirms by means of its reflexive view of the historical development of our civilisation. We literally move along with this reference system, and the cultural systems established outside it are perceptible to us only through the distortions imprinted upon them by our system. Indeed it may even make us incapable of seeing those systems.[40]

Cultures are sealed compartments which separates 'us' from 'them'. Cultures impose upon us (even from before birth) ways of being and modes of thinking from which we cannot escape. We may understand other cultures if they are close to us; those far away remain incomprehensible.

We can see here the implicit similarity between the concept of race and that of culture. But Lévi-Strauss is not content to allow this similarity to remain implicit. The relationship between race and culture is not incidental but at the very core of his philosophy:

[C]ultures are comparable to irregular doses of the genetic traits that are designated 'races'. A culture consists of a multiplicity of traits, some of which it shares, in varying degrees, with nearby or distant cultures, and some of which distinguish it more or less sharply from others. These traits are balanced within a system that, in either case, must be viable if the culture is not to be gradually eliminated by other systems more capable of propagating or reproducing themselves. In order to develop differences, so that the boundaries enabling us to distinguish one culture from its neighbours may become sufficiently clear-cut, the conditions are roughly the same as those promoting biological differentiation between human groups: relative isolation for a long period, limited cultural and genetic exchange. Cultural barriers are almost of the same nature as biological barriers; the cultural barriers prefigure the biological barriers all the more as all cultures leave their mark on the human body: through styles of costume, hair and ornament, through physical mutilation, and through gestures, they mimic differences comparable to those that can exist between races and by favouring certain physical types, they stabilise and even spread them.[41]

Lévi-Strauss seems to be arguing here that culture mimics race even to the extent that it stamps on its members physical marks of distinction which are passed on from one generation to another. What is important to him, however, is the recognition not simply that culture acts in the same fashion as race but that culture *governs* race. Thus he argues that nineteenth-century racial formalists were looking through the wrong end of the telescope, as it were, when they wondered about the relationship between race and culture:

Throughout the nineteenth and the first half of the twentieth century, scholars wondered whether and in what way race influences culture . . . [W]e now realise that the reverse situation exists: the cultural forms adopted in various places by human beings, their ways of life in the past or in the present, determine to a very great extent the rhythm of their biological evolution and its direction. Far from having to ask whether culture is or is not a function of race, we are discovering that race . . . is one function among others of culture.[42]

Classical racial theorists had hoped to show that biological variation within humankind could account for social and cultural differences. Lévi-Strauss wants to show to the contrary that cultural differences underly biological dissimilarities. In a critique of sociobiological theories, Lévi-Strauss argues that 'it is not the gene for resistance to polar temperatures (assuming the gene exists) that gave the Inuit Eskimos their culture; rather it was their culture that favoured individuals with the greatest resistance to cold and handicapped others.'[43] This seems to suggest that Inuit culture has somehow selected for individuals who are biologically better adapted to polar conditions, and hence created racial difference. Rather than seeing culture as the outcome of human ingenuity, Lévi-Strauss sees human beings as the passive prisoners of their culture. Culture, for him, is a thing outside of humanity which nevertheless governs human beings' ability to adapt and be creative. In reality, however, the Inuit Eskimos' culture is the product of their attempts to adapt to living in polar conditions, not, as Lévi-Strauss would have it, the cause of their ability to survive.

It is true that the Inuit are physiologically better adapted to Arctic conditions than non-polar peoples. They are short in stature and compact, compared to, say, the tall, lean Massai who live in the hot, humid conditions of the African savannah, and they are physiologically better able to withstand extremes of cold. But such features would have been selected for not by culture but by non-cultural natural selection. Culture, far from creating people more adapted to cold, allows those less adapted to survive. The Masai, for instance, would be able to survive in the Arctic, despite their lack of biological adaptation, if they were to adopt Inuit customs and habits – the wearing of fur, techniques for fishing, using snow for construction, and so on.

It is true too that cultural and social development can shape genetic variation within a population – migration, the coming of agriculture, or marriage rules have all had an impact on human genetic variation. However, cultural change does not, as Lévi-Strauss suggests, make a population better adapted to a particular environment, by 'selecting' for certain biological attributes. The main impact of cultural and social development is on the contrary to free human populations from the constraints of their natural endowments. The result is that human biological change has become increasingly less meaningful. As geneticist Steve Jones has put it, '[M]ost social changes seem to be conspiring to slow down human evolution . . . It may even be that economic advance and medical progress mean that humans are almost at the end of their evolutionary road.'[44]

Lévi-Strauss accepts racial difference at face value, but seeks to subordinate its significance to that of cultural difference, which he nevertheless regards as rigid and as inflexible as racial formalists had previously conceived distinctions of race to be. His concept of culture as thing *sui generis*, his belief in the inflexibility of cultural difference and his advocacy of cultural pluralism all lead Lévi-Strauss to deny the possibility of making judgements about different societies. 'We must accept the fact', he believes, 'that each society has made a certain choice, within the range of existing human possibilities and that the various choices cannot be compared to each other'.[45] Moreover, it is 'impossible' to deduce any 'moral or philosophical criterion by which to decide the respective values of the choices which have led each civilisation to prefer certain ways of life and thought while rejecting others'.[46]

The consequence of Lévi-Strauss's argument is that it is impossible to distinguish morally between, say, a fascist and a democratic society, between a nation under colonial rule and one that is exercising formal independence. None 'is fundamentally good, but none . . . is absolutely bad.' All societies 'offer their members certain advantages' (no doubt the trains would run on time under fascism) and in every society 'there is inevitably a residue of evil, the amount of which seems to remain more or less constant'.[47]

As soon as he declares the impossibility of judging different forms of societies, however, Lévi-Strauss is forced to abandon his own strictures. For if there is one sort of society that, according to Lévi-Strauss, is fundamentally bad it is one that aspires to a rational form of equality and freedom. In a speech to the French National Assembly's special commission on liberties in 1976, Lévi-Strauss argued that

> We cannot adopt a rationalist definition of freedom – thus claiming universality – and simultaneously make a pluralist society the place of its flowering and its exercise. A universalist doctrine evolves ineluctably toward a model equivalent to the one party state or toward a corrupt and rampant freedom where ideas, left to themselves, will fight one another until they lose all substance.[48]

For Lévi-Strauss the 'rich content' of society lies in the differences it embodies. Freedom and equality inevitably serve to diminish such difference and diversity. Instead Lévi-Strauss wants us to preserve 'those minute privileges, those possibly ludicrous inequalities that, without infringing upon general equality, allow individuals to find their general anchorage'.[49]

This is not simply a plea against grey uniformity. It is, as Lévi-Strauss makes clear elsewhere, a rejection of the very idea of equality:

> The struggle against all forms of discrimination is part of the same movement that is carrying humanity towards a global civilisation – a civilisation that is the destroyer of those old particularisms, which had

the honour of creating the aesthetic and spiritual values that make life worthwhile.[50]

For Lévi-Strauss, then, the essence of being human lies in our inequality. Hence 'the struggle against all forms of discrimination' must be necessarily detrimental to humankind since it helps destroy 'the aesthetic and spiritual values that make life worthwhile'. For the Enlightenment *philosophes* human creativity arose out of human sociability. Human beings were uniquely creative because they were uniquely capable of co-operating in a conscious manner, because the essence of humanity was the desire to overcome differences. In Lévi-Strauss's antihumanist philosophy, co-operation is itself a danger to humanity: 'In order to progress, men must collaborate; and in the course of this collaboration they see a gradual pooling of their contributions whose initial diversity was precisely what made their contributions fecund and necessary.'[51]

This paradoxical relationship between progress and regression is exactly the same as that which had troubled Gobineau. For Gobineau, 'civilisation' arose through conquest and hence through racial mixture: 'Thus mixed, mixed everywhere, always mixed, there is the clearest, most assured, most durable work of the great societies and powerful civilisations, the work that, unquestionably, lives after them.' But intermixing begat the degeneration of the race: 'Peoples only degenerate as a result of, and in proportion to, the intermixings they undergo.' Such intermixing meant that a 'people no longer possesses the intrinsic value it once had, because it no longer has in its veins the same blood, for successive alloys have gradually modified its values.'[52]

From the standpoint of civilisation, then, intermixture provided the fuel for advancement. What made the 'white race' the most civilised was its ability to assimilate other peoples and races: 'The essentially civilising tendencies of this elite race have continually driven it to mix with other peoples.'[53] From the standpoint of the race, however, intermixing was fatal because it caused racial degeneration and the creation of a 'mongrel race'.

The result, in Gobineau's eyes, is what Tzvetan Todorov calls 'a tragic paradox' for humanity: 'As soon as society is strong enough it tends to subjugate others; but as soon as it subjugates others its own identity is threatened, and it loses its strength'.[54] If we replace in Gobineau's reasoning the concept of race with that of culture, we can see that Lévi-Strauss's argument expresses the same paradox for humanity: progress requires what Lévi-Strauss calls a 'coalition' of cultures. But contact between different cultures weakens them, often fatally.

Lévi-Strauss's answer is to encourage the creation of barriers between different human groups to minimise the impact of cultural mongrelisation. The ideal situation, he argues, would be where 'communication had become adequate for mutual stimulation by remote partners, yet was not so frequent or so rapid as to endanger the indispensable obstacles between individuals and groups or to reduce them to the point where overly facile exchanges might equalise and nullify their diversity'.[55] Unfortunately, '[t]he upheavals unleashed by an expanding industrial civilisation, and the rising speed of transportation and communication, have knocked down these barriers'.[56] Lévi-Strauss therefore calls on 'international institutions' to see the 'necessity of preserving the diversity of cultures in a world threatened by monotony and uniformity'.[57]

For Lévi-Strauss, then, different cultures and peoples should only communicate if there was no danger of one contaminating the other. Peoples and cultures should, as far as possible, remain where they 'belong'. Every culture needs to ensure that there are not too many foreign elements undermining its distinctive cultural identity. 'One might wonder about the political opportuneness of this doctrine', Todorov observes, 'in an era when the nations of Western Europe are seeking to protect themselves against human invasions originating in the Third World'.[58] This is a theme I shall pick up again in the next chapter.

In the work of Lévi-Strauss we can not only see articulated the various themes of the discourse of culture but also their consequences being drawn out. We can see clearly the relationship between the discourse of culture and the discourse of race and the antihumanist belief that animates both. We can see how the rejection of universalism is linked to a despair about social progress. We can see, too, how the advocacy of cultural particularism leads to support for social inequality.

THE MEANING OF MULTICULTURALISM

The discourse of culture provided in the postwar era a new language for the discussion of social differences and a new basis for considerations of social policy. Cultural pluralism, value relativism, mutual tolerance – these became the fundamentals of the postwar liberal approach to social and cultural differences. When, in 1963, US president John F. Kennedy told his audience that 'if we cannot end our differences, at least we can help make the world safe for diversity',[59] he was drawing upon the tradition of pragmatism and relativism that has informed much political discourse in the wake of the collapse of nineteenth-century positivism. When in 1968 the British home secretary Roy Jenkins announced that Britain had abandoned a policy of assimilation for immigrants, and instead had embarked on a policy of pluralism which he described as the promotion of 'cultural diversity, coupled with equal opportunity, in an atmosphere of mutual tolerance',[60] he was adopting a language familiar to anthropologists from Boas to Lévi-Strauss.

There are few beliefs more entrenched in the modern liberal imagination than that of the virtues of a 'multicultural' society. The degree to
which the Bosnian city of Sarajevo has assumed symbolic significance in
contemporary Western discourse expresses the measure of attachment to
the principles of a multicultural, multiethnic community, which the city
is said to embody. Just as in the thirties the struggle for Barcelona during
the Spanish Civil War became symbolic of the defence of democracy
against fascism, so the siege of Sarajevo has assumed a mythic status as
a struggle between pluralism and barbarism. On the other hand there are
few crimes which contemporary society regards as more monstrous than
that of 'ethnic cleansing', the attempt to eliminate diversity and difference and to create an ethnically and culturally homogenous society.
From Bosnia to Rwanda, 'the forcible expulsion of rival ethnic groups'
has become the measure of the breakdown of civilised values.[61]

The idea of a plural or multicultural society is, however, a deeply
ambiguous one. Just as the discourse of culture has recast the concept of
race in a new form, so multiculturalism represents not a means to an
equal society, but an alternative to one, where equality has given way to
the toleration of difference, and indeed of inequality. From a racial viewpoint, economic, social and technological inequalities are the natural
outcome of racial differences. From the standpoint of multiculturalism,
on the other hand, differences are welcomed as expressions of cultural
diversity. In the final analysis both philosophies attempt to impute rational meaning to inequality.

We may recall that Franz Boas had confronted the racist implications
of nineteenth-century positivism by turning the Victorian evolutionary
ladder on its side. Humanity, for Boas, was stratified vertically, not
horizontally. This idea lies also at the heart of the concept of a 'plural
society':

> According to this tradition, what we are concerned with in the study
> of race relations ... are neither hierarchically arranged castes, nor
> classes in conflict, nor a system of roles arranged hierarchically accord-
> ing to their evaluation in terms of some set of ideal values [but]
> segments which cut across the strata, producing vertical rather than
> horizontal divisions within the society.[62]

The concept of a plural society first emerged through the analysis of
colonial societies. In a study of Indonesia and Burma, the anthropologist
J. S. Furnivall wrote that 'the first thing that strikes the visitor is the
medley of peoples – European, Chinese, Indian and native' that constitute the society. The different groups, Furnivall wrote, 'mix but do not
combine'. Each group, 'holds by its own religion, its own culture and
language, its ideas and ways'. The result was 'a plural society, with

different sections of the society living side by side but separately within the same political unit.'[63]

The concept of a plural society proved attractive both to colonial administrators, grappling with the problem of imposing law and order on their territories, and to Western liberals keen to protect colonial subjects from the ravages of imperialism. Pluralism quickly moved from being a *description* of colonial society to an *explanation* for it. The inequalities of colonial society were rationalised as products of the different cultural outlooks and lifestyles of the various groups that constituted that society. For colonial administrators this provided a rationale for the policy of 'indirect rule', the maintenance of Western control through 'traditional' African or Asian institutions. For Western liberals it was an argument for preserving 'native' cultures and allowing them to follow their own path to modernity.

The pluralists adopted what we might call the *Star Trek* principle of cultural development. In that popular sci-fi series, Starfleet's 'Prime Directive' forbids the crew of the Starship Enterprise from interfering in any way in the development of any other cultures they might meet, each of whom must proceed on it's own unique path. In particular our heroes are proscribed from imparting their superior knowledge to less-developed peoples, in case this should disrupt the normal functioning of that particular society. The same belief animated many early twentieth-century scholars and colonial administrators.

In 1926 the International Institute of African Languages and Cultures was established in London to research African societies and cultures and to devise policies for their preservation. In its five-year research plan published in 1932 the Institute feared that 'the interpenetration of African life by the ideas and economic forces of European civilisation' could lead to the 'complete disintegration' of African societies. The Institute aimed, therefore, to determine 'the right relations between the institutions of African society and alien systems of government, education and religion, in preserving what is vital in the former and eliminating unnecessary conflict between the latter and African tradition, custom and mentality'.[64] Like functionalists, and *Star Trek* scriptwriters, the Institute believed that every culture was adapted to its particular environment, and so primitive Africans had to be protected from the ravages of modern Western ideas.

In reality, however, the so-called 'African tradition, custom and mentality' were not relics from an ancient past but the products of the colonial epoch. Tribal units, village elders, ancient rituals – all were the fruits of the confrontation between the pre-existing African societies and colonial society. The people of Uganda, Adam Southall notes, 'have been almost universally misrepresented as primeval tribes, each with their distinctive language, culture, sense of identity and clear-cut boundaries'.

However, Southall continues, 'There is no evidence that the peoples of Uganda – or for that matter the rest of Africa – could ever be so categorised, until the exigencies of colonial administration forced some of these qualities upon them'.[65] Wim van Bimsbergen similarly observes that 'Modern central African tribes are not so much survivals from a pre-colonial past but largely colonial creations by colonial officers and African intellectuals.'[66] Throughout Africa, Terence Ranger has observed, 'customary law, customary land-rights, customary political structures and so on were in fact *all* invented by colonial codification'.[67] The aim of colonial policy, Frantz Fanon has observed, was not so much to destroy pre-existing cultural forms, as to mummify 'native' culture as a form frozen in time, and thereby to deny its creative character:

> The setting up of the colonial system does not of itself bring about the death of the native culture. Historic observation reveals, on the contrary, that the aim sought is rather a continued agony than a total disappearance of the pre-existing culture. This culture, once living and open to the future, becomes closed, fixed in the colonial status, caught in the yoke of oppression. Both present and mummified, it testifies against its members. It defines them without appeal . . . Thus we witness the setting up of archaic, inert institutions, functioning under the oppressor's supervision and patterned like a caricature of formerly fertile institutions.[68]

The plural outlook ignored the dynamic interplay of the various groups making up colonial society, and instead represented the products of their mutual interaction as cultural forms created by autonomous segments of society, each supposedly following its own particular path in isolation.[69] The social and economic cleavages caused by colonial rule, and the limits on social development imposed by colonial policy, were reread as the fruits of such autonomous cultural development. Like racial theory, plural theory provided an apology for social inequalities, portraying them as the inevitable result of cultural differences.

In the interwar years the concept of a plural society was applied almost exclusively to colonial states. Certainly some anthropologists were inclined to see plural forms in Western nations. According to Furnivall, for example,

> one finds a plural society in the French provinces of Canada, where two peoples are separated by race, language and religion, and an English lad, brought up in an English school, has no contact with French life; and in countries such as Ireland where, with little or no difference of race or language, the people are sharply divided in their religious allegiance.

He added that:

Even where there is no difference of creed or colour, a community may still have a plural character, as in Western Canada, where people of different racial origin tend to live in distinct settlements and, for example, a North European cannot find work on the railway, because this is reserved for Dagoes or 'Wops'.[70]

In America, Horace Kallen coined the term 'cultural pluralism' to describe the way that different immigrants groups had integrated into American society while also maintaining their particularist identity.[71] Such arguments, however, had little broader impact. Indeed, the idea of a plural society was developed in contrast to the concept of the homogenous nation-state, regarded as characteristic of Western Europe. Kallen was an isolated figure in the interwar years, while Furnivall himself considered 'typically' plural societies to be 'tropical dependencies where the rulers and the ruled are of different races'.[72]

In the years following the Second World War, however, the concept of a plural society became applied in an increasingly promiscuous way to Western societies as 'the notion of pluralism . . . passed into the anthropologists' *lingua franca* (or pidgin?) as a loose and apparently useful descriptive term for labelling all multi-ethnic societies'.[73] Not just anthropological but sociological and political discourse now appropriated the concept of a plural society. A currently popular sociological textbook tells us that 'virtually all modern societies are pluralistic to some extent',[74] while few politicians today would dissent from the view that multiculturalism is a 'good thing'.

The impact of mass immigration and the political context in which this immigration took place combined to engineer this transformation. Eleven million foreign workers came to Europe in the fifties and sixties, encouraged by the economic boom. One in seven of all manual workers in Britain and West Germany today originally entered as immigrants. In France and Belgium a quarter of the industrial workforce is of foreign origin. Switzerland's foreign population rose from 90 000 in 1950 to over one million (16 per cent of its population) by 1973.[75]

The political context in which this mass immigration occurred was an ambiguous one. On the one hand, immigrants were seen as 'different' or alien, a view that, as we saw in Chapter 1, was promoted by the dominant 'race relations' paradigm. The racialisation of immigration heightened the sense of the heterogeneity of society. On the other hand, in the liberal climate of the postwar years, racial arguments could not be openly expressed. Pluralism provided a language through which to understand social differences without having to refer to the discredited discourse of race. It provided both a sense of continuity with prewar racial discourse and a means of asserting the aversion to racism that exemplified the postwar years.

Key to such an ambiguous use of pluralism has been the presentation of social differences in terms neither of culture nor of race but of *ethnicity*. 'Ethnicity' is a peculiarly postwar word. The Oxford English Dictionary gives a first recorded usage in 1953. In fact the American Chicago school of social anthropologists had used the term in the forties, but Nathan Glazer and Daniel Moynihan, writing in the mid-seventies, could still claim that 'ethnicity seems to be a new term'.[76] Malcolm Chapman observes that both the terms 'ethnic' and 'ethnicity' came into use in the postwar period as 'the discourse of race became very properly self-conscious about the employment of its central terms during the 1930s and 1940s'.[77]

Huxley and Haddon first suggested that 'race' should be replaced by 'ethnic group' in their influential book, *We Europeans*. As we saw in Chapter 4, Huxley and Haddon were not so much opposed to the concept of racial differences as to its political uses, particularly by Nazi Germany. Introducing the term 'ethnic group' in place of 'race', they suggested, would remove the political connotations of racial difference, and allow social distinctions to be studied in a neutral, value-free fashion. In the postwar years ethnicity has indeed come to replace race as a politically acceptable means of describing social differences. In contemporary discourse, a 'plural' society is generally considered to be a 'multiethnic' one. As Anthony Giddens puts it, 'Plural societies are those in which there are several large ethnic groupings, involved in the same political and economic order but otherwise largely distinct from one another'.[78]

Like race, ethnicity is a term that is used in a fairly promiscuous way, without there ever being a consensus as to its meaning, and there continue to be fierce debates among sociologists and anthropologists as what exactly ethnicity is. However, there is a general sense that if race describes differences created by imputed biological distinctions, ethnicity refers to differences with regard to cultural distinctions. Sandra Wallman has noted that in ordinary discourse, the distinction between race and ethnicity is akin to the distinction between immutable and mutable differences:

> The word 'race' is still used when the speaker wishes to indicate objective and immutable differences between human groups and individuals, ie it continues to denote difference that *seems to be* immutable. In the same popular language, ethnicity . . . implies a degree of choice and a possibility for change which 'race' precludes.[79]

The same distinction between race and ethnicity is reproduced in academic and political discourse too. The anthropologist M. G. Smith, for instance, distinguishes between 'race relations' and 'ethnic relations', 'reserving the first term for relations between peoples of differing racial stock and the second for relations between people of the same racial stock who feel themselves, and are felt by others, to differ ethnically by virtue of their differing descent and culture'. 'Unlike ethnic identity', Smith continues, 'racial identity and/or difference is immutable, manifest and *normally* unambiguous in multiracial societies and contexts'. By comparison, 'ethnicity is generally latent and situational in its assertion'.[80] John Rex, whose approach to the study of race relations is in contrast to that of Smith and who acknowledges that neither race nor ethnicity has any objective reality, nevertheless also uses the term 'ethnicity' to describe 'race relations situations' in which group differences are seen in terms of culture or behaviour rather than physical appearance.[81] Milton Yinger delineates an ethnic group as being defined by three conditions:

[A] segment of a larger society is seen by others to be different in some combination of the following characteristics – language, religion, race and ancestral homeland with its related culture; the members also perceive themselves in that way; and they participate in shared activities built around their (real or mythical) common origin and culture.[82]

Similarly, Giddens argues that 'ethnicity refers to cultural practices and outlooks that distinguish a given community of people':

Members of ethnic groups see themselves as culturally distinct from other groupings in a society, and are seen by those others to be so. Many different characteristics may serve to distinguish ethnic groups from one another, but the most usual are language, history or ancestry (real or imagined), religion, and styles of dress or adornment.[83]

Both these definitions are tautological: an ethnic group is that which is defined as an ethnic group. But their very utility lies in their tautology. Defining ethnicity in this fashion allows us to divide humanity into discrete groups without feeling the taint of racial ideology. Ethnicity does away with objective, biological distinctions and instead introduces subjective, cultural differences. As Giddens puts it, 'Ethnic differences are *wholly learned,* a point which seems self-evident until we remember how often some such groups have been regarded as "born to rule" or, alternatively, have been seen as "unintelligent", innately lazy, and so forth'.[84] Ethnicity is defined through learned or cultural criteria and boundaries between ethnic groups are fluid. Yet in actual use, the concept of ethnicity is not so different from that of race. When, for instance,

Giddens gives examples of ethnic groups, he draws heavily on popular conceptions of racial difference:

> Most modern societies include numerous different ethnic groups. In Britain, Irish, Asian, West Indian, Italian and Greek immigrants, among others, form ethnically distinct communities within a wider society. The United States is considerably more differentiated ethnically than Britain, and incorporates immigrant communities from all corners of the globe.[85]

Ethnicity here seems to be defined through the status of being an immigrant and determined by differences of 'race' or nationality. The concept of ethnicity therefore allows Giddens to proclaim differences according to cultural practices that are wholly learned, while in practice using it to define social groups according to old-fashioned criteria of race or nationality. Yinger's argument that ethnicity allows us to distinguish between 'socially defined and biologically defined races'[86] shows how ethnicity provides a politically acceptable way of referring to imputed racial differences. As Malcolm Chapman notes, 'In many ways, "ethnicity" is "race" after an attempt to take the biology out'.[87]

 Indeed it is more than that, for ethnicity incorporates biological notions of race as another aspect of identity. Harold Abramson has argued that while 'race is the most salient ethnic factor, it is only one of the dimensions of the larger cultural and historical phenomenon of ethnicity'.[88] Or, as Sandra Wallman puts it, 'Once it is clear that ethnic relations follow on the *social* construction of difference, phenotype falls into place as one element in the repertoire of ethnic boundary markers'.[89]

 Ethnicity bridges the gap between racial and cultural definitions of social difference. The ambiguous relationship between race, culture and ethnicity within the pluralist framework can be seen in the seminal Swann report on British education, which spelt out the essential attributes of a pluralist society:

> [A] multi-racial society such as ours would in fact function most effectively and harmoniously on the basis of a pluralism which enables, expects and encourages members of all ethnic groups, both minority and majority, to participate fully in shaping the society as a whole within a framework of commonly accepted values, practices and procedures, whilst also allowing and, where necessary, assisting the ethnic minority communities in maintaining their distinct ethnic identities within this common framework.[90]

This passage is a remarkable hodgepodge of contradictions. Britain is a 'multi-racial society'. Its multiracial character is expressed through a patchwork, not of races, but of 'ethnic groups'. Both the differences between ethnic groups, and their common integration into British society, is expressed through 'values, practices and procedures' – in other words through cultural norms. Ethnic groups, however, retain a homogeneous, essentialist character, each with its own 'distinct identity'. The passage reveals how ideas of race, ethnicity and culture all elide into the concept of multiculturalism. As in the discussion of pluralism in colonial society, the multiculturalist approach overestimates the homogeneity and autonomy of the various ethnic groups and underestimates the degree to which all groups are reciprocally implicated in the creation of cultural forms within a common framework of national political, social and economic institutions. The multicultural approach sees immigrant communities as somehow external to the nation. Thus the Swann Report regards the values of the various ethnic groups as distinct from 'British' values. Similarly, a discussion of French immigration considered immigrants to 'be torn between two cultural and social worlds' since 'they wish (as is only normal) to enter into the new world without losing their identity, to transform themselves whilst remaining faithful to themselves'.[91] But as Maxim Silverman, who cites the quote, notes, 'it is difficult to see what "their identity" was before becoming split, or what is meant by "whilst remaining faithful to themselves"'.[92]

The 'nation' and 'immigration', Silverman argues, 'are not opposites but part of a more complex whole'.[93] He adds that

> Just as 'nations as a natural, God-given way of classifying men, as an inherent though long-delayed political destiny, are a myth' so too should it be recognised that the inherent destiny of minorities is also a myth. Their 'essence' and 'roots' are as dependent on a retrospective unity as are those of the nation. The frontiers (both geographical and metaphorical) defining the nation-state and minorities are produced at the same time and by the same process.[94]

The tendency within multiculturalist discourse to portray ethnic groups or 'minorities' as external to the national body arises from the nature of the discourse. Pluralism developed in the postwar years not as a means to establish equality but as an accommodation to the persistence of inequality. As immigrants remained ghettoised, excluded from mainstream society, subject to discrimination and clinging to their old habits and lifestyles as a familiar anchor in a hostile world, so such differences became rationalised not as the negative product of racism or discrimination but as the positive result of multiculturalism.

7
Cultural Wars

In 1975 Stanford University in California decided to rehabilitate its course on 'Western Civilisation' which had been abolished in 1970. By 1978 a two-year pilot programme had been approved and in 1980 a new, year-long, required course began for all incoming students. The core reading list for the course included what were considered to be the basic 'Great Books' of the Western tradition – the Bible, Plato and Homer, Augustine's *Confessions*, Dante's *Inferno*, More and Machiavelli, Luther and Galileo, Voltaire's *Candide*, *The Communist Manifesto*, Freud's *Civilisation and its Discontents*, Darwin's *The Origin of Species*.

The revived course, and in particular the core reading list, generated considerable opposition from both students and faculty members who objected to its European orientation and who demanded that black, Third World and women's literature should be included in the core curriculum. This dispute over what constituted 'Western Civilisation' became a national *cause célèbre*, pitting luminaries such as philosopher Allan Bloom, Republican secretary of state for education William Bennett, novelist Saul Bloom – whose infamous comment that 'When the Zulus have a Tolstoy, we will read him' caused an outcry – and Robert Bork, Ronald Reagan's nominee for the US Supreme Court, against what the African-American scholar Henry Louis Gates called a 'rainbow coalition of feminists, deconstructionists, Althusserians, Foucauldians, people working in ethnic or gay studies, etc'.[1] On the one side, conservatives such as Dinesh D'Souza lambasted 'the new barbarians who have captured the humanities, law and social science departments of so many of our universities'. Students, D'Souza claimed, were being 'exposed to an attempted brainwashing that deprecates Western learning . . . in the name of multiculturalism'.[2] D'Souza's popular polemic *Illiberal Education* launched a fierce conservative backlash against 'political correctness', the supposed attempt by liberals to stifle free speech and replace American values with dogmatic assertions about racism and sexism. Allan Bloom's *The Closing of The American Mind*, a meditation on the state of American culture and education, and a book that included long disquisitions on Plato, Socrates and Nietzsche, became a surprise national best seller.

On the other side, opponents of the Stanford course argued that it was necessary to take into account the changing nature of American society. 'The character of US society is changing', one speaker in the Stanford debate claimed. 'More and more North Americans insist on affirming the specificity of their class, ethnicity, gender, religion, race or sexual orientation, rather than melting into the homogenising pot. They see such affirmation as intrinsic to their citizenship.'[3] For such critics the European orientation of the course was an expression of the racist nature of American society, the attempt, in the words of Molefi Kete Asanti, 'to maintain a Eurocentric hegemony over the curriculum'.[4]

Why did a debate about a university course generate such fierce passions and become transformed in the national imagination into what Pat Buchanan, the rightwing candidate for the 1992 Republican presidential nomination, called a 'cultural war'? Because, as liberal historian Arthur Schlesinger has put it, 'The debate about the curriculum is a debate about what it means to be American'.[5] In the anxious and fragile mood that transfixed an America coming out of the Cold War and into a New World Order, the debate about what constituted 'Western Civilisation' became symbolic of a struggle to determine and define the very identity of America as a nation.

The controversy over university curricula and political correctness has revealed the instability of the multicultural project. For the past half century pluralism has been a central tenet of faith for Western societies, and one which has shaped their ethos and identities in the wake of the Nazi experience. Yet in the turbulent political waters of the post-Cold War era there is greater pressure than ever before on Western politicians to articulate a coherent and singular national identity. The 'cultural war' reflects the difficulty in reconciling these two conflicting political demands in contemporary society.

America's original self-image, forged in the optimistic afterglow of independence, was that of a land in which old-world differences were eradicated in the creation of a new nation. America, Ralph Waldo Emerson wrote, was 'an asylum of all nations' in which 'the energy of the Irish, the Germans, Swedes, Poles, & Cossacks, & all the European tribes – of the Africans, & and the Polynesians, will construct a new race'.[6] Of course, there never was a time in American history in which the various groups – in particular black people – had an equal claim to citizenship. Nevertheless, equality through assimilation was, rhetorically at least, the national creed, defined by the slogan *E Pluribus Unum* – 'Out of many, One'. But as the many failed to fuse into the one, and as social inequality remained a central aspect of American society, so the assimilationist ideology of the melting pot (or the 'smelting pot' as Emerson called it) gave way to the pluralist notion of an America created out many nations, each maintaining their distinct identity while partaking of American citizenship.

In the postwar period pluralism became institutionalised as a pragmatic response to the discrediting of racial theory. This pragmatic assertion of pluralism was well-expressed by historian Lawrence Fuchs when he observed that 'No nation before had ever made diversity itself a source of national identity and unity'.[7] Economic expansion generated by the postwar boom, the sense of a national mission created by the Cold War and the USA's international ascendency which allowed American values to acquire universal status, all helped minimise the divisive consequence of the multicultural project. It was possible to believe, in Diane Ravich's words, that 'Paradoxical as it may seem, the United States has a common culture that is multicultural'.[8]

By the end of the eighties, however, such an argument was no longer plausible. The breakdown of postwar consensus, the end of the Cold War, the demise of social movements and the onset of economic recession all helped to undermine national cohesion and encourage social fragmentation. As Schlesinger put it, 'The rising cult of ethnicity was a symptom of decreasing confidence in the American future'.[9] The failure of the movement for equality, and disillusionment with prospects for social change, turned minority groups inwards, seeking to find in their particular histories and identities that which they had failed to gain from the ideology of equality. At the same time, cutbacks in public and welfare spending led to a scramble for resources among different social groups, strengthening the sense of a nation composed of competing tribes. 'The battle over multiculturalism', Elizabeth Fox-Genovese has observed, 'is a battle over scarce resources and shrinking opportunities'.[10]

Conservatives, on the other hand, and even many liberals, came to see 'the cult of ethnicity' not as the product but as the cause of national decline. The problem, in their view, was that the relativist outlook of the multicultural approach had destroyed the common values and shared traditions that denoted the American nation. 'The multiethnic dogma', Schlesinger argued, 'abandons [America's] historic purposes, replacing assimilation by fragmentation, integration by separatism. It belittles *unum* and glorifies *pluribus*'.[11] For such critics of multiculturalism, the disorientation caused by the collapse of the postwar order was experienced in terms of the disintegration of American society. The very existence of rival cultures and histories called into question the integrity of society. As William Bennett put it, a singular 'national memory' is 'the glue that holds our political community together'.[12]

The attack on multiculturalism displaced the real problem facing American conservatives. The end of the Cold War deprived America of a common external enemy around which to articulate its identity. At the same time, the uncertainties of the post-Cold War era required even more than before the expression of an assertive national identity. Targeting multiculturalism and political correctness provided both an enemy around which to articulate American values and a scapegoat for America's decline. 'As Communism collapses', Adam Meyerson, editor of the conservative *Policy Review,* has written, 'the greatest ideological threat to western civilisation comes from within the West's own cultural institutions'.[13] Speaking at the 1992 Republican National Convention, Pat Buchanan urged fellow Americans to take back their cities, culture and country 'block by block'.

The conflict between an entrenched pluralism and an assertive nationalism has been at the heart of political debate, not just in America, but throughout the Western world and has been the source of considerable social tension over the past decade. It has led to fierce debates about, for example, the impact of immigration on Western cultures and whether adherence to Islam is compatible with loyalty to Western liberal democracy. The campaign against Salman Rushdie's *The Satanic Verses* in Britain and *l'affair foulard* in France (the controversy generated by the ban on Muslim girls wearing their traditional headscarves in school) have polarised society in the same way as has the debate about political correctness in the USA. As in America, European conservatives have come to see plurality as the cause of national decline. One British newspaper, for instance, bemoaned the impact of immigration on the sense of national identity:

> Barely a generation ago these islands were occupied by a single people who despite differences of region, background and expectation were bound by common loyalties and affection, by a shared history and memory. Thirty years on and the English have become 'the white section of the community' and Britishness is something to be had from the bazaar.[14]

But if pluralism has come to be regarded as the cause of national disintegration, it has at the same time also provided conservatives with a language through which to articulate their concern for a coherent national identity and culture. The pluralist idea that every people has a unique and discrete culture has been transformed into a potent weapon in the conservative armoury. 'Every society, every nation is unique', the British politician Enoch Powell has claimed. 'It has its own past, its own story, its own memories, its own ways, its own languages or ways of speaking, its own – dare I use the word – culture.'[15] The preservation of diversity, such nationalists argue, is a common good. But, they claim, preserving diversity requires the destruction of the multicultural society. 'It is because we respect ourselves and others', Pierre Pascal, a leading rightwing thinker in France contends, 'that we refuse to see our country transformed into a multiracial society in which each group loses their specificity'.[16] The 'true racists', Pascal argues, are those who would deny the uniqueness of each culture by submerging it into a multicultural whole. Such arguments do not reject pluralism as such. Rather they reject pluralism *within* a society in favour of pluralism *between* societies. The ambiguity of multicultural arguments has made possible such a transformation. Take, for instance, Allan Bloom's argument that cultural relativism is an eccentricity of Western liberalism:

> One should conclude from the study of non-Western cultures that not only to prefer one's own way but to believe it best, superior to all others, is primary and even natural – exactly the opposite of what is intended by requiring students to study these cultures. What we are really doing [in promoting relativism] is applying a Western prejudice – which we covertly take to indicate the superiority of our culture – and deforming the evidence of those other cultures to attest to its validity.[17]

The problem with relativists, Bloom seems to be saying, is that they do not take notice of their own arguments. The evidence of pluralism shows that it is natural for every culture to assert its own superiority, and this applies as much to Western societies as it does to non-Western ones. Indeed, Bloom argues, in a twist to the argument, liberals take relativism itself to be an expression of Western superiority. The real pluralists, Bloom is suggesting, are those who oppose a standard multicultural society in favour of a plurality of unitary societies.

The ability of conservatives to purloin pluralist themes to assert a sense of exclusivity should not surprise us. As I have shown in previous chapters, racial discourse and the pluralist outlook have common roots in particularist philosophy. In this chapter I want to examine how pluralist themes are being recast in the 'cultural war' to breathe new life into racial ideology. The new discourse of race has appropriated the language of cultural pluralism and refashioned it into a language of cultural exclusion. Politicians and academics alike now look at clashes between cultures or civilisations as the real root of human differences. Culture, history, tradition – these are the means of delineating one people from another. They have also become a means of authenticating social legitimacy. For societies bereft of a positive vision of what they represent, and unable to galvanise their populations around a common purpose, representing other cultures, histories and traditions as dangerous or alien provides a useful mechanism of establishing a common social bond. Presenting national, or Western, culture as under threat provides a means of drawing society behind a single mission.

To understand these issues, I shall return to a number of themes I first raised in Chapter 1 – in particular perceptions of immigration, the underclass, and the Third World – and re-examine them to show how cultural difference has become the form through which racial ideas acquire contemporary meaning. The first two sections in this chapter will contrast the debate on immigration and national identity in Britain and France, a contrast that helps bring out the underlying themes and contradictions of contemporary racial discourse. I shall then look at the underclass debate in the USA, a debate which reveals new forms for old arguments about moral degeneracy. The attempt to resurrect racial arguments is not without its difficulties. The debates about immigration and the underclass both reveal the manner in which the public expression of difference can be both socially divisive and politically uncomfortable. In the final section of the chapter I shall look at the one field of discussion in which the rehabilitation of racial arguments has proved the least problematic – the debate about the nature of the Third World.

IMMIGRATION, ASSIMILATION AND NATIONAL HISTORY

The novelist Toni Morrison has suggested that in American literature the figure of the Negro or the African is often a device to discuss themes central to American society itself but which are difficult openly to broach. The 'Africanist presence' is, she notes,

> both a way of talking about and a way of policing matters of class, sexual licence and repression, formation and exercises of power, and meditations on ethics and accountability . . . It provides a way of contemplating chaos and civilisation, desire and fear, and a mechanism for testing the problems and blessings of freedom.[18]

We might consider the 'immigrant' as playing a similar role in contemporary, particularly European, discourse.

Immigration has become a cipher, a means through which deeper social concerns are revealed. It is a mirror to the fears and hopes of a society, and in particular to those of the ruling élite. The insecurities unleashed by the profound changes of recent decades have thrown into disarray the carefully articulated visions that previously bound society. This profound dislocation has been experienced to a great degree as a disruption of 'who we are'. The debate about immigration, like that about multiculturalism, has become a means of articulating these concerns. At the same time it has also become a means of remaking national history to present a more cogent sense of 'who we are'. In Britain it was the Conservative politician Enoch Powell who first raised the question 'Who are we?' in a series of explosive speeches in the late 1960s in which he linked immigration and national decline. The controversy he detonated cost Powell his seat in the shadow cabinet and effectively ended his political career. But Powell's intervention was to set the themes of the subsequent discussion on British national identity.[19]

Since Powell's seminal speeches, both the extent of Britain's decline and the disorienting impact of decline on national identity have become manifest. The reshuffling of the world order in the post-Cold War era has revealed more starkly than ever Britain's weaknesses. The end of the Cold War has raised questions about the very significance of what it means to be 'British'. Popular attachment to the idea of Britishness can no longer, as in the past, be sustained by reference to imperial greatness or to the nation's special mission. Indeed there is little in present-day society that can inspire people to say 'I am proud to be British'. Instead British identity has to be recast through its *past*. History is Britain's priceless possession. Politicians who extol the importance of the 'mother of parliaments', laud the virtues of Britain's unwritten constitution or remind the world of the pluckiness of the country that stood up to Nazi tyranny recognise that in its history Britain possesses a unique and incomparable asset. By reworking Britain's past greatness, politicians and policy-makers hope to recast the sense of self. Geoffrey Elton, the late Regius Professor of History at Cambridge University, elaborated this view of history in proposing that 'the historian's task consists among other things, if I may so put it, in a crude rekindling of a certain respect for a country whose past justifies that respect'.[20] Implicit in Elton's view is the observation that the *present* does not justify such respect. Indeed in the inaugural lecture of his Regius Professorship, Elton made explicit this precise point. 'A *New Statesman* era like ours', he claimed, 'full of self-deprecation and envy, can do with the corrective of a past that demonstrates virtue and achievement'.[21]

The importance of history to Britain's image today was demonstrated by Margaret Thatcher, who in a speech after the Falklands War of 1982 drew parallels between the Conservative mission to revitalise the nation and Britain's glorious age of Empire:

> When we started out, there were the waverers and the fainthearts . . . the people who thought we could no longer do the great things we once did. Those who believed our decline was irreversible – that we could never again be what we were . . . that Britain was no longer the nation that had built an Empire and ruled a quarter of the world. Well they were wrong. The lesson of the Falklands is that Britain has not changed and that this nation has those sterling qualities that shine through our history.[22]

Britain's sterling past provides a means of buttressing its less than sterling present. The invocation of history in this fashion transforms it into a living thing with the capacity to reach out from the past and shape our lives today. It is a view of history that is very important for conservatives, and in particular for present-day conservatives. Once the nature and identity of a people or a nation is conceived of in terms of a fixed 'essence', then little can change it. The fact that Britain today is a middle-ranking nation cannot hide the fact that its essence lies in it greatness. 'Britishness' becomes something far removed from the reality of closed factories, run-down housing estates and politicians touched by sleaze.

It is in this context that we need to understand the debate on immigration. Britain's postwar immigrants, for conservatives, disrupt the sense of a shared greatness. Not only are immigrants gatecrashers who are not part of the glorious past, but they are the very symbols of Britain's tumble from glory. Like the other great icons of contemporary conservative demonology—the 1960s and the welfare state—immigrants are symbolic of the time that the nation lost faith in itself and stopped believing in its essential greatness.

Immigrants are the yardstick against which is measured 'Britishness'. A society in decline cannot offer a positive vision of itself; it can only do so through the past—or through a contemporary vision of what it is *not*. And immigrants are what 'we' are not. 'We cannot fail to recognise the deep bitterness', the MP Winston Churchill has claimed, 'that exists among ordinary people who one day were living in Lancashire and woke up the next day in New Delhi, Calcutta or Kingston, Jamaica'.[23] The need to measure Britishness in opposition to immigration explains why so much of conservative discussion of black settlement is couched in the language of war and invasion. 'It is . . . truly when he looks into the eyes of Asia', thundered Enoch Powell, 'that the Englishman comes face to face with those who would dispute with him the possession of his native land.'[24]

It is not possible, say the conservatives, for immigrants to have an unalloyed attachment to Britain. 'The presence of a common status where there was no common nationhood', Enoch Powell has claimed, 'has produced in the cities of England a concentration of other nationals who assert the contradictory claim to belong—and not belong—to this nation.' Oxford don John Casey has written of Asians, that 'by their large numbers and their profound difference in cultures, they are most unlikely to identify themselves with the traditions and loyalties of the host nation.' Similarly, Casey has argued, Afro-Caribbean behaviour is alien to the British way of life, because of their family structure, their educational standards and their proclivity for crime.[25] Former Conservative minister Norman Tebbit's infamous 'cricket test'—his demand that black people in Britain should demonstrate their loyalty by supporting England rather India, Pakistan or the West Indies—may have displayed a poor appreciation of the finer arts of the game but it gave a populist form to the argument that immigration inevitably entails a contradictory sense of belonging.

Such conservatives draw on a concept of culture that derives from Burke, Renan and Barrés. Culture, here, is more than simply a way of life.

It is that which gives a sense of attachment, of belonging and of rooted-ness; that which links the present with the past and creates a unique heritage. 'Britain is not a geographical expression or a New-World terri-tory open to all comers with one foot in their old home and one foot in the new', wrote Alfred Sherman, former adviser to Margaret Thatcher. 'It is the national home and birthright of its indigenous people.' Along with family and religion, argued Sherman in a self-conscious echo of Edmund Burke, the nation is 'man's main focus of identity, his roots, his sense of history, his link with the wider world, with past and future, "a partner-ship between those who are living, those who are dead and those who are to be born".' For Sherman, national consciousness is the 'sheet-anchor for the unconditional loyalties and acceptance of duties and responsibilities, based on personal identification with the national com-munity, which underlie civic duty and patriotism'.[26]

The problem with immigration, for such critics, is that it denies the singularity of this vision of culture. 'Multicultural identity', rightwing educationalist Ray Honeyford argues, 'appears to have no attachment to history, tradition, natural development or actual common experience—in other words, no attachment to those things which give the concept "culture" real human meaning.'[27] Different peoples have different cul-tures, runs the argument, and it is nigh on impossible for someone from one culture to acquire another. 'A West Indian or an Asian does not by being born in England become an Englishman', claimed Powell. 'In law he becomes a United Kingdom citizen by birth; in fact he is a West Indian or an Asian still.'[28] Culture is something you are born into, not something you acquire, the conservatives argue. Viewed in this fashion culture inherits the role of race in the nineteenth century, and history the power of biology. Culture becomes particularist and exclusive, delineating a common past to which some can belong and some cannot. And that past becomes determinist and teleological, holding power over the present through tradition and rootedness.

Those who conceive of culture in this fashion deny that they are 'racist' in the old sense of the word. Asked whether he considered himself a racist, Enoch Powell maintained that 'If by a racialist you mean a man who despises a human being because he belongs to another race, or a man who believes that one race is inferior to another or that only one has the capacity for civilisation, then the answer is emphatically no'.[29]

The key merit of a cultural view of difference is that it does not appear to have any connection with 'race' at all. By eliding the idea of 'race' and 'nation', race can be made to disappear, as conservative philosopher Roger Scruton has made clear. 'Nobody who defends the national idea', he argues, 'is now likely to explain himself in terms of kinship or race.' This is not simply 'through fear of the thought-police'. Rather 'the idea that mankind divides into biological "races" has been put into such absurd use by the Gobinistes and their followers, and entangled itself with so much nonsense and pseudo-science, as to have lost all credibility.' Indeed, writes Scruton, because biological races are defined 'without reference to history', the idea 'offers nothing to those searching for an historical identity, upon which to found a state which owes its legitimacy to birthright alone.' Nevertheless, the idea of race 'accurately reflects *ways of conceiving* social unity':

> It denotes a continuity across generations, based in kinship and intermarriage, but supported by a consciousness of common descent. This common descent creates the obligation of inheritance: we must receive from our forefathers that which we also pass to our children. Only the idea that the inheritance is entirely *biological* rather than cultural renders the concept suspect to those of open mind.[30]

By divesting the concept of race of its biological heritage, and conceiving it in terms of cultural inheritance ('an endlessly transferable set of beliefs and burdens'), the new discourse of race has reshaped the concept into a form usable in the post-Nazi era. The debate on culture has recreated the assumptions of racial thinking but in a form that can allow cultural exclusivists to deny that they are racist. 'The whole question of race' maintains Robin Page, 'is not a matter of being superior or inferior, dirty or clean, but of being different.'[31] The result, as Paul Gilroy has observed, is that

> we increasingly face a racism which avoids being recognised as such because it is able to link 'race' with nationhood, patriotism and nationalism, a racism which has taken a necessary distance from the crude ideas of biological inferiority and superiority and now seeks to present an imaginary definition of the nation as a unified *cultural* community.[32]

The use of culture in this fashion can be seen in the debate about *The Satanic Verses*. The imposition of a death sentence by fatwa on Salman Rushdie, and the public burning of a copy of *The Satanic Verses* during a Muslim demonstration in Bradford in January 1989, enraged British commentators. Former Labour MP Robert Kilroy-Silk was incensed to have 'our reading dictated by the tastes of non-English speaking Muslims many of them not long out of the villages of Bangladesh'. He complained that 'British traditions, culture and laws have had to be amended to meet the needs of those with values and mores fashioned in less civilised times and places.' 'There is nothing racist', Kilroy-Silk maintained, 'in believing and asserting that the culture that has evolved in Britain over the past 1000 years and more is to be preferred to that created elsewhere'. After all,

who could possibly argue that the culture that embraces a parliamentary democracy, in which the values of freedom, justice, fairness and
toleration are pre-eminent, is not better than one which enjoins the
burning of books, that passes a death sentence on a man for having
unorthodox views, and whose British adherents can cheerfully proclaim that it is their intention to carry out the Ayatollah's wishes?[33]

Britishness was defined through its culture, one which 'evolved over the
past 1000 years'. This culture was unique to Britain and distinct from
other cultures, such as Islam. British culture was to be preferred to any
other, partly because it was 'ours' and partly because it was superior, embodying as it did 'the values of freedom, justice, fairness and toleration'.

If the British way of life was patently superior, then equally the Muslim
way of life became in its entirety a bastion of reaction and intolerance.
Feminist novelist Fay Weldon painted a bar-room picture of the Muslim
community with 'their arranged marriages, their children in care, their
high divorce rates, the wife-beatings, the intimidations, the penalties for
recalcitrance, the unregulated work in Dickensian workshops'. Muslim
women, said Weldon, are 'one step above slaves, two above camels'.[34]

Critics described Muslims in the same terms as crowd psychologists
had used to talk of the 'mob' a century earlier. For novelist Anthony
Burgess, the 'sheeplike docility and wolflike aggression' of Muslims
explained their fanatical devotion to their faith. Fay Weldon, noting 'the
blank and puzzled look on the face of the devout Muslim when you tried
to reason with him', believed that

> The Koran, that terrifying book, is beaten (often literally) into the small
> male child at the mosque, every day after school, and if you ask me it's
> terror, not unreason, which looks out of even the most sophisticated
> Muslim eyes when you try to suggest that you can't kill an idea by
> killing the person who gives voice to it.[35]

In her pamphlet *Sacred Cows*, Weldon found the Bible to be a 'superior
revelatory work to the Koran – or at least [one that] reveals a kinder,
more interesting, less vengeful, less cruel God, one worth studying and
worshipping.' Weldon added that 'You can build a decent society around
the Bible', because it provided a 'blueprint for building heaven on earth'
unlike the Koran which simply 'gives weapons and strength to the
thought police'.[36] The cultural distinction between Britishness and Islam
allowed critics of Islam to treat all Muslims as irrational, fanatical, intolerant and illiberal. British, Christian culture by contrast was portrayed
as essentially rational, tolerant and guided by the principles of modern
liberal democracy.

The Rushdie affair became the focus for a celebration of British, Western, Christian culture, and a denigration of Islamic values (and by implication those of all non-Western peoples). Yet what was notable about it was how low-key the debate remained. It never became politicised in the way that, as we shall later in this chapter, the debate about Islam has become a hot political issue in France. Few senior politicians entered the debate. There was no real attempt to question the right of Muslims to remain British citizens. Official concern about Britain's Muslim communities rarely translated into a national political matter. Compared to the debate in France, the anti-Islamic undercurrents in British politics were relatively understated.

What is true of the Rushdie affair is also true of the entire debate on race and immigration in the eighties and nineties. The Conservative governments of this period (rightly) have a reputation for being tough on 'race'. As opposition leader, Margaret Thatcher played on growing racial fears in her infamous radio interview of 1978 in which she warned of a Britain 'swamped' by alien cultures. In power, the Conservatives introduced harsh new immigration and nationality laws, such as the 1981 Nationality Act, the 1987 Carriers Liability Act and the 1992 Asylum Act. They imposed visas on visitors from black Commonwealth countries, refused the Commission for Racial Equality the right to investigate immigration rules on the grounds that these were necessarily racist, and supported a series of tough crackdowns on 'illegal' immigration. Conservative politicians have consistently attacked their opponents for being too liberal on issues such as asylum rights, and inner-city crime.

Yet the Conservatives were also very skilful in preventing race from turning into a socially divisive political problem. The issue of race barely featured in Conservative manifestos for the general elections in 1983, 1987 or 1992. Ministers who indulged in racist rhetoric, such as Norman Tebbit or Alan Clark, were largely marginal. When a politician did make an overtly racist speech, he was quickly isolated. When, for instance, in 1991, Conservative MP Winston Churchill delivered a high-profile speech resurrecting the 'swamping' arguments of Margaret Thatcher's 1978 radio interview, a whole host of senior politicians and ministers as well as Conservative-leaning newspapers launched a ferocious attack on his arguments, claiming that his comments could only damage race relations in Britain.

The Conservatives also maintained pragmatic support for a 'multiculturalist' approach to social problems. They consistently balanced their hardline policies or pronouncements on race with softer, pragmatic responses to racial issues. When, for instance, the Swann report on ethnic minority education published its findings in 1985, education minister Keith Joseph was critical of the report's 'simplistic' understanding of racism and claimed that he had seen 'precious little evidence of any

racist prejudice' among teachers. Nevertheless he wanted schools in
Britain to 'transmit national values in a way which accepted Britain's
ethnic diversity and promoted tolerance and racial harmony'. The government also required the training of teachers to be reworked to take into
account the ethnic diversity of British society.[37] The following year Conservative Party chairman Norman Tebbit launched his party's manifesto
for local elections in London with a blistering attack on the teaching of
'anti-sexist, anti-racist, gay, lesbian, CND rubbish in school'. Yet a few
days later the schools minister, Chris Patten, confirmed that the government would be providing funds for antiracist teacher training programmes. He added that schools in all-white areas would have to pay as
much attention to multicultural education as those in inner cities. The
government would take a 'dim view', he said, of councils which avoided
multicultural education because they had few black children in their
areas. Such areas could become a breeding ground for racism unless
schools embraced multicultural education, he implied.[38]

One academic study of race relations in Britain and France observes
that during the eighties in Britain 'official multiculturalism moved from
a denial that diversity is a threat to the quite different claim that diversity
is in itself a value that must be promoted'. The study notes that 'minority
demands that could not have been expressed a decade earlier took a
prominent place on the agenda, including such controversial issues as
same-race adoption, separate schooling, specific family law, black sections in the Labour Party etc'. It adds that 'despite considerable debate,
mainstream opinion acquired, by French standards, a remarkable tolerance for such demands'.[39]

This is not to say that British society has been any less 'racist' than that
in France or Germany. Racial violence, police harassment, and discrimination in housing and employment have been as severe in Britain as
elsewhere in Europe. Indeed Britain's immigration and asylum laws are
probably the most restrictive and discriminatory of any European Community member.[40] What is different, however, is that race has not become
politicised to the extent it has in Europe. Racial discrimination is a fact of
life in Britain, but it has rarely been a political fact of life.

A number of factors account for the British authorities' impressive
ability to maintain the depoliticisation of race. First, most immigrant
workers came to Britain as British citizens; the issue of citizenship has
therefore never become a political issue as it has in France or Germany.
Secondly, the fact that immigrants possess citizenship has combined
with a conscious policy of integration on the part of successive governments to stabilise the relationship between black communities and
British society to a greater extent than elsewhere in Europe. Black people
are much more a part of social life, and more integrated into mainstream
society, than in other European countries. There is, for example, a signif-

icantly greater black presence in politics, the media, the professions and business than, say, in France. The result, as Weil and Crowley note, is greater 'social interaction and shared practices – including shared debates and constructive political conflict'.[41] Britain's black population may not be fully considered as equal citizens, but they are rarely completely rejected.

Perhaps most importantly, however, the degree to which the issue of race has remained depoliticised in Britain expresses the way in which British politicians have successfully been able to use the ideals of cultural pluralism for the project of constructing a cohesive national identity. The ideas of tolerance and diversity are at the heart of Britain's self-image. In the *Lion and the Unicorn* George Orwell emphasised 'the gentleness of the English civilisation' which was 'its marked characteristic' and which was 'rooted deep in history'.[42] This Orwellian notion of the essential goodness and tolerance of English civilisation became entrenched after fascism and war swept through Europe in the thirties and it became a central motif of postwar discourse. 'We are a sovereign country', an editorial in a national newspaper recently claimed, 'also a rather decent, humane country which owes nobody an apology for the treatment of black or brown people. Orwellian decency runs very deep in the British.'[43]

By drawing on these motifs of decency and tolerance as essential British characteristics, the discourse of British nationalism has paradoxically been able to appropriate antiracist themes for chauvinist ends. Racism is seen as an outlook foreign to the British tradition, the product of extremist politics alien to the culture of moderation, compromise and consensus that supposedly characterises the British polity. In particular racism is associated with fascism, which has been seen as a foreign, anti-British and, above all, German ideology. Antiracist organisations have characteristically exaggerated the political or physical threat posed by far-right groups, and at the same time portrayed racism as largely emanating from fascist organisations. The result has been the creation of what Paul Gilroy calls 'the coat of paint theory of racism', which sees racism as 'always located on the surface', 'an embarrassing excrescence on the otherwise unblemished features of British democracy'.[44]

The conflation of racism and fascism has allowed antiracism to be recast in a patriotic guise. Central to antiracist arguments has been the idea that British Nazis are merely sham patriots who soil the British flag. The literature of the Anti-Nazi League, Britain's leading antifascist organisation formed in 1977 to stem the electoral influence of the far-right National Front, bears this out. 'The NF says they are putting Britons first', read one ANL leaflet. 'But their Britain will be just like Hitler's Germany'. Antiracist literature – particularly that of the ANL – constantly harks back to the Second World War, using its memory to alert us to the dangers of racists in our midst. As Gilroy has put it, 'it is hard to gauge

what made [the National Front] more abhorrent to the ANL, their Nazism or the way they were dragging British patriotism through the
mud'.[45]

The patriotism of antifascism and antiracism made it easily assimilated
into the discourse of cultural nationalism. We have already seen how the
Second World War and the narrative of Britain's lone stand against Nazi
tyranny is a central component of modern national identity. In the eighties antifascism and antiracism became part of that narrative. As race
became more politicised, and as the European far-right began to march,
antiracism (cast as antifascism) became a source of chauvinistic pride in
Britain. Conservatives traded on their anti-German chauvinism to present their antiracist credentials. Rightwing ministers such as Norman
Tebbit and Nicholas Ridley warned of 'jackboots marching across Europe' in the wake of German reunification and the rise of fascist groups.
British culture was superior because it was tolerant and non-racist.
Rather than challenging British chauvinism, antiracism became a component of national identity.

A small example illustrates well the way that antiracism and chauvinism have become melded together. The day after the England football
team was bundled out of the World Cup qualifying competition by
Holland in October 1993, the black England footballer Ian Wright was
asked why he thought they had lost. 'Because of the German referee', he
replied. 'The Germans have done it to us again. We stuck it to them in the
war and they don't like it.' Wright is a leading black celebrity, known for
his strong antiracist views. That he should casually tap into the under-
current of anti-German chauvinism that infuses British culture to explain
yet another national humiliation, and look to past glories to lessen the
pain of current failure, shows how fluid the relationship between antiracism and cultural chauvinism has become, and how Britain's black
population themselves can partake in the rewriting of British history.

The achievement of the British polity in fusing nationalism and antiracism, and the continuing ability of the authorities to keep race off the
political agenda, has limited the resonance of the arguments of the more
rigid nationalists such as Enoch Powell. The logic of Powell's reasoning
would suggest that black British citizens should not be considered British. This would be both socially divisive and would run counter to a
central strand of Britain's modern self-image – that of a tolerant, decent
nation. The new discourse of British nationalism, contrary to Powell's
expectations, has managed, at least for now, to re-invent British history
in a way that can accommodate the histories of postwar immigrants,
even while using immigration as a yardstick against which to measure
Britishness. This is why the likes of Powell have only held the political
centre-stage for the briefest of moments, in contrast to the fortunes of
politicians such as Jean-Marie Le Pen in France.

This is not to deny, however, the influence of Powell and his fellow thinkers in shaping the way that British politicians, and the public, have come to think about national identity. The understanding of the relationship between national identity and national decline, the fashioning of national identity in response to an alien threat, the conception of Britishness as a cultural property, the very language through which debates about immigration and national culture take place, derive to a great extent from the arguments of Powell, Sherman and others. The conception of Britishness that has been forged since the late sixties has managed to absorb the ideals of antiracism and cultural pluralism as an essential aspect of British history and culture. But it remains an identity that derives its strength from a sense of *difference,* indeed of *superiority,* and is often as inflexible and as unthinkingly chauvinistic as that derived from theories of biological destiny.

ISLAM, ENLIGHTENMENT AND CITIZENSHIP

In France, even more clearly than in Britain, the concepts of difference and plurality have become recycled through the new discourse of race. But in France, unlike in Britain, ideas of pluralism cannot simply or easily be absorbed into a particularist national identity. French history places a particular burden, and often contradictory demands, on the understanding of French nationhood. French identity draws heavily on the Enlightenment and the universalist principles of the 1789 Revolution. In this tradition, citizenship is a political contract and an individual is considered without any reference to his or her origin, race or culture. The concept of nationhood, however, requires, by definition, a particularist formulation, a delineation of a collective identity, different from other collective identities. As a result of this clash between universalist principles and the demands of nationhood, French society is, as Maxim Silverman observes, 'perhaps the clearest manifestation of the contradictions in the formation of all modern nation-states: contradictions which emerge within Enlightenment formulations of the individual and the collectivity'.[46]

The ambiguous relationship between universalism and particularism in the concept of French nationhood has been highlighted throughout the postwar years by the policy of assimilation, the bedrock of French immigration policy. The demand for assimilation, Jacques Barou has observed, is the form in which insistence on difference is expressed:

There is therefore a paradox in the policies of the French state with regard to minority groups, who are both invited to merge into the national fabric by renouncing their attachment to origins, yet who are

also the object of particularist designations with which they are subsequently reproached.[47]

The very denial of racial difference, the very insistence that France treats
its citizens without regard to their race, is a means of highlighting the
difference of immigrants. The debate on immigration and assimilation,
as we saw in Chapter 1, has been a way of establishing a mythical
homogeneity of French society through the assertion of immigrants'
'difference'. I now want to look at how this process, in the context of the
political and social demands made by the post Cold-War era, has led to
a revision of notions of citizenship.

In France, as much as in Britain, the understanding of national and
social decline has been mediated through the question of 'Who are we?'
and 'What does it mean to be French?'. This became particularly evident
from the mid-eighties onwards when, in the wake of economic crisis and
the collapse of François Mitterrand's leftwing economic and social
policies, the issue of assimilation became reframed around questions of
nationality and citizenship. Many began to question the right of Muslims
to be treated as French citizens, because of their perceived refusal to
acculturate to French values and ideals. In 1985 *Le Figaro* magazine put
on its cover a picture of Marianne, the female symbol of the French
Revolution, wearing a veil and posed the question 'Will we still be
French in twenty years time?'. The richness of the allusions could not be
missed – the importance of the Enlightenment and the 1789 Revolution
for the sense of national identity, the disfigurement (even rape?) of
Frenchness by Islamic culture, the threat of a France that would no
longer be French.

Both those favourable, and inimical, to Islam have tended to view
the clash between Islamic and French values that has characterised
recent years as being deep-rooted in history. In fact the idea of Islam as
the Other to French identity is specific to contemporary discourse.
France's relationship to Islam has been a pragmatic one, and at times
quite benign. In 1922 the French government built and funded the first
mosque in Paris. 'Far from separating us', wrote Pierre de Foucauld at
the time of its opening, 'our religions, if we may lift ourselves high
enough to see only the community of feeling of which they are the
high expression, teach us the mutual respect of our convictions'.[48] In
the postwar years Islam was seen as a useful bulwark against radical
socialist and nationalist movements. In the 1950s, during the Algerian
war of liberation, the independence movement FLN was rarely
demonised as Islamic. Rather, the French authorities regarded Muslims
as more likely to be pro-French and viewed secular Algerians with
suspicion, rightly believing them to be more influenced by nationalist
ideas.

As late as the 1970s Islam was seen as a stabilising influence on immigrant communities, diminishing the prospect of political activity. Government ministers encouraged North Africans to maintain their Islamic affiliations. 'The right to a cultural identity', declared Paul Dijoud, minister for immigrant workers in Valéry Giscard d'Estaing's government, 'allows the immigrant, despite his geographical distance, to stay close to his country'.[49] The government sought in Islam a 'stabilising factor which would turn the faithful from deviance, delinquency, or membership of unions or revolutionary parties'.[50] Employers were particularly keen to encourage Islam. 'We have never had any problems with our religious leaders nor with the worshippers' a Renault official noted. 'They are very responsible people'.[51]

In the seventies, therefore, Islam, far from being seen as a threat to national unity, was regarded as a mechanism for the integration of immigrants into French society. The transformation of Islam in French political imagination in the eighties had less to do with the nature of Islam than with the problems of French decline, and the way that decline was perceived in terms of the fragmentation of national identity. Jacques Chirac's centre-right RPR–UDF coalition won a general election in March 1986 on a manifesto which promised to create a 'national community more certain of its identity'. After the election, Chirac spoke of the necessity 'to preserve the identity of our national community'.[52] Such rhetoric reflected both the sense of crisis of national identity and the way this crisis was refracted through perceptions of identity and citizenship. The Nationality Commission which Chirac established in 1986 to report on the state of French nationality worried that 'We barely hear any more talk of patriotism':

> National institutions, like school or the army, are willingly questioned
> ... This weakening of the institutions and the universal values around
> which the national tradition has been built ... constitutes the real
> danger for our national life.[53]

Such concerns were not confined to the right. Socialist president François Mitterrand, in his New Year speech to the nation in 1992, warned that 'We must take care not to lose all sense of unity. A population which does not recognise itself in the unitary state must take care not to ... break all links which bind, returning us to a pre-Middle Ages situation'.[54] The debate on immigration became the means of discussing the national crisis, symbolising as it did 'the danger for the order, unity and even the existence of the French national community'.[55] In this context the 'Islamic presence' in France came to be reframed as a threat to France's national tradition and cohesion.

In reframing Islam in this fashion, the right was able to use the language of cultural pluralism for its own ends. From the early 1980s the far-right had astutely been exploiting the right to maintain cultural difference, which had been a major plank for antiracist defence of immigrant rights, by asserting the right of the French to their cultural identity. Muslims, they declared, were 'Français de papier' (paper Frenchmen) or 'Français malgré eux' (French despite themselves). They belonged to a different culture and tradition and one inimical to that of France. The right adopted the language of pluralism and turned it against immigrants. 'I love North Africans', claimed Le Pen. 'But their place is in the Mahgreb'.[56] Muslims in France did not deserve to become French because of their adherence to Islam. They were culturally different from previous immigrants in that they had not assimilated in the 'normal' way and therefore they warranted different treatment.

These themes became crystalised in *l'affair foulard* (the headscarves affair) which first hit the headlines in 1989, and has since repeated itself in several instances. In October 1989, three female Muslim students were excluded from their school in Creil, near Paris, for wearing their traditional headscarf. The school authorities claimed that this violated the secular tradition of the French education system. The affair polarised the nation between those who supported the school's action and those who opposed it. But for all the intensity of the argument, there was, as Silverman has observed, 'a much deeper consensus over the French model of universalist secularism [which] united the warring factions'.[57] For both sides, the French tradition expressed secularism, universalism, reason and tolerance while Islam embodied obscurantism, particularism, unreason and intolerance. Those who supported the exclusion of the Muslim girls believed that only such action could defend French tradition from contamination by Islam. Antiracists who opposed exclusion did so because they believed that Muslims had to be educated out of their backwardness. Harlem Desir, leader of the largest antiracist organisation, SOS Racism, argued that 'schools must welcome all children for it is only in that way that they can escape from obscurantism'.[58] Bernard Henri-Lévy similarly argued that Muslims had to be inculcated with French values if they were not to be 'trapped in their ghettos': 'We have young "beurs" who arrive at school impregnated with beliefs, taboos and a form of servitude inherited from their families. The secular school must speak to them and liberate them.'[59] Both sides of the debate therefore accepted the dualism between France and Islam, the one positive, the other negative. In fact the image constructed here of the secular French tradition and an obscurantist Muslim population is a mythical one. There is no clear-cut separation between religion and the state, between the public and the private in the French tradition. As Silverman, among others, has pointed out, religion, and in particular Catholicism, has left its traces right across French life, including the education system:

[T]he major holidays in France are Christmas, Easter, Assumption and All Saints; the traditional half-day at school was arranged to accommodate catechism classes; the contractual relationship between the private schools (predominantly Catholic) and the state includes a certain amount of state subsidy for private (religious) education; the taxpayer similarly contributes to the maintenance of the (Catholic) church and so on.[60]

Equally, those marked out as 'Muslim' are rarely the fundamentalist obscurantist figures of the republican stereotype. The social mores of young North Africans in France today are little different from those of their white counterparts. The demonisation of Islam does not arise from a substantial division between French and Islamic values but from the need to establish the validity of French identity through its opposition to supposed Islamic traditions. Creating a binary opposition between Islam and French republicanism helps to construct a French tradition that does not exist in reality and to define the values and purpose of the French nation which cannot otherwise be defined.

In practical terms the reframing of Islam has led to the remaking of the concept of French citizenship. Traditionally, French citizenship has been a political contract, based on the principle of *jus soli* – those born in France are automatically accorded French citizenship. Until 1993, Article 44 of the French Nationality Code guaranteed French-born children of foreigners living in France French nationality by right between the ages of 16 and 21 if they had lived in the country for the previous five years. The right objected to such a definition of citizenship because it made into French citizens those who were not deemed to be French by culture. In 1986, Jacques Chirac proposed a bill to 'safeguard' national identity by turning the automatic right to citizenship to a voluntary request which the authorities could refuse. The bill sought to institutionalise the idea that nationality depended on assimilation and that contemporary immigrants, particularly those from North Africa, were different from previous immigrants because they refused, or were unable, to assimilate, and hence did not deserve French citizenship.

The bill caused an outcry and was rejected by the *Conseil d'État*. Chirac set up a nationality commission to look into the matter. When the commission reported in 1988 it noted that there had been significant changes in the origins and character of immigration, that it was now 'predominantly non-European' and from cultures 'less sensitive to European influence'. It recommended therefore that French-born children of foreigners should be obliged to seek French nationality at the age of sixteen. Significantly, such had been the ideological transformation over the eighties, that even sections of the antiracist movement, such as MRAP, backed the commission's proposals. In 1993, when a centre–right coalition returned to power, the Nationality Code was reformed on the lines of Chirac's 1986 proposals, suppressing automatic access to French nationality.

French citizenship has been remade not as a political but as a cultural contract. It is a notion of citizenship that has made legitimate the idea that those 'closer' in culture (such as Europeans) are more deserving of citizenship that those whose culture is supposedly more removed from that of France, such as North African Muslims, or indeed any Third World immigrant. The rewriting of French citizenship is a clear expression of what Pierre Taguieff calls 'cultural' or 'differential' racism.[61] The irony is that the motive force for the new discourse of race has been the supposed defence of the enlightened principles of the French Revolution against the dark forces of Islamic unreason.

ÉLITISM AND THE UNDERCLASS

The debate about immigration has reworked racial themes into cultural arguments about national identity. The debate about the underclass, which has developed into a marked feature of political and academic discourse on both sides of the Atlantic, has in a similar fashion linked the discussion about moral degneracy to the debate about national identity. In this section I want to consider how the underclass discussion, particularly in the USA, has become a key component in the recasting of race through allowing the élite to define the meaning of moral degeneracy and moral superiority, and their relation to the values that define the nation, in terms of immutable cultural difference.

The 'underclass' is a term similar to 'race' in that it is a concept that is universally used, one that most people understand, yet few would be able to define. Even in academic discourse the underclass is rarely defined in precise terms. As Lydia Morris has pointed out, 'one of the problems facing attempts to unravel [the underclass] debate is the looseness of definition, which in turn complicates the problem of explanation'. According to Morris, 'Economic marginality, alternative values and deviant behaviour appear in some combination in almost all discussions of the underclass; deviance broadly embracing both criminal behaviour and single parenthood, which are implicitly associated'. The concept of underclass, Morris argues, is used not so much to define a sociological category as to denote a sense of estrangement from social norms and values:

> In much of its usage, those to whom the label is applied not only stand outside of mainstream society and its central institutions, they reject its underlying norms and values. In Victorian England these social outsiders were sometimes termed the dangerous classes. They are now

doubly dangerous, posing not only a threat to social organisation, but
also a challenge to our models for portraying and understanding
social structure. Through a construction of a category of 'outsiders',
this threat is located outside of society, which may then be perceived
as internally cohesive and free from significant challenge.[62]

The term 'underclass' is used therefore to express the idea of marginality,
of social groups who exist at the edge, or outside, of society's normal
structures, and has acquired through such usage 'a sense both pejorative
and threatening'.[63] Morris, and similarly critical authors such as Michael
Katz,[64] are very much to the point in their claim that what defines the
underclass in both popular and academic debate is not its poverty or its
lack of resources, but its supposedly alien moral values. A major feature
in *Time* magazine, for instance, defined the underclass primarily by its
values and behaviour, which it believed differed sharply from those of
other Americans:

> Behind the ghetto's crumbling walls lives a large group of people who
> are more intractable, more socially alien and more hostile than almost
> anybody has imagined. They are the unreachables: the American
> underclass. Their bleak environment nurtures values that are often at
> odds with those of the majority – even the majority of the poor. Thus
> the underclass produces a highly disproportionate number of the na-
> tion's juvenile delinquents, school dropouts, drug addicts and welfare
> mothers, and much of the adult crime, family disruption, urban decay
> and demand for social expenditure.[65]

The underclass is not simply the category of poor or marginalised
people. The distinction is made between 'the majority of the poor' and
the underclass. The underclass is treated as somehow different from the
rest of society and indeed as standing outside of society. The very term
'underclass' denotes people who do not fit in to the scheme of things.
The underclass is seen as composed of aliens and outcasts: 'A Nation
Apart' as one US newspaper described it.[66]

The parallels between the debate on immigration and that on the
underclass should already be apparent. Both immigrants and the underclass are regarded as alien to the body of the nation, as groups whose
difference imperil the cohesion of the nation and its sense of community.
And just as the supposed difference of immigrants helps retrospectively
establish the mythical homogeneity of the national community, so the
difference of the underclass helps define the supposed meaning of
citizenship. The very inarticulacy of what one British newspaper described as 'the Calibans in our midst'[67] gives voice to the 'real' norms and
values that guide our society.

The parallels are also apparent between the contemporary debate on the underclass and the Victorian debate on the 'residuum'. Compare the description of the underclass (or 'lower class' as he termed it) given by Edward Bansfield, a one-time adviser to US president Richard Nixon, with Victorian writer Henry Mayhew's description of the poor. Bansfield writes:

> The lower class person lives from moment to moment, he is either unable or unwilling to take account of the future or to control his impulses. Improvidence and irresponsibility are direct consequences of this failure to take the future into account . . . and these consequences have further consequences: being improvident and irresponsible, he is likely also to be unskilled, to move frequently from one dead end job to another, to be a poor husband and father.[68]

Compare that with Mayhew's description:

> The poor man is distinguished from the civilised man by his repugnance to regular and continuous labour – by his want of providence in laying up a store for the future – by his inability to perceive consequences ever so slightly removed from immediate apprehension – by his passion for stupefying herbs and roots and, when possible, for intoxicating liquor.[69]

Not simply the description but the very language seems to span a century. Both the residuum and the underclass are descriptions not of the poor but of the morally degenerate, a class of people which by its nature is dissolute, debauched, depraved and sinful. In both the discussion of the residuum and that of the underclass, poverty and deprivation are seen as the responsibility not of society but of individuals. In both, poverty is portrayed as a moral, not a social, issue. Members of the residuum or the underclass are disadvantaged because they do not have the personal qualities or the moral fibre necessary to make themselves into good citizens. 'You become a member of the underclass when you are severed from the moral pressures of society', wrote British commentator Brian Appleyard. What was needed for the underclass was not money but 'purpose, discipline and a moral code to guide their behaviour.'

But if the discussion of the underclass shows striking parallels with the debate about the 'dangerous classes' in Victorian times, we should not regard the former as simply a rerun of the latter. Though the similarities between the two are clear, I want to look at the differences too, for in these differences we can see the new shape of contemporary racial theory.

The most arresting difference between the two debates lies in the manner in which 'difference' is conceived. In Victorian discourse the dangerous classes were seen as physically distinct, their moral decadence arising from their biological inferiority. They were a race apart because they were anthropologically discrete. Some proponents of the underclass thesis have, as we shall see, attempted to establish a genetic basis for social differences. But, in general, the difference of the underclass has been cast in cultural, not biological, terms. The underclass is seen as culturally distinct from the rest of society. The habits and morals that make it different are seen as being passed on from generation to generation through cultural, not genetic, transmission.

Today the demonisation of the underclass is a central component of the conservative backlash against the postwar consensus. But the origins of the idea that the poor belong to a distinct culture lies, as Katz has noted, 'among liberals who advocated more active, generous, and interventionist policies on behalf of the poor'.[70] The lineage of the contemporary concept of the underclass lies with the liberal discourse which formed the foundation of the postwar consensus.

Katz points to anthropologist Oscar Lewis as pre-eminent in introducing the idea of the culture of poverty. In Lewis's account of the slum-dwellers of Mexico and Puerto Rico the poor were characterised by a set of attitudes and behaviour that was bred by the struggle to survive and which became a 'way of life . . . passed down from generation to generation along family lines'.[71] This culture of poverty played a causal role in the disadvantage of succeeding generations. 'By the time slum children are aged six or seven', wrote Lewis, 'they have usually absorbed the basic values and attitudes of their subculture and are not psychologically geared to take full advantage of the changing conditions or increased opportunities that may occur in their lifetime'.[72]

Lewis mainly studied poverty in Third World societies. Michael Harrington applied the idea of the culture of poverty to communities in the USA. In *The Other America*, the seminal liberal account of poverty in America, Harrington argued that 'poverty in the United States is a culture, an institution, a way of life'. According to Harrington 'The family structure of the poor' was 'different from that of the rest of society.' He added that there was 'a language of the poor, a psychology of the poor, a world view of the poor.'[73]

Lewis and Harrington were liberals. Their aim was to formulate a programme of state intervention which could alleviate poverty by undermining the culture of poverty and by acculturating the poor into middle-class, middle American values. The proponents of the culture of poverty thesis were all fierce supporters of the War on Poverty and the Great Society, president Lyndon B. Johnson's sixties crusade against poverty. But the argument that the poor were different from the rest of society, that they belonged to a different culture, subscribed to a different world view and formed different social structures had ominous undertones. It appropriated the old idea that social inadequacies were the function of racial differences and recast it in the language of postwar liberalism. The culture of poverty, observes Katz, 'did not capture all poor people'. Rather, 'it placed in a class by themselves those whose behaviours and values converted their poverty into a self-perpetuating world of dependence'. Underlying this thesis was the liberal assumption that 'dependent people were mainly helpless and passive, unable, without the leadership of liberal intellectuals, to break the cycles of deprivation and degradation that characterised their lives'.[74]

In the political context of the postwar consensus the culture of poverty thesis was an argument for government intervention to eradicate poverty. But as postwar liberalism began to ebb the same concept came to underpin the argument that no amount of intervention could transform poverty. Since the poor were distinct, different, apart from society, they could not be considered as part of a common community but should be regarded as a threat to the integrity of society. Through this process the poor became *racialised*. For sixties liberals the poor were different but they believed that philanthropic intervention could alleviate their cultural deprivation and inculcate them with new values. For nineties conservatives the underclass is different and no amount of intervention can eradicate that difference.

The very failure of the liberal hopes of the sixties has given rise to the racialisation of the underclass. Today's conservatives ask themselves the same question that has puzzled all proponents of racial theory: why is it that, despite a political goal of equality and improving social and economic conditions, social differences seem stubbornly unwilling to be eradicated? Back in the seventies, the British secretary of state for education Sir Keith Joseph asked 'Why ... in spite of long periods of full employment and relative prosperity and the improvement in community services since the Second World War, [do] deprivation and problems of maladjustment so conspicuously persist?'[75] Two decades later, Richard Herrnstein and Charles Murray faced up to the same question in the picture they drew of contemporary America in their controversial book *The Bell Curve*:

A great nation, founded on principles of individual liberty and self-government that constitute the crowning achievement of statecraft, approaches the end of the twentieth century. Equality of rights – another central principle – has been implanted more deeply and more successfully than in any other society in history. Yet even as the principle of equal rights triumphs, strange things begin to happen to two small segments of the population.

In one segment life gets better in many ways. The people in this group are welcomed at the best colleges, then at the best graduate and professional schools, regardless of their parents' wealth. After they complete their education they enter fulfilling and prestigious careers. Their incomes continue to rise even when income growth stagnates for everyone else . . .

In the other group, life gets worse, and its members collect at the bottom of society. Poverty is worse, drugs and crime are rampant, and the traditional family all but disappears. Economic growth passes them by . . . They live together in urban centres or scattered in rural backwaters, but their presence hovers over other parts of town and countryside as well, creating fear and resentment in the rest of society that is seldom openly expressed but festers nonetheless.[76]

I shall return to the controversy surrounding *The Bell Curve* later. What is important here (and the reason that I have quoted the passage at length) is that Herrnstein and Murray express with devastating clarity the central conundrum of racial thinking: how to equate a belief in equality with growing inequality. The answer for Herrnstein and Murray, as for Joseph and for all underclass theorists, as indeed it has been for all racial thinkers, is that difference is in the nature of things. Social inequality persists because society is by nature unequal. The élitism of classical racial formalism was expressed in biological terms. Today élitist arguments are more likely to be cast in cultural or moral terms – the breakdown of the family structure of the underclass or its propensity for criminality.

The ease with which conservative explanations of social inequality have become accepted rests on the fact that liberal discourse itself held that the poor were in some way different. The transformation of the liberal concept of the culture of poverty into the conservative idea of the underclass can be seen most obviously in the changing terms of the discussion of black disadvantage in the USA. There has long been a tradition in liberal discourse to see the particularities of black life in America as the product of slavery. In the postwar era this became transformed into the thesis that slavery had imposed upon American blacks a particular culture and set of social institutions that made them unfit for entering modern American life.

In the 1950s historian Stanley Elkins compared the destructive impact of slavery to that of Nazi concentration camps. Slavery, he claimed, had created a unique personality type among American blacks. The force of oppression had disintegrated the black personality and through a process of mass infantilisation had created the black individual as 'a perpetual child incapable of maturity'. African Americans had been transformed into 'Sambos', incapable of independent thought or action because slavery had forced them simply to please their masters.[77]

Elkins's thesis that slavery had imposed a unique negative structure on American black communities was adopted by senator Daniel Moynihan in his 1965 report on the black family, *The Negro Family: The Case for National Action*.[78] Moynihan, then assistant secretary for labour, wrote the report for president Lyndon B. Johnson as part of the Great Society programme to combat poverty. The fundamental problem with black communities, argued Moynihan, was that 'the Negro family in the urban ghettos is crumbling': 'For vast numbers of the unskilled, poorly educated city working class the fabric of conventional social relationships has all but disintegrated'.[79] Moynihan's indices of family breakdown are startlingly like the conservative indices of underclass formation two decades later: 'Nearly a quarter of urban Negro marriages are dissolved'; 'Almost one-fourth of Negro families are headed by females'; 'the breakdown of the Negro family has led to a startling increase in welfare dependence'.[80]

Moynihan traced the breakdown of black family life to the particular brutality of slavery. Racism and slavery, Moynihan argued, had emasculated the black male:

The very essence of the male animal, from the bantam rooster to the four-star general, is to strut. Indeed in 19th century America a particular type of exaggerated male boastfulness became almost a national style. Not for the Negro male. The 'sassy nigger' was lynched.[81]

The effeminisation of the black male and the subsequent disintegration of the black family structure had woven a 'tangle of pathology', creating a black 'subculture' at odds with mainstream American society:

Ours is a society which presumes male leadership in private and public affairs . . . A subculture such as that of the Negro American, in which this is not the pattern, is placed at a distinct disadvantage . . . In essence the Negro community has been forced into a matriarchal structure which, because it is so out of line with the rest of American society, seriously retards the progress of the group as a whole.[82]

According to Moynihan the 'tangle of pathology' revealed itself not simply in the matriarchal family structure but also in 'the failure of youth', 'juvenile delinquency', and 'narcotic addiction'. 'So long as this situation persists', Moynihan believed, 'the cycle of poverty and disadvantage will continue to repeat itself'.[83] To overcome the pathology at the heart of black communities, Moynihan called for a programme of national action 'to strengthen the Negro family so as to enable it to raise and support its members as do other families'.[84]

Both Elkins' and Moynihan's theses were controversial and were widely rejected at the time. They were nevertheless immensely influential. They provided the link between 'structural' and 'moral' interpretations of black disadvantage and hence the bridge to the racialisation of the underclass. Structural theories locate social inequalities in economic or social factors. Moral theories regard the individual as to blame for his own misfortune. By rooting black disadvantage in the legacy of slavery, the Elkins-Moynihan thesis appealed to liberal proponents of structural explanations. But by regarding that legacy as a pathological personality and family structure, it also provided ammunition for moral explanations. As government intervention failed to improve the position of blacks, so moral explanations gained credence. For conservatives, liberal policies of the sixties not only failed to address the problems of the inner cities but actually generated those problems. By undermining traditional American moral values, sixties legislation created the underclass.

One of the key popularisers of the conservative version of the underclass thesis has been Charles Murray. Murray has used Moynihan's arguments about 'the tangle of pathology' at the heart of the black family structure to launch an assault on welfare programmes. In his 1984 book, *Losing Ground: American Social Policy 1950–1980*, Murray argued that poverty, unemployment and other social pathologies were the result not of policy failure but of the personal failings of the poor. The underclass, he claimed, was different from the rest of American society in its values and norms. This difference was particularly revealed in its amoral behaviour, the best indices of which were the rising illegitimacy rates, increased crime and drug addiction, and welfare dependency. Murray subsequently brought his analysis to Britain, arguing that Britain too had created its own underclass and was heading for a social crisis similar to that which already existed in the USA.[85]

Murray's thesis has been controversial, but it has also proved to be highly influential, particularly in the context of the conservative backlash against postwar liberalism and welfare policies that characterised the Reagan/Thatcher years. Robert Greenstein observed in March 1985 that 'Congress will soon engage in bitter battles over where to cut the federal budget, and *Losing Ground* is already being used as ammunition by those who would direct more reductions to programmes for the poor'.[86] Murray's ideas have influenced not only conservatives, but liberals too. The social policies of both US Democratic president Bill Clinton and of Tony Blair's new-look Labour Party in Britain have been shaped by the underclass thesis.

In contrast to *Losing Ground*, Murray's latest work, *The Bell Curve*, which he co-authored with the late Richard Herrnstein, was met with almost unanimous condemnation. A series of responses to the book from eminent scholars and authors in the American magazine *New Republic*

ranged from descriptions of *The Bell Curve*'s vision as 'alien and repellent' to denunciations of Herrnstein and Murray for their 'neo-Nazi'
outlook.[87] There were many calls on both sides of the Atlantic for the
book to be banned.

Why has there been such hostility to the work of an author who
previously had been so influential? The answer lies in the way that the
book confused cultural arguments for racial difference with old-fashioned biological arguments. The core thesis in *The Bell Curve* is the
belief that America is being stratified (or 'partitioned' in Herrnstein and
Murray's terminology) by intellectual ability, with a 'cognitive élite' of
highly educated professionals at the top and a growing underclass –
which Herrnstein and Murray estimate to be 12.5 million strong – of
dullards at the bottom. The authors relentlessly insist that it is personal
intelligence, not social or economic factors, that explains the disparity
between rich and poor.

According to Herrnstein and Murray social pathologies such as poverty, welfare dependency, unemployment, illegitimacy and crime are all
strongly related to low IQ. Indeed they claim that IQ is the best single
explanation of why some people never get off welfare, why crime is
rampant in the inner city and why some teenage girls get pregnant. They
claim too that differences in IQ are largely genetic and passed on from
generation to generation.

At the same time as linking antisocial attitudes to low IQ, Herrnstein
and Murray also resurrect traditional explanations for underclass behaviour:

> A lack of foresight, which is often associated with low IQ, raises the
> attractions of immediate gains from crime and lowers the strength of
> deterrents, which come later (if they come at all). To a person of low
> intelligence, the threats of apprehension and prison may fade to
> meaninglessness. They are too abstract, too far in the future, too uncer-
> tain . . .
>
> Perhaps the ethical principles for not committing crimes are less
> accessible (or less persuasive) to people of low intelligence. They find
> it harder to understand why robbing someone is wrong, find it harder
> to appreciate the values of civil and cooperative social life, and are
> accordingly less inhibited from acting in ways that are hurtful to other
> people and to the community at large.[88]

Such arguments may be distasteful but they differ little from mainstream, including liberal, explanations for underclass behaviour. The
most explosive argument in *The Bell Curve*, and the one that has drawn
all the critical flak, is the assertion that differences between different
'racial' groups can also be explained by differences in intelligence.

Observing that there is a consistent gap between the IQ levels of black and white populations in America, Herrnstein and Murray argue that this is the result of inherent racial differences in intellectual ability. Reworking figures for unemployment, wage levels and imprisonment, they claim that differences between black and white populations all but disappear once IQ levels are taken into account. The conclusion is that black disadvantage is the result not of racism but of innate intellectual inferiority.

In an article in the magazine *New Republic,* Herrnstein and Murray took further their argument about the permanence of inequality. The world, they claimed, is made up of a myriad of 'clans' — 'Arab, Chinese, Jew, Welsh, Russian, Spanish, Zulu, Scots, Hungarian (the list could go on indefinitely)' — each of which possesses a unique mix of qualities, which are 'incomparable across clans': 'The Irish have a way with words . . . ; the Russians see themselves as soulful . . . The Scotch-Irish who moved to America tended to be cantankerous, restless and violent.' Drawing on the work of Afrocentrist Wade Boydkin, Herrnstein and Murray believe that black people have a distinct value system that puts them 'at odds with the prevailing Eurocentric model'. Among black qualities are 'spirituality . . . ; a belief in the harmony between humankind and nature; an emphasis on the importance of movement, rhythm, music and dance; . . . verve and affect.' Rather than bemoaning the fact that blacks are intellectually inferior to whites, we should celebrate the fact that they possess different qualities: 'It is possible to look ahead to a world in which the glorious hodgepodge of inequalities of ethnic groups – genetic and environmental, permanent and temporary – can be not only accepted but celebrated.'[89]

Murray and Herrnstein have thrown together a hodgepodge of everyday prejudices, framed it with an impressive-looking set of statistics, and presented it as an academic thesis. The fundamental methodological flaws of *The Bell Curve* – such as Herrnstein and Murray's treatment of race as a biological entity, their failure to understand intelligence as a social product and their conflation of correlation and causation – are all too apparent.[90] The real theme of *The Bell Curve*, however, is neither the attempt to understand the role of intelligence in social life nor the study of black inferiority, but an attack on what Herrnstein and Murray term the 'perversions of the egalitarian ideal that began with the French Revolution':

> The egalitarian ideal of contemporary political theory underestimates the importance of the differences that separate human beings. It fails to come to grips with human variation. It overestimates the ability of political intervention to shape human character and abilities . . . People who are free to behave differently from one another in the

important affairs of daily life inevitably generate the social and economic inequalities that egalitarianism seeks to suppress. That, we believe, is as close to an immutable law as the uncertainties of sociology permit.[91]

Combining their common and garden prejudices with a welter of statistics, Herrnstein and Murray have in *The Bell Curve* produced an 845-page tome in defence of social inequality. Beginning by asking why it is that, in a nation that prides itself on providing equal opportunities for all, social disaggregation is tugging at the very fabric of society, Herrnstein and Murray, like all racial thinkers, come to the conclusion that difference is in the nature of things. Inequality persists because society is by nature unequal.

Liberal intellectuals (and indeed many conservatives) were repelled by the book's crude ethnographic stereotypes, its unintentional parody of multicultural arguments, and most of all by its seeming throwback to Victorian eugenics and prewar racial theory. Yet if the book were stripped of its vulgar racial claims, most of its critics would have been drawn to the underlying élitism of Herrnstein and Murray's argument, and to the book's basic proposition that America's underclass is morally inferior and alien to the American tradition. As a review by Malcolm Browne in the *New York Times Book Review* suggested, 'one of the strengths of *The Bell Curve* is that it devotes an entire section to the relationship between IQ and behaviour among whites alone, thereby eliminating the complications arising from interracial comparisons'. Herrnstein and Murray's analysis of the white underclass made it difficult, Browne believed, 'to challenge the notion that IQ plays a statistically important role in the shaping of society'. Similarly, in *New Republic*, Leon Wiesseltier made a scorching attack on the book, which he called 'old, dreary and indecent, philosophically shabby and politically ugly'. Yet he painted a picture of underclass America very little different from that of Herrnstein and Murray. 'This is what is happening in the [ghetto] streets', he claimed: 'guns, drugs, rape, rats, demagogues, babies, a collapsing pit of decadence and despair'.[92]

Such critical responses show the ambiguity of contemporary thought to racial ideas. There is widespread revulsion at any attempt to revive scientific racism, to promote eugenic arguments or to prove the biological inferiority of blacks and superiority of whites. But there is at the same time an increasing tendency towards more élitist theories of social differentiation, and a willingness to see social differences as in some way resting on inherent moral and cultural dispositions. In accepting the argument that the underclass is different from the rest of society, *The Bell Curve*'s critics too are promoting the racialisation of social differences. Liberal theorists may prefer to articulate their élitist beliefs around moral issues, such as family structure, illegitimacy and crime – as Murray did in *Losing Ground* – rather than around claims of biological superiority and inferiority, as Herrnstein and Murray do in *The Bell Curve,* but the racial consequences are little different. In preferring the Murray of *Losing Ground* to the Murray of *The Bell Curve,* liberal critics signal that they prefer a hidden, coded form of racial argument based on the grounds of cultural and moral difference to upfront claims of racial inferiority and superiority based on biological theories. *The Bell Curve,* and the response to it, provides a warning that racial theory can come in more than one guise.

THE BIFURCATED WORLD

The debates about immigration and the underclass reveal the manner in which racial ideas are being recast today. They also reveal the inherent difficulties in rehabilitating a public discourse of race. Assertions of racial difference are both socially divisive and politically troublesome. During the French presidential elections in March 1995, a Moroccan student was murdered in Paris by Front National supporters who dumped his body in the river Seine. The killing caused a national outcry. The two protagonists for the presidency, conservative Jacques Chirac and socialist Leonid Jospin, both of whom had previously made a play for the racist vote by attempting to outdo each other on the toughness of their immigration policies, had quickly to backtrack and adopt a much lower key on the issue. Tough talk on immigration may be electorally popular, but no politician can afford to be seen flirting openly with racial politics in the wake of a racist murder. Race remains a sensitive issue in domestic Western politics.

The one area in which there are fewer restraints in the expression of racial ideas is the discussion of the Third World. Arguments about the cultural and moral superiority of the West to the Third World have not only become commonplace, they have also become acceptable. There is little recognition that such assertions are resurrecting old-fashioned racial notions. The debate about the relationship between the West and the Third World has therefore become a key part of the cultural war and central to the contemporary recasting of race. The open, unabashed manner in which many politicians and media pundits today propose colonial rule as an answer to Third World problems is symbolic of the striking transformation in political culture that has taken place in recent years. When, in December 1993, the United Nations launched Operation Restore Hope, the American-led military programme designed to end famine and civil war in Somalia, the *Wall Street Journal* was clear about the implications of the endeavour: 'There is one word for this:

colonialism. Modern-day colonialism . . . may be the only policy that can
prevent more tragedies in Somalia, and perhaps elsewhere in Africa.'[93]
Similarly, after the failure of the Bangladeshi government to build sufficient
shelters to protect its population from a devastating cyclone in 1991, a
leader in a liberal British newspaper suggested that 'neo-colonialism' might
be the only answer: 'If the government of Bangladesh is too muddled and
inept, as well as too poor, to build such shelters, then some foreign agency
should intervene and build them directly. This is called neo-colonialism . . .
But in this case it is hard to see why anyone should complain.'[94]

Twenty years ago colonialism was regarded as an unmitigated evil;
today it is a seen in many quarters as the only solution for the Third
World. For Western politicians the new climate in which 'neo-colonialism' can be seen, not as a denial of the interests of Third World states, but
as the assertion of the West's legitimate rights, has been welcome. As
former British foreign secretary Douglas Hurd put it, 'we are slowly
putting behind us a period of history when the West was unable to
express a legitimate interest in the developing world without being
accused of "neo-colonialism".'[95]

The transformation in the perceptions of the Third World has become a
new source of legitimacy for racial ideas. In contemporary discourse, the
West is presented as superior, the Third World as inferior, the West as
modern, the Third World as premodern, the West as democratic, the
Third World as lawless, and so on. The distinction between the two is
seen as the product of immutable cultural differences. A series of articles
in academic journals has suggested that 'cultural wars' between the West
and the Third World may replace the Cold War as the distinctive characteristic of the new millennium. Writing in the journal *Foreign Policy*,
William Lind has suggested that the 'defence of Western culture abroad'
should replace anticommunism as the defining feature of Western
foreign policy in the post-Cold War era. For Lind, the First and Second
World Wars and the Cold War were all examples of 'civil wars' because
they pitted one set of 'Western' nations against another. Now the West
faced a threat from other 'cultures' such as Africa, Asia, India and Islam,
from which it would have to defend itself. In an equally contentious
article in *Foreign Affairs*, Samuel Huntingdon similarly declared 'the
clash of civilisations' to be the key conflict in the post-Cold War era,
while in *International Affairs* Barry Buzan foresaw the 'clash of cultures'
creating 'a kind of societal cold war' as we move towards the new
millennium.[96]

As in other areas of contemporary racial discourse, the difference between the West and the non-Western world is expressed not in biological,
but in cultural terms. Nevertheless it is a divide conceived of as being as
absolute as any in the Victorian racial imagination. As we saw in Chapter
4, Victorian society viewed itself as a benign, civilising influence, making

sacrifices for the good of the sullen, slothful and ungrateful heathens in the colonies. The imperialist relationship between the West and its colonies cemented the idea that non-Western peoples were inferior to those of European and American stock. Given the natural superiority of the West, imperialism was seen less as conquest than as a humanitarian mission, a means of bringing civilisation to the uncivilised world. It was widely accepted that the Great Powers had a duty to introduce the rule of law to foreign parts, to suppress the slave trade, to put down piracy, to convert heathens to Christianity and through the development of trade to uplift Africans and Asians from what was considered to be degrading idleness. It was this idea of the West's moral responsibility arising out of its natural superiority that Rudyard Kipling captured in the idea of the 'White Man's burden'.

This rosy vision of the benefits of imperialism, as well as the assertion of natural superiority, was gradually undermined through the twentieth century. By the postwar period such a view was no longer tenable. A number of factors, which we discussed earlier in the book, were important in effecting this transformation. The three key developments important for our discussion here are the undermining of the Western claim to be the arbiters of civilised values, the growing anti-colonial revolt in the Third World and the impact of the Cold War.

The actions of the imperialist powers themselves undermined their claim to an inherent superiority. After the horrors of the Holocaust, the deathcamps, the dropping of nuclear bombs on Hiroshima and Nagasaki, it was hard to argue that the West should be responsible for setting standards of civilised behaviour. The Japanese victory against Russia in 1905, and its humiliation of Britain in Singapore during the Second World War, had tremendous impact on anti-colonial struggles, undermining the notion of the invincibility of the White Man. The success of nationalist movements in the Third World both sapped further faith in Western superiority and gave the lie to the idea that Africans and Asians could not manage their own affairs.

Finally, and perhaps most importantly, the onset of the Cold War in the late forties helped transform the relationship between the West and the Third World. The support that the Soviet Union gave to the ideas of racial equality and national self-determination won Moscow widespread support in the former Western colonies. Terrified that the newly emergent nations of Africa and Asia would be drawn into the Soviet bloc, the Western powers were forced publicly to adopt the same ideals and to acquiesce to the process of decolonisation. At the same time the very existence of the Soviet Union gave expression to the possibility of an alternative social system to the West which spurred many liberation movements. In many cases the Soviet Union also gave moral, and occasionally, military assistance to Third World movements.

The consequence of all this was, at the ideological level, acceptance in public of the concepts of equality and of national sovereignty. At a practical level these developments led to the process of decolonisation, a process that for the first time allowed the Third World a voice on the world stage. As never before advocates of the imperial ideal found themselves on the defensive. The West was forced to accommodate to nationalist forces in Africa, Asia and the Middle East. Just as the enforced liberalism of the postwar political climate constrained the public discourse on race and immigration, so it helped shape public perceptions of the Third World. Third World countries were now regarded as independent states with the right to national sovereignty and the privilege to be heard in the international political arena.

The tarnishing of the imperial ideal, the impact of the Cold War and the rise of Third World liberation movements all acted as checks to the idea of a beneficent imperialism, but they never extinguished it entirely. The ideas underlying the notion of the imperial ideal were simply held at arm's length by the *realpolitik* of the Cold War era. Throughout this period, the spectre of Third World primitiveness and backwardness constantly reasserted itself in Western discourse. In the fifties the Mau Mau rebellion in Kenya was presented by Western politicians and press as evidence of the barbarism that inhabited the African psyche. The Congo crisis of 1960 again seemed to provide confirmation of the real nature of African people. As Rupert Emerson remarked, 'for many Americans the entire Congo experience, and the murder of hostages in particular, had a drastic effect in rearousing the image of Africans as a savage and primitive people'.[97] In the seventies the image of the 'Third World terrorist' caught the public and media imagination. More recently, issues such as Islamic fundamentalism, drug cartels and ethnic warfare have all been manipulated to heighten fears about the Third World. As the influence of the Soviet Union waned in the eighties, and particularly since the end of the Cold War, these underlying sentiments about Third World barbarism have been fully drawn out.

If the onset of the Cold War gave the Third World a voice on the world stage, the end of the Cold War rolled back the political terrain of the postwar years. As Oxford academic John Casey has observed, Western 'deference' to the Third World in the postwar years was largely a pragmatic response to the Cold War. With the demise of communism, the West is no longer constrained in its attitudes:

The deference liberals in the West have shown towards the various nationalisms of the Third World could be understood, not as the application of highminded principle but as part of the Western, and especially American, strategy of wooing those who might otherwise succumb to communist blandishments.

But, along with the collapse of Soviet communism, the old colonial powers, along with America, can now do what they like. There is no longer any need to take seriously things like Arab nationalism, or the allegedly unjust divisions imposed on the Arab world by the colonial powers.[98]

Ideas of Western superiority and of Third World inferiority that were only hinted at previously are now being openly developed. One academic review of the relationship between the West and the Third World in the post-Cold War era observes that as the 'euphoria of independence has faded' for Third World states, so the 'reality of continued inferiority has reasserted itself'.[99] Another notes that 'the West is now more secure and confident in the superiority of its values than it has been at any time since the end of the Second World War'.[100]

The problems of African societies are portrayed as the specific products of African culture or the African mentality. Many argue that the attempts of Third World states to modernise have been misplaced as the people of the Third World have remained stubbornly premodern. One account of West Africa has described the area as caught in a web of 'premodern formlessness',[101] while an editorial in an American newspaper considered that Third World pretensions to modernity were simply a 'mask' beneath which hid ancient ethnic divisions and tribal customs:

In the Third World, there had been grand ideas of new states and social contracts among communities, post-colonial dreams of what men and women could do on their own. There were exalted notions of Indian nationalism, Pan-Arabism and the like. Ethnicity hid, draped in the colours of modern nationalism, hoping to keep the ancestors – and the troubles – at bay. But the delusions could not last. What was India? The India of its secular founders – or the 'Hindu Raj' of the militant fundamentalists? What exactly did the compact communities of Iraq– the Kurds, the Sunnis, the Shias – have in common? The masks have fallen, the tribes have stepped to the fore.[102]

The reversion to tribalism and savagery is an enduring motif in contemporary discussion of the Third World. *Newsweek* described tribalism as 'an ancient plague' which 'continues to afflict the people of sub-Saharan Africa'.[103] According to David Kaplan, the examples of 'the chetniks in Serbia, "technicals" in Somalia, Tontons Macoutes in Haiti, or soldiers in Sierra Leone' show that 'in places where the Western Enlightenment has not penetrated, and where there has always been mass poverty, people find liberation in violence'. He adds that 'the intense savagery of the fighting' in the Third World indicates that 'a large number of people on this planet, to whom the comfort and stability of a middle class life is

entirely unknown, find war and a barracks existence mere a step up than
a step down'.[104] Military historian Martin von Creveld believes that
Third World societies show examples of 'reprimitivised man'.[105]

The idea that peoples of the Third World remain in thrall to ancient
urges was a particularly strong theme in the discussion of the Rwandan
tragedy which unfolded in 1994. In the summer of that year, Rwanda
descended into a bloody civil war between the majority Hutu and minority Tutsi populations. Thousands were killed, often brutally, and
several hundred thousand defeated Hutus fled to refugee camps in
neighbouring Zaire.

The roots of the conflict between Hutus and Tutsis lie in colonial policy
and in the postcolonial relationship between Rwanda and the West. The
very division of the Rwandan into Hutus and Tutsis is largely the product of colonial rule.[106] Media descriptions of the civil war, however,
preferred to portray it as an incomprehensible horror, the venting of an
ancient bloodlust. In the hands of Western journalists Rwanda became a
symbol of bestiality, terror and evil. The Hutus in particular were singled
out as a people for whom the most monstrous of acts came naturally.

Reports from Rwanda described Hutu soldiers laughing as they casually dismembered their living victims and of Western peacekeepers
finding bodies of Tutsi children with their penises rammed into their
mouths.[107] The reports suggest that such actions were the products of an
incomprehensible predilection for savagery. 'Conflict was ingrained in
precolonial Africa', suggested *Sunday Times* columnist Barbara Amiel,
and now it had resurfaced in the postcolonial world. Another journalist
suggested that the Hutu people could not tell the difference between
right and wrong because they found it 'more natural to tell lies than tell
the truth'. The Kinyarwandan dictionary, he wrote, 'does not include a
word that is equivalent to our concept for truth, and it is said that a
Rwandan boy comes of age when he can lie convincingly to his grand-
mother'. As a result 'In Rwanda, deceit and the nurturing of hatred is far
more institutionalised and sophisticated than in Europe' and the 'dehumanisation' of the people 'begins at birth'.[108] For one television reporter
the people of Rwanda were so dehumanised that they compared unfa-
vourably to the local gorillas: 'While the people of Rwanda have
plumbed the depths of bestial savagery, these gentle noble beasts have
survived with their dignity intact.'[109]

Rwandans, then, are a people who are not really human, who are worse
than beasts, who have an ingrained tendency to violence, who do not
have 'our' moral capacities. Not only is the division between 'us' and
'them' clear, but the tendency to treat 'them' not simply as different but
as less than fully human harks back painfully to the racial imagination of
the Victorians. Contemporary writers may eschew the biological rhetoric
of nineteenth-century racial science but in the new discourse of imperial-

ism the world is divided into two as absolutely as in the old discourse of race.

Drawing on Francis Fukuyama's 'end of history' thesis,[110] David Kaplan argues that we are 'entering a bifurcated world': 'Part of the globe is inhabited by Hegel's and Fukuyama's Last Man, healthy, well fed, and pampered by technology. The other, larger, part is inhabited by Hobbes's First Man condemned to a life that is "poor, nasty, brutish, and short".'[111] The Last Man, Kaplan adds, lives 'in cities and suburbs in which the environment has been mastered and ethnic animosities have been quelled by bourgeois prosperity' while the First Man is 'stuck in history', living in 'shantytowns where attempts to rise above poverty, cultural dysfunction, and ethnic strife' are 'doomed'. The Last Man will be able to master the challenges of the future; the First Man will not. Thomas Fraser Homer-Dixon, head of the Peace and Cultural Conflict Studies Programme at the University of Toronto, describes the division of the world with a telling metaphor:

> Think of a stretch limo in the potholed streets of New York City, where homeless beggars live. Inside the limo are the air-conditioned post-industrial regions of North America, Europe and the emerging Pacific Rim, and a few other isolated places, with their trade summitry and computer-information highways. Outside is the rest of mankind going in a completely different direction.[112]

The distinction between First Man and Last Man, historical and posthistorical societies, premodern and modern cultures, interprets the division between the West and the non-Western world as something inherent in the nature of those societies and peoples. The different destinies of the two worlds do not lie, as they did in Kipling's days, in biology but in culture or civilisation. Western Enlightenment has allowed the Last Man to overcome his animal drives and desires and enter the stretch limo. The incapacity of the First Man to embrace modernity dooms the people of the Third World to be slaves to nature.

Homer-Dixon's analogy about the stretch-limo in the pot-holed streets of New York suggests the fear of the barbarism abroad is intimately bound up with the fear of the collapse of values at home. Just as the Victorian debate about the inferiority of the colonial peoples was a transmutation of the fear of the domestic masses, so today the demonisation of the Third World arises to a large extent from the transposition to the international stage of domestic fears. The impulse to racialise social divisions has emerged from underlying insecurities about Western society.

In a speech in Britain at the end of 1993, former US president Ronald Reagan stressed the need to establish a new moral purpose for the West in the post-Cold War era. The end of the Cold War, he admitted, 'has robbed much of the West of its common uplifting purpose.' The result was a sense of moral drift in Western societies. How, asked Reagan, could the West rediscover a common purpose? By uniting, he said, 'to impose civilised standards of behaviour on those who flout every measure of decency' – and pointing to Africa as an example.

The West needs an 'uplifting purpose', suggested Reagan, which – like the old fight against the 'evil empire' – can be used to galvanise public opinion. One way of understanding the tendency to treat the Third World as the embodiment of darkness, and to portray Third World people as primitive and backward, needing the civilising influence of the West – the tendency to *racialise* the division between the West and the Third World – is that by turning events in Africa or Asia into a sort of morality play, Western politicians are attempting to give a sense of moral purpose to their own societies.

8

Universalism, Humanism and the Discourse of Race

A few weeks after the riot that shook Los Angeles in May 1992, I gave a lecture on racism in America to a group of students at a north London college. The audience was largely young and black. In the discussion that followed, there was a lively debate over my view that the fragmentation of American society into competing ethnic groups – African-Americans, Hispanic-Americans, Korean-Americans, and so on – was a fatal blow to the struggle for black rights. Almost the entire audience disagreed. 'African-Americans', one student explained, 'are different. Our problems are different, our experiences are different, our history is different and our culture is different. We have to gain respect ourselves before we can unite with other people.'

Here was summed up the core ideas that underpin much of current radical thinking on race: first, that social groups define themselves by their history and identity; second, that the particular history and identity of each group sets them apart from other social groups; third, that it is important to recognise this plurality of differences as a positive aspect of society today; and finally, that the struggle for racial equality takes the form of a struggle for group identity.

The 'assertion of difference' has become, for many radicals, the principal dynamic in society today. 'The emergence of new subjects, new genders, new ethnicities, new regions, new communities', claims sociologist Stuart Hall, has given hitherto invisible groups 'the means to speak for themselves for the first time'.[1] Radicals such as Hall have welcomed the contemporary flowering of ethnic differences as an expression, not of social discord, but of a new form of democracy through which sections of society previously silenced have been given voice. In Britain for example, the 'new ethnicities', Hall writes, posit a 'non-coercive and a more diverse conception of ethnicity, to set against the embattled, hegemonic conception of "Englishness" which ... stabilises so much of the dominant political and cultural discourses'.[2]

During the eighties, the so-called 'politics of difference' emerged to provide an intellectual and philosophical rationale for the kind of arguments expressed by my north London students. The advocates of the politics of difference argue that we are living in a form of society

217

radically different from that of half a century ago – a postindustrial or, more fashionably, *postmodern* society. Though postmodernism is an ambiguous term and few have tried to define it with any great clarity, for most of its theorists the postmodern society is characterised by its very heterogeneity and diversity.

The postmodern condition is one in which the 'grand narratives' have become discredited.[3] Grand narratives are attempts to grasp society in its totality, to give coherence to our observations of the objective world. Nationalism is one such grand narrative because it attempts to impose a collective sense of belonging on disparate individuals. Postmodernists reject all the 'great collective social identities of class, of race, of nation, of gender, and of the West'.[4] They reject Marxism too, and in fact any form of emancipatory theory the aim of which is the *total* liberation of humankind.

For postmodernists, the Enlightenment project of pursuing a rational, scientific understanding of the natural and social world, and of creating a universal outlook from fragmented experience, has failed. It has failed because no one can grasp society as a whole; the world is too complex and too varied to be subsumed under a single, totalising theory. 'Everybody intuitively knows that everyday life is so complex', argues Kobena Mercer, 'that no singular belief system or Big Story can hope to explain it all'.[5] There can be no single theoretical discourse, say postmodernists, which can encompass all forms of social relations and every mode of political practice. Indeed some reject the idea of theory altogether: '[T]heory is simply that which is labelled theory by institutions that empower themselves to do so.'[6]

Not only are totalising theories a fantasy, they are a dangerous fantasy. Universalism is a 'Eurocentric' viewpoint, a means of imposing Euro-American ideas of rationality and objectivity on other peoples. Universalism is racist because it denies the possibility of non-European viewpoints. The intellectual arrogance of universalism, argue such critics, has led to the attempt to eliminate not just non-European thought, but also non-Aryan people. The science and technology that flowed from Enlightenment rationalism was inevitably tainted with the spirit of savagery. Not just for postmodernists, but for many postwar social theorists, the road that began with Enlightenment rationalism ends in Nazi deathcamps. 'Concentration camps, mass exterminations, world wars, and atom bombs are no "relapse into barbarism"', wrote Herbert Marcuse, 'but the unrepressed implementation of the achievements of modern science, technology and domination'.[7]

Hostility to universalism has led many contemporary social theorists to celebrate plurality or fragmentation. Social fragmentation, they argue, is a way of giving voice to those who have been previously excluded from the political arena. 'The idea that all groups have a right to speak for themselves, in their own voice, and have that voice accepted as authentic and legitimate', notes David Harvey, 'is essential to the pluralistic stance of postmodernism'.[8] The politics of difference has evolved as the intellectual embodiment of social fragmentation.

The advocates of plurality argue that the assertion of difference helps undermine the grip of the dominant groups over political and social discourse. Traditional politics, they say, serves to silence the voices of the weak and the oppressed, to consign their histories and experiences to the margins and to subsume all experience to the dominant outlook. Because British history is written by those who want to create a singular national identity it denies the experiences and histories of, for example, black people who are not part of that singular identity. By 'decentring' discourse and giving hitherto marginalised groups centre-stage, it is possible to create a more democratic form of social dialogue.

This embrace of difference obviously stands in stark contrast with the argument that I have developed in this book. Whereas I have argued that it is the degradation of universalism that has given rise to the discourse of race, poststructuralist and postmodernist theories take universalism itself to be the source of a racial outlook. Where I have placed stress on ideas of difference as lying at the heart of racial theories, many contemporary theorists regard the right to be different as an essential part of any antiracist strategy. I want in these final two chapters, therefore, to engage with poststructuralist and postmodern theories of difference. I want through such critical engagement both to reveal the flaws of contemporary theories of difference and to rearticulate the main themes of my thesis.

I will in the course of this chapter be examining the ideas of a number of writers from a variety of theoretical outlooks and academic disciplines – structuralism and poststructuralism, Marxism and deconstructionism, phenomenology and postmodernism. My intention is not to erase the differences between the authors and outlooks, nor to ignore the often heated debates that have taken place between the various protagonists. Rather it is to demonstrate the common threads that link the diverse strands of contemporary theory and to suggest that, for the purposes of our discussion of racial theories, these commonalities far outweigh in importance the differences that are often expressed. In this spirit I shall use the terms 'poststructuralist' and 'postmodernist' interchangeably to refer to discourses and theorists influenced by the work of such as Claude Lévi-Strauss, Jacques Lacan, Jacques Derrida, Michel Foucault and similar thinkers. Their work, though varied and often conflictual, is characterised by a number of themes, including a critique of reason, a hostility to universalism, a rejection of humanism, an antirealist epistemology and a radical relativism. I have not sought to provide a comprehensive critique of these ideas but rather simply to engage with them in such a fashion that the main themes of my own thesis are clarified.

THE WEST AND ITS 'OTHERS'

'The world begins to be decolonised', Stuart Hall writes, at 'that moment when the unspoken discovered that they had a history which they could speak' and that they had 'languages other than the languages of the master'.[9] The central argument in contemporary theories of difference is the idea that Enlightenment discourse, by establishing universal norms and by equating such norms with European societies and cultures, has ensured the silence of non-European peoples and cultures. 'Without significant exception', Edward Said has argued,

> the universalising discourses of modern Europe and the United States assume the silence, willing or otherwise, of the non-European world. There is incorporation; there is inclusion; there is direct rule; there is coercion. But there is only infrequently an acknowledgement that the colonised people should be heard from, their ideas known.[10]

Western science and philosophy, such critics believe, have established a form of knowledge whereby non-Western societies and cultures are represented solely in terms of the categories of Western thought, and in which Western society acts as a standard against which all other societies are judged. This inevitably leads to the silencing of other voices. At the same time the differences between Western and non-Western cultures are rationalised through non-Western peoples being defined as the 'Others', distinguished solely through their antagonism to the dominant image of the 'self', and against whose peculiarities the self-image of the West is created. The result has been the acquisition of an aura of superiority for Western cultures and an imposition of a sense of inferiority upon non-Western ones.

From the Renaissance onwards, Stuart Hall explains, Europe began to define itself in relation to a new idea – 'the existence of many new "worlds" profoundly different from itself'.[11] This gave rise to the discourse of the Other, which 'represents what are in fact very differentiated (the different European cultures) as homogeneous (the West)'. Further 'it asserts that these different cultures are united by one thing: the fact that *they are all different from the Rest*'. At the same time the 'Other' (or the 'Rest' in Hall's terminology) 'though different among themselves, are represented as the same in the sense that they are all different from the West'.[12]

The sense of 'otherness' that Western discourse imposes on non-Western peoples and cultures is seen as the source of the modern ideas of race. 'The figure of the "Other"', writes Hall, was 'constructed as the absolute opposite, the negation of everything the West stood for'.[13] Through the representation of an absolute difference between the West and its Others, the idea of difference took on a racial form. '[R]ace emerged with and has served to define modernity by insinuating itself in various fashions into modernity's prevailing conceptions of moral personhood and subjectivity', David Goldberg believes. 'By working itself into the threads of liberalism's cloths just as that cloth was being woven, race and the various exclusions it licensed became naturalised in the Eurocentric visions of itself and its self-defined others, in its sense of Reason and rational direction.'[14]

Since the framework of 'the West and its Others' is so central to contemporary theories of the meaning of race, I want to examine more closely some of its assumptions. The concept of the Other was developed in the phenomenological tradition, particularly by Edmund Husserl, as a constitutive factor in the subject's self-image. The Other was conceived as the perceiving, conscious, meaning-conferring other person who helps, or forces, the conscious subject to define its own world picture and its view of its place in it. Through the work of writers such as Jean-Paul Sartre, Claude Lévi-Strauss, Jacques Lacan and Michel Foucault, the concept of the Other entered poststructuralist discourse.[15]

In poststructuralist discourse the Other is a social object, the difference against which the Self is measured. In Michel Foucault's seminal work, *Folie et Deraison,* lepers were the Others of medieval society, a prime source of contamination, whose exclusion from everyday life helped provide society with a sense of its normality. As leprosy became less common, so it was less able to play its previous symbolic role. Instead, argues Foucault, a new Other was born: those who were non-productive – the criminal, the homeless and, especially, the mad. 'A new leper is born', writes Foucault, 'who takes the place of the first.'[16]

The Other, then, is that which lies outside a particular culture or society's epistemological boundaries. Not only is everything beyond the boundary treated as the Other, but society requires an Other without which there can be no sense of Self. A single category that can encapsulate the idea of an object of study, an object of exclusion and an object through the perception of whose difference self-identity can be affirmed has proved very attractive in the study of race. Most contemporary studies define racial difference in terms of the Other.

The distinction between the West and its Other is, for many contemporary theorists, implicit in the categories of Enlightenment universalism. Stuart Hall has pointed how the establishment of the Other was fundamental to the development of Enlightenment thought:

This 'West and the Rest' discourse greatly influenced Enlightenment thinking . . . In Enlightenment discourse, the West was the model, the prototype and the measure of social progress. It was western progress, civilisation, rationality and development that were celebrated. And yet . . . without the Rest (or its own internal 'others') the West would not have been able to recognise and represent itself as the summit of human history. The figure of 'the Other', banished to the edge of the conceptual world and constructed as the absolute opposite, the negation, of everything which the West stood for, reappeared at the very centre of the discourse of civilisation, refinement, modernity and development in the West. 'The Other' was the 'dark' side – forgotten, repressed and denied; the reverse image of enlightenment and modernity.[17]

According to such critics, through the discourse of universalism the characteristics of the West and its Others were eternalised and the differences established as absolute. Thus Peter Hulme observes that Western understanding of non-Western cultures creates a distinction between 'self' and 'other' by 'establish[ing] characteristics as eternal verities immune from the irrelevances of the historical moment: "ferocious", "hostile" "truculent and vindictive" – these are present as innate characteristics irrespective of circumstances'.[18]

Many of these ideas have been central to my thesis in this book. I have argued, for instance, that the discourse of race helped recast social differences as natural ones, eternalising what were historically contingent features. I have argued, too, that in certain circumstances the notion of the 'other' has helped established a sense of self-identity. Despite this I want to argue that the framework of 'the West and its Others' is unhelpful in understanding the concept of race. The category of the Other is ahistorical and takes little account of the specificities of time and place in the creation of the discourse of race. Instead it steamrollers historical, social and geographical differences into a single discourse of 'the West and its Others'.

The category of the Other eternalises human modes of perception. It takes historically specific ways of constructing identity and endows them with an eternal validity. In *Britons*, her entertaining study of the development of British national identity, Linda Colley argues that the idea of being British arose in opposition to perceived enemies:

It was an invention forged above all by war. Time and time again, war with France brought Britons, whether they hailed from Wales or Scotland or England, into a confrontation with an obviously hostile Other and encouraged them to define themselves collectively against it . . . And, increasingly as the wars went on, they defined themselves in contrast to the colonial peoples they conquered, peoples who were manifestly alien in terms of culture, religion and colour . . . Britishness was superimposed over an array of internal differences in response to contact with the Other, and above all in response to conflict with the Other.[19]

Colley's reconstruction of the forging of British national identity seems to me to be largely correct, if somewhat one-sided. Indeed I argued in previous chapters that, in a similar fashion, contemporary British (and Western) identity is being recast in opposition to immigrants, the Third World, and other 'outsiders'.

What is fallacious in Colley's argument, however, is her assumption that the creation of national identity in the modern world should act as a template that is true for all time and all forms of identities: '[M]en and women decide who they are by reference to who and what they are not. Once confronted by an obviously alien "Them", an otherwise diverse community can become a reassuring or merely desperate "Us".'[20] This suggests that the perception of 'Them' and 'Us' is in some way an epistemological constant, built into human 'nature'. It is an argument that derives partly from the work of Claude Lévi-Strauss, who believed that the human brain operates by classifying the world in terms of pairs of opposites. Both pre-literate and modern societies, argued Lévi-Strauss, think of the world in terms of binary opposites: solid/liquid, clean/dirty, truth/lie, body/soul, white/black, male/female. One side of the opposition, for instance clean, or white, is privileged, or given positive affirmation, while the other, dirty or black, has negative connotations. The meaning of the positive element is generally established through the exclusion of the negative half. In other words, clean means 'not-dirty' and white means 'not-black'. This provides the epistemological template for thinking about the world exclusively in terms of Us and Them, or Self and Other.[21]

For Edward Said this epistemological constant has become the basis for the distinction between the West and its Others. The distinction is not simply epistemological but ontological, woven into the very being of the West. In *Culture and Imperialism* Said posits the existence of 'a fundamental ontological distinction between the West and the rest of the world' whose boundary we may consider 'absolute':

Throughout the exchange between Europeans and their 'others' that began systematically half a millennium ago, the one idea that has scarcely varied is that there is an 'us' and a 'them', each quite settled, clear, unassailably self-evident. As I discuss it in *Orientalism*, the division goes back to Greek thought about barbarians, but, whoever originated this kind of 'identity' thought, by the nineteenth century it had become the hallmark of imperialist cultures as well as those cultures trying to resist the encroachments of Europe.[22]

Having established a transhistorical, ontological distinction that collapses the subtleties of two millennia of history, Said subsequently reads history backwards, conceiving of the past in terms specific to the present so that all encounters between Europeans and their Others, whatever their form, comprise part of 'the distinction between the West and the rest of the world'. For instance, the acquisition of Ireland by England's Henry II in the twelfth century is deemed to be an imperialist conquest and the English nobility's attitudes towards the Irish is assumed to be racial in form:

> The high age of imperialism is said to have begun in the late 1870s, but in English-speaking realms it began well over seven hundred years before . . . Ireland was ceded by the Pope to Henry II of England in the 1150s; he himself came to Ireland in 1171. From that time on an amazingly persistent cultural attitude existed towards Ireland as a place whose inhabitants were a barbarian and degenerate race.[23]

Said does not tell us what it is about the Pope's award of Ireland to Henry II that is of the same moment as the European powers' scramble for Africa from the 1870s onwards. Nor does he explain in what way twelfth-century perceptions of the Irish show a continuity with nineteenth-century perceptions of Africans. That continuity is simply *assumed*. Such assumptions are rarely valid. Human consciousness is not static or innate but is constantly recreated through changing social and historical circumstances. Without investigating social phenomena in their specificity, we fall into the trap of projecting specifically contemporary values and judgements on to past epochs.

In Herman Melville's *Moby Dick* the narrator Ishmael observes sourly that 'a purse is but a rag unless you have something in it'. The outward appearance of something tells us little. Only through understanding an object or phenomenon in its context can we appreciate its content or meaning. This is particularly so with social phenomena, such as 'race'. 'A Negro is a Negro', wrote Marx. 'He only becomes a slave in certain circumstances'.[24] Possessing a black skin does not mean that one is a slave, nor indeed that one is an object of racism. However, we have a tendency to assume this because we mistakenly assume that the contemporary signification of blackness has always been so.

Take, for instance, the contemporary reading of Shakespeare's *Othello*. Today the play is generally taken to be an example of the racist outlook of the Elizabethan period.[25] Yet as C. L. R. James has pointed out, this interpretation is simply the product of our own 'race-ridden consciousness'. For Elizabethan audiences, what was important was not Othello's 'race' but the fact that he was a stranger:

> [Y]ou could strike out every single reference to his black skin and the play would be essentially the same. Othello's trouble is that he is an outsider. He is not a Venetian. He is a military bureaucrat, a technician hired to fight for Venice, a foreign country. The senate has no consciousness whatever of his colour. That is a startling fact but true. They haven't to make allowances for it. It simply has no place in their minds.[26]

The meaning of a black skin has not always been the same. Nor have the concepts of self and of difference. In the past people perceived of themselves and of others in very different fashion, indeed in ways that would strike us as irrational and incomprehensible. In Chapter 2 we saw how precapitalist, pre-Enlightenment views of difference resonated with ideas and fears we could barely conceive of today. We saw in the tale of Bemoin how it was possible for Europeans to regard the same African both as 'one of us' and as an 'other' depending literally on where he stood in relation to the mental map of Europe.

//We saw too how the idea of difference became transformed in the Enlightenment through the idea of equality and a single humanity. I argued in Chapter 3 that the discourse of race did not arise out of the categories of Enlightenment discourse but out of the relationship between Enlightenment thought and the social organisation of capitalism. The disparity between the abstract belief in equality and the reality of an unequal society slowly gave rise to the idea that differences were natural, not social. The emergence of the modern idea of race was predicated on a wide number of social, political and economic developments which I discussed in Chapters 3 and 4; the consequence of these developments was the degradation of the universalistic outlook.

We saw how the idea of race emerged not so much with reference to populations which were *external* to Western society, populations which were exotic or distant or physically distinct, but rather in relation to social gradations *within* European society. The modern discourse of race developed through the racialisation of social and class differences, through the attribution of racial inferiority to the lower orders of society – the 'dangerous classes'. Such attribution of inferiority came not from some imputed need to posit an image of self in opposition to an Other, but as a way of making sense of social differences.\\

The racial categories developed in relation to differences within European societies were subsequently transposed to the non-European world. I argued that there was a dialectical relationship between the two: the process of European modernisation established Europe's superiority over the non-Western world at the same time as it revealed the differences and divisions within European societies.

The coming of mass democracy, on the one hand, and of imperialist expansion, on the other, helped transform the nature of the discourse of race. It was at this point that racial difference became identified with the distinction between the West and the Rest. It was also at this point that the Western élites began to understand their own identity primarily in terms of the inferiority of others. This process, we saw, was the consequence of social, political and economic changes which undermined the optimism and self-belief of élite groups in Western society. This process of casting identity in opposition to an Other has become, as we saw in Chapter 7, a principal source of Western identity in the post-Cold War era. At the same time disillusionment with ideas of social progress, together with the impact of the Nazi experience, has helped recast the discourse of race, so that social differences are today explained more in cultural or moral terms than in biological ones.

We can see in this quick resumé of my argument in this book that it is simply not possible to understand the discourse of race within a single framework of the 'West and its Others'. Any such attempt not only disregards the complexities of the development of the discourse of race, but misreads the origins of race, transposing it from differences within Europe to differences between Europe and the non-European world.

There might appear to be a contradiction in this critique of the framework of the 'West and its Others'. On the one hand I am claiming that contemporary theorists of difference regard the idea of the Other as a product of Enlightenment universalism – in other words, as a specifically modern development. On the other hand, I am also arguing that theirs is an ahistoric understanding of the relationship between Self and Other in that they view the dichotomy as an epistemological constant. There is indeed a contradiction here, but it arises out of the very use of the idea of the Other. Poststructuralist and postmodernist discourse tend to regard the Other as both a product of post-Enlightenment philosophy and as a constant in human perception. The conflation of these two ideas in fact plays a major part in the confusion about the relationship between Enlightenment discourse and the discourse of race.

We can understand better both the ahistoricity of the concept of the Other, and the contradictions it embodies, by looking in some depth at a text that was key to developing the framework of the 'West and its Others' – Edward Said's *Orientalism*. Published in 1978, the book became very influential in its discussion of the way in which Western understanding of the Orient – by which Said meant the Middle East – imposed upon it a reality created in the West. The confusions and contradictions in *Orientalism* reflect the broader problems with poststructuralist theories of difference.

ORIENTALISM AND AHISTORICISM

In *Orientalism* Said argues that Western historians, philologists and philosophers have fabricated a complex set of representations about the Orient which for the West have effectively become the Orient. Said suggests that the creation of the Orient in literary, historical and scholarly accounts established a discourse through which the West could assert political and military control over the Orient:

> My contention is that, without examining Orientalism as a discourse, one cannot possibly understand the enormously systematic discipline by which European culture was able to manage – and even produce – the Orient politically, sociologically, militarily, ideologically, scientifically and imaginatively during the post-Enlightenment period. Moreover, so authoritative a position did Orientalism have that I believe that no one writing, thinking, or acting on the Orient could do so without taking account of the limitations on thought and action imposed by Orientalism. In brief, because of Orientalism, the Orient was not (and is not) a free subject of thought and action . . . [T]his book . . . also tries to show that European culture gained in strength and identity by setting itself off against the Orient as a sort of surrogate and even underground self.[27]

For Said, then, Orientalism constitutes a body of thought which both limits how those in the West are able to think about the Orient and allows the West to establish physical power over it. The discourse of Orientalism establishes a dualism between the West and the Orient which strengthens Western cultures and imprisons those of the Orient. This dualism shapes the reality of the Orient for the peoples of both the West and the Orient itself.

Despite such major claims there is, however, a total lack of precision in Said's work as to what he means by 'Orientalism' and what are the historic and epistemic boundaries that delimit it as a discourse. Said himself observes in his Introduction that 'by Orientalism I mean several things'. But these 'several things' are often so contradictory, and sometimes mutually exclusive, that the term 'Orientalism' is rendered meaningless.

Central to Said's argument would seem to be the idea that Orientalism is a post-Enlightenment discourse, the product of the Enlightenment's universalising categories and one which allowed the West to establish colonial power over the Orient:

> Taking the late eighteenth century as a very roughly defined starting point Orientalism can be discussed and analysed as the corporate institution for dealing with the Orient – dealing with it by making

statements about it, authorizing views of it, describing it, by teaching it, settling it, ruling over it: in short, Orientalism as a Western style for dominating, restructuring and having authority over the Orient.[28]

But Said also argues that 'the demarcation between the Orient and the West . . . already seems bold by the time of the *Iliad*.' In Aeschylus's *The Persians* and Euripides's *The Bacchae*, 'Asia speaks through and by virtue of the European imagination, which is depicted as victorious over Asia, that hostile "other" world beyond the seas.' The two plays, writes Said, distil the distinctions between Europe and the Orient which 'will remain essential motifs of European imaginative geography':

> A line is drawn between the two continents. Europe is powerful and articulate; Asia is defeated and distant . . . It is Europe that articulates the Orient; this articulation is the prerogative, not of a puppet master, but of a genuine creator, whose life giving power represents, animates, constitutes the otherwise silent and dangerous space beyond familiar boundaries . . . Secondly there is the motif of the Orient as insinuating danger. Rationality is undermined by Eastern excesses, those mysteriously attractive opposites to what seem to be normal values.[29]

Orientalism now no longer seems to be the specific product of Enlightenment categories but originates at the very dawn of what Said conceives of as European civilisation. Within the earliest of Athenian plays appear the concepts that were to be articulated later by the Enlightenment *philosophes*. This allows Said to suggest that Orientalism 'can accommodate Aeschylus, say, and Victor Hugo, Dante and Karl Marx'.[30]

Any concept of a discourse that can accommodate four writers as historically, politically and philosophically diverse as Aeschylus, Hugo, Dante and Marx can but be profoundly ahistoric. The specificities of Aeschylus's understanding of the barbarian, Dante's view of Islam and Marx's analysis of India disappear beneath the swamp of an all-encompassing 'Orientalism'. And if the concept of the non-Western world as the 'Other' derives from the universalising impulse of the Enlightenment, yet is premised on 'a line . . . drawn between two continents' by Ancient Greek playwrights and philosophers, in what way is Enlightenment discourse specific to the Enlightenment? Said seems here to posit a view of 'Western thought' essentially untouched since its creation.

The ahistoricism of Orientalism leads Said to mimic the very discursive structures against which he polemicises. Said creates a 'Western tradition' which runs in an unbroken line from the Ancient Greeks through the Renaissance, the Enlightenment to modernism. It is a tradition which defines a coherent Western identity through a specific set of beliefs and values which remain in their essence unchanged through two millennia of European and Western history. This of course is the myth of 'Western civilisation' propagated by many an advocate of Western superiority, from Gobineau to Goebbels and beyond.

In reality there is no such continuous tradition. The idea that modern Western culture has its roots in Greek learning is, as Martin Bernal has shown, the product of post-Enlightenment Romantic thought.[31] Nineteenth-century racial discourse expunged from history the roots of Greek learning in Afro-Asiatic cultures and the Enlightenment's debt to Arab learning, and fabricated instead the myth of an organic 'Western' tradition from ancient Greece to modern Europe.

Said not only accepts the reality of such a tradition, but he also erases, as Aijaz Ahmad observes, the fractures, conflicts and divisions within European societies and treats Europe as a homogenous maker of history:

> It is rather remarkable how constantly and comfortably Said speaks . . . of *a* Europe, or the West, as a self-identical, fixed being which has always had an essence and a project, an imagination and a will; and of the 'Orient' as its object – textually, militarily, and so on. He speaks of the West, or Europe, as the one that produces that knowledge, the East as the object of that knowledge. In other words, he seems to posit stable subject–object identities, as well as ontological and epistemological distinctions between the two. In what sense, then, is Said himself not an Orientalist – or at least as Sadek el-Azm puts it, an 'Orientalist-in-reverse'? Said quite justifiably accuses the 'Orientalist' of essentialising the Orient, but his own essentialising of the 'West' is equally remarkable. In the process Said of course gives us the same 'Europe' – unified, self-identical, transhistorical, textual – which is always rehearsed for us in the sort of literary criticism which traces its own pedigree from Aristotle to T. S. Eliot.[32]

For Said a European, by virtue of being European, must necessarily be racist. '[E]very European', he writes, 'in what he could say about the Orient, was consequently a racist, an imperialist, and almost totally ethnocentric.'[33] *Every* European? Surely even Gobineau or Renan, Chamberlain or Knox would have been somewhat more circumspect about making such sweeping statements. As Ahmad observes, 'These ways of dismissing entire civilisations as diseased formations are unfortunately far too familiar to us, who live on the other side of the colonial divide, from the history of imperialism itself.'[34]

Elsewhere, Said himself has argued cogently against such ahistoric attitudes:

> If you know in advance that the African or Iranian or Chinese or Jewish or German experience is fundamentally integral, coherent,

separate, and therefore comprehensible only to Africans, Iranians, Chinese, Jews or Germans you first of all posit as essential something which, I believe, is both historically created and the result of interpretation – namely the existence of Africanness, Jewishness, of Germanness, or for that matter Orientalism or Occidentalism.[35]

Yet such cautionary reminders of the dangers of an unhistorical approach are all too often lost amidst the rush to establish that the categories of Western thought are in and of themselves imbricated with racial thought. A few chapters on from his warning against thinking of cultures as 'fundamentally integral, coherent, separate', Said argues that there exists a 'fundamental ontological distinction between the West and the rest of the world' and that 'we may consider' 'the geographical and cultural boundaries between the West and its non-Western peripheries' as 'absolute'.[36]

DISCOURSE, POWER AND KNOWLEDGE

The filiation between the discourse of difference and that of race that is suggested by the ahistoricism of both is strengthened by the idealism which permeates contemporary radical thinking about race. Rather than being rooted in the real world, discourse often appears, as Salman Rushdie writes of the migrant imagination in *Shame,* to have 'floated up from history, from memory, from Time'. We can see this quite clearly in Said's work, in which the relationship between the discourse of Orientalism and the reality of the West's domination of the Orient is often obscure.

At first sight it might seem strange to accuse Said of ignoring the social and material realities which gave rise to the discourse of Orientalism. After all, one of the significant features of *Orientalism* is its insistence that literary and scholarly criticism must take into account the context of imperialism which has shaped their objects of study. Yet such are the contradictions within Said's work that one sometimes wishes he himself would take heed of his strictures on the need for contextual reading.

On the one hand Said holds that Orientalism is a representation, a fabrication by Western writers and travellers of an Orient that has no real existence. On the other hand he argues that knowledge contained within the discourse of Orientalism played a key part in allowing Europe to subjugate the non-Western world. But if the discourse of Orientalism was effective in allowing Western politicians and generals to take actual control over the Orient, then it must have been more than simply a 'representation'. As Robert Young has asked, 'How can Said argue that the "Orient" is just a representation, if he also wants to claim that

"Orientalism" provided the necessary knowledge for actual colonial conquest?'[37]

Said attempts to circumvent this problem by arguing that the texts of Orientalism 'can *create* not only knowledge but the reality they appear to describe'.[38] What does Said mean by this? He could be suggesting that the reality of the Orient is *contained* within the texts of Orientalism. If so, this would seem to be a highly textualised understanding of reality, especially coming from an author who has been critical of Orientalism precisely for its textuality. If indeed the texts contained the reality, there would be no need for contextual reading, for the context would lie in the texts themselves.

Alternatively Said could mean that the texts of Orientalism *impose* on the Orient its reality. When Orientalists conceive of the Orient in a particular fashion, the Orient succumbs to that vision. David Goldberg clearly reads Said in this way:

> Naming the racial Other, for all intents and purposes, *is* the Other. There is, as Said makes clear in the case of the Oriental, no Other behind or beyond the invention of the Other in the Other's name. / These practices of naming and knowledge construction deny all autonomy to those so named and imagined, extending power, control, authority and domination over them. To extend Said's analysis of the 'Oriental' to the case of race in general, social science of the Other establishes the limits of knowledge about the Other, for the Other is just what the racialised social science knows.[39] /

Goldberg transforms European colonialists into the witchdoctors of modernity who, through the invocation of 'names', extend 'power, control, authority and domination' over their subject peoples. A very potent magic indeed. In Salman Rushdie's novel *The Satanic Verses*, one of the central characters, Saladin, finds himself incarcerated in a detention centre for illegal immigrants. Saladin discovers that his fellow inmates have been transformed into beasts – water buffaloes, snakes, manticores. He himself has become a hairy goat. How do they do it, Saladin asks a fellow prisoner. 'They describe us', comes the reply, 'that's all. They have the power of description and we succumb to the pictures they construct.' Similarly Said and Goldberg seem to be suggesting that the only role allotted to the 'Other' is to succumb to the picture constructed by the Western 'self'. It is a picture of the relationship between the West and its Other in which the Other is transformed into simply a passive victim.

Elsewhere Said has claimed that 'Representation itself [keeps] the subordinate subordinate, the inferior inferior.'[40] But in what way is this an understanding of the Orient different from that contained in the discourse of Orientalism itself, an understanding of the Orient as a passive, submissive Other moulded entirely by the history-making West? Said and Goldberg complain that the universalising discourse of the West silences the voices of the Other. Yet it is Said and Goldberg themselves who silence the Other by conceiving of it as a compliant, inert object constituted solely by Western knowledge. The West produces its image of the Orient as the Other, and the Orient meekly accepts the image that is constructed.

Whichever way we might interpret them, Said's comments also raise, as Ahmad notes, the question of the very relationship between Orientalism and colonialism:

> In a revealing use of the word 'delivered', Said remarks at one point that Orientalism *delivered* the Orient to colonialism, so that colonialism begins to appear as a product of Orientalism itself – indeed, as the realisation of the project already inherent in Europe's perennial project of inferiorizing the Orient first in discourse and then in colonisation.[41]

For Said, Orientalism seems to be not the product of social developments or material forces but their creator. Just as the West is ontologically incapable of understanding the non-Western world except as its Other, so the West is ontologically driven to impose its power over the rest of the globe. Said's argument that 'psychologically, Orientalism is a form of paranoia',[42] an argument that he repeats frequently, suggests that he views Orientalism as the compulsion of a diseased European psyche. The drive to colonisation arises out of a psychological need in the Western mind, a need that is already present at the time of the Greeks with their view of the barbarian Other, and which becomes manifest through post-Enlightenment colonial power. Having detached the discourse of race from real social movement, Said provides us with a theory of race and imperialism which sounds like nothing so much as the Romantic vision of a people's destiny unfolding through history, except that where the Romantics saw this as the positive affirmation of a people's heritage, Said regards it as the destructive consequence of a deranged mind.

There is yet another problem that arises from Said's idealism. 'The real issue' he claims, 'is whether there can be a true representation of anything, or whether any or all representations, because they are representations, are embedded first in the language and then in the culture, institutions and political ambience of the representer.' Said plumps for the second definition and argues that 'a representation is *eo ipso* implicated, intertwined, embedded, interwoven with a great many other things beside "truth", which is itself a representation'. Representations cannot be 'truthful', and 'truth' is but a representation, constituted 'by some common history, tradition, universe of discourse'.[43] Having established that Orientalists' 'objective discoveries . . . are and always have been conditioned by the fact that its truths, like any truths delivered by language, are embodied in language', Said then quotes Nietzsche to the effect that language is but 'a mobile army of metaphors, metonyms and anthropomorphisms' and that 'truths are but illusions about which one has forgotten that this is what they are.'[44]

But if true representations are not possible, and truth itself is but a representation, then in what way can we criticise Orientalism? After all, one representation is as good as another and there is no objective means by which to challenge the picture that Orientalists provide us of the Orient. The relativism of Said's outlook (a relativism with which, as we shall see later, he is not entirely comfortable) denies the possibility of challenging the very discourse he despises.

The problem in comprehending the relationship between the representation and the real arises from the concept of 'discourse' which Said derives from Michel Foucault. I have used the term 'discourse' throughout this book in a relatively loose sense, meaning a coherent body of knowledge which shapes and limits the ways of understanding a particular topic. Central to Foucault's concept of a discourse, however, is the idea that social facts can never be conceived of as being 'true' or 'false'. The very language we use to describe facts imposes truth or falsity upon those facts. Hence it is the discourse itself that creates the truth about a particular topic and competing discourses create competing truths. Truth lies not in the relationship between discourse and social reality but in the relationship between discourse and power. It is the relationship between discourse and power which decides which one of the many truths is accepted as *the* truth. For Foucault 'power produces knowledge' and 'power and knowledge directly imply one another' because 'there is no power relation without the correlative constitution of a field of knowledge, nor any knowledge that does not presuppose and constitute . . . power relations'.[45]

For Foucault, a discourse is a way of constituting power, and is at the same time verified by that power. The knowledge which a discourse produces constitutes a kind of power, exercised over those who are 'known'. When that knowledge is exercised in practice, those who are known in a particular way will be subject to it. Those who produce the discourse also have the power to make it true, to enforce its validity:

Truth isn't outside power . . . [I]t induces regular effects of power. Each society has its regime of truth, its 'general politics' of truth; that is, the types of discourse which it accepts and makes function as true; the mechanisms and instances which enable one to distinguish between 'true' and 'false' statements; the means by which each is sanctioned; and the techniques and procedures accorded value in the acquisition of truth; the status of those who are charged with saying what counts as true.[46]

But what does Foucault mean by 'power'? He is very vague about this. Power, for Foucault, cannot be conceived of in class or social terms. It is not the property of an individual or a class, nor does it emanate from an identifiable source or institution, such as the state. Power is simply omnipresent. Its threads are everywhere and it is only through power that 'reality' is constituted. Given the omnipresence of power, and its role in constituting reality, Foucault is forced to conceive of power relations in arbitrary terms. Power struggles do not emanate from social or historical movement, but simply pit all against all: 'There aren't immediately given subjects of the struggle, one the proletariat the other the bourgeoisie. Who fights against whom? We all fight each other. And there is always within each of us something that fights something else.'[47] I shall return to the consequences of Foucault's understanding of power later. What is important now is to grasp how belief in the arbitrary nature of both power and truth leads to an extreme relativism. If power is simply the constituting element in all social systems, how can we choose between one society and another? And if a discourse makes its own truth, whose validity is given by the strength of an arbitrary power, how are we to distinguish between different representations or discourses? We can neither relate ideas and representations to real social movements, nor can we pass value judgements on different sets of ideas.

The logic of the Foucauldian argument would lead us to suppose that it is the very act of attempting to establish an objective truth that is the problem. And this indeed is the argument that the more extreme proponents of a relativistic outlook use against Enlightenment discourse. The phenomenologist Emmanual Levinas objected to the very idea of knowledge in the traditional Western sense because in the process of understanding, he argued, Western philosophy undermines and devalues whatever societies, cultures or modes of living it comes across: 'Western philosophy coincides with the disclosure of the other where the other, in manifesting itself as a being, loses its alterity. From its infancy philosophy has been struck with a horror of the other that remains other.'[48]

What Levinas means is that Western thought cannot allow objects of study to remain outside of its epistemological boundaries or to be defined in their own terms. For Levinas conventional knowledge, conceived of as the relationship between subject and object, always involves appropriating one to the other. This he calls 'the imperialism of the same', drawing a parallel between the physical subjugation of the Third World and the intellectual subordination of its ideas, history and values. Just as Western politicians and generals annex foreign lands, so the West's intellectuals and philosophers appropriate all other knowledge.

Robert Young similarly argues that Western universalism 'articulates a philosophical structure which uncannily simulates the project of nine-teenth-century imperialism; the construction of knowledges which all operate through forms of expropriation and incorporation of the other mimics at a conceptual level the geographic and economic absorption of the non-European world by the West.'[49]

Since all knowledge and understanding requires the appropriation of the object by the subject, implicit in every act of understanding, says Levinas, is an act of violence. The only solution to this problem for Levinas, and for other theoreticians of difference, such as Robert Young and Gayatri Chakravorty Spivak, is to abjure entirely knowledge in the conventional sense. Instead of 'grasping' the object, says Levinas, we must 'respect' it; in the place of assimilation there should be 'infinite separation'.

'Respect' for the other means a refusal to judge others' values or norms. It has become normal now for backward habits, reactionary institutions, illogical beliefs all to be defended on the grounds that they may not make sense in our culture, but they do in others'. Even inequality can be seen as a culturally valid belief. American philosopher Richard Rorty has observed how what he calls 'Enlightenment liberals' seem to be caught in a dilemma over equality:

> Their liberalism forces them to call any doubts about human equality a result of irrational bias. Yet their connoisseurship [of diversity] forces them to realise that most of the globe's inhabitants do not believe in equality, that such a belief is a Western eccentricity. Since they think it would be shockingly ethnocentric to say, 'So what? We Western libe-rals do believe in it, and so much the better for us', they are stuck.[50]

Rorty himself, a self-avowed 'postmodern bourgeois liberal', solves the dilemma by arguing that equality is good for 'us' but not necessarily for 'them'.

At this point difference becomes resolved into *indifference*, an unwill-ingness to engage with what any one else has to say. It is an outlook described much more succinctly and lucidly than by any postmodern professor by the TV character Archie Bunker in the American sitcom *All in the Family*. In one particular episode, Edith tells Archie to lace his bowling shoes 'over' rather than 'under'. 'What's the difference?' de-mands Archie. When Edith tries to explain, Archie cuts her short: 'I didn't say "what's the difference – explain it to me". I said "What's the difference – who the hell cares?".'

In the indifference of postmodernism, Christopher Miller perceptively observes, the politics of difference mirrors the arguments of racial think-ing. 'The impulse to leave the other alone', he writes, 'rejoins the impulse to obliterate the other on the ground that they have in common: the inability to describe something outside the self, to see in Clifford Geertz's words "ourselves among others, as a local example of the forms human life has locally taken".'[51] In other words, the advocates of racial thinking and the theorists of difference seem equally indifferent to our common humanity. While one posits the notion of a 'Britishness' or 'Frenchness' or 'Americanness' accessible only to those privileged by race or history, the other renounces any possibility of access across the divide of cultural or ethnic difference. Said himself is well-aware of the dangers of such an outlook:

> Let us begin by accepting the notion that although there is an irreducible subjective core to human experience, this experience is also historical and secular, it is accessible to analysis and interpretation, and – centrally important – is not exhausted by totalising theories, not marked or limited by doctrinal or national lines, nor confined once and for all to analytical constructs. If one believes with Gramsci that an intellectual vocation is socially possible as well as desirable, then it is an inadmissible contradiction at the same time to build analyses of historical experience around exclusions, exclusions that stipulate, for instance, that only women can understand feminine experience, only Jews can understand Jewish suffering, only formerly colonial subjects can understand colonial experience.[52]

Again, Said has reminded us that the pluralist approach of privileging every voice, far from ensuring a more democratic society, would simply create a modern-day Tower of Babel: '[I]f everyone were to insist on the radical purity or priority of one's own voice, all we would have would be the awful din of unending strife, and a bloody political mess'.[53] Social dialogue requires, not that all voices are equal, but a willingness to engage in critical debate and to accept that some views are more valid than others. If all voices are to be heard and all views are equally valid, we may have cacophony but there can be no dialogue. Unfortunately, Said's more reasoned approach has got submerged, both in his work and that of other poststructuralist writers, beneath the inexorable logic of the anti-universalist argument.

HUMANISM, COLONIALISM AND THE HOLOCAUST

Associated with the anti-universalist stance of poststructuralist theories has been an unremitting hostility to a humanist approach. Humanism, we should recall, is a philosophy which takes human experiences as the starting point for humankind's knowledge of itself and its relation to nature. This anthropocentric outlook underpinned the scientific and philosophical revolution unleashed by the Renaissance and the Enlightenment.

At the heart of humanism are two key beliefs. First, humanists hold that human beings, while an inherent part of nature and subject to its laws, nevertheless have an exceptional status in nature because of their unique ability, arising out of human sociability, to overcome the constraints placed upon them by nature. Second, humanists believe in the unity of humankind, holding that all humans possess something in common, a something which is often described as a common 'human nature'.

The humanist outlook has expressed itself in a variety of political forms, from liberalism to Marxism. Liberal humanists tend to view human nature as a static, eternal quality given by nature. David Hume, for instance, argued that 'there is a great uniformity among the acts of men, in all nations and ages, and that human nature remains the same in its principles and operations'.[54]

Marx, on the other hand, saw the human essence as a social or historical construction. In his 'Theses on Feuerbach', for example, Marx criticised the German philosopher Ludwig Feuerbach for 'abstract[ing] from the historical process' and assuming that the human essence was 'an internal dumb generality which naturally unites the many individuals'. But, argued Marx, 'the human essence is no abstraction inherent in each single individual. In its reality it is the ensemble of the social relations.'[55] In other words, 'historical humanism', as Georg Lukács called it, sees 'man' not as naturally given but 'as a product of himself and of his own activity in history'.[56]

Whether liberal or Marxist, underlying all humanistic strands is a belief in human emancipation – the idea that humankind can rationally transform society through the agency of its own efforts. Indeed, no emancipatory philosophy is possible without a humanist perspective, for any antihumanistic outlook is forced to look outside humanity for the agency of salvation. Conversely, no humanist outlook is possible without an accompanying belief in human rationality and capacity for social progress.

Antihumanistic strands developed from the Enlightenment onwards, largely in opposition to the idea of rational human emancipation. Just as there have been a number of different strands of humanism, so there have been a number of different strands of antihumanism, ranging from the conservatism of Burke, the Catholic reaction of de Maistre to the nihilism of Nietzsche and the Nazism of Martin Heidegger. All rejected Enlightenment rationalism and the idea of social progress because they despaired of the capacity of humankind for such rational progress. As we have seen in earlier chapters, such despair was in general an expression of either fear of or contempt for the masses, who were seen as irrational, atavistic and a threat to civilised society. Antihumanism rejected ideas of equality and human unity, celebrating instead difference and divergence and exalting the particular and the authentic over the universal.

Antihumanism developed therefore as a central component of élite theories and hence of racial theories. In the postwar era, however, antihumanism came to represent a very different tradition – the liberal, indeed radical, anti-colonialist and antiracist outlook. In the hands of such critics of Western society as Frantz Fanon, Jean-Paul Sartre, Michel Foucault, Jacques Derrida and Louis Althusser, among others, antihumanism became a central thread of structuralist and poststructuralist theories, and a key weapon in the interrogation of racist and imperialist discourses. 'Humanism', Sartre wrote in his famous preface to Fanon's *The Wretched of the Earth*,' is nothing but an ideology of lies, a perfect justification for pillage; its honeyed words, its affectations of sensibility were only alibis for our aggression'.[57]

How did a philosophical outlook which originated within conservative anti-emancipatory politics, and which was a key component of racial theory, become a central motif of radical antiracist, anti-imperialist doctrines? And how did philosophers such as Nietzsche and Heidegger, whose work had previously been seen as paving the way for twentieth-century racist and fascist ideologies, become icons of antiracist discourse? Understanding this puzzle will take us a long way towards explaining the relationship between theories of race and the contemporary discourse of difference.

There were two main strands to postwar radical antihumanism. One developed out of anti-colonial struggles, the other through Western (and in particular French) academic philosophy and was subsequently elaborated by the 'new social movements' such as feminism and environmentalism which emerged in the late sixties and seventies.

In *The Wretched of the Earth*, Martinique-born Algerian nationalist Frantz Fanon gave voice to the rage of colonial peoples against their inhuman treatment at the hands of the imperialist powers. The humanist idea of 'Man', wrote Fanon, which lay at the heart of the Western post-Enlightenment tradition, was achieved through the dehumanising of the non-Western Other:

> That same Europe where they were never done talking of Man, and where they never stopped proclaiming that they were only anxious for the welfare of Man: today we know what sufferings humanity has paid for every one of their triumphs of the mind.[58]

Europeans only became human, suggested Fanon, by denying humanity to their colonial Other. As Sartre put it, 'Humanism is the counterpart of racism: it is a practice of exclusion'.[59] According to Sartre, 'There is nothing more consistent than a racist humanism since the European has only been able to become a man through creating slaves and monsters.'[60] To maintain a belief in humanism while treating non-European peoples as animals, Europeans declared that non-Europeans were in fact sub-human. Herein lies the source of racial theory in humanism. At the same time, argued Fanon, humanists salved their conscience, by inviting the sub-human colonial Other to become human by imitating 'European Man':

> Western bourgeois racial prejudice as regards the nigger and the Arab is a racism of contempt; it is a racism which minimises what it hates. Bourgeois ideology, however, which is the proclamation of an essential equality between men, manages to appear logical in its own eyes by inviting the subhuman to become human, to take as their prototype Western humanity as incarcerated in the Western bourgeoisie.[61]

The category 'human' was empty of meaning, such critics asserted, because it was ahistoric. The invocation of a common human nature hid the fact that human nature is socially and historically constructed. According to James Clifford, '[I]t is a general feature of humanist common denominators that they are meaningless, since they bypass local cultural codes that make personal experience articulate'.[62] When humanists assert the universality of human nature, what they are really talking about are the particular human values expressed in European society. '[T]hose universal features which define the human', argues Robert Young, 'mask over the assimilation of human itself with European values.' The category of the human, he believes, 'however exalted in its conception' is 'too often invoked only in order to put the male before the female, or to classify other "races" as sub-human, and therefore not subject to the ethical prescriptions applicable to humanity at large'.[63]

Third World critics, however, did not reject humanism in its entirety. Fanon, for instance, recognised that the contradiction lay not so much in humanism itself as in the disjuncture between the ideology of humanism and the practice of colonialism:

> All the elements of a solution to the great problems of humanity have, at different times, existed in European thought. But Europeans have not carried out in practice the mission which fell to them, which consisted of bringing their whole weight to bear violently upon these elements, of modifying their arrangement and their nature, of changing them and, finally, of bringing the problem of mankind to an infinitely higher plane.[64]

Fanon called therefore for a new humanism stripped of its racist, Eurocentric aspects:

Let us decide not to imitate Europe; let us combine our muscles and
our brains in a new direction. Let us try to create the whole man,
whom Europe has been incapable of bringing to triumphant birth.[65]

For Fanon, then, the humanist idea of 'the whole man' was key to
emancipation. Despite the critique of Western humanism as a camouflage for the dehumanisation of non-Western peoples, humanism remained a central component of the ideology of Third World liberation
struggles of the postwar era, virtually all of which drew on the emancipatory logic of universalism. Indeed Western radicals were often
shocked by the extent to which anti-colonial struggles adopted what the
radicals conceived of as tainted ideas. The concepts of universalism and
unilinear evolutionism, Lévi-Strauss observed, found 'unexpected support from peoples who desire nothing more than to share in the benefits
of industrialisation; peoples who prefer to look on themselves as tempo-
rarily backward rather than permanently different'.[66] Elsewhere he
noted ruefully that the doctrine of cultural relativism 'was challenged by
the very people for whose moral benefit the anthropologists had established it in the first place'.[67]

The willingness of Third World radicals to maintain at least a residual
support for a humanistic outlook stemmed from their continued engagement in the project of liberation. Postwar radicals in the West, however,
increasingly rejected humanism, not simply in its guise as a cover for
racism and colonialism, but in its entirety. For postwar European intellectuals the most pressing problem was not that of establishing the
ideological foundations of liberation struggles but rather of coming
to terms with the demise of such struggles in Western democracies.
Western intellectuals had, on the one hand, to excavate the social and
intellectual roots of the Nazi experience, an experience which more
than any other weighed upon the European intellectual consciousness in
the immediate postwar period, and on the other, to explain why the
possibilities of revolutionary change, which had seemed so promising in
the early part of the century, appeared to have been extinguished. For
many the explanation lay in some deep-seated malaise in European
culture.

Postwar radicals asked themselves why it was that Germany, a nation
with deep philosophical roots in the Enlightenment project and a strong
and vibrant working-class movement, should succumb so swiftly and so
completely to Nazism. The answer seemed to be that it was the logic of
Enlightenment rationalism itself and the nature of democratic politics
that had given rise to such barbarism. As Theodor Adorno and Max
Horkheimer, members of the 'Frankfurt School' of radical German scholars, put it in their seminal work, *Dialectic of Enlightenment*, 'Enlightenment is totalitarian'.[68] In *Dialectic of Enlightenment* Adorno and

Horkheimer developed the two motifs – a critique of Enlightenment rationality and social progress, on the one hand, and of mass society, on the other – which were to become immensely influential in shaping postwar discourse.

The idea that the Holocaust – and indeed all Western barbarism – found its roots in Enlightenment rationalism and humanism became a central tenet of postwar radicalism, as Lévi-Strauss expressed in an interview in *Le Monde*:

> All the tragedies we have lived through, first with colonialism, then with fascism, finally the concentration camps, all this has taken shape not in opposition to or in contradiction with so-called humanism in the form in which we have been practising it for several centuries, but I would say almost as its natural continuation.[69]

According to Lévi-Strauss, the Enlightenment ambition of mastering nature, of setting humanity above nature, inevitably had destructive consequences for humanity itself. A humanity which could enslave nature was quite capable of enslaving fellow human beings. As David Goldberg has put it, 'Subjugation ... defines the order of the Enlightenment: subjugation of nature by human intellect, colonial control through physical and cultural domination, and economic superiority through mastery of the laws of the market'.[70] Mastery of nature and the rational organisation of society, which in the nineteenth century was seen as the basis for human emancipation, now came to be regarded as the source of human enslavement.

The idea that technological and social progress could be the cause of barbarism has led many critics to find evidence not simply of humanism but of the whole project of 'modernity' behind the Holocaust. Zygmunt Bauman has suggested that the Final Solution was the 'product' not 'failure' of modernity and that 'it was the rational world of modern civilisation that made the Holocaust thinkable':

> The truth is that every ingredient of the Holocaust – all those many things that rendered it possible – was normal ... in the sense of being fully in keeping with everything we know about our civilisation, its guiding spirit, its priorities, its immanent vision of the world – and of the proper ways to pursue human happiness together with a perfect society.[71]

Bauman's hint that 'civilisation' itself may have been responsible for the barbarism of the Final Solution is made explicit by Richard Rubinstein who (in a phrase approvingly quoted by Bauman) argues that the Holocaust 'bears witness to the *advance of civilisation*':

The world of death camps and the society it engenders reveals the progressively intensifying night side of Judeo-Christian civilisation. Civilisation means slavery, wars, exploitation, and death camps. It also means medical hygiene, elevated religious ideas, beautiful art, and exquisite music. It is an error to imagine that civilisation and savage cruelties are antitheses . . . Both creation and destruction are inseparable parts of what we call civilisation.[72]

Here again in the debate on the origins of the Holocaust, as in the discussion about the Other, we can see the conflation of arguments about the post-Enlightenment discourse with those about a supposed tradition that has existed from the beginnings of the Western (or Judeo-Christian) history. But what can it mean to suggest that barbarism is an inseparable part of civilisation? It is, on the one hand, logically meaningless, since the two concepts are defined in opposition to each other. On the other hand, to suggest that 'the advance of civilisation' inevitably leads to 'slavery, wars, exploitation, and death camps' can only mean that barbarism is an eradicable part of human nature. But is this not to posit a concept of human nature that is as ahistoric as that supposedly held by humanists? Condemning civilisation as forever imbricated with inhumanity is certainly an argument that sits uneasily with a critique of humanism which claims that an ahistoric notion of 'Man' has been used to deny humanity to the West's Others.

The argument that humanism and rationalism (or 'modernity') are the causes of the Holocaust implies, in the words of Tzvetan Todorov, 'not only that the speaker is disregarding or repressing the ideological origins of fascism in nineteenth century *antihumanism* . . . but also that the speaker is wilfully cultivating a logical paradox, since he is complacently deducing the thesis of the *inequality* of man on the basis of human *equality*'.[73]

We have seen in previous chapters how the discourse of race was a product of the degradation of Enlightenment humanism, universalism and reason. Scientific racism, which was much propounded by Nazi theoreticians, was not the application of science and reason to the question of human difference, but the use of the discourse of science to give legitimacy to irrational, unscientific arguments.

The 'Final Solution' was implicit in the racial policies pursued by the Nazis. To engage in mass extermination it was necessary to believe that the objects of that policy were less than human. But to say that it was a rationally conceived plan is to elevate the prejudices of the Third Reich to the status of scientific knowledge – in other words to accept as true the very claims of racial discourse. As Todorov has put it, to attribute such ideas to Enlightenment humanism 'is to take at face value what was only propaganda: an attempt, most often a clumsy one, to replaster the facade of a building constructed for quite a different purpose'.[74]

The second motif in the Frankfurt School analysis of fascism which came to dominate postwar thought was the critique of mass society. The concept of mass society began to win acceptance among sociologists in the 1950s. Stuart Hughes has pointed out both the ambiguity and irrationality of the concept and the underlying disillusionment with the soullessness of modern capitalist society which it expressed:

> [T]he ways in which it was used were imprecise, overlapping and frequently contradictory. Sometimes its emphasis was on undifferentiated numbers, sometimes on mechanisation, sometimes on bureaucratic predominance. Yet for all their fuzziness of language the analysts of mass society agreed on a few defining characteristics: what they saw about them was a situation at once uniform and fluid – a state of social 'nakedness' in which the notion of community seemed to be slipping away and the individual lacked a cushion of intermediate groups to protect him against direct and overwhelming pressures from the wielders of political and economic power.[75]

For the sociologists of the mass society, technological progress and mass democracy had combined to debase society, creating a mass of people with little intellectual depth, spiritual involvement or cultural profundity. The creation of such a mass society had taken humanity to the abyss of barbarism. Behind the rise of Nazism lay the willingness of the unthinking masses to follow herd-like behind demagogic leaders such as Adolf Hitler. This idea was first expressed in the Frankfurt School's analysis of the 'authoritarian personality' – a personality type characterised by extreme obedience and unquestioning respect for authority and usually accompanied by rigidity, conventionality, prejudice, and intolerance of weakness or ambiguity.[76] According to the authors of *The Authoritarian Personality*, the potential of fascism lay in the presence of such a personality type within the mass of the people. Given that democratic societies, such as the USA, were also mass societies, the sociologists of the Frankfurt School believed that the potential existed for the rise of fascism there too.

The critique of Enlightenment rationality and the critique of mass society became fused into the 'totalitarian' theory of fascism. Popularised by Hannah Arendt in her book *The Origins of Totalitarianism*, the theory suggested that fascism was a species of totalitarianism, similar to the Soviet Union, Communist China or (a comparison that later totalitarian theorists would make) the Ayatollah Khomeini's Iran and Saddam Hussein's Iraq. The components of a totalitarian state were a herd-like mass, a compelling totalising ideology that subsumed all under its cold logic and a machine-like society that effaced all individuality in the name of a higher rationality. For Arendt totalitarianism represented the 'madness of the mob', the 'refuse of all classes', falling under the leadership of *déclassé* intellectuals. The members of the mob sought to merge into something larger than themselves, to give up their individualism to belong to the mass.[77] The critique of totalitarianism – and of totality – was to become a defining feature of poststructuralist discourse.

The irony in this is that the critique of totalitarianism is in substance a reworking of the nineteenth-century critique of Enlightenment rationalism and of mass society pursued by philosophers such as Nietzsche and Heidegger, whose work, as we saw in Chapter 4, flowed from the hostility of the intelligentsia to equality and mass democracy. Arendt was a student of Heidegger's and her theory of totalitarianism carries over the main themes of Heidegger's thought in its anti-mass character, its incipient anti-rationalism and in particular its hostility to the Enlightenment as the embodiment of both.

The idea of the authoritarian personality, and of the masses as the 'refuse of all classes', clearly has close parallels with the themes of crowd psychology which we discussed in Chapter 4. Both are a cry against what Heidegger called the 'anonymity of the They': 'an endless etcetera of indifference and always-the-sameness . . . the domination of the indifferent mass . . . that destroys all rank and every world-creating impulse of the spirit'.[78] The antihumanist belief that the technical forms of modernity arising from the human mastery of nature underlay the implementation of the Holocaust is also taken from Heidegger. Compare, for instance, Heidegger's analysis of the barbarism of the twentieth century with a sociological interpretation of the same:

> Agriculture is now a mechanised food industry; in essence it is no different from the production of corpses in gas chambers and death camps, the embargoes and food reductions to starving countries, the making of hydrogen bombs.[79]

> There is more than a wholly fortuitous connection between the applied technology of the mass production line, and its vision of universal material abundance, and the applied technology of the concentration camp, with its vision of a profusion of death.[80]

I find it odious that scholars can in all seriousness equate mass extermination with the production of McDonald's hamburgers or of Ford Escorts, or make a comparison between technology aimed at improving the material abundance of society and political decisions taken to annihilate whole peoples and destroy entire societies. But what is interesting is that the second quote, from Edmund Stillman and William Pfaff, comes from a liberal interpretation of the Holocaust, whereas the first quote, from Heidegger himself, comes from an apologia for his Nazi past.

Heidegger had been an active member of the Nazi Party until 1943. After the war he attempted to rehabilitate his reputation and in the document *Rectoral Addresses – Facts and Thoughts* he marshalled the arguments which he hoped would distance himself from the Third Reich. The key piece of evidence for the defence was the assertion that Nazism was simply another manifestation of the spirit of modernity. According to Heidegger there existed a 'universal will to power within history, now understood to embrace the planet' and that 'everything stands in this historical reality, no matter whether it is called communism, fascism or world democracy'.[81] It is a telling measure of the degree of confusion in postwar theory that liberal and Nazi explanations of the Holocaust can barely be prised apart. As James Heartfield observes, 'Heidegger's thought, having tried to articulate – or spiritualise – national socialism, went on to a more remarkable achievement. Through Hannah Arendt and the totalitarian thesis, Heidegger's ideas shaped the interpretation and critique of fascism after its defeat.'[82]

Indeed, it did more than that. The antihumanism of Heidegger, and his fellow thinkers, became a central theme of poststructuralist and postmodernist discourse, of colonial discourse analysis and of the theories of difference and cultural pluralism. As Heartfield remarks, 'how perverse that the rejection of . . . barbarism should preserve the very prejudices that gave rise to it'.

Underlying the commonality of themes in racial and poststructuralist theory is their attempt to come to terms with the same problem – the disjuncture between a belief in equality and progress, and a society that can seem to deliver neither. Read the whole of the passage in which Sartre rails against the hypocrisy of Western humanism and this becomes clear:

> Liberty, equality, fraternity, love, honour, patriotism and what have you. All this did not prevent us from making anti-racial speeches about dirty niggers, dirty Jews and dirty Arabs. High-minded people, liberal or just soft-hearted, protest that they were shocked by such inconsistency; but they were either mistaken or dishonest, for with us there is nothing more consistent than a racist humanism since the European has only been able to become a man through creating slaves and monsters.[83]

Nineteenth-century thinkers who held fast to Enlightenment principles – whether liberal or revolutionary – argued that the disjuncture could be closed by social transformation. By the end of the century, however, liberals had by and large come to despair of the possibility of any such transformation and were drifting over to the long-held conservative belief that inequalities were both inevitable and necessary. By the midpoint of this century, the experience of Nazism and the defeat of

working-class movements had led radicals to similar pessimistic conclusions. As Stuart Hughes observes in his wonderfully lucid study of
postwar intellectual thought, there was within the radical intelligentsia
a widespread

> disappointment in the course of recent history, in the strategy of the
> political parties that laid claim to the inheritance of Marx, and, most
> particularly, in the proletariat itself. The class which Engels had cel-
> ebrated as the 'heirs of classical philosophy' had failed to perform in
> the style expected of it.[84]

Postwar developments entrenched such views. The experience of the
failure of the student revolts of May 1968, the collapse of both Stalinist
and social democratic parties in the eighties and the demise of Third
World liberation movements all added to the belief that social transformation was a chimera.

The very goals of 'modernity' seemed unattainable. As Bauman has put
it, 'Postmodernity is modernity coming to terms with its own impossibility: a self-monitoring modernity, one that consciously discards what it
was once unconsciously doing'.[85] For postwar theorists the gap between
belief and reality could be closed not by transforming the reality but by
relinquishing their beliefs. Despairing of social change, poststructuralist
and postmodernist thinkers asserted instead that equality and humanity
had no meaning, and that difference and diversity should be our goal.

Despair about social transformation also led postwar theorists to see
the barbarism of the twentieth century not as a product of specific social
relations, but unspecifically as the consequence of 'modernity'. In Chapter 2, I suggested that the claim that the categories of modernity necessarily give rise to a racial division of humanity conflates two different
meanings of 'modernity'. On the one hand there is modernity in the
sense of an intellectual or philosophical outlook which holds that it is
possible to apprehend the world through reason and science – what has
come to be called the 'Enlightenment project' – and the technological
advance that such an outlook has engendered. On the other hand modernity has also come to mean the particular society in which these ideas
found expression – in other words, capitalism.

By conflating the social relations of capitalism with the intellectual and
technological progress of 'modernity', the product of the former can be
laid at the door of the latter. The specific problems created by capitalist
social relations became dehistoricised. In poststructuralist discourse
racial theory, colonialism or the Holocaust are not investigated in their
specificity, as products of distinctive tendencies within capitalist society,
but are all lumped together as the general consequence of 'modernity'. In
this way the positive aspects of capitalist society – its invocation of

reason, its technological advancements, its ideological commitment to equality and universalism – are denigrated while its negative aspects – the inability to overcome social divisions, the propensity to treat large sections of humanity as 'inferior' or 'subhuman', the contrast between technological advance and moral turpitude, the tendencies towards barbarism – are seen as inevitable or natural.

APPEARANCE, ESSENCE AND EQUALITY

An insistent theme of poststructuralist and postmodernist discourse, and one that is closely linked to its antihumanism, is its opposition to *essentialism*:

> Poststructuralist thinking, opposes the notion that a person is born with a fixed identity – that all black people, for example, have an essential underlying black identity which is the same and unchanging. It suggests instead that identities are floating, that meaning is not fixed and universally true at all times for all people, and that the subject is constructed through the unconscious in desire, fantasy and memory.[86]

The reminder that our identities are not naturally given but socially constructed is a useful antidote to the idea that human differences are fixed and eternal. But the understanding of the 'social' in poststructuralist discourse is, as we shall see, an inadequate one. Instead of viewing society as a totality, poststructuralists regard it as inherently heterogeneous and diverse and incapable of being grasped as a whole, 'a product of practices of regulation, resistances and representation rather than a pre-given entity which reproduces itself through agencies of socialisation'.[87] Such a conception of society has undermined the capacity of poststructuralist discourse to challenge naturalistic explanations of difference. Indeed, it has driven poststructuralists to posit an understanding of identity which in substance is barely different from that of nineteenth-century racial theorists.

The problem can be seen in the very concept of 'anti-essentialism'. Sociologist Ali Rattansi has described anti-essentialism as a 'manoeuvre cutting the ground from conceptions of subjects and social forms as reducible to timeless, unchanging, defining and determining elements or ensembles of elements – "human nature", for example, or in the case of the social, the logic of the market or mode of production'.[88]

On the one hand Rattansi characterises anti-essentialism as opposition to the idea of timeless or unchanging social forms, as hostility to an ahistoric understanding of social phenomena. On the other hand he believes that an anti-essentialist outlook is also opposed to the view that social forms can be 'defining' or 'determining'. In other words, Rattansi believes that anti-essentialism espouses indeterminacy. In this he reflects much postmodern thinking which regards uncertainty and ambivalence as central – and positive – features of contemporary society. It is a view that suggests that phenomena can never be fully pinned down and that it is in the uncertainties (or 'differences') that we can elucidate the meanings of social forms.

But it is precisely indeterminacy that is the foundation of ahistoric explanations. In order to be historically or socially specific one must understand the determinations of any social fact and its relationship with the totality in which it appears. Repudiating such certainty, and celebrating ambivalence, denies us the ability to grasp social phenomena in their specificity.

We could, for instance, argue about whether the essence of capitalism should be seen in the logic of the market, in the particular mode of production, in some other aspect, or in some combination of these. But unless we can characterise the essence of capitalist society, in other words the specific content of capitalism as a social form, we cannot distinguish it from other types of societies, nor understand how any particular social phenomenon or fact is rendered specific within the context of capitalist society. We would be unable to understand, for instance, what is specific about the modern concept of race, and would instead be forced into an ahistoric explanation of the sort we have seen previously in this chapter, in which race becomes an eternal feature of human societies.

The roots of anti-essentialism lie in the hostility to naturalistic explanations of social phenomena, particularly positivism. Positivism reduced social laws to natural laws. The founder of positivism, August Comte, for example, saw the laws determining human relations as being as quantifiable and as permanent as those determining nature. The positivist view of society, we saw in Chapter 3, underpinned nineteenth-century racial theories. Opponents of racial theory have therefore always been hostile to naturalistic theories of society. As Theodor Adorno and Max Horkheimer observed, 'the extreme model of rendering society "natural" . . . is the racist insanity of national socialism'.[89]

But in its haste to despatch naturalistic theories, poststructuralist discourse (and indeed much of modern sociology) has thrown the baby out with the bathwater. Poststructuralists hold that naturalistic explanations of society fail because they posit an essence that underlies social phenomena. Positivism is considered to have held that social relations are merely the surface appearance of a natural essence. In fact this is a misapprehension of positivism, which if anything is defined by its empiricism, and which reduces laws to the subjective arrangement of phenomena by the observer. 'I personally believe that the doctrine of indeterminacy is true', wrote Karl Popper, the principal twentieth-century proponent of positivism.[90] Having defined positivism as the belief in a natural essence underlying social phenomena, anti-essentialists then argue against not simply naturalistic explanations of society, but any essentialistic explanation. All determination is considered to be essentialistic and therefore illegitimate.

Anti-essentialism is therefore a critique not simply of the idea of natural essence but of any and all essentialist viewpoints. Anti-essentialists hold that theory can have no recourse to determinants beyond empirically given phenomena. Essences and forces, whether natural or metaphysical, spiritual or historical, are fictitious. At best social 'laws' are convenient fictions that allocate an order to empirical phenomena. At worst they are self-serving illusions that only seek to shield us from facing reality. For poststructuralists, then, social phenomena are not reducible to another property that bestows them with meaning. It is an outlook that renders all determinate relations contingent, bereft of any inner necessity.

The indeterminacy of poststructuralism is well-encapsulated in the methodology of deconstructionism, a movement initiated in the late sixties by Jacques Derrida's reading of Martin Heidegger. Deconstructionism denies the possibility of language embodying any true meaning. The French structuralist and linguist Frederick Saussure had established a distinction between the *signifier* and the *signified* in language. The sound image made by 'black' is the signifier, the concept of 'blackness' is the signified. The relationship between the two constitutes a sign, and language is made up of these. Since for Saussure the crucial distinction was not between word and object but between signified and signifier, his structuralist linguistics opened the way for non-realist theories of meaning.

In Saussure's conception of the sign, the signifier and the signified operate according to a relatively stable relationship. Deconstruction, however, denies any correspondence between the signifier and the signified. The signifier (the word) does not yield the signified (the meaning). No text or utterance can have any definite meaning, because it can have an infinity of meaning. For deconstructionists there can be no single meaning, or 'essence', to a text.

Derrida denies determinacy for two reasons. First the meaning of any signifier is contained in what it is not as much as in what it is, in the difference between signifiers. The meaning of 'black' is constituted in what it is not ('white'). The meaning of a signifier always lies outside of itself and is therefore indeterminate. Secondly the meaning of any signifier can only be defined in terms of other signifiers, and hence there is a whole cascade of signifiers or texts, through which meaning is dispersed. Derrida uses the term *différance,* to convey the idea both of 'difference' and of 'deference', in the sense of a meaning that is always deferred, or made inaccessible.

The methodology of deconstruction is to examine texts minutely, to break it down into its component parts and to reveal meanings that were neither intended nor previously grasped, often by making marginal aspects of the text central. Such a method is not simply applied to texts. Society itself is deconstructed in a similar fashion.

It was Lévi-Strauss who first argued that a culture or a society can be read like a language. He took from Saussure the idea that language has a given structure – a set of grammatical and other rules about how to communicate which lie below the consciousness of any individual speaker and which operates independently of them – and applied this concept to cultural artifacts, such as myths, rituals and kinship structures. Social forms, argued Lévi-Strauss, are in fact social signs embodying a relationship between signifier, the external structure, and the signified, the inner meaning. It is an argument, as we saw in Chapter 6, that tends towards an antihumanist interpretation in the sense that it regards culture as an entity working through human beings rather than it being a product of humanity.

Deconstructionism takes this argument a few stages further, both idealising social forms and making them indeterminate. Rather than seeing social processes operating *like* a language, deconstructionism regards them as constituted *in* language. Taking their cue from Nietzsche's dictum that 'the world as a work of art gives birth to itself', deconstructionists posit human subjects, and human society, as made out of language. Poststructuralist theorists emphasise 'the materiality of language itself, the impossibility of simply referring it back to some primal anterior reality, "social being" '.[91] Hence Gareth Stedman Jones, a prominent social historian, dismisses 'the prevalent treatment of the "social" as something outside of, and logically – and often, though not necessarily, chronologically – prior to its articulation through language'.[92] In this way, as one critic of the postmodernist outlook notes, 'the cultural becomes the material; the ideological becomes *the* real'.[93] Language and discourse become reified into the only reality while 'social beings' become illusions, something 'constituted in the world of language and symbols'. Reality is simply a discursive form so that, as Neville Kirk put it in a critique of such arguments, there is 'no economy, no society, no cultural or political systems and structures, but only economic, social, cultural and political discourses'.[94]

Since discourse and language themselves are indeterminate, so are social forms. As with a linguistic sign, the meaning of a social form depends as much on what it is not as with what it is. Social meaning therefore lies in the differences between social forms and is deferred or made inaccessible in the same way as is linguistic meaning. Further, any social process can have a multiplicity of meanings since meaning depends on context, and the context is different for every human subject. The result is, in E. P. Thompson's words, 'a self-generating conceptual universe ... [which] imposes its own identity upon the phenomena of material and social existence, rather than engaging in a continual dialogue with them'.[95]

Poststructuralists are particularly keen to deconstruct or *decentre* the human subject. Arising from the rejection of humanist values, the decentring of the subject involves 'the deflation of a rationalist/Cartesian pretension to unproblematic self-knowledge' and 'a critique of the conception of a linear connection of subjects to the external world, in which reality is made transparent from a uniquely privileged vantage point through the application of rationality and empirical disciplines'.[96] The human subject, say poststructuralists, is not a unitary, given entity acting rationally upon the world, but a site of conflict and difference which is constituted through discourse. 'Society does not influence the autonomous individual', writes Jeffrey Weekes; 'on the contrary the individual is constituted in the world of language and symbols which come to dwell in, and constitute, the individual'.[97] Or, as Kobena Mercer has put it, 'the subject is constituted in language'.[98]

Poststructuralists deny the concept of an 'essential' identity and stress instead 'the phenomenon of *multiple social identities*'. As Robin Cohen notes, 'the modern study of identity has ... dished the old "essentialisms" – for example the Marxist idea that all social identity could essentially be reduced to class identity'. Instead it holds that 'there are competing claims for affiliation that cannot be reduced to epiphenomena' and 'gender, age, disability, race, religion, ethnicity, nationality, civil status, even musical styles and dress codes' are all 'very potent axes of organisation and identification'.[99]

The concept of conflicting social pressures and identities is clearly valid. The problem arises, however, when all 'identities', of whatever form, are treated as of equal social validity, so that personal lifestyle preferences such as 'musical styles', physical attributes such as 'disability' and social products such as 'race' and 'class' are seen as being of the same moment, while, at the same time, the determinate relations between identity and society are denied. The result is that fundamental social relations such as racial oppression become reduced to lifestyle choices. The 'social' seems to mean nothing more than a particular decision that an individual may make, and 'society' is reduced to the aggregate of individual relationships.

The consequence of the poststructuralist notion of society is that many contemporary writers treat social distinctions as personal or political choices. There is a scene in Woody Allen's film *Bananas,* in which our luckless hero, played by Allen, bemoans the fact that he dropped out of

college. 'What would you have been if you had finished school?', someone asks him. 'I don't know', sighs Allen. 'I was in the black studies
programme. By now I could have been black.' This seems to be the
essence of the contemporary view of identity. As Cohen notes, poststructuralists suggest that

> an individual constructs and presents any one of a number of possible
> social identities, depending on the situation. Like a player concealing
> a deck of cards from the other contestants, the individual pulls out a
> knave – or a religion, or an ethnicity, a lifestyle – as the context deems
> a particular choice desirable or appropriate.[100]

In this spirit an increasing number of writers now view racial division as
cultural exclusiveness. Winston James, employing Benedict Anderson's
notion of an 'imagined community', argues that, 'Like all nations, nationalities and ethnic groups, Afro-Caribbean people in Britain have
erected boundaries in relation to those with whom they identify'.[101] The
suggestion is that Afro-Caribbeans have *chosen* to establish distinctive
cultural patterns, that they have asserted their right to be different, as a
way of confirming their 'imagined community', of establishing what
James calls a *'new* sense of fellowship'.

If this were true, however, then racism would not be a problem. If we
could choose identities like we choose our clothes every morning, if we
could erect social boundaries from a cultural Lego pack, then racial
hostility would be no different from disagreements between lovers of
Mozart and those who prefer Charlie Parker, or between supporters of
different football clubs. In other words there would be no social content
to racial differences, simply prejudice borne out of a plurality of tastes or
outlooks.

But we know that in reality racial divisions do have a social content,
that they are not simply the product of personal preferences, and that
blackness amounts to more than a semester on a black studies programme. It is not Afro-Caribbeans, or any other racialised group, who
have 'erected boundaries' with the rest of society. It is society which has
established those boundaries by racialising certain social groups, and
signifying them as 'different' – as James himself acknowledges when
he notes 'the powerful centripetal forces of British racism'.[102] Black youth
in Brixton or the Bronx have no more 'chosen' their difference than
Jews did in Nazi Germany. Certainly oppressed communities have
often reacted to racial division by adopting particular cultural forms.
In his autobiography Miles Davis recounts how black jazz musicians
in the forties responded to racism by developing bebop as a style
that would exclude white players.[103] Similarly many Jews today continue
to observe Jewish cultural rituals less out of religious faith than in

response to anti-Semitism and in memory of the victims of the Holocaust. But such cultural assertion is not the cause of racial identification, it is its product.

The corollary of the argument that oppressed people choose their racialised identities is the belief that racism is the result of a political conspiracy. Thus, Theodore Allen, writing about Ireland, argues that 'racial oppression [was] introduced as a deliberate ruling class policy'. The ruling class, even if it desired to do so, could not (and cannot) simply 'invent' racial divisions. Racial differentiation emerges out of real social and economic mechanisms, out of dialogue and struggle between different social groups, out of the interaction between ideology and social processes. The ruling class can no more 'introduce' racial oppression than Afro-Caribbeans can invent their blackness – or Woody Allen become a black man.

Far from demonstrating identity and the human subject as socially constructed, poststructuralist discourse reduces (or deconstructs) society to the accidental interaction of individuals and removes the subject from the terrain of the social. Since there is no mediation between the individual and the social, determinate social relations are reduced to contingent relations between individuals and the 'social' itself is seen as having a discursive, not a real, existence.

The celebration of idealism and indeterminacy is reinforced by hostility to universalising theory, or totality. Indeed the stress on indeterminacy arises from the belief that we cannot comprehend social reality in any holistic sense. We saw in the previous section how repugnance to fascism was recast as rejection of totalitarianism, seen as the product of Enlightenment universalism. In poststructuralist theory all attempts at grasping social reality as a totality are rejected. All such attempts are 'totalitarian' because they impose a single vision of the world upon what is in fact a plurality.

In a famous critique of Jean-Paul Sartre, Lévi-Strauss claimed that the argument for a single or universal history in Sartre's *Critique of Dialectical Reason* was tautological because the universal had only been established by excluding all that lay outside the self-defined total:

A truly total history would . . . [be] chaos. Every corner of space conceals a multitude of individuals each of whom totalises the trend of history in a manner that cannot be compared to the others . . . Even history which claims to be universal is still only a juxtaposition of a few local histories within which (and between which) very much more is left out than put in . . . In so far as history aspires to meaning, it is doomed to select regions, periods, groups of men and individuals in these groups and to make them stand out, as discontinuous figures, against a continuity barely good enough to be used as a backdrop.

A truly total history would cancel itself out – its product would be nought.[104]

When we consider history or society, we cannot study everything, only those aspects which we deem to be important. A universal history, argues Lévi-Strauss, is therefore an oxymoron. Sartre, like all Western and Marxist thinkers, had created his universal history only by excluding all histories except that of the West. Hence, Sartre, like all those who attempt to grasp social reality within a single frame, must necessarily be ethnocentric and any discourse of universality necessarily racist.

It is true that any history or sociology – whether Lévi-Strauss's, Sartre's, Marx's or indeed mine in this book – requires the use and interpretation of facts in a selective manner. 'What I want is Facts', exclaims Mr Gradgrind in Charles Dickens' *Hard Times*, 'Facts alone are wanted in life.' But in the real world facts do not come in a 'pure' form and with their meaning readily apparent. Facts, the historian E. H. Carr has written, 'are not at all like fish on the fishmonger's slab'. Rather,

> they are like fish swimming about in a vast and sometimes inaccessible ocean; and what the historian catches will depend, partly on chance, but mainly on what part of the ocean he chooses to fish in and what tackle he chooses to use – these two factors being, of course, determined by the kind of fish he wants to catch'.[105]

Facts need to be interpreted, and there is an intimate relationship between fact and interpretation. The meaning of a fact is not necessarily apparent in its outward appearance, but is often hidden. For example, it is a fact that the people of the world could be divided according to the colour of their skin. Whether we think that this fact is important, and that skin colour is a useful way of dividing up humanity, depends on how we interpret the facts of skin colour. Within the discourse of race, skin colour (like headform in earlier times) is deemed an important fact. In the argument I have presented in this book, the fact of skin colour is irrelevant in any assessment of humanity.

Again, African-Americans as a group have a lower IQ than white Americans. That is a fact. But what that fact means is not apparent from the fact itself. For some authors, like Charles Murray, the difference in IQ is an indication that black and white Americans are naturally different in their intellectual ability. For others it means that IQ tests are poor measures of intellectual ability. For yet others, the difference between the IQ scores of black and white Americans is a product of their differential treatment by society. The true meaning of a fact is not necessarily apparent and requires interpretation.

The real issue raised by Lévi-Strauss, then, is not that we are forced to select and interpret facts but about what criteria we use to do so. In rejecting a universalistic outlook, Lévi-Strauss suggests that one fact is as important as another and that all selections and interpretations of facts are as valid as any other. Without a universalist theory there can be no frame within which to measure the truth or importance of any social fact. The 'regions, periods, groups of men and individuals in these groups' which we select to be historically important would be entirely arbitrary, as Lévi-Strauss himself acknowledges:

> When one proposes to write a history of the French Revolution one knows (or ought to know) that it cannot, simultaneously and under the same heading, be that of the Jacobin and that of the aristocrat. *Ex hypothesi,* their respective totalisations . . . are equally true. One must therefore choose between two alternatives. One must select as the principal either one or a third (for there are an infinite number of them) and give up the attempt to find in history a totalisation of the set of partial totalisations; or alternatively one must recognise them all as equally real: but only to discover that the French Revolution as commonly conceived never took place.[106]

Different facts or episodes are important to different social groups and we are simply left with a plurality of competing histories, each 'equally real' and none of which can 'be compared to the others'. As Robert Young has put it, 'history may be made up of the multiple meanings of specific, particular histories – without their necessarily being in turn part of a larger meaning of an underlying Idea or force'.[107]

Lévi-Strauss and Young propose here an 'anything goes' theory of meaning, in which there is no commensurability between different worlds of meaning. As George and Ira Gershwin put it, 'You say pot-ay-to/I say po-tah-to/You say to-may-to/I say to-mah-to/. . . Let's call the whole thing off.' But if this were true, how would we be able to distinguish between a racist history and a non-racist one? Each would be valid in its own context, just as Lévi-Strauss believes that a Jacobin and aristocratic interpretation of the French Revolution would. We return to the problem we encountered in our discussion of Said's notion of representation. Just as the logic of Said's argument in *Orientalism* undermined his capacity rationally to criticise Orientalism, so the relativity of meaning given by the arguments of Derrida, Lévi-Strauss and others undermines their capacity to challenge racist discourse. Different interpretations are not, however, equally valid or equally true, as Carr understood:

> It does not follow that, because a mountain appears to take on different shapes from different angles of vision, it has objectively either no

shape or an infinity of shapes. It does not follow that, because interpretation plays a necessary part in establishing the facts of history, and because no existing interpretation is wholly objective, one interpretation is as good as another, and the facts of history are not amenable to objective interpretation.[108]

A racist and non-racist interpretation of history are not equally valid, and neither are Jacobin and aristocratic interpretations of the French Revolution. We are required to choose between them, to decide which is true and which is not. A totalising theory gives us the capacity to make such choices.

A totalising theory does not mean, as Young claims, that 'it [must] include every historical fact', something which Young and Lévi-Strauss rightly observe 'would be chaos'.[109] Such would be the empiricist's approach. Rather, a totalising theory provides a framework in which we can decide which facts and interpretations are objectively important or true. We require a standard of significance to distinguish between real or significant facts and irrelevant ones. But a standard by which we establish truth cannot, as the positivists believed, be absolute or eternal, such as Reason or Nature. The standard itself is historically specific, a standard which evolves as humanity evolves. A totalising theory, by grasping social reality as a whole, can provide for us principles which, at any specific time, operate across human boundaries and hence act as standards by which we can gauge the truth or falsity of any interpretation.

Equality is a value that would have been meaningless in precapitalist society. It is the specific historic product of modern or capitalist society. Even within capitalist society the concept of equality has evolved, from the view that it was a natural concept to the contemporary realisation that it is socially defined. The historical specificity of the concept of equality, however, does not deny its universal quality or its objective significance. It is a standard by which we are able to judge political arguments and social practices. It is a measure by which we can objectively gauge historical and social progress. And it is a criterion by which we can pass judgement on different interpretations of the French Revolution or of IQ differentials in contemporary America.

Conversely, the idea of inequality is also historically specific. Inequality in precapitalist society has a different meaning from inequality under capitalism. The fact of inequality or difference does not yield up its inner meaning or essence. This only becomes apparent when we study it in its particular historical context. To do this we need to be able to grasp social reality as a whole, in other words to understand capitalist society or precapitalist society in its totality. Without a conception of totality it is not possible to develop a historical understanding of social relations. There becomes an inevitable tendency to treat all the partial social categories as having been always present in every society. It is only in the context of the whole that our understanding of the particular can develop. Lukács has put this argument well:

> [T]he objective forms of all social phenomena change constantly in the course of their ceaseless dialectical interactions with each other. The intelligibility of objects develops in proportion as we grasp their function in the totality to which they belong. This is why only a dialectical conception of totality can enable us to understand *reality as a social process.*[110]

To understand the specificity of any fact we need therefore to detach it from the form in which it appears and to discover the intervening links which connect it with its core, its essence. Without such a determinate relationship between appearance and essence, there can be no understanding of facts in their context. We have already seen in the ahistorical rendering of categories such as 'difference', 'the Other' and indeed 'race' how relativism gives way to ahistoricism.

The critical flaw in poststructuralist theory is the collapse of historical specificity into a relativistic epistemology. Or, to put it another way, poststructuralists are mistaken in rejecting not simply the eternalisation of social relations over time, but also their universalisation throughout society. In poststructuralist discourse social relations are seen not just as historically specific but also as particular to an immediate cultural environment. Such particularism inevitably, and paradoxically, gives rise to ahistoricism. In denying essentialism, in the sense of a meaning beyond surface appearance, poststructuralism is forced to adopt an essentialist methodology, in the sense of an ahistoric outlook.

The very nature of deconstructionist methodology imposes an eternal framework on its object of investigation. The starting point of poststructuralism is the search for difference. As Derrida has put it, it is futile to ask who or what differs, since difference is prior to any subject.[111] But this is to smuggle the conclusion of the investigation into the method. Rather than the method of investigation taking its cue from the object of investigation, it exists prior to it. If you set out to find difference in anything and everything, then that is exactly what you will find. Difference becomes the absolute in history, the objective force which makes history intelligible. It is the avatar in poststructuralist discourse of Nature in positivist thought.

The paradox of poststructuralist anti-essentialism, then, is this: it is an outlook that arises from a desire to oppose naturalistic explanations and to put social facts in social context. But in rejecting all essentialist explanations, in celebrating indeterminacy and in opposing the idea of totality it has undermined its own ability to explain social facts historically.

Facts, wrenched from their living context, are apprehended only in their isolation. The irony is that this methodology resembles nothing so much as the empiricism of the positivists, the very outlook anti-essentialism sought to overturn.

Poststructuralist theory identifies nature and society in the same way as positivism does, albeit with different consequences. Take, for instance, David Goldberg's argument that 'Open incorporative standards [in society] will discourage individuals or groups from extending their values over others, as though they constituted a human or social essence, a natural condition'.[112] What this suggests is that for Goldberg, 'a human or social essence' is equivalent to 'a natural condition'. Goldberg, as much as Comte or Knox, equates the natural and the social.

Goldberg adds that 'we are not to convert the contingency of prevailing identities into those deemed ethically essential by universalising them'.[113] What matters, then, are the immediate superficial appearances, not any underlying essential quality. Equality, however, presumes the existence of a 'human essence'. Without such a common essence, equality would be a meaningless concept. If humanity did not form a single category, if in Foucault's words 'Nothing in man – not even his body – is sufficiently stable to act as the basis for self-recognition or for understanding other men',[114] then equality between different human individuals and groups would be as meaningless as equating apples and pears or, to use Lévi-Strauss' analogy in his critique of Sartre, such 'different domains' as 'natural and irrational numbers'.[115]

In the early days of the development of capitalist society, human essence was seen as natural ('human nature'). Democrats such as Rousseau and Tom Paine saw equal rights as 'inalienable', as given by nature. A more historical understanding indicates that these rights are socially constructed, and that our essential character as political equals is something we make ourselves. As Marx put it, 'the human essence is no abstraction inherent in each single individual' but 'is the ensemble of the social relations'.[116] But once essential explanations, whether natural or social, are excluded, the very idea of equality also becomes subordinate to the 'contingency of prevailing identities'.

The appearance of difference is taken at face value and, given that no inner essence exists, taken as evidence of a multiplicity of categories of humanity. This, we should recall, is precisely the method employed by positivist racial theory, which deduced from the appearance of difference (skin colour, headform, and so on) the division of humanity into different categories or 'races'. Of course, contemporary theorists of difference deny that superficial biological differences define categorical distinctions, preferring instead to see historical or cultural factors as important. But cultural formalism is in substance no different from racial formalism.

Both move from the apprehension of formal difference to posit the existence of different ontological categories. This is why the anti-humanist, anti-essentialist tendencies of poststructuralist thought inevitably leads to the questioning of equality itself.

9
Equality and Emancipation

One of the more notable film releases of the nineties has been *Schindler's List*, Stephen Spielberg's magisterial account of the emergence of hope from inhumanity in the Second World War. The film, based on Thomas Keneally's Booker prize winning novel *Schindler's Ark*, tells the story of German businessman Oskar Schindler's attempt to save the lives of the Jewish workers in his forced-labour factory in Poland during the closing years of the war. We see the transformation of Schindler from a womanising, hedonistic, money-grabbing businessman and Nazi Party member into someone who risked his life to save those of his Jewish workers, many of whom he came to regard as his friends.

I remember reading Keneally's novel in the early eighties and being struck by the optimism which infused the story. Schindler becomes a heroic figure because he discovers his humanity in the midst of unparalleled inhumanity. The novel seemed to suggest that we all possess the capacity to transcend our moral frailties and to seek redemption in our common humanity. It came as a shock, therefore, to read an article by Keneally more than a decade later in which he suggested that the message of his novel was that 'mankind is naturally racist'. 'Racism', wrote Keneally, 'is as human as love. In defining ourselves, the tribe we belong to, its mores, we are tempted to believe in the inferiority of the culture and mores of other groups'.[1]

It may be that I had misread *Schindler's Ark*, failing to see the darkness within it. It is more likely, however, that Keneally's pessimism was new-found and that it is symbolic of changing perceptions of racism. The political, social and economic changes of recent years, and in particular the turmoil unleashed in many parts of the world in the post-Cold War period, has created a sense of melancholy about human relations. Those who previously had been optimistic about the nature of humanity now find themselves downcast about the human potential. 'The hostility of one tribe for another is among the most instinctive human reactions', writes liberal American historian Arthur Schlesinger. With the end of the Cold War, he believes, 'ethnic and racial conflict' will 'replace the conflict of ideologies as the explosive issue of our times':

> Lifting the lid of ideological repression in eastern Europe releases
> ethnic antagonisms deeply rooted in experience and in memory. The

disappearance of ideological competition in the Third World removes superpower restraints on national and tribal confrontations. As the era of ideology subsides, humanity enters – or more precisely re-enters – a possibly more dangerous era of ethnic and racial animosity.[2]

As the framework of the postwar order breaks up, so disorder seems to be unleashed upon the world. As the movements for liberation, in the East, in the West and in the Third World all fade away, so it appears that the maladies of the world spring from the dark demons within us. As the German essayist and poet Hans Magnus Enzensberger has put it, 'Self-interest and xenophobia are anthropological constants; they are older than all known societies.'[3]

This pessimism about human nature has transformed the character of antiracist struggles. We saw in the last chapter how the philosophy of difference has come to provide a rationale for social fragmentation. In this concluding chapter I want to consider how this privileging of difference has influenced the meaning of antiracism and how this transformation of antiracism has been fuelled by disillusionment about social change. I want to examine too how it may be possible to transcend the discourse of race and view human differences under a different light.

FROM THE 'RIGHT TO BE EQUAL' TO THE 'RIGHT TO BE DIFFERENT'

The terrain of antiracist struggle today is no longer that of social equality but of cultural diversity. Indeed the very meaning of social equality has come into question: for many the concept of equality in the old sense is a form of discredited universalism which does not take into account the differences within society. Equality has come to be redefined from 'the right to be the same' to mean 'the right to be different'.

In the sixties and seventies, the struggle for equal rights meant campaigns against immigration laws or against segregation through which different 'races' were treated differently; today it means campaigns for separate schools, demands to use different languages, the insistence on maintaining particular cultural practices. The black American critic bell hooks observes that in the past, 'civil rights reform reinforced the idea that black liberation should be defined by the degree to which black people gained equal access to material opportunities and privileges available to whites – jobs, housing, schooling, etc.' This strategy could never bring about liberation, argues hooks, because such 'ideas of "freedom" were informed by efforts to imitate the behaviour, lifestyles and most importantly the values and consciousness of white colonisers.'[4] In the Alice in Wonderland world of postmodern discourse, the struggle for equality is likened to the racist practices of the 'white colonisers' while the rejection of equal rights is seen as the hallmark of social advancement. 'Equality' has come to mean oppression, 'difference' liberation.

The shift from campaigning for the 'right to be equal' to proclaiming the 'right to be different' is predicated on the antihumanist, anti-essentialist tendencies in poststructuralist discourse. But these tendencies themselves are a product of the disillusionment with social change which has become an increasingly prominent feature of postwar politics. Campaigning for equality requires one to believe that it is possible to effect social change, to transform society through humanity's collective efforts. Conversely proclaiming difference requires us to accept society as it is, to accept as given the divisions and inequalities that characterise our social world. In this sense the philosophy of difference is a rationalisation of the demise and defeat of social movements over the past decade which has led radicals to renounce the very idea of social struggle. The ideas of difference seek to accommodate to this new political era.

Poststructuralists and postmodernists seem to suggest that change can rarely be for the better. Struggle, they say, is as dominating as subjugation. '[T]here is no question here of proposing a "pure" alternative to the system', Lyotard wrote in his seminal book, *The Postmodern Condition*. 'We all know, as the 1970s come to a close, that an attempt at an alternative of that kind would end up resembling the system it was meant to replace'.[5] Any attempt to change society, he suggests, can at best leave things as they are, at worst inflict greater pain upon us. Similarly Derrida has written that 'discourses . . . [which] state their opposition to racism, to totalitarianism, to Nazis, to fascism . . . do this in the name of the Spirit, in the name of an axiomatic'.[6] Derrida means that to take a stand against racism or fascism is to adopt the totalitarian outlook of the racist or the fascist.

The logic of Foucault's argument would suggest the same conclusion. Foucault, we have already observed, believes in the existence of an all-encompassing Power, through which society and its subjects are constituted. Foucault believes that 'the power is "always already there"', that one is never "outside" it, that there are no "margins" for those who break with the system to gambol in'.[7] For Foucault power itself breeds resistance, but that resistance is always within the framework constituted by power. In the end 'we all fight each other'.[8] There is therefore nothing but an endless round of power and resistance, with no direction or goal. The consequence, as Jeffrey Isaacs observes, is the 'abandonment of *criticism* as a guiding ideal for theory':

> If there are no metanarratives, no underlying reasons for us to do what we should do then the theorist or political writer is under no obligation to offer such reasons in support of his or her proposals. Theory

then becomes rhetoric, or poetry, or perhaps a game in which the writer's will to power or self-expression becomes his or her primary motivation.[9]

The consequence is a withdrawal from political struggle. '[I]n spite of all their talk of context and concreteness', Isaac notes, 'these writers fail to address contemporary political realities in anything like a substantive manner'.[10] Renouncing struggle, poststructuralists and postmodernists demand instead 'space' within a 'plural' society. 'We cannot transform society', runs the argument, 'so we want to claim our place within society as it is.' Thus Caroline Knowles and Shamira Mercer offer what they call 'a deconstructionist approach to any notion of oppression.' They dismiss what they term 'the general "isms"', which see the issue of oppression as 'reaching beyond the manifestations of the problem to the structures of the system itself'. This they regard as an overly pessimistic view: 'There is no need to accept these inequalities as inevitable or to develop strategies that strike at the very root of capitalist and patriarchal society.' Instead 'we need only to identify the practices and procedures throughout a range of social institutions . . . which have the effect of producing racial and gender inequalities.' Once these have been identified, they 'can then be monitored and challenged'.[11] We do not have to tackle oppression at its roots, simply prune a few of the unfortunate branches.

For all their desire to be different, what pluralists really want is to be included in. They want their particular history, their particular culture, their particular story to be acknowledged. Pluralism is about accepting the common framework of society but arguing that we want to be included in it too. Hence Edward Said, despite a lifetime of political campaigning on behalf of the Palestinian people, seems to accept the inevitability of oppression:

> There is the possibility of a more generous and pluralistic vision of the world, in which imperialism courses on, as it were, belatedly in different forms (the North–South polarity of our own time is one), and the relationship of domination continues, but the opportunities for liberation are open.[12]

There is little we can do about imperialist domination, suggests Said. So why not accept the inevitable and simply make the best of it? In practical terms Said's accommodation to 'the relationship of domination' can be seen in Palestine. Said has been very critical of the 1994 peace treaty between the Palestine Liberation Organisation and the Israeli government, which provided the Palestinians with 'autonomous' areas in Jericho and the Gaza strip. The peace treaty, Said has rightly pointed out, institutionalises the denial of rights to the Palestinian people. Yet such institutionalisation of oppression is surely the logic of Said's plea for a 'pluralistic vision of the world' in which 'the relationship of domination continues' but 'opportunities for liberation are open'.

In this world of limited opportunities and low horizons, the state of being marginal is now seen as a cause for celebration. 'Paradoxically', writes Stuart Hall, 'marginality has become a powerful space. It is a space of weak power, but is a space of power nonetheless'.[13] What Hall is really saying is that the weak and the oppressed have been confined to the margins of society and have no recourse to the levers of power. The defeats of the liberation struggles, of the social movements and of working-class action mean that there is little possibility of the marginalised groups achieving power. We should make the best of what we have and celebrate 'marginality' as powerful. The fate of the Palestinian people in Gaza and Jericho should remind us that 'marginality' is anything but a 'powerful space'.

Unable to transform society, postmodern critics accommodate to, and occasionally even celebrate, oppression. bell hooks writes nostalgically of the segregated South of her childhood as a 'marginal space where black people (though contained) exercised power, where we were truly caring and supportive to one another':

> I had come from an agrarian world where folks were content to get by on little, where Baba, mama's mother, made soap, dug fishing worms, set traps for rabbits, made butter and wine, sewed quilts, and wrung the necks of chickens . . . The sweet communion we felt (that strong sense of solidarity shrouding and protecting my growing up years was something I thought all black people had known) was rooted in love, relational love, the care we had towards one another.[14]

hooks might have added that this was also a world where poverty was endemic, starvation common and lynching an ever-present threat. hooks goes on to contrast the romanticised black community of her childhood with the 'corrosive' nature of sixties black militancy:

> Looking back, it is easy to see that the nationalism of the sixties and seventies was very different from the racial solidarity born of shared circumstance and not theories of black power. Not that an articulation of black power was not important; it was. Only it did not deliver the goods; it was too informed by corrosive power relations, too mythic, to take the place of that concrete relational love that bonded black folks together in communities of hope and struggle.[15]

For hooks, struggle itself becomes the problem. The aspiration to power is necessarily 'corrosive' in contrast to the 'concrete relational love' that characterised black communities in the past. In the face of social movements that failed to 'deliver the goods', poststructuralist and postmodernist thinkers are forced to romanticise oppression, decry equality and accept difference and marginality. bell hooks makes this clear when she derives the politics of difference from the defeat of the sixties' black liberation movement:

> In the wake of the black power movement, after so many rebels were slaughtered and lost, many of these voices were silenced by a repressive state; others became inarticulate. It has become necessary to find new avenues to transmit the messages of black liberation struggle, new ways to talk about racism and other politics of domination. Radical postmodern practice, most powerfully conceptualised as a 'politics of difference' should incorporate the voices of displaced, marginalised, exploited, and oppressed black people.[16]

The philosophy of difference is the politics of defeat, born out of defeat. It is the product of disillusionment with the possibilities of social change and the acceptance of the inevitability of an unequal, fragmented world. Unable to pursue the goal of equality, postmodernists have simply refashioned its meaning and embraced difference. The consequence has been the celebration of marginality, of parochialism and indeed of oppression. Transcending such an outlook requires not simply intellectual conviction but political aspiration.

TRANSCENDING 'RACE'

Throughout this book I have insisted that the meaning of 'race' cannot be confined to a simple definition or reduced to a single property or relationship. Rather, race arises out of complex contradictions within capitalist society and articulates those contradictions in complex ways. In previous chapters I have considered the contradictions primarily in terms of the conflict between an abstract belief in equality and the reality of an unequal society. In Chapter 8, I reframed the dichotomy in a slightly different way – as that between the belief in historic specificity and the need for universalist forms of thinking. The biological discourse of race and the cultural discourse of difference both arise from the inability to reconcile the two. Both take the existence of human specificity, that is the particular forms of human existence, as evidence for the denial of human universality, of a common human essence.

The difficulty in reconciling belief in the abstract principle of universality with the actual, concrete, particular expressions of humanity reveals one of the central problems of Western philosophy. Throughout this book we have encountered this dichotomy in a variety of forms – as between the subject and the object, the ideal and the material, the individual and society, fact and interpretation, the empirical and the theoretical. This dichotomy was one expression of the conflict between Enlightenment and Romantic viewpoints. On the one hand, a commitment to universality, to which Enlightenment *philosophes* were attached, seemed to suggest the need for an eternalising approach. Universalists seemed blind to the specific, historical aspects of human activity. The French Catholic conservative Joseph de Maistre famously mocked the Revolutionary belief in the 'rights of Man' because of its abstract nature:

> There is no such thing as *man* in the world. During my life I have seen Frenchmen, Italians, Russians, and so on; thanks to Montesquieu I even know that one can be *Persian;* but I must say, as for *man,* I have never come across him anywhere; if he exists he is completely unknown to me.[17]

The critics of Enlightenment discourse argued that 'man' was a social not a natural being, and that all social phenomena must be considered in their historical context. On the other hand, the introduction of the social and the historical into Romantic discourse seemed to dissolve universalism by privileging difference. For the Romantics all peoples had their own cultures which were incommensurate, their own values which were incompatible.

Early liberal discourse simply assumed a reconciliation between the universal and the particular. Eighteenth-century radicals and nineteenth-century liberals both argued, for instance, that there existed an identity between individual desire and the social good. The anthropologist E. B. Tylor defended free trade on the grounds that 'what serves the general profit of mankind serves also the private profit of the individual man'.[18] Similarly nineteenth-century liberals agreed that nationalism could reconcile both particular and universal interests. Whereas Rousseau had recognised in the nation-state a tension between the rights of man and the rights of citizens, liberal nationalists agreed with Condorcet that 'Nature could not have wished to found the happiness of one people on the unhappiness of its neighbours, nor to set in opposition two virtues that it equally inspires: love of the fatherland and love of humanity.'[19]

As we have already seen in Chapter 3, historical development helped undermine this belief in the implicit reconciliation of particular interests and the universal good. The emergence of the working class, the growth of social conflict, the fears for social progress, all made manifest the growing friction between narrow parochial interests and broader social aims. As the intelligentsia grew increasingly apprehensive of social transformation it began to distance itself from the emancipatory logic of

Enlightenment discourse. In this context the belief in universalism became transformed into the concept of the natural or the eternal, while historical specificity became degraded to the idea of particularism or 'difference'. This process gave rise to the biological discourse of race, on the one hand, and the cultural discourse of difference on the other. Both wrenched apart the particular and the universal, and treated each category in isolation. In the absence of any mediation between the particular and the universal, what we had was the eternalisation of difference.

Standing betwixt the Enlightenment and Romantic traditions, Rousseau had already anticipated the difficulties in reconciling the concepts of universalism and of historical specificity. He agreed, on the one hand, that social differences had to be acknowledged in order to understand the commonality of humanity: 'When one wants to study men, one must consider those around one. But to study man, one must extend the range of one's vision. One must first observe the differences in order to discover the properties.'[20] In other words, humanity manifests itself in concrete, local forms and these must be the starting point in understanding the abstract concept of human universality. On the other hand, Rousseau was adamant that the commonalities of humankind could not simply be deduced from the particularities of different societies. '[O]ne can know Peter and James thoroughly', he wrote, 'and yet have made little progress in the knowledge of men'.[21] Understanding purely the specific, concrete manifestations of humanity gives us little understanding of its universal properties.

To reconcile the one with the other, Rousseau argued that the universal and the particular must be seen in dynamic relation to each other, as different moments of the same process: 'Society must be studied in the individual and the individual in society.'[22] What Rousseau is arguing is that the individual has no meaning except within the context of society, but society only manifests itself through the individual. Tear one apart from the other and neither becomes comprehensible.

The idea that Rousseau is developing here (though he never used the term) is that of the *dialectic*. The dialectical approach to humanity sees the universal and the particular as in a state of constant tension and dialogue. Human universality expresses itself in specific concrete aspects. Concrete human activity can only be understood within the context of the totality provided by the concept of universality. 'Only in this context which sees the isolated facts of social life as aspects of the historical process and integrates them in a *totality*, can knowledge of the facts hope to become knowledge of *reality*', wrote Georg Lukács. He added that 'The knowledge of the real, objective nature of a phenomenon, the knowledge of its historical character and the knowledge of its actual function in the totality of society form, therefore, a single undivided act of cognition.'[23]

This concept of the dialectic was developed within the German idealist tradition, notably by Hegel. It was subsequently appropriated by Marx (who famously wrote that he 'stood Hegel on his head') as a tool to study the contradictions within capitalist society from a materialist viewpoint. Marx married the Enlightenment commitment to universalism to the Romantic insistence that social phenomena had to be studied historically. The same social laws, he argued, bound all humanity, but such laws were historically specific.

In Marx's work we find the full flowering of the idea which was first intimated by Rousseau. For Marx, human beings were conscious active subjects constantly making and remaking the world around them. The logic of Marx's approach suggested, on the one hand, that every society was transient and, on the other, implied not just the possibility but the need for social transformation. This process of conscious human activity to transform society was, for Marx, the link between the particular and the universal.[24]

The logic of the argument I have presented in this book suggests that only a dialectical understanding of the relationship between the particular and the universal can allow us to transcend the concept of 'race'. Such an understanding forces us to see the universal and the particular not as separate categories but existing only in a reciprocal relationship. It allows us to see human differences as socially constructed, while at the same time reminding us that humans possess a social essence, arising out of their sociability, which is the basis for human equality.

Developing such a dialectical understanding is not simply an intellectual problem. Throughout this book, I have stressed the intimate relationship between intellectual progress and wider social and political developments. One cannot be reduced to the other, but neither can the two be understood in isolation. The significance of race only becomes apparent in the interaction of the two. The aim of this book has been to tease out the meaning of race through studying the interaction of intellectual and social developments over the past two centuries.

Contemporary celebration of difference, irrespective of whether that difference is mediated through culture or biology, is the product of the social and political changes that have shaken the world over the past period. It is an intellectual outlook that has been forged out of the seeming impossibility of transforming social relations. For two centuries after the French Revolution radicals defined themselves by their belief in human progress, their support for collective action and their commitment to social transformation. From the Enlightenment onwards a radical intellectual tradition embodied those hopes and aspirations. Today that intellectual tradition is dead. The cumulative legacy of defeats has destroyed not simply the organisations and movements that espoused social change but also the intellectual tradition that guided it. The philosophy of difference is the ideological embodiment of that defeat. To transcend the concept of race we require not just an intellectual revolution, but a social one too.

Notes and References

INTRODUCTION

1. Walter Bagehot, *Physics and Politics* (London: King, 1887) pp. 20–1.
2. Lancelot Hogben, *Genetic Principles in Medicine and Social Science* (New York: Knopf, 1932) p. 123.
3. For an elaboration of the race relations paradigm see Michael Banton, *Racial and Ethnic Competition* (Cambridge University Press, 1983); John Rex, *Race Relations in Sociological Theory* (London: Weidenfeld & Nicolson, 1970). For a more radical perspective see CCCS, *The Empire Strikes Back: Race and Racism in 70s Britain* (London: Hutchinson, 1982); Michael Omi and Howard Winant, *Racial Formation in the United States: From the 1960s to the 1980s* (London: Routledge & Kegan Paul, 1986). For Robert Miles' critique, see *Racism and Migrant Labour: A Critical Text* (London: Routledge & Kegan Paul, 1982); *Racism after 'Race Relations'* (London: Routledge, 1993).
4. Miles, *Racism after 'Race Relations'*, p. 2.
5. Michael Banton, 'The Race Relations Problematic', *British Journal of Sociology*, vol. 42 no. 1 (1991).
6. Miles, *Racism after 'Race Relations'*, pp. 5–6.
7. Johann Friederich Blumenbach, *The Anthropological Treatises of Johann Friederich Blumenbach*, trans and ed. by Thomas Bendyshe (London: Anthropological Society, 1865) p. 98.
8. William Z. Ripley, *The Races of Europe: A Sociological Study* (New York: D. Appleton, 1899) p. 111.
9. See Stephen Rose, R. C. Lewontin and Leon J. Kamin, *Not in Our Genes: Biology, Ideology and Human Nature* (Harmondsworth: Penguin, 1984) pp. 119–27.
10. Steve Jones, *The Language of the Genes: Biology, History and the Evolutionary Future* (London: Harper Collins, 1993).
11. Blumenbach, *Anthropological Treatises*, p. 99.
12. Robert Miles, *Racism* (London: Routledge, 1989) p. 71.
13. Hogben, *Genetic Principles*, p. 124.
14. George W. Stocking Jnr, *Race, Culture and Evolution: Essays in the History of Anthropology* (University of Chicago Press, 1982) p. 45.

1. BEYOND THE LIBERAL HOUR

1. Geoff Mulgan, 'Nazi Business', *Marxism Today*, (November 1991).
2. *European*, 27 Sep. 1991.
3. *The Economist*, 28 Sep. 1991.
4. *Bosnia's Last Testament*, BBC, 11 Apr. 1993.

5. Frank Furedi, *Mythical Past, Elusive Future: History and Society in an Anxious Age* (London: Pluto Press, 1990) p. 172.

6. Cited in John Stevenson, 'Has Planning a Future?', in J. C. D. Clark (ed.), *Ideas and Politics in Modern Britain* (London: Macmillan, 1990) p. 235.

7. Furedi, *Mythical Past*, p. 130.

8. Daniel Bell, *Sociological Journeys: Essays 1960–1980* (London: Heinemann, 1980) p. 149.

9. Karl Pearson, *National Life from the Standpoint of Science* (London: A. & C. Black, 1905) p. 21.

10. Theodore Roosevelt, 'The Winning of the West', in *The Works of Theodore Roosevelt* (New York: Scribner's, 1926) vol. 9, p. 57.

11. UNESCO, *Conference for the Establishment of the United Nations Educational, Scientific and Cultural Organisation*, 16 Nov. 1945, p. 93.

12. See Paul Gordon Lauren, *Power and Prejudice: The Politics and Diplomacy of Racial Discrimination* (London: Westview Press, 1988) pp. 76–101.

13. Ashley Montagu, *Statement on Race*, (London: Oxford University Press, 1972).

14. *Pravda*, 17 Nov. 1946.

15. Cited in Lauren, *Power and Prejudice*, p. 190.

16. *Spectator*, 25 Jan. 1957.

17. *Spectator*, 5 Jul. 1957.

18. Lauren, *Power and Prejudice*, p. 189.

19. President's Committee on Civil Rights, *To Secure These Rights* (Washington DC: Government Printing Office, 1947) pp. 111, 166.

20. N. Deakin, *Colour, Citizenship and British Society* (London: Panther, 1969).

21. I. Katznelson, *Black Men, White Cities: Race Relations and Migration in the United States 1900–1930 and Britain 1948–68* (London: Oxford University Press for the Institute of Race Relations, 1973) p. 126; Michael Banton, *Promoting Racial Harmony* (Cambridge University Press, 1985) p. 126.

22. Anthony Thwaite (ed.), *Selected Letters of Philip Larkin* (London: Faber & Faber, 1992).

23. Anthony Thwaite, 'Introduction', *Larkin at Sixty* (London: 1982) p. 11; Alan Gardiner, 'Larkin's England' in Linda Cookson and Bryan Loughrey (eds), *Critical, Essays on Philip Larkin: The Poems* (London: Longman, 1988) p. 62; Andrew Motion, *Larkin* (London: Routledge, 1982) p. 20.

24. J. Murray *et al.*, PRO HO 213/244, 22 Jun. 1948.

25. PRO CO 876/88, 5 Jul. 1948.

26. Cited in Keith Tompson, *Under Seige: Racial Violence in Britain Today* (Harmondsworth: Penguin, 1988) p. 62.

27. Cmnd 7695, *Report of the Royal Commission on Population* (London: HMSO, 1949) p. 124.

28. Cited in Shirley Joshi and Bob Carter, 'The Role of Labour in the Creation of a Racist Britain', *Race and Class*, vol. 25, no. 3 (1984).

29. Cited in Zig Layton-Henry, *The Politics of Immigration* (Oxford: Blackwell, 1992) p. 34.

30. PRO CAB 128/29, 3 Nov. 1955.

31. Cited in Joshi and Carter, 'The Role of Labour in the Creation of a Racist Britain', *Race and Class* (1984)

32. Ibid.

33. Cited in Tompson, *Under Seige*, p. 64.

34. Cited in Robert Miles and Annie Phizacklea, *White Man's Country: Racism in British Politics* (London: Pluto, 1984) pp. 27–8.

35. Cited in Layton-Henry, *The Politics of Immigration*, p. 32.

36. *Daily Mail*, 7 Feb. 1961.

37. For an excellent account of the background to the Notting Hill riots see Edward Pilkington, *Beyond the Mother Country: West Indians and the Notting Hill White Riots* (London: I. B. Tauris, 1988).
38. Cited in Pilkington, *Beyond the Mother Country*, p. 127.
39. *Daily Sketch*, 2 Sep. 1958.
40. Cited in Miles and Phizacklea, *White Man's Country*, p. 35.
41. Richard Crossman, *The Diaries of a Cabinet Minister* (vol. 1) (London: Jonathan Cape, 1975).
42. Cited in Sheila Patterson, *Immigration and Race Relations in Britain 1960–1967* (London: Oxford University Press for the Institute of Race Relations, 1969) p. 113.
43. *Spectator*, 1 Mar. 1968.
44. *The Times*, 1 Mar. 1968.
45. Miles and Phizacklea, *White Man's Country*, p. 58.
46. Sir Arthur Hoare, Chairman of Middlesex County Council's Education Committee, *Middlesex County Times*, 2 Nov. 1963; cited in Patterson, *Immigration and Race Relations in Britain*, pp. 110–11.
47. Cmnd. 2739, *Immigration from the Commonwealth* (London: HMSO, Aug. 1965).
48. Reginald Maudling, speaking in the parliamentary debate on the 1968 Commonwealth Immigrants Act, cited in Miles and Phizacklea, *White Man's Country*, p. 62.
49. *Libération*, 19 Feb. 1991.
50. Ministère du Travail/Secrétariat d'Etat aux Travailleurs Immigrés, *Immigration et 7e Plan* (Paris: La Documentation Français, 1977).
51. *Le Monde*, 9 Feb. 1990.
52. Ministère du Travail, *Immigration et 7e Plan*, p. 156.
53. *L 'Usine Nouvelle*, 26 March 1970; cited in F. Gaspard and C. Servan-Schreiber, *La Fin des Immigrés* (Paris: Seuil, 1985).
54. C. Wihtol de Wenden, *Les Immigrés et la Politique* (Paris: Presses de la Fondation Nationale des Sciences Politiques, 1988).
55. C. Calvez, 'Extraits du Rapport de Corentin Calvez sur le Problème des Traivailleurs Étrangers', *Hommes et Migrations*, no. 768 (1969).
56. Calvez, 'Extraits d'u Rapport de Corentin Calvez', *Hommes et Migration* (1969).
57. Maxim Silverman, *Deconstructing the Nation: Immigration, Racism and Citizenship in France* (London: Routledge, 1992) p. 86.
58. T. Nairn, *The Break-up of Britain* (London: Verso, 1981) p. 274.
59. *Daily Mail*, 10 Oct. 1991.
60. *Sunday Telegraph*, 6 Sep. 1992.
61. *Time*, 17 Aug. 1977.
62. *Sunday Telegraph*, 3 May 1992.
63. Midge Decter, 'How the Rioters won', *Commentary* (Fall 1992).
64. James G. Shields, 'Anti-Semitism in France: the Spectre of Vichy', *Patterns of Prejudice*, vol. 24, nos. 2–4 (1990).
65. *Libération*, 21 Jun. 1991.
66. Thomas Byrne Edsall, 'Willie Horton's Message', *New York Review of Books*, 13 Feb. 1992.
67. Norman Tebbit, 'Fanfare for Being British', *The Field* (May 1990).
68. Colin Holmes, *John Bull's Island: Immigration and British Society, 1871–1971* (London: Macmillan, 1988); J. Garrard, *The English and Immigration 1880–1910* (Oxford University Press, 1971); B. Gainer, *The Alien Invasion: The Origins of the Aliens Act 1905* (London: Heinemann, 1972); A. Dummet and

A. Nichol, *Subjects, Citizens, Aliens and Others: Nationality and Immigration Law* (London: Weidenfeld and Nicolson, 1990); L. Sponza, *Italian Immigrants in Nineteenth-Century Britain: Images and Realities* (Leicester University Press, 1988); P. Panayi, *The Enemy in Our Midst: Germans in Britain During the First World War* (New York: Berg, 1991); D. Cesarani, 'Anti-Alienism in England After the First World War', *Immigrants and Minorities*, vol. 6 (1987).

69. Silverman, *Deconstructing the Nation*, p. 81.
70. G. Noiriel, *Le Creuset Français: Histoire de l'Immigration XIXe – XXe Siècles* (Paris: Seuil, 1988); C Wihtol de Wenden, *Les Immigrés et La Politique* (Paris: Presses de la Fondation National des Sciences Politiques, 1988).
71. Mark Almond, 'Europe's Immigration Crisis', *National Interest*, no. 29 (Fall 1992)
72. Barry Buzan, 'Global Security in the New World Order', *International Affairs*, vol. 67, no. 3 (Jul. 1991).
73. Paul Johnson, 'How to restore the good name of colonialism', *Spectator*, 9 Jan. 1993.

2. THE SOCIAL LIMITS TO EQUALITY

1. *Daily Mail*, 15 Jun. 1995.
2. George L. Mosse, *Toward the Final Solution: A History of European Racism* (London: J. M. Dent & Sons, 1978); Leon Poliakov, *The Aryan Myth: A History of Racist and Nationalist Ideas in Europe* (New York Library, 1971); David Theo Goldberg, *Racist Culture: Philosophy and the Politics of Meaning* (Oxford: Blackwell, 1993).
3. Mosse, *Toward the Final Solution*, p. 3.
4. Goldberg, *Racist Culture*, pp. 29, 28.
5. Ibid., p. 24.
6. Ibid., p. 3.
7. Ibid., p. 3.
8. E. J. Hobsbawm, *The Age of Revolution 1789–1848* (London: Sphere, 1973 [first pub. 1962]) p. 35.
9. Cited in Peter Fryer, *Staying Power: The History of Black People in Britain* (London: Pluto Press, 1984) pp. 137–8.
10. Anthony Pagden, *European Encounters with the New World* (New Haven: Yale University Press, 1993) pp. 4–5.
11. Irving Zeitlin, *Ideology and the Development of Sociological Theory* (Englewood Cliffs, NJ: Prentice-Hall, 1968) pp. 2–3; the quote is from Cassirer, *The Philosophy of the Enlightenment*, p. viii.
12. Cited in N. Hampson, *The Enlightenment: An Evaluation of its Assumptions, Attitudes and Values* (Harmondsworth: Penguin, 1968) p. 36.
13. Charles de Secondat Montesquieu, *The Spirit of the Laws*, trans Anne M. Cohler, Carolyn Miller and Harold S. Stone (Cambridge University Press, 1989).
14. Zeitlin, *Ideology and Development of Sociological Theory*, p. 7.
15. Hampson, *The Enlightenment*, p. 39.
16. Nathan Tarcov, *Locke's Education for Liberty* (University of Chicago Press, 1984) p. 1.
17. George-Louis Leclerk de Buffon, *A Natural History, General and Particular*, trans by William Smellie (London: Richard Evans, 1817) pp. 107, 306, 398.
18. David Hume, *Inquiry Concerning Human Understanding* (Oxford University Press; 1994, orig. pub. 1748).

19. Cited in Ashley Montagu, *Man's Most Dangerous Myth: The Fallacy of Race* (Cleveland: World Publishing, 1964), p. 44.
20. Cited in Montagu, *Man's Most Dangerous Myth*, p. 44.
21. Louis-Armand de Lom D'Acre Lahontan, *New Voyages to North America* (London: H. Bonwicke, 1703) vol. 2, p. 8.
22. Jean-Jacques Rousseau, *The Social Contract*, trans by Maurice Cranston (Harmondsworth: Penguin, 1968 [orig. pub. 1770]) p. 49.
23. Jean-Jacques Rousseau, *A Discourse on Inequality*, trans by Maurice Cranston (Harmondsworth: Penguin, 1984; orig. pub. 1755) p. 160.
24. Ibid., n. J, pp. 154–155.
25. Jean-Jacques Rousseau, *On the Origin of Language*, trans by John H. Moran and Alexander Gode (New York: Frederick Unger, 1966; orig. pub. 1761).
26. Rousseau, *A Discourse on Inequality*, n. J, p. 159.
27. Joseph-Marie Degerando, *The Observation of Savage Peoples*, trans by F. C. T. Moore (Berkeley: University of California Press, 1969; orig. pub. 1300) p. 66.
28. Degerando, *The Observation of Savage Peoples*, p. 84.
29. Stocking, *Race, Culture and Evolution*, p. 28.
30. Degerando, *The Observation of Savage Peoples*, p. 97.
31. François-Marie Arouet Voltaire, 'Essays on the Customs and Spirit of the Nations', in *The Age of Louis XIV and Other Selected Writings*, trans and abridged by J. H. Brumfitt (New York: Washington Square Press) p. 243.
32. David Hume, 'Of National Characters', in *Selected Essays* (Oxford University Press, 1993) n. 120, p. 360.
33. Hume, *Selected Essays*, p. 166.
34. Tzvetan Todorov, *On Human Diversity: Nationalism, Racism and Exoticism in French Thought*, trans Catherine Porter (Cambridge Mass.: Harvard University Press, 1993; orig. pub. 1989), p. 103.
35. Georges-Louis Leclerk de Buffon, *The History of Man and Quadrupeds*, trans William Smellie (London: T. Caddell and W. Davies, 1812) p. 373.
36. Michael Banton, *Racial Theories* (Cambridge University Press, 1987) pp. 8–9; Robert Miles, *Racism* (London: Routledge, 1989); Anthony Barker, *The African Link: British Attitudes to the Negro in the Era of the Atlantic Slave Trade, 1550–1807* (London: Frank Cass, 1978).
37. T. H. Huxley, 'Emancipation – Black and White', in *Lay Sermons, Addresses and Reviews*, (New York: D. Appleton, 1871) p. 24.
38. Hobsbawm, *The Age of Revolution*, p. 36.
39. Ibid.
40. Isaiah Berlin, *Vico and Herder: Two Studies in the History of Ideas* (London: Hogarth, 1976) p. 215.
41. Adam Smith, *An Inquiry into the Nature and Causes of the Wealth of Nations*, ed. Kathryn Sutherland (Oxford University Press, 1993; orig. pub. 1776) p. 408.
42. The Early Draft of the *Wealth of Nations* is presumed to have been written in 1773 (three years before the final version was published). It was published in 1937.
43. Cited in Lucio Colletti, *From Rousseau to Lenin: Studies in Ideology and Society* (London: Monthly Review Press, 1972; orig. pub. 1969) p. 155.
44. Smith, *The Wealth of Nations*, p. 408.
45. Rousseau, *A Discourse on Inequality*, p. 77.
46. Ibid., p. 137.
47. Fryer, *Staying Power*.
48. Barker, *The African Link*, pp. 157–8.
49. William Blackstone, *Commentaries on the Laws of England* (Oxford: Clarendon Press, 1765–9) p. 23.

50. Seymour Drescher, *Capitalism and Antislavery: British Mobilisation in Comparative Perspective*, (Oxford University Press, 1987; orig. pub. 1986) p. 20.
51. Fryer, *Staying Power*, pp. 133–90.
52. David Brion Davis, *The Problem of Slavery in the Age of Revolution 1770–1823* (Oxford University Press, 1989) p. 461.
53. Drescher, *Capitalism and Antislavery*, p. 20.
54. Montesquieu, *The Spirit of the Laws*, pp. 394–5.
55. Drescher, *Capitalism and Antislavery*, p. 25.
56. Ibid., pp. 39–40.
57. Cited in Reginald Coupland, *Wilberforce, A Narrative* (Oxford University Press, 1923) pp. 144–5.
58. Cited in Robin Blackburn, *The Overthrow of Colonial Slavery, 1776–1848* (London: Verso: 1988) p. 148.
59. Cited in Hampson, *The Enlightenment*, p. 153.
60. Cited in Blackburn, *The Overthrow of Colonial Slavery*, p. 49.
61. Cited in Blackburn, *The Overthrow of Colonial Slavery*, p. 49.
62. Blackburn, *The Overthrow of Colonial Slavery*, pp. 49–50.
63. Cited in Blackburn, *The Overthrow of Colonial Slavery*, p. 50.
64. Cited in Blackburn, *The Overthrow of Colonial Slavery*, p. 50.
65. Cited in David Brion Davis, 'New Sidelights on Early Antislavery Radicalism', *William and Mary Quarterly*, 3rd Series, no. 28 (Oct. 1971).
66. Cited in James Walvin, 'British Popular Sentiment for Abolition', in Christine Bolt and Seymour Drescher (eds), *Anti-slavery Religion and Reform* (Hampden: Archon, 1980) pp. 152–3.
67. See Blackburn, *The Overthrow of Colonial Slavery*, esp. pp. 131–60 and pp. 293–330; Drescher, *Capitalism and Antislavery*, esp. pp. 89–110.
68. Blackburn, *The Overthrow of Colonial Slavery*, p. 170.
69. Abbé Raynal, *The Philosophical and Political History of the Settlements and Trade of the Europeans in the East and West Indies* (London, 1776) vol. 13, pp. 466–67.
70. Michael L. Kennedy, *The Jacobin Clubs in the French Revolution: The First Years* (Princeton University Press, 1982) p. 202.
71. M. B . Garrett, *The French Colonial Question, 1789–1791* (Ann Arbor, Michigan: George Wahr, 1921) p. 51.
72. C. L. R. James, *The Black Jacobins: Toussaint L'Ouverture and the San Domingo Revolution* (London: Allison & Busby, 1980; orig. pub. 1938) p. 80.
73. Cited in James, *The Black Jacobins*, p. 76.
74. James, *The Black Jacobins*, p. 120.
75. Ibid., p. 70.
76. Robin Blackburn, 'The French Revolution and New World Slavery' in Peter Osborne (ed.), *Socialism and the Limits of Liberalism* (London: Verso, 1991) p. 89.
77. Jean-Jacques Rousseau, *Émile, or, On Education*, trans Allan Bloom (New York: Basic Books, 1979) p. 39.
78. Thomas Paine, 'Agrarian Justice', in Michael Foot and Isaac Kramnick (eds), *The Thomas Paine Reader* (Harmondsworth: Penguin, 1987) p. 484.

3. THE MAKING OF A DISCOURSE OF RACE

1. Rousseau, *A Discourse on Inequality*, p. 77.
2. Karl Marx and Friedrich Engels, 'Manifesto of the Communist Party' in Marx and Engels, *Selected Works* (London: Lawrence & Wishart, 1968) p. 38.

3. 'Introduction' to Roy Porter and Mikulas Teich (eds), *Romanticism in National Context* (Cambridge University Press, 1988) pp. 4–5.
4. Cited in Russel Kirk, *The Conservative Mind* (London: Faber & Faber, 1954) p. 47.
5. Smith, *The Wealth of Nations*, p. 227.
6. Zeitlin, *Ideology and the Development of Sociological Theory*, p. 36.
7. Edmund Burke, 'Reform of Representation in the House of Commons', in *Collected Works*, (London: Rivington, 1815–27) vol. VI, p. 141.
8. Cited in Berlin, *Vico and Herder*, p. 182.
9. Cited in Berlin, *Vico and Herder*, p. 159.
10. Edmund Burke, *Reflections on the Revolution in France* (Harmondsworth: Penguin, 1968 [orig. pub. 1790]) p. 106.
11. Cited in Berlin, *Vico and Herder*, p. 165.
12. Cited in Hampson, *The Enlightenment*, p. 240.
13. Cited in Berlin, *Vico and Herder*, p. 180.
14. Cited in Mosse, *Toward the Final Solution*, p. 37.
15. Cited in Berlin, *Vico and Herder*, pp. 160–161.
16. Cited in Claude Blanckaert, 'On the Origins of French Ethnology', in George W. Stocking (ed.), *Bones, Bodies and Behaviour: Essays on Biological Anthropology (History of Anthropology*, vol. 5) (Madison, Wis.: University of Wisconsin Press, 1988) p. 26.
17. Cited in Blanckaert, 'On the Origins of French Ethnology', pp. 30–31.
18. Cited in Blanckaert, 'On the Origins of French Ethnology', p. 25.
19. Johannes Fabian, *Time and the Other: How Anthropology Makes its Object* (New York: Columbia University Press, 1983) p. 28.
20. Edward Said, *Culture and Imperialism* (London: Chatto & Windus, 1993) p. 120.
21. Fryer, *Staying Power*, p. 144.
22. Daniel Pick, *Faces of Degeneration: A European Disorder, c1848–1918* (Cambridge University Press, 1989) pp. 38, 39.
23. Eugen Weber, *Peasants into Frenchmen: The Modernisation of Rural France 1870–1914* (Stanford University Press, 1976).
24. Cited in Pick, *Faces of Degeneration*, p. 60.
25. Pick, *Faces of Degeneration*, p. 41.
26. Cited in Blanckaert, 'On the Origins of French Ethnology', p. 42.
27. Count Arthur de Gobineau, *The Inequality of Races* trans Adrian Collins (Los Angeles: Noontide Press, 1966) p. 5.
28. Gobineau, *The Inequality of Races*, p. 120.
29. Ibid., p. 78.
30. Cited in Georg Lucaks, *The Destruction of Reason* (London: Merlin, 1980) p. 676.
31. Cited in Pick, *Faces of Degeneration*, p. 12.
32. Cited in Gertrude Himmelfarb, *The Idea of Poverty: England in the Early Industrial Age* (London: Faber & Faber, 1984) p. 362.
33. Cited in Greta Jones, *Social Darwinism and English Thought: The Interaction Between Biological and Social Theory* (New Jersey: Harvester, 1980) p. 42.
34. Pick, *Faces of Degeneration*, p. 57.
35. Cited in Pick, *Faces of Degeneration*, p. 68.
36. Cited in Zeitlin, *Ideology and the Development of Sociological Theory*, p. 74.
37. Cited in Zeitlin, *Ideology and the Development of Sociological Theory*, p. 75.
38. Cited in Jones, *Social Darwinism*, p. 1.
39. Cited in Lucaks, *The Destruction of Reason*, p. 687.
40. Nancy Stepan, *The Idea of Race in Science: Great Britain 1800–1960* (London: Macmillan, 1982), p. 4.
41. *Spectator*, 16 Sep. 1865.
42. Cited in Stepan, *The Idea of Race*, p. 24.

43. William Smellie, *The Philosophy of Natural History* (Boston: Brown, Taggard & Chase, 1885) pp. 308–9.

44. Douglas A. Lorimer, *Colour, Class and the Victorians: English Attitudes to the Negro in the Mid-Nineteenth Century* (Leicester University Press, 1978) pp. 67–68.

45. *British Mother's Magazine*, 1 Apr. 1853.

46. 'American Slavery and European Revolutions', *Englishmen's Magazine* (Sep. 1852).

47. *Uncle Tom in England: or Proof that Black's White* (1852) p. 206; cited in Lorimer, *Colour, Class and the Victorians*, p. 97.

48. *Saturday Review*, 16 Jan. 1864.

49. Cited in Asa Briggs, 'Middle Class Consciousness in English Politics 1760–1846', *Past and Present*, no. 9 (Apr. 1956).

50. Henry Mayhew, *London Labour and the London Poor*, ed. by John D. Rosenberg (New York: Dover, 1968) vol. 1, p. 1.

51. Mayhew, *London Labour and the London Poor*, vol. 1, p. 2.

52. *Report on the Sanitary Condition of the Labouring Population of Great Britain*, ed. M. W. Flinn (Edinburgh: 1965) p. 202.

53. Himmelfarb, *The Idea of Poverty*, p. 356.

54. Cited in Jones, *Social Darwinism and English Thought*, pp. 148–9.

55. Thomas Huxley, 'On the Methods and Results of Ethnology', *Proceedings of the Royal Institute of Great Britain* IV (1862–66) pp. 461–3.

56. Bernard Semmel, *The Governor Eyre Controversy* (London: McGibbon & Kee, 1962) pp. 134–5.

57. F. D. Lugard, *The Dual Mandate in British Tropical Africa* (London: William Blackwood & Sons, 1922) pp. 18, 69, 88.

58. Cited in Lorimer, *Colour, Class and the Victorians*, p. 195.

59. *Saturday Review*, 13 Oct. 1866.

60. *Daily Telegraph*, 21 Aug. 1866.

61. Lorimer, *Colour, Class and the Victorians*, p. 195.

62. Cited in Fryer, *Staying Power*, p. 178.

63. V. G. Kiernan, *The Lords of Humankind: European Attitudes Towards the Outside World in the Imperial Age* (London: Weidenfeld & Nicolson, 1969) p. 316.

64. Cited in Jan Nederveen Pieterse, *Empire and Emancipation: Power and Liberation on a World Scale* (London: Pluto, 1989) p. 254.

65. Gustav LeBon, *The Psychology of Peoples* (New York: G. E. Stechert, 1912 [orig. pub. 1894]) pp. 29, 43.

66. Henrika Kuklick, *The Savage Within: The Social History of British Anthropology 1885–1945* (Cambridge University Press, 1991) pp. 85–6.

67. Kuklick, *The Savage Within*, p. 86.

68. Cited in Jones, *Social Darwinism and English Thought*, p. 144.

69. Cited in Allan Chase, *The Legacy of Malthus: The Social Costs of the New Scientific Racism* (Chicago: University of Illinois Press, 1980) p. 14.

70. J. G. Spurzheim, 'Phrenological Note by Dr Spurzheim', *Phrenological Journal*, no. 6 (1829–30).

4. RACE IN THE AGE OF DEMOCRACY

1. Robert Knox, *The Races of Men: A Philosophical Enquiry into the Influence of Race over the Destinies of Nations* (London: Henry Renshaw, 1850) pp. 234–6.

2. Cited in Daniel Jo Kevles, *In the Name of Eugenics: Genetics and the Uses of Human Heredity* (Harmondsworth: Penguin, 1986) p. 90.
3. Jones, *Social Darwinism*, 53.
4. Cited in 'Introduction', in Peter Keating (ed.), *Into Unknown England* (Manchester University Press, 1976) p. 14.
5. Himmelfarb, *The Idea of Poverty*, p. 366.
6. Beatrice Webb, *My Apprenticeship* (London: Penguin, 1971) pp. 186–7.
7. Houston Stewart Chamberlain, *The Foundations of the Nineteenth Century*, trans John Lees (London: Lane, 1910) vol. 1, p. 319.
8. C. F. Masterman, *The Condition of England* (London: Methuen 1909). p. 118.
9. John Carey, *The Intellectuals and the Masses: Pride and Prejudice Among the Literary Intelligentsia, 1880–1939* (London: Faber & Faber, 1992).
10. Jose Ortega y Gasset, *The Revolt of the Masses* (London: Allen & Unwin, 1932) p. 54.
11. Cited in Herbert Lottman, *Flaubert: A Biography* (London: Methuen, 1989) p. 237.
12. LeBon, *The Psychology of the Peoples*, pp. 215–16.
13. Cited in Carey, *The Intellectuals and the Masses*, p. 29.
14. Beatrice Webb, *Diaries* (London: Virago, 1983–6), vol. 1, p. 15.
15. W. B. Yeats, *Autobiographies* (London: Macmillan, 1977) p. 229.
16. Aldous Huxley, 'Aristocracy', in *Proper Studies* (London: Chatto & Windus, 1927) p. 159.
17. Cited in 'Introduction', in David Bradshaw (ed.), *The Hidden Huxley: Contempt and Compassion for the Masses* (London: Faber & Faber, 1994) p. xx.
18. Aldous Huxley, 'The Outlook for American Culture: Some Reflections in a Machine Age', *Harper's Magazine* (Aug. 1927).
19. T. S. Eliot, *Christianity and Culture* (New York: Harcourt Brace, 1968) p. 185.
20. William Bateson, *Biological Fact and the Structure of Society* (Oxford: Clarendon Press, 1912) p. 31.
21. Gaetano Mosca, *The Ruling Class*, trans Hannah D. Kahn and Arthur Livingstone (New York: McGraw-Hill, 1965) p. 416.
22. Pick, *Faces of Degeneration*, p. 20.
23. Eugenics Education Society, 'Investigation into the Pauper Family Histories', *Papers on the Report of the Poor Law Commission* (1911) pp. 187–8.
24. Cited in Pick, *Faces of Degeneration*, p. 51.
25. Émile Zola, *Nana* (Harmondsworth: Penguin, 1933; orig. pub. 1880) p. 222.
26. Cited in Pick, *Faces of Degeneration*, p. 41.
27. Aldous Huxley 'What is Happening to Our Population?', *Nash's Pall Mall Magazine*, XCIII (Apr. 1934).
28. R. A. Fisher, *Genetical Theory of Natural Selection* (Oxford University Press, 1930) p. 222.
29. H. J. Laski, 'The Scope of Eugenics', *Westminster Review*, vol. LXXIV (1910).
30. Alfred Marshall, *The Economics of Industry* (London: Macmillan, 1881) p. 31.
31. Cited in 'Introduction', in David Bradshaw (ed.), *The Hidden Huxley*, xiii–xiv.
32. Cited in Carey, *The Intellectuals and the Masses*, p. 12.
33. Carey, *The Intellectuals and the Masses*, p. 12.
34. Cited in Chase, *The Legacy of Malthus*, p. 127.
35. Chase, *The Legacy of Malthus*, p. 134.
36. Joseph Chamberlain, cited in *The Times*, 12 Nov. 1895.
37. *Daily Mail*, 23 Jun. 1897.
38. E. J. Hobsbawm, *The Age of Empire, 1875–1914* (London: Cardinal, 1989; orig. pub. 1987) p. 70.
39. Cited in Paul B. Rich, *Race and Empire in British Politics* (Cambridge University Press, 1986) p. 24.

40. Gilbert Murray, 'The Exploitation of Inferior Races in Ancient and Modern Times', in Gilbert Murray, Francis W. Hirst and J. L. Hammond, *Liberalism and the Empire: Three Essays* (London: Johnson, 1900).
41. Theodore Rooselvelt, 'The Winning of the West', in *The Works of Theodore Roosevelt* (New York: Scribner's, 1926), vol. 9, pp. 56–7.
42. James Morris, *Pax Britannica: The Climax of an Empire* (Harmondsworth: Penguin, 1979) p. 134.
43. *Sydney Daily Telegraph*, 14 Oct. 1896.
44. *The Times*, 12 Sep. 1910.
45. T. Lothrop Stoddard, *The Rising Tide of Color Against White World Supremacy* (New York: Scribner's, 1921) p. 9.
46. Cited in Lauren, *Power and Prejudice*, p. 55.
47. Stepan, *The Idea of Race*, p. 84.
48. Stocking, *Race, Culture and Evolution*, p. 57.
49. Cited in Lukacs, *The Destruction of Reason*, 693.
50. W. J. Solas, *Paleolithic Races and their Modern Representatives* (London: reprinted from *Science Progress*, 1908–1909) p. 505.
51. Cited in Ripley, *The Races of Europe*, 111.
52. Richard Dixon, *The Racial History of Man*, (New York: Scribner's, 1923) p. 8.
53. Elazar Barkan, *The Retreat of Scientific Racism: Changing Concepts of Race in Britain and the United States Between the World Wars* (Cambridge University Press, 1991) p. 101.
54. Cited in Lucaks, *The Destruction of Reason*, 694.
55. Stepan, *The Idea of Race*, xx–xxi.
56. Stephen Jay Gould, *Ontogeny and Phylogeny* (Cambridge, Mass.: Harvard University Press, 1977).
57. See Stephen Jay Gould, 'Racism and Recapitulation', in *Ever Since Darwin: Reflections in Natural History* (Harmondsworth: Penguin, 1980) pp. 214–21.
58. Barkan, *The Retreat of Scientific Racism*, 228.
59. Ibid., pp. 279–80.
60. *Spectator*, 29 Nov. 1934.
61. *Spectator*, 20 Dec. 1924.
62. Julian Huxley, *Africa View* (New York: Harpers, 1931) p. 395.
63. Barkan, *The Retreat of Scientific Racism*, p. 300.
64. J. Huxley and A. C. Haddon, *We Europeans: A Survey of 'Racial Problems'* (London: Jonathan Cape, 1935) pp. 169–70.
65. *Nature*, 12 Dec. 1936.
66. Ruth Benedict, *Race and Racism* (London: Routledge & Kegan Paul, 1983 [orig. pub. 1942]) pp. 6, 97.
67. Huxley and Haddon, *We Europeans*, p. 89.
68. Julian Huxley, 'Eugenics and Society' in *Man Stands Alone* (New York: Harpers, 1940) p. 53.

5. RACE, CULTURE AND NATIONHOOD

1. *Guardian*, 27 Aug. 1994.
2. Ernest Renan, 'What is a nation?', trans Martin Thom, in Homi K. Babha (ed.), *Nations and Narration* (London: Routledge, 1990) p. 13; all subsequent quotes are from this edition.
3. Silverman, *Deconstructing the Nation*, p. 20.
4. Todorov, *On Human Diversity*, p. 226.

5. E. J. Hobsbawm, *Nations and Nationalism since 1780: Programme, Myth, Reality* (Cambridge University Press, 1922 [2nd edn; 1st edn 1990]).
6. Hobsbawm, *Nations and Nationalism since 1780*, p. 20.
7. Cited in Todorov, *On Human Diversity*, p. 24.
8. Hobsbawm, *Nations and Nationalism since 1780*, p. 20.
9. Cited in Hobsbawm, *Nations and Nationalism since 1780*, p. 33.
10. J. S. Mill, 'Utilitarianism, Liberalism and Representative Government', in *On Liberty and Other Essays* (ed. John Grey) (Oxford University Press, 1993).
11. Silverman, *Deconstructing the Nation*, p. 27.
12. Todorov, *On Human Diversity*, p. 175.
13. Silverman, *Deconstructing the Nation*, p. 28.
14. Eric Hobsbawm, 'Mass-Producing Traditions: Europe, 1870–1914', in Eric Hobsbawm and Terence Ranger (eds), *The Invention of Tradition* (Cambridge University Press, 1983) p. 264.
15. Hobsbawm, 'Mass-Producing Traditions', p. 265.
16. Cited in Hobsbawm, *The Age of Capital*, p. 111.
17. Jules Michelet, *France Before Europe* (Boston: Roberts Brothers, 1871) p. 59.
18. Jules Michelet, *The People*, trans John P. McKay (Urbana: University of Illinois Press, 1973 [first pub. 1846]) p. 210.
19. Ibid., p. 180.
20. Maurice Barrès, *Scènes et Doctrines du Nationalisme* (Paris: Plon-Nourrit, 1925 [orig. pub. 1902]) vol. 1, pp. 84, 129.
21. Jules Michelet, *History of France*, trans Walter Kelly (London: Chapman & Hall, 1844). vol. 1, p. 1.
22. Hobsbawm, *Nations and Nationalism Since 1780*, p. 54.
23. Renan, 'What is a Nation?', in Babha (ed.), *Nations and Narration*, p. 11.
24. See Hobsbawm, 'Mass-Producing Traditions', in Hobsbawm and Ranger (eds) *The Invention of Tradition*.
25. D. Lochak, 'Etrangers et citoyens au regard du droit', in C. Wihtol de Wenden (ed), *La Citoyenneté* (Paris: Edilig/Fondation Diderot, 1988) p. 78.
26. Ernest Renan, *The Future of Science* (Boston: Roberts Brothers, 1891) pp. xiv–xv.
27. Ernest Renan, 'Des service rendus aux sciences historiques par la philologie', in *Oeuvres Complètes* (Paris: Calmann-Levy, 1947–61) vol. 8, 1220.
28. Ernest Renan, 'Histoire du peuple d'Israël', *Oeuvres Complètes*, vol. 6, p. 32.
29. Todorov, *On Human Diversity*, p. 144.
30. Barrès, *Scènes et Doctrines du Nationalisme*, vol. 1, p. 14.
31. Ibid., vol. 1, p. 12.
32. Cited in Todorov, *On Human Diversity*, p. 190.
33. Barres, *Scènes et Doctrines du Nationalisme*, vol. 1, pp. 43–4.
34. Cited in Stocking, *Race, Culture and Evolution*, p. 115.
35. E. B. Tylor, *Researches into the Early History of Mankind* (London: John Murray, 1865) p. 361.
36. Hippolyte Taine, *History of English Literature*, trans H. van Laun (Philadelphia: Gebbie Publishing, 1897 [first pub. 1864]) vol. 1, p. 8.
37. Todorov, *On Human Diversity*, pp. 156–7.
38. Enoch Powell, Speech at Eastbourne, 16 Nov. 1968.
39. Renan, *The Future of Science*, p. 169.
40. LeBon, *The Psychology of Peoples*, pp. 216–17.
41. Ibid., p. 35.
42. Barrès, *Scènes et Doctrines du Nationalism*, vol. 1, 64; vol. 2, p. 177.
43. See Todorov, *On Human Diversity*, pp. 57–8.
44. Barrès, *Scènes et Doctrines du Nationalisme*, vol. 1, p. 60.

45. Ernest Gellner, *Relativism and the Social Sciences* (Cambridge University Press, 1985) p. 83.
46. Cited in Stocking, *Race, Culture and Evolution*, p. 117.
47. Stocking, *Race, Culture and Evolution*, p. 88.
48. Eric Hobsbawm, *Age of Extremes: The Short Twentieth Century* (London: Michael Joseph, 1994) pp. 6, 7.

6. FROM BIOLOGICAL HIERARCHY TO CULTURAL DIVERSITY

1. M. Gibson, 'Approaches to Multicultural Education in the United States: Some Concepts and Assumptions', *Anthropology and Education Quarterly*, vol. 7, no. 4, (1976).
2. Cited in Barry Troyna and Jenny Williams, *Racism, Education and the State* (London: Croom Helm, 1986) p. 36.
3. Rick Simonson and Scott Walker, 'Introduction', in Rick Simonson and Scott Walker (eds), *Multicultural Literacy: Opening the American Mind* (St. Paul, Minn.: Gray Wolf Press, 1988) p. xi.
4. George Stocking, *Race Culture and Evolution*; Melville J. Herskovits, *Franz Boas; The Science of Man in the Making* (New York: Scribner's, 1952); Walter Goldschmidt (ed.), *The Anthropology of Franz Boas* (San Francisco: American Anthropological Association, Memoir no. 89, 1959).
5. Carl Degler, *In Search of Human Nature: The Decline and Revival of Darwinism in American Social Thought* (Oxford University Press, 1991) p. 61.
6. Stocking, *Race, Culture and Evolution*, p. 214.
7. Cited in Stocking, *Race, Culture and Evolution*, p. 148.
8. Franz Boas, 'Changes in the Bodily Form of Descendants of Immigrants', *American Anthropologist*, vol. 14, no. 3 (1912).
9. Franz Boas, *The Mind of Primitive Man* (New York: Free Press 1965 [revd edn; original edn pub. 1911]) p. 281.
10. E. B. Tylor, *Anthropology: An Introduction to the Study of Man and Civilisation* (New York: D. Appleton, 1913; orig. pub. 1881) pp. 439–40.
11. Franz Boas, 'Some Traits of Primitive Culture', *Journal of American Folklore*, XVII (1904).
12. Stocking, *Race, Culture and Evolution*, 227.
13. Emile Durkheim, *The Elementary Forms of Religious Life* (London: Allen & Unwin, 1976 [orig. pub. 1912]); *The Rules of Sociological Method* (London: Macmillan 1982 [orig. pub. 1895]).
14. Cited in Adam Kuper, *Anthropology and Anthropologists: The Modern British School* (London: Routledge, 1983 [2nd edn, 1st edn, 1973]) p. 43.
15. Franz Boas, 'The Mind of Primitive Man', *Science*, vol. 113, no. 321 (Feb. 1901).
16. Boas, *The Mind of Primitive Man*, p. 76.
17. George Stocking (ed.), *The Shaping of American Anthropology 1883–1911: A Franz Boas Reader* (New York: Basic Books, 1974) p. 213.
18. Barkan, *The Retreat of Scientific Racism*, p. 67.
19. Charles Davenport, 'Euthenics and Eugenics', *The Popular Science Monthly*, vol. 78, no. 2 (Jan. 1911).
20. Charles Davenport, 'Euthenics and Eugenics', *Popular Science Monthly*, (Jan. 1911).
21. J. B. Lamarck, *Zoological Philosophy: An Exposition with Regard to the Natural History of Animals*, trans Hugh Elliot (London: Macmillan, 1914) pp. 11, 113.
22. Cited in Jones, *Social Darwinism and English Thought*, p. 88.

23. Degler, *In Search of Human Nature*, p. 191.
24. Stocking, *Race, Culture and Evolution*, pp. 265–6.
25. Alfred Kroeber, 'Inheritance by Magic', *American Anthropologist*, vol. 18, no. 1 (1916).
26. Alfred Kroeber, *The Nature of Culture* (University of Chicago Press, 1952) p. 34.
27. See Stocking, *Race, Culture and Evolution*, pp. 259–260.
28. Claude Levi-Strauss, *The View from Afar*, trans Joachim Neugroschel and Phoebe Hoss (Harmondsworth: Penguin, 1987; orig. pub.1962) p. 27.
29. Robert H. Lowie, *Culture and Ethnology* (New York: Boni & Liveright, 1917) p. 66.
30. Cited in Degler, *In Search of Human Nature*, p. 102.
31. Melville J. Herskovits, *The Myth of the Negro Past* (Boston: Beacon Press, 1990; orig. pub. 1941).
32. Ruth Benedict, *Patterns of Culture* (Boston: Houghton Mifflin, 1934) pp. 10, 13.
33. Benedict, *Patterns of Culture*, pp. 254–255.
34. Leslie White, *The Science of Culture: A Study of Man and Civilisation* (New York: Farrar, Strauss, 1949) p. 181.
35. Ibid.
36. Claude Lévi-Strauss, *The Savage Mind* (London: Weidenfield & Nicolson, 1966 [orig. pub. 1962]); *Structural Anthropology*, vol. 1, trans by Claire Jacobson and Brooke Grundfest Schoepf (Harmondsworth: Penguin, 1972 [orig. pub. 1963]); *Structural Anthropology*, vol. 2, trans by Monique Layton (Harmondsworth: Penguin, 1978 [orig. pub. 1973]); *The View From Afar*.
37. Lévi-Strauss, *Structural Anthropology*, vol. 2, p. 25.
38. Lévi-Strauss, *Structural Anthropology*, vol. 1, p. 13.
39. Lévi-Strauss, *Structural Anthropology*, vol. 2, p. 63.
40. Lévi-Strauss, *The View From Afar*, pp. 10–11.
41. Ibid., p. 17.
42. Ibid., p. 15.
43. Ibid., p. 33.
44. Steve Jones, *The Language of the Genes: Biology, History and the Evolutionary Future* (London: Harper Collins, 1993) pp. 237–8.
45. Claude Lévi-Strauss, *Triste Tropiques* (Harmondsworth: Penguin, 1955) p. 385.
46. Claude Lévi-Strauss, *The Naked Man*, trans by John and Doreen Weightman (London: Harper & Row, 1981; orig. pub. 1971) p. 636.
47. Lévi-Strauss, *Tristes Tropiques*, p. 387.
48. Lévi-Strauss, *The View From Afar*, p. 285.
49. Ibid., p. 285.
50. Ibid., p. 23.
51. Lévi-Strauss, *Structural Anthropology*, vol. 2, p. 360.
52. Gobineau, *The Inequality of the Races*, p. 159.
53. Ibid., p. 163.
54. Todorov, *On Human Diversity*, pp. 137–138.
55. Lévi-Strauss, *The View From Afar*, p. 24.
56. Ibid., p. 23
57. Lévi-Strauss, *Structural Anthropology*, vol. 2, p. 362.
58. Todorov, *On Human Diversity*, p. 72.
59. Commencement Address, American University, Washington DC, 10 June 1963.
60. Cited in John Rex, 'The Political Sociology of a Multi-Cultural Society', *European Journal of Intercultural Studies*, vol. 2, no. 1 (1991).
61. Noel Scott and Derek Jones (eds), *Bloody Bosnia: A European Tragedy* (London: *Guardian*/Channel 4 Television, 1994).

62. John Rex, *Race Relations in Sociological Theory* (London: Routledge & Kégan Paul, 1970) p. 19.
63. J. S. Furnivall, *Colonial Policy and Practice: A Comparative Study of Burma and Netherlands India* (New York University Press, 1956) p. 304.
64. Cited in Kuper, *Anthropology and Anthropologists*, pp. 106–7.
65. Adam Southall, 'The Current State of National Integration in Uganda', in David Smock and Kwamena Bentsi-Enchill (eds), *The Search for National Integration in Africa* (New York: The Free Press, 1975) p. 309.
66. *African Social Research*, Jun. 1976.
67. Terence Ranger, 'The Invention of Tradition in Colonial Africa', in Hobsbawm and Ranger (eds), *The Invention of Tradition*, p. 250.
68. Frantz Fanon, *Toward the African Revolution*, trans Haakon Chevalier (New York: Grove Press, 1969 [orig. pub. 1964]) p. 34.
69. H. Adam, *Modernising Racial Domination* (Berkeley: University of California Press, 1972).
70. J. S. Furnivall, *Netherlands India: A Study of Plural Economy* (Cambridge University Press, 1939) p. 446.
71. Horace Kallen, *Cultural Pluralism and the American Idea: An Essay in Social Philosophy* (University of Pennsylvania, 1956).
72. Furnivall, *Netherlands India*, p. 446.
73. Richard Jenkins, 'Social Anthropological Models of Inter-Ethnic Relations', in John Rex and David Mason (eds), *Theories of Race and Ethnic Relations* (Cambridge University Press, 1986) p. 180.
74. Anthony Giddens, *Sociology* (Cambridge: Polity Press, 1993 [2nd edn; 1st edn. 1989]) p. 253.
75. Figures from S. Castles, *Here For Good: Western Europe's New Ethnic Minorities* (London: Pluto, 1984).
76. 'Introduction' to Nathan Glazer and Daniel Moynihan (eds), *Ethnicity: Theory and Experience* (Cambridge, Mass.: Harvard University Press, 1975) p. 1.
77. Malcolm Chapman, 'Social and Biological Aspects of Ethnicity', in Malcolm Chapman (ed.), *Social and Biological Aspects of Ethnicity* (Oxford University Press, 1993) p. 19.
78. Giddens, *Sociology*, p. 253.
79. Sandra Wallman, 'Ethnicity and the Boundary Process in Context', in Rex and Mason (eds), *Theories of Race and Ethnic Relations*, p. 227.
80. M. G. Smith, 'Pluralism, Race and Ethnicity in Selected African Countries', in Rex and Mason (eds), *Theories of Race and Ethnic Relations*, pp. 190, 191.
81. John Rex, 'Race and Ethnicity', in P. Worsley (ed.), *Introducing Sociology* (Harmondsworth: Penguin, 1986).
82. J. Milton Yinger, 'Intersecting strands in the theorisation of race and ethnic relations', in Rex and Mason (eds), *Theories of Race and Ethnic Relations*, p. 22.
83. Giddens, *Sociology*, pp. 252–3.
84. Ibid., p. 253.
85. Ibid.
86. Yinger, 'Intersecting Strands in the Theorisation of Race and Ethnic Relations', in Rex and Mason (eds), *Theories of Race and Ethnic Relations*, p. 22.
87. Chapman, 'Social and Biological Aspects of Ethnicity', in Chapman (ed.), *Social and Biological Aspects of Ethnicity*, p. 21.
88. Harold J. Abramson, *Ethnic Diversity in Catholic America* (London: John Wiley, 1973) p. 175.
89. Wallman, 'Ethnicity and the Boundary Process in Context', in Rex and Mason (eds), *Theories of Race and Ethnic Relations*, p. 229.

90. Lord Swann, *Education for All: The Report of the Committee of Inquiry Into the Education of Children from Ethnic Minority Groups* (London: HMSO, 1985 [Cmnd. 9453]) p. 5.
91. Cited in Silverman, *Deconstructing the Nation*, pp. 13–14.
92. Silverman, *Deconstructing the Nation*, p. 14.
93. Ibid., p. 18.
94. Ibid., pp. 18–19; the quote is from Ernest Gellner, *Nations and Nationalism* (Oxford: Blackwell, 1983), pp. 48–9.

7. CULTURAL WARS

1. Cited in Richard Rorty, 'Two Cheers for the Cultural Left', in *The South Atlantic Quarterly*, vol. 89, no. 1 (Winter 1990).
2. Dinesh D'Souza, 'The Visigoths in Tweed', in Patricia Aufderheide (ed.), *Beyond PC: Towards a Politics of Understanding* (St. Paul, Minn.: Gray Wolf Press, 1992) pp. 11, 12.
3. Quoted in Mary Louize Pratt, 'Humanities for the Future', *The South Atlantic Quarterly*, (Winter, 1990).
4. *The American Scholar* (Spring 1991).
5. Arthur M. Schlesinger, *The Disuniting of America: Reflections on a Multicultural Society* (New York: Norton, 1992 [orig. pub. 1991]) p. 17.
6. Cited in Schlesinger, *The Disuniting of America*, p. 40.
7. Cited in Schlesinger, *The Disuniting of America*, p. 131.
8. Diane Ravich, 'Multiculturalism', *The American Scholar*, vol. 59, no. 3 (1990).
9. Schlesinger, *The Disuniting of America*, p. 41.
10. Elizabeth Fox-Genovese, 'The Self-Interest of Multiculturalism', *Tikkun*, vol. 6, no. 4 (Jul./Aug. 1991).
11. Schlesinger, *The Disuniting of America*, pp. 16–17.
12. William Bennett, 'Lost Generation', *Policy Review*, no. 33 (Summer 1985).
13. Adam Meyerson, 'The Vision Thing, Continued', *Policy Review*, no. 52 (Summer 1990).
14. *Sunday Telegraph*, 18 Feb. 1989.
15. *Sunday Express*, 24 Apr. 1983.
16. Pierre Pascal, 'Les Vrais Racistes', *Militant*, vol. 16, no. 156 (Jan. 1984)
17. Allan Bloom, *The Closing of the American Mind: How Higher Education has Failed Democracy and Impoverished the Souls of Today's Students* (New York: Simon & Schuster, 1987) p. 36.
18. Toni Morrison, *Playing in the Dark: Whiteness and the Literary Imagination* (Cambridge, Mass.: Harvard University Press, 1992) p. 7.
19. Anthony Messina, *Race and Party Competition in Britain* (Oxford: Clarendon Press, 1989); Zig Layton-Henry, *The Politics of Immigration: Immigration, 'Race' and 'Race' Relations in Post-war Britain* (Oxford: Blackwell, 1992); Paul Foot, *The Rise of Enoch Powell* (Harmondsworth: Penguin, 1969).
20. G. R. Elton, *The Future of the Past* (Cambridge University Press, 1966) p. 22.
21. G. R. Elton, *The History of England* (Cambridge University Press, 1984) p. 28.
22. Margaret Thatcher, Speech to a Conservative Rally at Cheltenham Race Course, 3 Jul. 1982; reprinted in Anthony Barnett, *Iron Britannia* (London: Allison & Busby, 1982) pp. 149–50.
23. Cited in Martin Barker, *The New Racism: Conservatives and the Ideology of the Tribe* (London: Junction Books, 1981) p. 15.
24. Enoch Powell, Speech in Southall, 4 Nov. 1971.

25. John Casey, *Salisbury Review*, no. 1 (Autumn 1982).
26. *Daily Telegraph*, 8 Sep. 1978.
27. Ray Honeyford, 'The Gilmore Syndrome', *Salisbury Review* (Apr. 1986).
28. Enoch Powell, Speech at Eastbourne, 16 Nov. 1968.
29. Cited in Paul Gordon and Francesca Klug, *New Right, New Racism* (London: Searchlight Publications, 1986) p. 20.
30. Roger Scruton, 'In Defence of the Nation', in J. C. D. Clark (ed.), *Ideas and Politics in Modern Britain* (Basingstoke: Macmillan, 1990) pp. 58–59.
31. Robin Page, 'To nature race is not a dirty word', *Daily Telegraph*, 3 Feb. 1977.
32. Paul Gilroy, 'The End of Antiracism', in Wendy Ball and John Solomos (eds), *Race and Local Politics* (Basingstoke: Macmillan, 1990) p. 196.
33. *The Times*, 17 Feb. 1989.
34. Fay Weldon, *Sacred Cows* (London: Chatto & Windus, 1989).
35. *New Statesman and Society*, 31 Mar. 1989.
36. Fay Weldon, *Sacred Cows*, p. 18.
37. *Runnymede Trust Bulletin*, May 1985.
38. Ibid., May 1986.
39. Patrick Weil and John Crowley, 'Integration in Theory and Practice: A Comparison of France and Britain', in Martin Baldwin-Edwards and Martin Schain (eds), *The Politics of Immigration in Western Europe* (Ilford: Frank Cass, 1994) p. 123.
40. Liberty, *The Last Resort: Violations of the Human Rights of Migrants, Refugees and Asylum Seekers* (London: Liberty, 1994).
41. Weil and Crowley, 'Integration in Theory and Practice' in Baldwin-Edwards and Schain (eds), *The Politics of Immigration in Western Europe*, p. 123.
42. George Orwell, *The Lion and the Unicorn* (Harmondsworth: Penguin, 1982) p. 141.
43. *Sunday Telegraph*, 3 Aug. 1986.
44. Paul Gilroy, 'The End of Antiracism', in Ball and Solomos (eds), *Race and Local Politics*, p. 195; *There Ain't No Black in the Union Jack: The Cultural Politics of Race and Nation* (London: Hutchinson, 1987) p. 148.
45. Gilroy, *There Ain't No Black in the Union Jack*, p. 131.
46. Silverman, *Deconstructing the Nation*, p. 6.
47. Cited in Silverman, *Deconstructing the Nation*, p. 103.
48. Cited in Richard Ings, *L'Islam: Une Menace Pour la France?* (unpub. paper, 1994).
49. Cited in Gilles Kepel, *Les Banlieues d'Islam* (Paris: Seuil, 1991) p. 140.
50. Ibid., p. 17.
51. Cited in Yves Gonzales-Quiljano, 'Les Musulmans dans la Société Française', *Revue Française des Science Politiques* (Dec. 1987).
52. Cited in Silverman, *Deconstructing the Nation*, p. 142.
53. Cited in Ings, *I'Islam: Une Menace Pour la France?*
54. Ibid.
55. Patrick Weil, *La France et ses Étrangers* (Paris: Calmann-Levy, 1991) p. 21.
56. Cited in Pierre-Andre Taguieff, 'The New Cultural Racism in France', *Telos*, no. 83 (Spring 1990).
57. Silverman, *Deconstructing the Nation*, p. 111.
58. *Le Figaro*, 20 Oct. 1989.
59. *L'Événement du Jeudi*, 9–15 Nov. 1989.
60. Silverman, *Deconstructing the Nation*, p. 115.
61. Taguieff, 'The New Cultural Racism in France', *Telos*, no. 83.
62. Lydia Morris, *Dangerous Classes: The Underclass and Social Citizenship* (London: Routledge, 1994) pp. 81, 80, 1–2.

63. Ibid., p. 1.
64. Michael B. Katz, *The Undeserving Poor: From the War on Poverty to the War on Welfare* (New York: Pantheon, 1989).
65. 'The American Underclass', *Time*, 19 Aug. 1977.
66. *US News and World Report*, cited in Katz, *The Undeserving Poor*, p. 197.
67. Gordon Sinclair, 'No Excuses for this Caliban Culture', *London Evening Standard*, 12 Sep. 1991.
68. Edward C. Banfield, *The Heavenly City Revisited* (Boston: Little, Brown, 1970) p. 54.
69. Mayhew, *London Labour and the London Poor*, p. 2.
70. Katz, *The Undeserving Poor*, p. 17.
71. Oscar Lewis, *La Vida: A Puerto Rican Family in the Culture of Poverty–San Juan and New York* (New York: Random House, 1966), p. xlii.
72. Oscar Lewis, *A Study of Slum Culture* (New York: Random House, 1968) p. 6.
73. Michael Harrington, *The Other America* (Harmondsworth: Penguin, 1963; orig. pub. 1962) pp. 22, 23.
74. Katz, *The Underserving Poor*, pp. 16, 17.
75. Cited in M. Rutter and M. Madge, *Cycles of Disadvantage* (London: Heinemann, 1976) p. 3.
76. Richard J. Herrnstein and Charles Murray, *The Bell Curve: Intelligence and Class Structure in American Life* (New York: Free Press, 1994) pp. xxi-xxii.
77. Stanley M. Elkins, *Slavery: A Problem in American Institutional and Intellectual Life* (Chicago University Press, 1959).
78. The full text of the Moynihan Report can be found in Lee Rainwater and William L. Yancey, *The Moynihan Report and the Politics of Controversy* (Cambridge, Mass.: MIT Press, 1967) pp. 39–125.
79. Rainwater and Yancey, *The Moynihan Report*, p. 43.
80. Ibid., p. 45.
81. Ibid., p. 62.
82. Ibid., pp. 72, 80.
83. Ibid., p. 43.
84. Ibid., p. 94.
85. Charles Murray, *Losing Ground: American Social Policy 1950–1980* (New York: Basic Books, 1984); *The Emerging British Underclass* (London: IEA Health and Welfare Unit, 1990).
86. Cited in Katz, *The Undeserving Poor*, p. 152.
87. *New Republic*, 31 Oct. 1994.
88. Herrnstein and Murray, *The Bell Curve*, pp. 240–1.
89. Charles Murray and Richard J. Herrnstein, 'Race, Genes and IQ – An Apologia', *New Republic*, 31 Oct. 1994.
90. Kenan Malik, 'Racialising the Poor', *Paradigm*, no. 1 (Autumn 1995).
91. Herrnstein and Murray, *The Bell Curve*, p. 532.
92. 'The Lowerers', *The New Republic*, Oct. 1994.
93. *Wall Street Journal*, 21 Dec. 1993.
94. *Independent on Sunday*, 12 May 1991.
95. Cited in *Financial Times*, 1 Nov. 1990.
96. William Lind, 'Defending Western Culture', *Foreign Policy* (Fall 1991); Samuel Huntingdon, 'The Clash of Civilisations', *Foreign Affairs*, vol. 72 no. 3 (Jul. / Aug. 1993); Barry Buzan, 'New Patterns of Global Security', *International Affairs*, vol. 67, no. 3 (Jul. 1991).
97. Rupert Emerson, *Africa and United States Policy* (Englewood Cliffs, NJ: Prentice-Hall, 1967) p. 2.

98. John Casey, 'All Quiet on the Liberal Front', *London Evening Standard*, 20 Aug. 1990.
99. Buzan, 'New Patterns of Global Security', *International Affairs* (July 1991).
100. R. H. Jackson, 'Juridical Statehood in Africa', *Journal of International Affairs* vol. 46, no. 1 (1992).
101. Robert D. Kaplan, 'The Coming Anarchy', *Atlantic Monthly* (Feb. 1994).
102. 'Tribal Nationalism, Balkanising the World', *US News and World Report*, 28 Dec. 1992.
103. 'Africa: The Curse of Tribal War', *Newsweek*, 21 Jun. 1993.
104. Kaplan, 'The Coming Anarchy', *Atlantic Monthly*, Feb. 1994.
105. Martin van Creveld, *On Future War* (London: Brassey's, 1991).
106. Catherine Newbury, *The Cohesion of Oppression: Clientship and Ethnicity in Rwanda 1860–1960* (New York: Columbia University Press, 1993); Alex de Waal, 'The Genocidal State', *The Times Literary Supplement*, 1 Jul. 1994.
107. *Daily Telegraph*, 22 Jul. 1994; *Guardian*, 30 Jul. 1994.
108. *The Sunday Times*, 31 Jul. 1994.
109. Jeremy Thompson, 'The Year in Review', *Sky News*, 26 Dec. 1994.
110. Francis Fukuyama. 'The End of History', *The National Interest*, no. 18 (1989).
111. Kaplan, 'The Coming Anarchy', *Atlantic Monthly* Feb. 1994.
112. Cited in Kaplan, 'The Coming Anarchy', *Atlantic Monthly*, (February 1994).

8. UNIVERSALISM, HUMANISM AND THE DISCOURSE OF RACE

1. Stuart Hall, 'The Local and the Global', in Anthony D. King (ed.), *Culture, Globalization and the World-System: Contemporary Conditions for the Representation of Identity* (Basingstoke: Macmillan, 1991) p. 34.
2. Stuart Hall, 'New Ethnicities', in James Donald and Ali Rattansi (eds), *'Race', Culture and Difference* (London: Sage Open University, 1992) p. 258.
3. Jean-François Lyotard, *The Postmodern Condition: A Report on Knowledge* (Manchester University Press, 1984) p. 23.
4. Stuart Hall, 'Old and New Identities, Old and New Ethnicities', in King (ed.), *Culture, Globalization and the World-System*, p. 44.
5. Kobena Mercer, 'Welcome to the Jungle: Identity and Diversity in Postmodern Politics', in Jonathan Rutherford (ed.), *Identity: Community, Culture, Difference* (London: Lawrence & Wishart, 1993) p. 50.
6. Christopher L. Miller, *Theories of Africans: Francophone Literature and Anthropology in Africa* (University of Chicago Press, 1990) p. 7.
7. Herbert Marcuse, *Eros and Civilisation* (London: Abacus, 1972) p. 23.
8. David Harvey, *The Condition of Postmodernity* (Cambridge: Basil Blackwell, 1989) p. 48.
9. Stuart Hall, 'The Local and the Global', in King (ed.), *Culture, Globalization and the World-System*, p. 35.
10. Edward W. Said, *Culture and Imperialism* (London: Chatto & Windus, 1993) p. 58.
11. Stuart Hall, 'The West and the Rest: Discourse and Power', in Stuart Hall and Bram Gieben (eds), *Formations of Modernity: Understanding Modern Societies* (Cambridge: Polity Press/Open University, 1992) p. 289.
12. Ibid., p. 280.
13. Ibid., p. 314.
14. Goldberg, *Racist Culture*, p. 10.

15. Lévi-Stauss, *Structural Anthropology*; Lévi-Strauss, *The Savage Mind*; Jean-Paul Sartre, *Being and Nothingness* (London: Methuen 1957); Jacques Lacan, *Écrits: A Selection* (London: Tavistock, 1977); Jacques Derrida, *Speech and Phenomena and Other Essays on Husserl's Theory of Signs* (Evanston: Northwestern University Press, 1973 [orig. pub. 1967]); Jacques Derrida, *Of Grammatology* (Baltimore: Johns Hopkins Press, 1976 [orig. pub. 1967]); Jacques Derrida, *Writing and Difference* (London: Routledge & Kegan Paul, 1978 [orig. pub. 1967]); Michel Foucault, *Madness and Civilisation* (London: Tavistock, 1967); Michel Foucault, *The Order of Things* (London: Tavistock, 1970); Michel Foucault, *The Archaeology of Knowledge* (London: Tavistock, 1972).

16. Michel Foucault, *Folie et deraison: Histoire de la folie à lâge classique* (2nd edn) (Paris: Galimard, 1972), p. 17; an abridged English version can be found in *Madness and Civilisation*, trans Richard Howard (London: Tavistock, 1967).

17. Hall, 'The West and the Rest', in King (ed.) *Culture, Globalization, and the World System* pp. 312–14.

18. P. Hulme, *Colonial Encounters: European and the Native Caribbean, 1492–1797* (London: Methuen, 1986) p. 49.

19. Linda Colley, *Britons: Forging the Nation 1707–1837* (New Haven, Conn.: Yale University Press, 1992) pp. 5–6.

20. Ibid., p. 6.

21. Claude Lévi-Strauss, *Totemism* (Harmondsworth: Penguin, 1969); *The Savage Mind* (London: Weidenfeld & Nicolson, 1966).

22. Said, *Culture and Imperialism*, p. 28.

23. Ibid., p. 266.

24. Marx and Engels, *Selected Works* p. 79.

25. See, for example, Ruth Cowing, 'Blacks in Renaissance Drama and the role of Shakespeare's Othello', in David Dabydeen (ed.), *The Black Presence in English Literature* (Manchester University Press, 1985).

26. C. L. R. James, *Spheres of Existence: Selected Writings* (London: Allison & Busby, 1980) p. 141.

27. Edward W. Said, *Orientalism: Western Concepts of the Orient* (Harmondsworth: Penguin, 1985 [orig. pub. 1978]) p. 3.

28. Ibid., p. 3.

29. Ibid., pp. 56,57.

30. Ibid., p. 3.

31. Martin Bernal, *Black Athena: The Afroasiatic Roots of Classical Civilisation* (London: Free Association Books, 1987).

32. Aijaz Ahmad, *In Theory: Classes, Nations, Literatures* (London: Verso, 1992) p. 183.

33. Said, *Orientalism*, p. 204.

34. Ahmad, *In Theory*, p. 182.

35. Said, *Culture and Imperialism*, p. 35.

36. Ibid., p. 129.

37. Robert Young, *White Mythologies: Writing History and the West* (London: Routledge, 1990) p. 129.

38. Said, *Orientalism*, p. 94.

39. Goldberg, *Racist Culture*, p. 150.

40. Said, *Culture and Imperialism*, p. 95.

41. Ahmad, *In Theory*, p. 181.

42. Said, *Orientalism*, p. 72.

43. Ibid., pp. 272, 273.

44. Ibid., p. 203.

45. Michel Foucault, *Power/Knowledge* (Brighton: Harvester, 1980) p. 27.

46. Ibid., p. 131.

47. Ibid., pp. 207–8.
48. Emmanual Levinas, 'The Trace of the Other', in Mark C. Taylor (ed.), *Deconstructing in Context* (Chicago University Press, 1986) p. 346.
49. Young, *White Mythologies*, p. 3.
50. Richard Rorty, *Objectivity, Relativism and Truth* (Cambridge University Press, 1991) p. 207.
51. Miller, *Theories of Africans*, p. 10.
52. Said, *Culture and Imperialism*, p. 35.
53. Ibid., p. 22.
54. Hume, *Inquiry Concerning Human Understanding*.
55. Karl Marx, 'Theses on Feuerbach', in Marx and Engels, *Selected Works*, p. 29.
56. Georg Lukacs, *The Historical Novel*, trans by Hannah and Stanley Mitchell (London: Merlin, 1962) pp. 28–29.
57. Jean-Paul Sartre, 'Preface', in Frantz Fanon, *The Wretched of the Earth* (Harmondsworth: Penguin, 1967 [orig. pub. 1961]) p. 21.
58. Fanon, *The Wretched of the Earth*, p. 251.
59. Jean-Paul Sartre, *Critique of Dialectical Reason*, vol. 1: *Theory of Practical Ensembles*, trans by Alan Sheridan-Smith (London: New Left Books, 1976) p. 752.
60. Sartre, 'Preface', in Fanon, *The Wretched of the Earth*, p. 22.
61. Fanon, *The Wretched of the Earth*, p. 131.
62. James Clifford, *The Predicament of Culture: Twentieth Century Ethnography, Literature, Art* (Cambridge, Mass. Harvard University Press, 1988) p. 263.
63. Young, *White Mythologies*, pp. 122, 123.
64. Fanon, *The Wretched of the Earth*, p. 253.
65. Ibid., p. 252.
66. Lévi-Strauss, *Structural Anthropology* vol. 2, p. 53.
67. Lévi-Strauss, *The View From Afar*, p. 28.
68. Theodor Adorno and Max Horkheimer, *Dialectic of Enlightenment* (London: Verso, 1979; orig. pub. 1944) p. 6.
69. Claude Lévi-Strauss, *Le Monde* 21–22 Jan. 1979; cited in Todorov, *On Human Diversity*, p. 67.
70. Goldberg, *Racist Culture*, p. 29.
71. Zygmunt Bauman, *Modernity and the Holocaust* (Cambridge: Polity Press, 1989) pp. 6, 13, 8.
72. Richard L. Rubenstein, *The Cunning of History* (London: Harper Row, 1978) pp. 91, 95.
73. Todorov, *On Human Diversity*, p. 68.
74. Ibid., p. 67.
75. H. Stuart Hughes, *The Sea Change*, in H. Stuart Hughes, *Between Commitment and Disillusionment* (Middletown, Conn.: Wesleyan University Press, 1987) pp. 134–5.
76. Theodor Adorno, Else Frenke-Brunswik, Daniel J. Levinson and R. Nevitt Sanford, *The Authoritarian Personality* (New York: Norton, 1950).
77. Hannah Arendt, *The Origins of Totalitarianism* (New York: Harcourt, Brace & Jovanovich, 1973) p. 309.
78. Martin Heidegger, *Introduction to Metaphysics* (New Haven, Conn.: Yale University Press, 1959) p. 45.
79. Martin Heidegger, cited in Jean-Francois Lyotard, *Heidegger and the 'Jews'* (New Haven Conn.: Yale University Press, 1994) p. 85.
80. Edmund Stillman and William Pfaff, *The Politics of Hysteria* (New York: Harper & Row, 1964) p. 34.
81. Cited in Thomas Rockmore, *On Heidegger's Nazism and Philosophy* (Berkeley: University of California Press, 1994) pp. 93–4.

82. James Heartfield, *The Heidegger Affair* (unpublished paper).
83. Sartre, 'Preface' in Fanon, *Wretched of the Earth*, p. 22.
84. Hughes, *The Sea Change*, pp. 135–6.
85. Zygmunt Bauman, *Modernity and Ambivalence* (Cambridge: Polity Press, 1991) p. 272.
86. David A. Bailey and Stuart Hall, 'The Vertigo of Displacement', *Ten8*, vol. 2, no. 3 (Spring 1992).
87. Ali Rattansi, '"Western" Racisms, Ethnicities and Identities', in Ali Rattansi and Sallie Westwood (eds), *Racism, Modernity and Identity: On the Western Front* (Cambridge: Polity Press, 1994) p. 30.
88. Ibid., p. 29.
89. Frankfurt Institute, *Aspects of Sociology* (London: Heinemann Educational, 1973) p. 23.
90. Karl Popper, *The Open Universe: An Argument for Indeterminacy*, ed. W. W. Batley, (London: Routledge, 1982) p. 41.
91. Gareth Stedman Jones, *Languages of Class: Studies in English Working Class History 1832–1982* (Cambridge University Press, 1983) p. 20.
92. Ibid., p. 7.
93. Bryan D. Palmer, 'The Eclipse of Materialism: Marxism and the Writing of Social History in the 1980s', in Ralph Milliband and Leo Panitch (eds), *The Retreat of the Intellectuals: Socialist Register 1990* (London: Merlin, 1990) p. 115.
94. Neville Kirk, 'History, Language, Ideas and Postmodernism: A Materialist View', *Social History*, vol. 19, no. 2 (May 1994).
95. E. P. Thompson, *The Poverty of Theory*, p. 205.
96. Rattansi, '"Western" Racism, Ethnicities, Identities', in Rattansi and Westwood (eds), *Racism and Modern Identity*, p. 29.
97. Jeffrey Weekes, *Sexuality and its Discontents: Meanings, Myths and Modern Sexualities* (London: Routledge & Kegan Paul, 1985) p. 170.
98. Kobena Mercer, 'Back to My Routes: A Postscript on the 80s', *Ten8*, vol. 2, no. 3 (Spring 1992).
99. Robin Cohen, *Frontiers of Identity: The British and the Others* (London: Longman, 1994) p. 205.
100. Ibid.
101. Winston James, 'Migration, Racism and Identity Formation: The Caribbean Experience in Britain', in Winston James and Clive Harris (eds), *Inside Babylon: The Caribbean Diaspora in Britain* (London: Verso, 1993) p. 266; Benedict Anderson, *Imagined Communities: Reflections on the Origins and Spread of Nationalism* (London: Verso, 1983).
102. James, 'Migration, Racism and Identity Formation', in James and Harris (eds), *Inside Babylon*, p. 266.
103. Miles Davis (with Quincy Troupe), *Miles: The Autobiography* (London: Macmillan, 1989).
104. Lévi-Strauss, *The Savage Mind*, p. 257.
105. E. H. Carr, *What is History?* (Harmondsworth: Penguin, 1987 [first pub. 1961]) p. 23.
106. Lévi-Strauss, *The Savage Mind*, p. 258.
107. Young, *White Mythologies*, p. 22.
108. Carr, *What is History?*, pp. 26–7.
109. Young, *White Mythologies*, p. 45.
110. Lukacs, *History and Class Consciousness*, p. 13.
111. Peggy Kamuf (ed.), *Between the Blinds – A Derrida Reader* (Brighton: Harvester Wheatsheaf, 1991) pp. 66–7.

112. Goldberg, *Racist Culture*, p. 223.
113. Ibid., p. 223.
114. Cited in Mark Philp, 'Michel Foucault', in Skinner (ed.), *The Return of Grand Theory in the Human Sciences* p. 78.
115. Lévi-Strauss, *The Savage Mind*, p. 260.
116. Marx, 'Theses on Feuerbach', in Marx and Engles, *Selected Works*, p. 29.

9. EQUALITY AND EMANCIPATION

1. Thomas Keneally, 'Schindler has much to tell us', *The Times*, 22 Mar. 1994.
2. Schlesinger, *The Disuniting of America*, pp. 9–10.
3. Hans Magnus Enzensberger, 'The Great Migration', *Granta* 42 (Winter 1992) p. 17.
4. bell hooks, *Yearning: Race, Gender and Cultural Politics* (London: Turnabout, 1991) p. 15.
5. Lyotard, *The Postmodern Condition*, p. 66.
6. Jacques Derrida, *Of Spirit: Heidegger and the Question* (University of Chicago Press, 1987), p. 40.
7. Foucault, *Power / Knowledge*, p. 85.
8. Ibid., p. 208.
9. Jeffrey C. Isaac, *Arendt, Camus and Modern Rebellion* (New Haven, Conn.: Yale University Press, 1992) pp. 8–9.
10. Ibid., p. 9.
11. Caroline Knowles and Sharmila Mercer, 'Feminism and Antiracism', in Donald and Rattansi (eds), *'Race', Culture and Difference*, pp. 109–10.
12. Said, *Culture and Imperialism*, pp. 277–8.
13. Hall, 'The Local and the Global', in King (ed.), *Culture, Globalisation and the World System*, p. 34.
14. hooks, *Yearning*, p. 35.
15. Ibid., p. 36.
16. Ibid., p. 25.
17. Joseph-Marie de Maistre, *The Works of Joseph de Maistre*, trans by Jack Lively (London: Macmillan, 1965) p. 80.
18. Tylor, *Anthropology*, 286.
19. Condorcet, 'Reception speech at the French Academy', in Keith Michael Baker (ed.), *Selected Writings* (Indianapolis: Bobbs-Merrill, 1976) 10–11.
20. Jean-Jacques Rousseau, *On the Origin of Language*, trans by John H Moran and Alexander Gode(New York: Frederick Unger, 1966 [orig. pub. 1755]) pp. 30–31.
21. Jean-Jacques Rousseau, 'Discourse on the Sciences and the Arts', in *The First and Second Discourses*, trans by Victor Gourevitch (New York: Harper&Row, 1986) p. 48.
22. Jean-Jacques Rousseau, *Émile, or, On Education*, trans by Allan Bloom (New York: Basic Books, 1986) p. 524.
23. Georg Lukacs, *History and Class Consciousness: Studies in Marxist Dialectics* (London: Merlin, 1971 [orig. pub. 1968]) pp. 8, 14.
24. See Lukacs, *History and Class Consciousness*, esp. pp. 1–24; Karl Korsch, *Marxism and Philosophy* (New York: Monthly Review Press, 1970).

Bibliography

Abramson, H. J., *Ethnic Diversity in Catholic America* (London: John Wiley, 1973).

Adam, H., *Modernising Racial Domination* (Berkeley: University of California Press, 1972).

Adorno, T. and Horkheimer, M. *Dialectic of Enlightenment* (London: Verso, 1979 [first pub. 1944]).

Adorno, T., Frenke-Brunswik, E., Levinson, D. J. and Sanford, R. N., *The Authoritarian Personality*, (New York, Norton 1950).

Ahmad, A. *In Theory: Classes, Nations, Literatures* (London: Verso, 1992).

Almond, M., 'Europe's Immigration Crisis', *National Interest*, no. 29 (Fall 1992).

Anderson, B., *Imagined Communities: Reflections on the Origins and Spread of Nationalism* (London: Verso, 1983).

Arendt, H., *The Origins of Totalitarianism* (New York: Harcourt Brace Jovanovich, 1973).

Aufderheide, P. (ed.), *Beyond PC: Towards a Politics of Understanding* (Saint Paul, Minnesota: Gray Wolf Press, 1992).

Babha, H. K. (ed.), *Nations and Narration* (London: Routledge, 1990).

Bagehot, W., *Physics and Politics* (London: King, 1887).

Bailey, D. A. and Hall, S., 'The Vertigo of Displacement', *Ten8*, vol. 2, no. 3 (Spring 1992).

Baldwin-Edwards, M. and Schain, M. (eds), *The Politics of Immigration in Western Europe* (Ilford: Frank Cass, 1994).

Ball, W. and Solomos, J. (eds), *Race and Local Politics* (Basingstoke: Macmillan, 1990).

Banfield, E. C. *The Heavenly City Revisited* (Boston, Mass.: Little, Brown, 1974).

Banton, M., *Racial and Ethnic Competition* (Cambridge University Press, 1983).

——, *Promoting Racial Harmony* (Cambridge University Press, 1985).

——, *Racial Theories* (Cambridge University Press, 1987).

Barkan, E. *The Retreat of Scientific Racism: Changing Concepts of Race in Britain and the United States Between the World Wars* (Cambridge University Press, 1991).

Barker, A., *The African Link: British Attitudes to the Negro in the Era of the Atlantic Slave Trade, 1550–1807* (London: Frank Cass, 1978).

Barker, M., *The New Racism: Conservatives and the Ideology of the Tribe* (London: Junction Books, 1981).

Barnett, A., *Iron Britannia* (London: Allison & Busby, 1982).

Barrès, M., *Scènes et Doctrines du Nationalisme* (Paris: Plon-Nourrit, 1925 [orig. pub. 1902]).

Bateson, W., *Biological Fact and the Structure of Society* (Oxford: Clarendon Press, 1912).

Bauman, Z., *Modernity and the Holocaust* (Cambridge: Polity Press, 1989).

——, *Modernity and Ambivalence* (Cambridge: Polity Press, 1991).

Bell, D., *The End of Ideology: On the Exhaustion of Political Ideas in the Fifties* (New York: Free Press, 1964).

——, *Sociological Journeys: Essays 1960–1980* (London: Heinemann, 1980).

Benedict, R., *Patterns of Culture* (Boston: Houghton Mifflin, 1934).
—— , *Race and Racism* (London: Routledge & Kegan Paul, 1983 [orig. pub. 1942]).
Bennett, W., 'Lost Generation', *Policy Review*, no. 33 (Summer 1985).
Berlin, I., *Four Essays on Liberty* (Oxford University Press, 1969).
—— , *Vico and Herder: Two Studies in the History of Ideas* (London: Hogarth Press, 1976).
Bernal, M., *Black Athena: The Afroasiatic Roots of Classical Civilisation* (London: Free Association Books, 1987).
Blackburn, R., *The Overthrow of Colonial Slavery, 1776–1848* (London: Verso, 1988).
—— , 'The French Revolution and New World Slavery', in Peter Osborne (ed.), *Socialism and the Limits of Liberalism* (London: Verso, 1991).
Blackstone, W. *Commentaries on the Laws of England* (Oxford: Clarendon Press, 1765–69) (4 vols).
Blumenbach, J. F. *The Anthropological Treatises of Johann Friederich Blumenbach*, trans and ed. by Thomas Bendyshe (London: Anthropological Society, 1865).
Blanckaert, C., 'On the Origins of French Ethnology', in G. W. Stocking (ed.), *Bones, Bodies and Behaviour: Essays on Biological Anthropology (History of Anthropology*, vol. 5) (Madison, Wis.: University of Wisconsin Press, 1988).
Bloom, A., *The Closing of the American Mind: How Higher Education has Failed Democracy and Impoverished the Souls of Today's Students* (New York: Simon Schuster, 1987).
Boas, F., *The Mind of Primitive Man* (New York: Free Press, 1965 [revised edn; original edn pub. 1911]).
—— ,'Some Traits of Primitive Culture', *Journal of American Folklore*, XVII (1904).
—— , 'The Mind of Primitive Man', *Science*, vol. 13, no. 321 (Feb. 1901).
—— , 'Changes in the Bodily Form of Descendants of Immigrants', *American Anthropologist*, vol. 14, no. 3 (1912).
Bolt C. and Drescher S. (eds), *Anti-Slavery, Religion and Reform* (Hampden: Archon, 1980).
Briggs, A., 'Middle Class Consciousness in English Politics 1760–1846', *Past and Present*, no. 9 (April 1956).
Buffon, G. L. L. de, *The History of Man and Quadrupeds*, trans William Smellie (London: T. Caddell & W. Davies, 1812).
—— , *A Natural History, General and Particular*, trans William Smellie (London: Richard Evans, 1817).
Burke, E., *Reflections on the Revolution in France* (Harmondsworth: Penguin, 1968 [orig. pub. in 1790]).
—— , *Collected Works* (London: Rivington, 1815–27).
Buzan, B., 'Global Security in the New World Order', *International Affairs*, vol. 67, no. 3 (July 1991).
Calvez, C., 'Extraits du Rapport de Corentin Calvez sur le Problème des Traivailleurs Étrangers', *Hommes et Migrations*, no. 768 (1969).
Carey, J., *The Intellectuals and the Masses: Pride and Prejudice Among the Literary Intelligentsia, 1880–1939* (London: Faber & Faber, 1992).
Carr, E. H., *What is History?* (Harmondsworth: Penguin, 1987 [orig. pub. 1961]).
Castles, S., *Here For Good: Western Europe's New Ethnic Minorities* (London: Pluto, 1984).
CCCS, *The Empire Strikes Back: Race and Racism in 70s Britain* (London: Hutchinson, 1982).
Cesarani, D., 'Anti-Alienism in England After the First World War', *Immigrants and Minorities*, vol. 6 (1987).
Chamberlain, H. S., *The Foundations of the Nineteenth Century*, trans John Lees (London: Lane, 1910).

Chapman, M. (ed.), *Social and Biological Aspects of Ethnicity* (Oxford University Press, 1993).

Chase, A., *The Legacy of Malthus: The Social Costs of the New Scientific Racism* (Chicago: University of Illinois Press, 1980).

Clark, J. C. D. (ed.), *Ideas and Politics in Modern Britain* (London: Macmillan, 1990).

Clifford, J., *The Predicament of Culture: Twentieth Century Ethnography, Literature, Art* (Cambridge, Mass.: Harvard University Press, 1988).

Cmnd. 7695, *Report of the Royal Commission on Population* (London: HMSO, 1949).

Cmnd. 2739, *Immigration from the Commonwealth* (London: HMSO, Aug. 1965).

Cohen, R., *Frontiers of Identity: The British and the Others* (London: Longman, 1994).

Colletti, L., *From Rousseau to Lenin: Studies in Ideology and Society* (London: Monthly Review Press, 1972).

Colley, L., *Britons: Forging the Nation 1707–1837* (New Haven, Conn.: Yale University Press, 1992).

Condorcet, M. -J. A. N. de C., *Selected Writings*, ed. Keith Michael Baker (Indianapolis: Bobbs-Merrill, 1976).

Cookson, L., and Loughrey, B. (eds), *Critical Essays on Philip Larkin: The Poems* (London: Longman, 1988).

Coupland, R., *Wilberforce, A Narrative* (Oxford University Press, 1923).

Creveld, M. van, *On Future War* (London: Brassey's, 1991).

Crossman, R., *The Diaries of a Cabinet Minister* (London: Jonathan Cape, 1975).

Davenport, C., 'Euthenics and Eugenics', *The Popular Science Monthly*, vol. 78, no. 2 (1911).

Davis, D. B., *The Problem of Slavery in the Age of Revolution 1770–1823* (Oxford University Press, 1989).

——, 'New Sidelights on Early Antislavery Radicalism', *William and Mary Quarterly*, 3rd Series, no. 28 (Oct. 1971).

Davis, M. (with Quincy Troupe), *Miles: The Autobiography* (London: Macmillan, 1989).

Deakin, N., *Colour, Citizenship and British Society* (London: Panther, 1969).

Degerando, J. -M., *The Observation of Savage Peoples*, trans F. C. T. Moore (Berkeley: University of California Press, 1969).

Degler, C. N., *In Search of Human Nature: The Decline and Revival of Darwinism in American Social Thought* (Oxford University Press, 1991).

Derrida, J., *Speech and Phenomena and Other Essays on Husserl's Theory of Signs* (Evanston: Northwestern University Press, 1973; orig. pub. 1967).

——, *Of Grammatology* (Baltimore: Johns Hopkins Press, 1976 orig. pub. 1967).

——, *Writing and Difference* (London: Routledge & Kegan Paul, 1978; orig. pub. 1967).

——, *Of Spirit: Heidegger and the Question* (University of Chicago Press, 1937).

——, *Between the Blinds: A Derrida Reader*, ed. Peggy Kamuf (Brighton: Harvester Wheatsheaf, 1991).

Dixon, R., *The Racial History of Man* (New York: Scribner's, 1923).

Donald, J. and Rattansi, A. (eds), *'Race', Culture and Difference* (London: Sage/ Open University, 1992).

Drescher, S., *Capitalism and Antislavery: British Mobilisation in Comparative Perspective* (Oxford University Press, 1987; orig. pub. 1986).

D'Souza, D., 'The Visigoths in Tweed', in Patricia Aufderheide (ed.), *Beyond PC: Towards a Politics of Understanding* (St. Paul, Minn.: Gray Wolf Press, 1992).

Dummet, A. and Nichol, A., *Subjects, Citizens, Aliens and Others: Nationality and Immigration Law* (London: Weidenfeld & Nicolson, 1990).

Durkheim, É. *The Elementary Forms of Religious Life*, (London: Allen & Unwin, 1976; orig. pub. 1912).
—— , *The Rules of Sociological Method* (London: Macmillan 1982; orig. pub. 1895).
Edsall, T. E., 'Willie Horton's Message', *New York Review of Books*, 13 Feb. 1992.
Eliot, T. S., *Christianity and Culture* (New York: Harcourt Brace, 1968).
Elkins, S. M., *Slavery: A Problem in American Institutional and Intellectual Life* (Chicago University Press, 1959).
Elton, G. R., *The Future of the Past* (Cambridge University Press, 1966).
—— , *The History of England* (Cambridge University Press, 1984).
Emerson, R., *Africa and United States Policy* (Englewood Cliffs, NJ: Prentice-Hall, 1967).
Enzensberger, H. M., 'The Great Migration', *Granta* 42 (Winter 1992).
Eugenics Education Society, 'Investigation into the Pauper Family Histories', *Papers on the Report of the Poor Law Commission* (1911).
Fabian, J., *Time and the Other: How Anthropology Makes its Object* (New York: Columbia University Press, 1983).
Fanon, F., *The Wretched of the Earth* (Harmondsworth: Penguin, 1967; orig. pub. 1961).
—— , *Toward the African Revolution*, trans Haakon Chevalier (New York: Grove Press, 1969; orig. pub. 1964).
Fisher, R. A., *Genetical Theory of Natural Selection* (Oxford: Clarendon Press, 1930).
Foot, P., *The Rise of Enoch Powell* (Harmondsworth: Penguin, 1969).
Foucault, M., *Madness and Civilisation*, trans Richard Howard (London: Tavistock, 1967).
—— , *The Order of Things* (London: Tavistock, 1970).
—— , *The Archaeology of Knowledge* (London: Tavistock, 1972).
—— , *Folie et deraison: Histoire de la folie à L'âge classique* (2nd edn; Paris: Galimard, 1972).
—— , *Power/Knowledge* (Brighton: Harvester Press, 1980).
Fox-Genovese, E., 'The Self-Interest of Multiculturalism', *Tikkun*, vol. 6, no. 4 (Jul. Aug. 1991).
Frankfurt Institute, *Aspects of Sociology* (London: Heinemann, 1973).
Fryer, P., *Staying Power: The History of Black People in Britain* (London: Pluto, 1984).
Fukuyama, F., 'The End of History', *The National Interest*, no. 18 (1989).
Furedi, F., *Mythical Past, Elusive Future: History and Society in an Anxious Age* (London: Pluto, 1990).
Furnivall, J. S., *Netherlands India: A Study of Plural Economy* (Cambridge University Press, 1939).
—— , *Colonial Policy and Practice: A Comparative Study of Burma and Netherlands India* (New York University Press, 1956).
Gainer, B., *The Alien Invasion: The Origins of the Aliens Act 1905* (London: Heinemann, 1972).
Gaspard, F. and Servan-Schreiber, C., *La Fin des Immigrés* (Paris: Seuil, 1985).
Garrard, J., *The English and Immigration 1880–1910* (Oxford University Press, 1971).
Garrett, M. B., *The French Colonial Question, 1789–1791* (Ann Arbor, Michigan: George Wahr, 1916).
Gasset, J. O. Y. *The Revolt of the Masses* (London: Allen & Unwin, 1932).
Gellner E., *Nations and Nationalism* (Oxford: Blackwell, 1983).
—— , *Relativism and the Social Sciences* (Cambridge University Press, 1985).
Gibson, M., 'Approaches to Multicultural Education in the United States: Some Concepts and Assumptions', *Anthropology and Education Quarterly*, vol. 7, no. 4, (1976).

Giddens, A., *Sociology* (Cambridge: Polity Press, 1993 [2nd edn; first pub. 1989]).

Gilroy, P., *There Ain't No Black in the Union Jack: The Cultural Politics of Race and Nation* (London: Hutchinson, 1987).

——, *The Black Atlantic: Modernity and Double Consciousness* (London: Verso, 1993).

——, 'The End of Antiracism', in Wendy Ball and John Solomos (eds), *Race and Local Politics* (Basingstoke: Macmillan, 1990).

Glazer, N and Moynihan, D (eds), *Ethnicity: Theory and Experience* (Cambridge, Mass: Harvard University Press, 1975).

Gobineau, A. de, *The Inequality of Races*, trans Adrian Collins (Los Angeles: Noontide Press, 1966).

Goldberg, D. T., *Racist Culture: Philosophy and the Politics of Meaning* (Oxford: Blackwell, 1993)

Goldschmidt, W. (ed)., *The Anthropology of Franz Boas* (San Francisco: American Anthropological Association, Memoir no. 89, 1959).

Gonzales-Quiljano, Y., 'Les Musulmans dans la Société Française', *Revue Française des Science Politiques* (Dec. 1987).

Gordon, P. and Klug, F., *New Right, New Racism* (London: Searchlight Publications, 1986).

Gould, S. J. *Ontogeny and Phylogeny* (Cambridge, Mass: Harvard University Press, 1977)

——, *Ever Since Darwin: Reflections in Natural History* (Harmondsworth: Penguin, 1980).

Hall, S, 'The Local and the Global', in King, A. D. (ed.), *Culture, Globalisation and the World System: Contemporary Conditions for the Representation of Identity* (Basingstoke: Macmillan, 1991).

——, 'Old and New Identities, Old and New Ethnicities', in King, A. D. (ed.), *Culture, Globalisation and the World System: Contemporary Conditions for the Representation of Identity* (Basingstoke: Macmillan, 1991).

——, 'New Ethnicities', in Donald, J. and Rattansi, A. (eds), *'Race', Culture and Difference* (London: Sage Open University, 1992).

Hall, S. and Gieben, B. (eds), *Formations of Modernity: Understanding Modern Societies* (Cambridge: Polity Press Open University, 1992).

Hampson, N., *The Enlightenment: An Evaluation of its Assumptions, Attitudes and Values* (Harmondsworth: Penguin, 1968).

Harrington, M., *The Other America* (Harmondsworth: Penguin, 1963; first pub. 1962).

Harvey, D., *The Condition of Postmodernity* (Cambridge: Basil Blackwell, 1989).

Heidegger, M., *Introduction to Metaphysics* (New Haven, Conn.: Yale University Press, 1959).

Herrnstein, R. J. and Murray, C., *The Bell Curve: Intelligence and Class Structure in American Life* (New York: Free Press, 1994).

Herskovits, M. J., *Franz Boas: The Science of Man in the Making* (New York: Scribner's, 1952).

Himmelfarb, G., *The Idea of Poverty: England in the Early Industrial Age* (London: Faber & Faber, 1984).

Hobsbawm, E. J. *The Age of Revolution, 1789–1848* (London: Sphere, 1973; orig. pub. 1962).

——, *The Age of Capital, 1848–1875* (London: Sphere, 1977; orig. pub. 1975).

——, *The Age of Empire, 1875–1914* (London: Sphere, 1989; orig. pub. 1987).

——, *Nations and Nationalism since 1780: Programme, Myth, Reality* (Cambridge University Press, 1992 [2nd edn; 1st edn 1990]).

——, *Age of Extremes: The Short Twentieth Century* (London: Michael Joseph, 1994).

Hobsbawm, E. J. and T. Ranger (eds), *The Invention of Tradition* (Cambridge University Press, 1983).

Hogben, L., *Genetic Principles in Medicine and Social Science* (New York: Knopf, 1932).

Holmes, C., *John Bull's Island: Immigration and British Society, 1871–1971* (London: Macmillan, 1988).

Honeyford, R., 'The Gilmore Syndrome', *Salisbury Review* (Apr. 1986).

hooks, b., *Yearning: Race, Gender and Cultural Politics* (London: Turnabout, 1991).

Hughes, H. S., *The Sea Change*, in H. S. Hughes, *Between Commitment and Disillusionment* (Middletown, Conn.: Wesleyan University Press, 1987).

Hume, D., *Selected Essays* (Oxford University Press, 1993).

——— , *Inquiry Concerning Human Understanding* (Oxford University Press, 1994; orig. pub. 1748).

Hulme, P., *Colonial Encounters: European and the Native Caribbean, 1492–1797;* (London: Methuen, 1986).

Huntingdon, S., 'The Clash of Civilisations', *Foreign Affairs*, vol. 72 no. 3 (Jul./ Aug. 1993)

Huxley, A., *Proper Studies* (London: Chatto & Windus, 1927).

——— , *The Hidden Huxley: Contempt and Compassion for the Masses*, ed. by David Bradshaw (London: Faber & Faber, 1994).

Huxley, J., *Africa View* (New York: Harper & Brothers, 1931).

——— , *Man Stands Alone* (New York: Harper & Brothers, 1940).

Huxley, J. and A. C. Haddon, *We Europeans: A Survey of 'Racial Problems'* (London: Jonathan Cape, 1935).

Huxley, T. H., *Lay Sermons, Addresses and Reviews* (New York: D. Appleton, 1871).

Huxley, T. H., 'On the Methods and Results of Ethnology', *Proceedings of the Royal Institute of Great Britain*, IV (1862–6).

Ings, R., *L'Islam: Une Menace Pour La France?* (unpub. paper, 1994).

Isaac, J. C. *Arendt, Camus and Modern Rebellion* (New Haven, Conn.: Yale University Press, 1992).

Jackson, R. H., 'Juridical Statehood in Africa', *Journal of International Affairs*, vol. 46, no. 1 (1992).

James, C. L. R., *The Black Jacobins: Toussaint L 'Ouverture and the San Domingo Revolution* (London: Allison & Busby, 1980; orig. pub. 1938).

——— , *Spheres of Existence: Selected Writings* (London: Allison & Busby, 1980).

James, W. and C. Harris (eds), *Inside Babylon: The Caribbean Diaspora in Britain* (London: Verso, 1993).

Jenkins, R., 'Social Anthropological Models of Inter-Ethnic Relations', in J. Rex and D. Mason (eds), *Theories of Race and Ethnic Relations* (Cambridge University Press, 1986).

Jones, G. *Social Darwinism and English Thought: The Interaction Between Biological and Social Theory* (New Jersey: Harvester Press, 1980).

Jones, S. *The Language of the Genes: Biology, History and the Evolutionary Future* (London: Harper Collins, 1993).

Joshi, S. and B. Carter, 'The Role of Labour in the Creation of a Racist Britain', *Race and Class*, vol. 25, no. 3.

Kallen, H. *Cultural Pluralism and the American Idea: An Essay in Social Philosophy* (University of Pennsylvania, 1956).

Kant I., *Critique of Practical Reason* (Basingstoke: Macmillan, 1993; orig. pub. 1788).

——— , *Critique of Pure Reason* (Basingstoke: Macmillan, 1991; orig. pub. 1781).

Kaplan, R. D. 'The Coming Anarchy', *Atlantic Monthly* (Feb. 1994).

Katz, M. B. *The Undeserving Poor: From the War on Poverty to the War on Welfare* (New York: Pantheon, 1989).

Katznelson, I. *Black Men, White Cities: Race Relations and Migration in the United States 1900–1930 and Britain 1948–68* (London: Oxford University Press for the Institute of Race Relations, 1973).

Keating, P. (ed.), *Into Unknown England* (Manchester University Press, 1976).

Kennedy, M. L., *The Jacobin Clubs in the French Revolution: The First Years* (Princeton University Press, 1982).

Kepel, G., *Les Banlieues d'Islam* (Paris: Seuil, 1991).

Kevles, D. J., *In the Name of Eugenics: Genetics and the Uses of Human Heredity* (Harmondsworth: Penguin, 1986).

Kiernan, V. G. *The Lords of Humankind: European Attitudes Towards the Outside World in the Imperial Age* (London: Weidenfeld & Nicolson, 1969).

King, A. D. (ed.), *Culture, Globalisation and the World System: Contemporary Conditions for the Representation of Identity* (Basingstoke: Macmillan, 1991).

Kirk, N., 'History, Language, Ideas and Postmodernism: A Materialist View', *Social History*, vol. 19, no. 2 (May 1994).

Kirk, R. *The Conservative Mind* (London: Faber & Faber, 1954).

Knowles, C. and S. Mercer, Feminism and Antiracism', in J. Donald and A. Rattansi (eds), *'Race', Culture and Difference* (London: Sage Open University, 1992).

Knox, R., *The Races of Men: A Philosophical Enquiry into the Influence of Race over the Destinies of Nations* (London: Henry Renshaw, 1850).

Korsch, K., *Marxism and Philosophy* (New York: Monthly Review Press, 1970).

Kroeber, A., *The Nature of Culture* (University of Chicago Press, 1952).

—— , 'Inheritance by Magic', *American Anthropologist*, vol. 18, no. 1 (1916).

Kuklick, H. *The Savage Within: The Social History of British Anthropology 1885–1945* (Cambridge University Press, 1991).

Kuper, A., *Anthropology and Anthropologists: The Modern British School* (London: Routledge, 1983) [2nd edn, 1st edn, 1973]).

Lacan, J., *Écrits: A Selection* (London, Tavistock, 1977).

Lahontan, L. -A. d'A., *New Voyages to North America* (London: H. Bonwicke, 1703).

Lamarck, J. B. *Zoological Philosophy: An Exposition with Regard to the Natural History of Animals*, trans Hugh Elliot (London: Macmillan; orig. pub. 1809, 1914).

Larkin, P., *Selected Letters*, ed. Anthony Thwaite (London: Faber & Faber, 1992).

Laski, H. J., 'The Scope of Eugenics', *Westminster Review*, vol. LXXIV (1910).

Lauren, P. G., *Power and Prejudice: The Politics and Diplomacy of Racial Discrimination* (London: Westview Press, 1988).

Layton-Henry, Z., *The Politics of Immigration: Immigration, 'Race' and 'Race' Relations in Post-war Britain* (Oxford: Blackwell, 1992).

LeBon, G., *The Psychology of Peoples* (New York: G. E. Stechert, 1912; orig. pub. 1894).

Levinas, E., 'The Trace of the Other', in M. C. Taylor (ed.), *Deconstructing in Context*, (Chicago University Press, 1986).

Lévi-Strauss, C. *Triste Tropiques* (Harmondsworth: Penguin, 1955).

—— , *The Savage Mind* (London: Weidenfeld & Nicolson, 1966, orig. pub. 1962).

—— , *Totemism* (Harmondsworth: Penguin, 1969).

—— , *Structural Anthropology*, vol. 1, trans by Claire Jacobson and Brooke Grundfest Schoepf (Harmondsworth: Penguin, 1972; orig. pub. 1963).

—— , *Structural Anthropology*, vol. 2, trans by Monique, London (Harmondsworth: Penguin, 1978; orig. pub. 1973).

—— , *The Naked Man*, trans by John and Doreen Weightman (London: Harper & Row, 1981; orig. pub. 1971).

—— , *The View From Afar*, trans by Joachim Neugroschel and Phoebe Hoss (Harmondsworth: Penguin, 1987; orig. pub. 1983).

Lewis, O., *La Vida: A Puerto Rican Family in the Culture of Poverty—San Juan and New York* (New York: Random House, 1966).
—— , *A Study of Slum Culture* (New York: Random House, 1968).
Liberty, *The Last Resort: Violations of the Human Rights of Migrants, Refugees and Asylum Seekers* (London: Liberty, 1994).
Lind, W., 'Defending Western Culture', *Foreign Policy* (Fall 1991).
Lochak, D., Étrangers et citoyens au regard du droit', in C. Wihtol de Wenden (ed.), *La Citoyenneté*, (Paris: Edilig/Fondation Diderot, 1988).
Lorimer, D. A., *Colour, Class and the Victorians: English Attitudes to the Negro in the Mid-Nineteenth Century* (Leicester University Press, 1978).
Lottman, H., *Flaubert: A Biography* (London: Methuen, 1989).
Lowie, R. H., *Culture and Ethnology* (New York: Boni & Liveright, 1917).
Lukacs, G., *The Historical Novel*, trans Hannah and Stanley Mitchell (London: Merlin, 1962).
—— , *The Destruction of Reason* (London: Merlin, 1980; orig. pub. 1962).
—— , *History and Class Consciousness: Studies in Marxist Dialectics* (London: Merlin, 1971; orig. pub. 1968).
Lugard, F. D., *The Dual Mandate in British Tropical Africa* (London: William Blackwood & Sons, 1922).
Lyotard, J. F. *The Postmodern Condition: A Report on Knowledge* (Manchester University Press, 1984).
—— , *Heidegger and the 'Jews'* (New Haven, Conn.: Yale University Press, 1994).
Maistre, J. M., de, *The Works of Joseph de Maistre*, trans Jack Lively (London: Macmillan, 1965).
Malik, K. 'Racialising the Poor', *Paradigm*, no. 1 (Autumn 1995).
Marcuse, H. *Eros and Civilisation* (London: Baacus, 1972).
Marshall, A, *The Economics of Industry* (London: Macmillan, 1881).
Marx, K. and Engels, F., *Selected Works* (London: Lawrence & Wishart, 1968).
Masterman, C. F., *The Condition of England* (London: Methuen, 1909).
Mayhew, H. *London Labour and the London Poor*, ed. John D. Rosenberg (New York: Dover, 1968).
Mercer, K., 'Welcome to the Jungle: Identity and Diversity in Postmodern Politics', in J. Rutherford (ed.), *Identity: Community, Culture, Difference* (London: Lawrence & Wishart, 1993).
—— , 'Back to My Routes: A Postscript on the 80s', *Ten8* vol. 2, no. 3 (Spring 1992).
Messina, A., *Race and Party Competition in Britain* (Oxford: Clarendon Press, 1989).
Meyerson, A., 'The Vision Thing, Continued', *Policy Review*, no. 52 (Summer 1990).
Michelet, J., *France Before Europe* (Boston: Roberts Brothers, 1871).
—— , *The People*, trans John P. McKay (Urbana: University of Illinois Press, 1973; orig. pub. 1846).
Miles, R., *Racism and Migrant Labour: A Critical Text* (London: Routledge & Kegan Paul, 1982).
—— , *Racism* (London: Routledge, 1989).
—— , *Racism after 'Race Relations'* (London: Routledge, 1993).
Miles, R., and A. Phizacklea, *White Man's Country: Racism in British Politics* (London: Pluto, 1984).
Mill, J. S., *On Liberty and Other Essays*, ed. John Grey (Oxford University Press, 1993).
Miller, C. L., *Theories of Africans: Francophone Literature and Anthropology in Africa* (University of Chicago Press, 1990).
Milliband, R., and L. Panitch (eds), *The Retreat of the Intellectuals: Socialist Register 1990* (London: Merlin, 1990).

Ministére du Travail/Secrétariat d'État aux Travailleurs Immigrés, *Immigration et 7e Plan* (Paris: La Documentation Français, 1977).

Montagu, A., *Man's Most Dangerous Myth: The Fallacy of Race* (Cleveland: World Publishing, 1964).

Montagu, A., *Statement on Race* (London: Oxford University Press, 1972).

Montesquieu, C. de S., *The Spirit of the Laws*, trans A. M. Cohler, C. M. and H. S. Stone (Cambridge University Press, 1989; orig. pub. 1748).

Morris, J., *Pax Britannica: The Climax of an Empire* (Harmondsworth: Penguin, 1979).

Morris, L., *Dangerous Classes: The Underclass and Social Citizenship* (London: Routledge, 1994).

Morrison, T., *Playing in the Dark: Whiteness and the Literary Imagination* (Cambridge, Mass.: Harvard University Press, 1992).

Mosca, G., *The Ruling Class*, trans H. D. Kahn and A. Livingstone (New York: McGraw-Hill, 1965).

Mosse, G. L., *Toward the Final Solution: A History of European Racism* (London: J. M. Dent & Sons, 1978).

Motion, A., *Larkin* (London: Routledge, 1982).

Moynihan, D., *The Negro Family: The Case for National Action*, in L. Rainwater and W. L. Yancey (eds), *The Moynihan Report and the Politics of Controversy* (Cambridge, Mass: MIT Press, 1967).

Murray, C., *Losing Ground: American Social Policy 1950–1980* (New York: Basic Books, 1984).

—— *The Emerging British Underclass* (London: Institute of Economic Affairs, 1990).

Murray, C. and R. J. Herrnstein, 'Race, Genes and IQ – An Apologia', *New Republic*, 31 Oct. 1994

Murray, G., F. W. Hirst and J. L. Hammond, *Liberalism and the Empire: Three Essays* (London: Johnson, 1900).

Nairn, T., *The Break-up of Britain* (London: Verso, 1981).

Newbury, C., *The Cohesion of Oppression: Clientship and Ethnicity in Rwanda 1960–1960* (New York: Columbia University Press, 1993).

Noiriel, G., *Le Creuset Francais: Histoire de l'Immigration XIXe—XXe Siècles* (Paris: Seuil, 1988).

Omi, M., and H. Winant, *Racial Formation in the United States: From the 1960s to the 1980s* (London: Routledge & Kegan Paul, 1986).

Orwell, G., *The Lion and the Unicorn* (Harmondsworth: Penguin, 1982).

Osborne, P. (ed.), *Socialism and the Limits of Liberalism* (London: Verso, 1991).

Pagden, A., *European Encounters with the New World* (New Haven Conn.: Yale University Press, 1993).

Paine. T., *The Thomas Paine Reader*, ed. Michael Foot and Isaac Kramnick, (Harmondsworth: Penguin, 1987).

Palmer, B. D., 'The Eclipse of Materialism: Marxism and the Writing of Social History in the 1980s', in R. Milliband and L. Panitch (eds), *The Retreat of the Intellectuals: Socialist Register 1990* (London: Merlin, 1990).

Panayi, P., *The Enemy in Our Midst: Germans in Britain During the First World War* (New York: Berg, 1991).

Patterson, S., *Immigration and Race Relations in Britain 1960–1967* (London: Oxford University Press for the Institute of Race Relations, 1969).

Pearson, K., *National Life from the Standpoint of Science* (London: A. & C. Black, 1905).

Pick, D., *Faces of Degeneration: A European Disorder, c1848–1918* (Cambridge University Press, 1989).

Pieterse, J. N., *Empire and Emancipation: Power and Liberation on a World Scale* (London: Pluto, 1989).

Pilkington, E., *Beyond the Mother Country: West Indians and the Notting Hill White Riots* (London: I. B. Taurus, 1988).

Poliakov, L., *The Aryan Myth: A History of Racist and Nationalist Ideas in Europe* (New York: New York Library, 1971).

Popper, K., *The Open Universe: An Argument for Indeterminacy*, ed. W. W. Batley (London: Routledge, 1982).

Porter, R., and M. Teich (eds), *Romanticism in National Context* (Cambridge University Press, 1988).

Pratt, M. L., 'Humanities for the Future: Reflections on the Western Culture Debate at Stanford', *The South Atlantic Quarterly*, vol. 89, no. 1 (Winter 1990).

President's Committee on Civil Rights, *To Secure These Rights* (Washington DC: Government Printing Office, 1947).

Rainwater, L. and W. L. Yancey *The Moynihan Report and the Politics of Controversy* (Cambridge, Mass.: MIT Press, 1967).

Rattansi, A. and S. Westwood (eds), *Racism, Modernity and Identity: On the Western Front* (Cambridge: Polity Press, 1994).

Ravich, D., 'Multiculturalism', *The American Scholar*, vol., 59 no. 3 (1990).

Raynal, A., *The Philosophical and Political History of the Settlements and Trade of the Europeans in the East and West Indies* (London, 1776).

Renan, E., *Oeuvres Complètes* (Paris: Calmann-Lévy, 1947–61).

—— , 'What is a nation?', trans Martin Thom, in H. K. Babha (ed.), *Nations and Narration* (London: Routledge, 1990).

—— , *The Future of Science* (Boston: Roberts Brothers, 1891).

Rex, J. *Race Relations in Sociological Theory* (London: Weidenfeld & Nicolson, 1970).

—— , 'Race and Ethnicity', in P. Worsley (ed.), *Introducing Sociology* (Harmondsworth: Penguin, 1986).

—— , 'The Political Sociology of a Multi-Cultural Society', *European Journal of Intercultural Studies*, vol. 2, no. 1.

Rex, J., and D. Mason (eds), *Theories of Race and Ethnic Relations*, (Cambridge University Press, 1986).

Rich, P. B., *Race and Empire in British Politics* (Cambridge University Press, 1986).

Ripley, W. Z., *The Races of Europe: A Sociological Study* (New York: D. Appleton, 1899)

Rockmore, T., *On Heidegger's Nazism and Philosophy* (Berkeley: University of California Press, 1994).

Roosevelt, T., *The Works of Theodore Roosevelt* (New York: Scribner's, 1926)

Rorty, R., *Objectivity, Relativism and Truth* (Cambridge University Press, 1991).

—— , 'Two Cheers for the Cultural Left' in *South Atlantic Quarterly*, vol. 89, no. 1 (Winter 1990).

Rose, S., R. C. Lewontin and L. J. Kamin *Not in Our Genes: Biology, Ideology and Human Nature* (Harmondsworth: Penguin, 1984).

Rousseau, J. J., *The Social Contract*, trans Maurice Cranston (Harmondsworth: Penguin, 1968; orig. pub. 1770).

—— , *A Discourse on Inequality*, trans Maurice Cranston (Harmondsworth: Penguin, 1984; orig. pub. 1755).

—— , *On the Origin of Language*, trans John H. Moran and Alexander Gode (New York: Frederick Unger, 1966; orig. pub. 1761).

—— , 'Discourse on the Sciences and the Arts' in *The First and Second Discourses*, trans by Victor Gourevitch (New York: Harper & Row, 1986; orig. pub. 1751).

—— , *Émile, or, On Education*, trans Allan Bloom (New York: Basic Books, 1979; orig. pub. 1761).

Rubinstein, R. L., *The Cunning of History* (London: Harper & Row, 1978).

Rutherford, J. (ed.), *Identity: Community, Culture, Difference* (London: Lawrence & Wishart, 1993).

Rutter, M. and M. Madge, *Cycles of Disadvantage*, (London: Heinemann, 1976)

Said, E. W., *Orientalism: Western Concepts of the Orient* (Harmondsworth: Penguin, 1985; orig. pub. 1978).

—— , *Culture and Imperialism* (London: Chatto & Windus, 1993).

Sartre, J. -P., *Being and Nothingness* (London: Methuen 1957).

—— , *Critique of Dialectical Reason*, vol. 1: *Theory of Practical Ensembles*, trans Alan Sheridan-Smith (London: New Left Books, 1976).

Schlesinger, A. M., *The Disuniting of America: Reflections on a Multicultural Society* (New York: Norton, 1992; orig. pub. 1991).

Scott, N. and D. Jones (eds), *Bloody Bosnia: A European Tragedy* (London: *Guardian*/Channel 4 Television, 1994).

Scruton, R. 'In Defence of the Nation', in J. C. D. Clark (ed.), *Ideas and Politics in Modern Britain* (Basingstoke: Macmillan, 1990).

Semmel, B., *The Governor Eyre Controversy*, (London: McGibbon & Kee, 1962).

Shields, J. G., 'Anti-Semitism in France: the Spectre of Vichy', *Patterns of Prejudice*, vol. 24, nos. 2–4 (1990).

Silverman, M., *Deconstructing the Nation: Immigration, Racism and Citizenship in France* (London: Routledge, 1992).

Simonson, R. and S. Walker (eds), *Multicultural Literacy: Opening the American Mind* (St. Paul, Minn.: Gray, Wolf Press, 1988).

Skinner, Q. (ed.), *The Return of Grand Theory in the Human Sciences* (Cambridge University Press, 1985).

Smellie, W., *The Philosophy of Nature History* (Boston: Brown, Taggard & Chase, 1885).

Smith, A. *An Inquiry into the Nature and Causes of the Wealth of Nations*, ed. Kathryn Sutherland (Oxford University Press, 1993; orig. pub. 1776).

Smith, M. G. 'Pluralism, Race and Ethnicity in Selected African Countries', in J. Rex and D. Mason, (eds), *Theories of Race and Ethnic Relations* (Cambridge University Press, 1986).

Smock, D. and K. Bentsi-Enchill (eds),*The Search for National Integration in Africa* (New York: Free Press, 1975).

Sponza, L. *Italian Immigrants in Nineteenth-Century Britain: Images and Realities* (Leicester University Press, 1988).

Stedman Jones, G., *Outcast London: A Study in the Relationship Between the Classes in Victorian Society* (Oxford University Press, 1971).

—— , *Languages of Class: Studies in English Working Class History 1832—1982* (Cambridge University Press, 1983).

Stepan, N., *The Idea of Race in Science: Great Britain 1800–1960* (London: Macmillan, 1982).

Stillman, E. and Pfaff, W., *The Politics of Hysteria* (New York: Harper & Row, 1964).

Stocking, G. W. Jnr, *Race, Culture and Evolution: Essays in the History of Anthropology* (University of Chicago Press, 1982).

—— , *Victorian Anthropology* (New York: Free Press, 1987).

—— , (ed.), *The Shaping of American Anthropology 1883–1911: A Franz Boas Reader* (New York: Basic Books, 1974).

—— , (ed.), *Bones, Bodies and Behaviour: Essays on Biological Anthropology (History of Anthropology*, vol. 5) (Madison, Wis.: University of Wisconsin Press, 1988).

Stoddard, T. L., *The Rising Tide of Color Against White World Supremacy* (New York: Scribner's, 1921).

Swann, Lord, *Education for All: The Report of the Committee of Inquiry Into the Education of Children from Ethnic Minority Groups* (London: HMSO, 1985 [Cmnd. 9453]).

Taguieff, P. A. 'The New Cultural Racism in France', *Telos*, no. 83 (Spring 1990).

Taine, H., *History of English Literature*, trans H. van Laun (Philadelphia: Gebbie Publishing, 1897, orig. pub. 1864).

Tarcov, N., *Locke's Education for Liberty* (University of Chicago Press, 1984).

Thompson, E. P., *The Poverty of Theory* (London: Merlin, 1976).

Todorov, T., *On Human Diversity: Nationalism, Racism and Exoticism in French Thought*, trans C Porter (Camb, Mass.: Harvard University Press, 1993).

Tompson, K., *Under Seige: Racial Violence in Britain Today* (Harmondsworth: Penguin, 1988).

Troyna, B. and J. Williams, *Racism, Education and the State* (London: Croon Helm, 1986).

Tylor, E. B., *Researches into the Early History of Mankind* (London: John Murray, 1865).

—— , *Anthropology: An Introduction to the Study of Man and Civilisation* (London: Macmillan, 1881).

Taylor, M. C. (ed.), *Deconstructing in Context* (Chicago University Press, 1986).

Voltaire, F. M. A., *The Age of Louis XIV and Other Selected Writings*, trans and abridged by J. H. Brumfitt (New York: Washington Square Press, 1963).

Waal, A. de, 'The Genocidal State', *The Times Literary Supplement* (1 Jul. 1994).

Wallman, S., 'Ethnicity and the Boundary Process in Context', in J. Rex and D. Mason (eds), *Theories of Race and Ethnic Relations* (Cambridge University Press).

Webb, B., *Diaries*, (London, Virago, 1983–86).

—— , *My Apprenticeship* (London: Penguin, 1971).

Weber, E., *Peasants into Frenchmen: The Modernisation of Rural France 1870–1914* (Stanford University Press, 1976).

Weekes, J., *Sexuality and its Discontents: Meanings, Myths and Modern Sexualities*, (London: Routledge & Kegan Paul, 1985).

Weil, P., *La France et ses Étrangers* (Paris: Calmann-Lévy, 1991).

Weil, P. and J. Crowley, 'Integration in Theory and Practice: A Comparison of France and Britain', in M. Baldwin-Edwards and M. Schain (eds), *The Politics of Immigration in Western Europe* (Ilford: Frank Cass, 1994).

Weldon, F., *Sacred Cows* (London: Chatto & Windus, 1989).

White, L., *The Science of Culture: A Study of Man and Civilisation* (New York: Farrar, Strauss, 1949).

Wihtol de Wenden, C., *Les immigrés et la Politique* (Paris: Presses de la Foundation Nationale des Sciences Politiques, 1988).

Wihtol de Wenden, C. (ed.), *La Citoyenneté* (Paris: Edilig/Fondation Diderot, 1988).

Worsley, P. (ed.), *Introducing Sociology* (Harmondsworth: Penguin, 1986).

Yeats, W. B., *Autobiographies* (London: Macmillan, 1977).

Yinger, J. M., 'Intersecting strands in the theorisation of race and ethnic relations', in J. Rex and D. Mason (eds), *Theories of Race and Ethnic Relations* (Cambridge University Press, 1986).

Young, R. *White Mythologies: Writing History and the West* (London: Routledge, 1990).

Zeitlin, I., *Ideology and the Development of Sociological Theory* (Englewood Cliffs, NJ: Prentice-Hall, 1968).

Index

Abramson, Harold 176
Academic philosophy 238
Acculturation 201
Acquired characteristics, inheritance of *see* Lamarckism
Action Français 141
Adoption *see* Transracial adoption
Adorno, Theodor 240–1, 248
Aeschylus 228
Affair Dreyfus, l' 144–5
Affair foulard, l' 181, 196
Africa 9, 17, 44, 81, 118, 210, 211–2, 213; indirect rule in 171; as premodern 171, 213–15; as tribal 171–2, 213–15; Western contempt for 36–7, 210, 212–16
African-Americans 38, 93, 178, 179, 183; breakdown of family structure 32, 204; as different 124–5, 157, 204, 217; impact of slavery on culture of 203–5; and IQ 206–7, 254; and 'tangle of pathology' thesis 204
African culture 162, 171–2, 213
Africanist presence (in American literature) 183
African mind, the 124, 149, 172, 212, 213
Africanness 230
Africans 28, 35, 54, 62, 81, 97, 125, 128–9, 163, 166, 179, 183, 194–5, 196, 197, 211; dehumanisation of 214; perception of as savage 43–4, 124, 212–15; pre-Enlightenment view of 43–5, 225; and the discourse of race 81, 97, 214–15, 224
Afro-Caribbeans 185, 252, 253
Afrocentrism 207
Age of Catastrophe, The 147
Ahistoricism 222–6, 227–30, 242, 247, 248, 255–8
Ahmad, Aijaz 229, 232
Algerians 194

Algerian war of liberation 194
Aliens Deportation Group (Britain) 38
Allen, Theodore 253
Allen, Woody 251–2, 253
All in the Family 235
Althusser, Louis 238
Ambivalence *see* Indeterminacy
America (USA) 119, 123, 149–50, 178; articles by Julian Huxley on 124–5; black 17, 30, 31–3, 162, 179, 203–5, 261–2, 264–5, *see also* African-Americans; Negroes); and the civil rights movement 261; Committee on Civil Rights 17; debate about immigration to 96, 126; fragmentation of 180–1, 217; and imperialism 115; as a mass society 243; as a melting pot 179; as a plural society 173; postwar sensitivity about race 15–17; support for eugenics in 114; and the underclass debate 31–3, 198–209
American Anthropologist 161
American Declaration of Independence 38–9, 47, 69
American national identity: debate about 179–82; the making of 138, 179; and pluralism 173, 179,
Americanness 236 (*see also* American national identity)
American patriots 57, 134
American Revolution 133
Amiel, Barbara 214
Ammon, Otto 96
Ammon's Law 96
Ancien régime 58, 73, 136
Anderson, Benedict 252
Anthropological Society (of London) 89, 96, 98
Anthropology 80, 81, 92, 99, 125, 147–8, 169, 170, 172, 173, 201,

240, 266; cultural 126, 147–8, 150–69; racial 87–9, 92, 99, 103, 119–21, 125, 147–8, 160; social 156, 160, 174; physical *see* racial; structural 163

Anti-colonialism 123, 211, 238, 240

Anti-essentialism 247–59, 262

Antifascism 191–2, 262

Anti-German chauvinism 191–2

Antihumanism 85, 87, 112, 160–9, 236, 237–47, 250, 259, 262

Anti-imperialism 117, 238

Anti-Nazi League, the 191–92

Antiracism 125, 145, 238, 262; and antifascism 191–2; as assertion of difference 217–19, 261–2; and chauvinism 192–3; as component of British national identity 191–3; as official policy 149–150, 190, 192; as response to experience of Nazism 123–4, 125–7; and science 122, 123–7; transformation of 261–5

Anti-Semitism 33, 253

Anti-universalism *see* Universalism, hostility to

Apartheid 17, 149, 150

Appearance (of social forms) 257–9

Appleyard, Bryan 200

Arendt, Hannah 243–4

Aristocratic reaction 83–4

Aryan 83, 120, 141

Asante, Molefi Kete 179

Asia 17, 118, 119, 185, 210, 211–12, 216; in Orientalist discourse 228

Asians 126, 128–9, 143, 176. 185, 186, 211

Assimilation 19, 169, 179, 180; as a means of maintaining difference 35–6, 193–4, 197

Associationist psychology 46, 76

Attlee, Clement 19

Auschwitz 101

Austen, Jane 70

Australia 112, 118, 119, 126

Authoritarian Personality, The 243

Authoritarian personality, theory of 243, 244

Azelio, Massimo d' 138

Bacchae (Euripedes) 228

Bagehot, Walter 2, 85, 102

Balfour, Arthur 114

Banfield, Edward 200

Banton, Michael 3, 18, 54

Barkan, Elazar 121, 122, 123, 125, 157

Barker, Anthony 54, 62

Barnave, Antoine 67

Barou, Jacques 193–194

Barrès, Maurice 139, 141, 142, 143, 144–5, 146, 147, 156, 186

Bastille Day 140

Bauman, Zygmunt 241, 246

Bebop 252

Belgium 115, 173

Bell Curve, The (Herrnstein and Murray) 202–3, 205–9; hostility to 205–9

Bell, Daniel 14

Bemoin, Prince 44–5

Benedict, Ruth 126, 162–3

Bennett, William 178, 180

Berlin, Isaiah 58

Bernal, Martin 229

Bethnal Green 93

Bimsbergen, Wim van 172

Biological concepts of society 88–9, 90–1, 95, 106–9, 111, 112, 127, 158–60, 162, 163, 206–7; relationship between biological and social concepts 158–60, 161–3, 186–7, 193

Biology 4–5, 15, 87–8, 89, 90, 96, 108–9, 112, 117, 123–7, 158

Black, as a category 1–2, 5, 119, 126, 247

Blackburn, Robin 64, 66, 68

Black immigration 18, 19–21, 23–4, 36, 185

Black Jacobins, The (James) 67–8

Blackness, the meaning of 224–5, 251–3

Black people 10, 30, 39, 49, 157, 179, 185; in Britain 19–20, 36, 38, 91–2, 185, 190–1, 192, 219 (*see also* African-Americans; America, black; Negroes)

Black power 264–265

Black race 83, 117, 118, 126

Blackstone, Sir William 62

Blair, Tony 205

Blake, William 74

Block, Maurice 135

Blood groups 4, 120
Bloom, Allan 178, 182
Bloom, Saul 178
Blumenbach, Johann Friederich 4, 5, 87, 88
Boas, Franz 150–6, 156–7, 161, 162, 163, 164, 169, 170
Boasians 157, 160–3
Boer War 110, 116
Bolk, Louis 122
Bonald, Louis de 74
Bork, Robert 178
Bosnia 10, 170
Bourgeoisie *see* Capitalist class
Boydkin, Wade 207
Brachycephalics 96
Britain 1, 2, 123, 149–50; contrast between race relations policies of Britain and France 26, 28–9, 190–1; fears for racial degeneration of 110; and immigration policy 18–25, 189–90; impact of immigration on 30, 173, 185; impact of imperialism on 115–17; importance of Commonwealth to 16–17; as a multiracial nation 176–7, 189–90; perceptions of Islam in 36, 187–9; in the post-Cold War era 181, 184; postwar sensitivity about race 15-17, 18, 21–2, 24, 189–91; and race relations policy 3, 17, 18–25, 176–7, 189–93; racial divisions in 252; rewriting immigration history of 34- 5; self-image of 191–3; and the Victorian belief in science 84–5
British Empire, the 114–17, 184
British national identity 20, 35, 177, 181, 184–6, 188, 191–3; antifascism as component of 191–2; and anti-German chauvinism 191–2; and the black population 20–1, 30–4, 192–3; and citizenship 190; constructing a sense of 138, 140, 222–3; contemporary debate about 183–7; impact of national decline on 183–7; importance of history to 184–7; pluralism as a component of 191–3; in the post-Cold War era 181, 183–93; Second World War as component of 191–2
Britishness 236 (*see also* British national identity)
Britons (Colley) 222–3
Broca, Paul 120
Browne, Paul 208
Bryce, Lord 116
Buchanan, Pat 179, 181
Buchez, Philippe 82
Buffon, G. L. 47–8, 54, 80
Burgess, Anthony 188
Burke, Edmund 63, 74–5, 77, 78, 85, 154, 186, 237
Burt, Cyril 114
Buzan, Barry 210

Calvez, Corentin 27
Calvez report 27
Canada 118, 119, 172
Cape Colony 98
Capitalism 6, 246–7; conflict between belief in equality and social organisation of 59–61, 69–70, 71, 102–3, 160; disenchantment with 13–14, 74, 241-4; essence of 248; as expression of Enlightenment ideology 55–7, 246-7; negative aspects of 247; positive aspects of 246–7; and race 70, 71–2, 102–3; transformative nature of 72
Capitalist class 100; appeal of Enlightenment philosophy to 57; contradictory attitudes towards equality of 59–61, 85–6, 93–4; and fear of progress 72, 85–6 (*see also* Élite, the)
Carey, John 106, 113
Carr, E. H. 254, 255–6
Casey, John 185, 212
Categorical imperative (Kant) 76
Cavour, Count Camillo 116
Cephalic index 88
Chamberlain, Houston Stewort 84, 105, 229
Chapman, Malcolm 174, 176
Chicago School (of social anthropology) 174
Chirac, Jacques 33, 195, 197, 198, 209

Christian Democrats 11, 12,
Christianity 188–9, 242
Churchill, Winston 185, 189
Citizenship 69, 134, 136–8, 140, 178,
    179, 185–7, 189, 190, 193–8
Civilisation 80, 84, 161;
    Enlightenment concepts of 52–3,
    142, 153, 154; hostility to
    universal forms of 78–9, 138–9,
    167–9; positivist view of 86;
    sense of precariousness of 82,
    85–6, 104, 109–10, 112; racial
    theories of 14, 36–7, 54–5, 83–4,
    85–6, 88, 115–16, 117, 168; as
    source of barbarism 241–7;
    Western 36–7, 79
Civilisational Cold War 36
Civilisation and its Discontents
    (Freud) 178
Civil rights movement (US) 261
Clark, Alan 189
Clash of civilisations, theory of 210
Class conflict and the discourse of
    race 57, 59–61, 85–96, 67–8, 104,
    116, 137
Class distinctions and the discourse
    of race 70, 80, 81–2, 83, 85–6,
    91–6, 98, 104–14, 115–16, 117, 119,
    121, 126, 198–209
Clinton, Bill 205
Closing of the American Mind, The
    (Bloom) 178
Cohen, Robin 251, 252
Cold War, the 7, 11, 180; corrosive
    effects of end of 9–10, 11–3,
    34, 179, 180-1, 184–5, 260–1;
    impact on perceptions of race
    10, 15–7, 21, impact on relations
    between West and the Third
    World 16–7, 211 (*see also*
    Post-Cold War era; Postwar
    consensus)
Coleridge, Samuel 74, 132, 154
Collective representations
    (Durkheim) 155–6
Colley, Linda 222–3
Colonialism 79, 81, 171, 246; calls for
    the return of 210; as ontological
    need of the West 224, 229, 232;
    as expression of legitimate
    Western interests 210 (*see also*
    Imperialism)

Colonial society 171
Colour bars 17, 21, 118
Coloured Races Restriction and
    Regulation Acts (Australia,
    1896) 118
Colour line, the 118
Commentaries on the Laws of England
    (Blackstone) 62
Commission for Racial Equality
    (British) 189
Commission on liberties (of French
    National Assembly) 167
Committee on Civil Rights (US) 17
Committee on Colonies (of the
    French National Assembly)
    66–7
Commonwealth, British 16–17, 23,
    189
Communist Manifesto, The (Marx and
    Engels) 72, 178
Comte, August 86, 258
Condorcet, Marquis de 47, 70, 134,
    266
Congo crisis, the 212
Conseil d'État (French) 27, 197
Conservatism: and collapse of the
    postwar consensus 12, 34, 180;
    and the culture concept 181–2,
    186–7; and democracy 106, 107;
    hostility to Enlightenment of
    74–9; 86; hostility to pluralism
    180–2, 185; hostility to relativism
    of 180–2; and inequality 74–5,
    102, 106, 107; origins of 74;
    postwar discrediting of 14; and
    the underclass debate 31–3,
    202–3, 205–8
Conservative Party, British 12;
    policies in government 20, 21,
    22–3, 189–91; postwar attitudes
    to race of 20, 21, 22–3, 189–91,
    192
Conservative/Romantic reaction *see*
    Romanticism
Cranial capacity 88
Creveld, Martin von 214
Cricket test, the (Norman Tebbit) 185
Criminality 1, 35, 85–6, 109–11, 114,
    185, 198–200, 203
Criticism, abandonment of 261–3
Critique of Dialectical Reason (Sartre)
    253–4

Critique of Practical Reason (Kant) 76

Critique of Pure Reason (Kant) 76

Crossman, Richard 23

Crowd psychology 106–7, 188

Crowd, the *see* Mob, the

Cultural anthropology *see* Anthropology, cultural

Cultural barriers, necessity for 77–9, 138–9, 143, 154–6, 168–9, 171, 181–2, 185, 196, 235–6, 261–2

Cultural difference 128–33, 138, 169–77; as an antiracist strategy 149–150, 167–8, 169–70 176–7, 217–19, 252, 253–4, 261–2; and apartheid 150; as basis of identity 76–9, 138–40, 141–4, 154–6, 168-9, 181–2, 185–7, 191–3, 195–8; and conservatism 76–9, 181–2, 185–7, 189–90, 195–98; as the essence of humanity 167–9; as language of the far right 196; as natural 150, 182, 206–7; and national identity 131, 133–40, 144–5, 185–7, 187–8, 193–8; as maintaining social stability 154–6, 171, 176–7, 186; in poststructuralist discourse 217–19, 223, 229–30, 235–6, 252, 253–4, 261–2; and segregation 264; and the underclass debate 198–209;

Cultural formalism 258–9

Cultural heritage 78, 154, 186–7

Culturalism 144

Cultural mixing, as a problem 77–9, 138–9, 143, 154–6, 168–9, 171, 185–6, 195–6, 234–6

Cultural pluralism 173 (*see also* Cultural difference; Multiculturalism; Pluralism)

Cultural racism 198

Cultural relativism 130, 144–8, 151–6, 160, 164–9, 180–1, 182, 217–9, 233–6, 240

Cultural superiority 36–7, 187–9, 192–3, 196, 209–16

Cultural war, the 179, 209, 210; as replacement for the Cold War 210

Culture 78; description of working-class inferiority in terms of 117, 198–209; and ethnicity 174–7; impact on human biology 166; and natural selection 166; functional role of 154–6, 171; of poverty 201–5; as transhistorical entity 133, 154–6, 164–5, 186–7, 222–6, 227–30

Culture and Ethnology (Lowie) 162

Culture and Imperialism (Said) 223–4

Culture concept, the: ambiguity of 144–8, 156–60, 161–3; and anthropology 150–6, 159–60, 161–9; antihumanist essence of 153–6, 160–1, 162–3, 166–9; as homologue of race 127, 128–30, 133, 140–48, 150, 156–63, 165–9, 172, 182, 186–7, 196, 198, 201, 208–9, 228–30, 232, 258–9; and Romanticism 131–3, 150, 151, 154 186, 229, 232; and social evolution 158–60

Curriculum, the, US debate over 178–9

Dangerous classes 110, 111, 198–201

Dante, Alighieri 106, 178, 228

Darwin, Charles 90–1, 101, 158, 178

Darwinism 90–1, 101, 158 (*see also* Social Darwinism)

Davenport, Charles 158

Davis, David Brion 62

Davis, Miles 252

Débâcle, The (Zola) 110

Decentring: discourse 219; the subject 251

Declaration of the Rights of Man *see* Rights of Man

Decolonisation 17, 211; in poststructuralist discourse 220

Deconstructionism 219, 249–51, 257–8

Degeneration 72–3, 83, 86, 105, 109–14, 168

Dégénérescence 86, 111

Degerando, Joseph-Marie 51–3, 80, 142

Degler, Carl 151, 159

Democracy 103, 104–9, 110, 114, 117, 170

Democratic Party (US) 205

Depoliticisation of race 7, 10, 18, 21–2, 28–9, 189–91
Depression, the 13
Derrida, Jacques 219, 238, 249–50, 255, 257, 262
Desir, Harlem 196
Dialectical view of society 257, 267–8
Dialectic of Enlightenment (Adorno and Horkheimer) 240–1, 248
Dicey, Alfred 116–17
Dickens, Charles 254
Diderot, Denis 47
Différance (Derrida) 249–50
Difference: assertion of 217–19, 261–2; comparison between concept in racial and cultural discourse 156, 156–60, 161, 164–9, 182, 186–7, 193, 203, 208–9, 228–30, 232, 258–9; cultural 76–9, 128–33, 154–6, 160, 161–2, 164–9, 177, 179–82, 185–7, 187–9, 193–8, 199–209, 213–16, 217–19, 223, 229–30, 235–6; moral 85–6, 94–5, 97, 109–11, 114, 213–16; as indifference 235–6; national 136–40; politics of 217–19; in poststructuralist discourse 217–19, 223, 229–30, 235-6, 247–59; as product of social defeats 261, 262, 264–5, 268–9; in pre-Enlightenment world 43–5, 225; and race 70, 81, 110, 160, 161, 174–7, 181–2, 186–7, 193, 206–7, 258; and the underclass 198–209
Differential racism 198
Diffusionism 160
Dijoud, Paul 195
Discourse, concept of 233–4, 250
Discourse on Inequality (Rousseau) 49, 59–60, 71
Disraeli, Benjamin 1
Dixon, Richard 120
Dolichephalics 96
Drescher, Seymour 62, 65
Dreyfus, Captain Alfred 144–5
D'Souza, Dinesh 178
Durkheim, Émile 154–6
Dutch Revolution 133

Ede, Chuter 19

Eden, Anthony 20, 22
Egalitarianism *see* Equality
Eliot, T. S. 106, 108, 114
Élite, the: ambivalence towards equality of 38–9, 59–61, 63–8, 69, 98, 102–3, 104–14, 202–3, 208–9; cognitive 206; fear of ability to govern 105, 109; fear of degeneration 72–3, 109–14; fear of the masses 85–6, 97–8, 104–14, 116–17; fear of social instability 85–6, 90, 106–8, 109–12, 183; impact of end of the Cold War on élite institutions 12; importance of race to 20–1, 105, 115, 117, 118; postwar attitudes to race of the British élite 18–19, 20–1, 23, 24; sense of racial superiority of 82, 97–100, 105, 112–14, 115, 117, 118; social pessimism of 72–3, 85–6, 104–5, 109–12, 123, 147; view of non-white races 97–100, 117–19
Élite theories 81–2, 93–4, 97, 99–100, 105, 116, 117, 203, 238; comparison of working class and non-white races in 98, 99–100; relationship between élitism and modernism 106
Elkins, Stanley 203–4, 205
Ellis, Havelock 102, 114
Elton, Geoffrey 184
Emancipation *see* Human emancipation
Emerson, Ralph Waldo 179
Emerson, Rupert 212
Empire Windrush, SS 19
Empiricism 40, 46, 47, 258
Engels, Friederich 72, 246
England football team 192
Englishness 143, 185, 186, 191, 217
Enlightenment, the 6–7, 40–61, 71–2, 73, 74, 76, 82, 102, 112, 130, 135, 146, 147; and capitalism 57–61; contemporary hostility to 40–2, 145, 218–19, 220, 221–2, 227–8, 234–5, 238–19, 240–2, 244–7; conservative/Romantic hostility to 54, 58–9, 74–9, 83, 85, 86, 145, 237–8; cosmopolitanism of 49; and European stability 55–6;

Enlightenment *cont.*
and feudalism 55–7; and the
French Revolution 57–9, 60; and
French national identity 133, 139,
193, 194; and human
emancipation 42, 57, 68–9, 154,
268; and the masses 57–8, 68–9;
and modernity 42, 45, 245–6;
and racism 40, 53, 54; as starting
point for the discussion of race
39–40, 42; as the source of
modern barbarism 240–3; and
the study of non-European
peoples 49–53
Enlightenment discourse: assumption
of reconciliation between the
universal and the particular in
266; blindness to human
specificity 265; concept of
civilisation in 52–3, 142, 153,
154; concept of equality in 42,
49–51, 53–5, 152; concept of
human nature in 42, 47–55, 168;
concept of human sociability in
47–8, 168; concept of nationhood
in 69, 131–3, 133–7; concept of
universalism in 42, 48–53, 68,
69, 79, 133, 135, 153, 154, 268;
contrast with nineteenth-century
philosophy 54–5, 86–90, 136–40;
contrast with the discourse of
culture 152–4, 157–60, 161,
162–3, 164–9; contrast with
pre-Enlightenment outlook 45;
critique of as a Western
philosophy 213; degradation of
69, 71–3, 75–9, 86–90, 103, 130–3,
140, 142, 152, 153–4, 156, 160,
163, 245–6, 266–7; and
humanism 160–1, 237; and
nationalism 69–70, 266; and
race 40, 51–5, 69; reification of
categories of 41–2, 266–7; and
Romanticism as contradictory
aspects of Western philosophy
265–8; transformative content of
154, 268
Environmentalism 238
Enzensberger, Hans Magnus 261
Epistemological constants, critique
of 223–6
Epistemology, poststructuralist

critique of 220–4, 226, 227–8,
232–5
Equality 42, 49–51, 53–5, 89–90,
93–4, 109, 110, 242; ambivalence
about 38–9, 102–3, 104–9, 135–7,
156–60, 170, 235; as both
universal and historically
specific 256; and capitalism
57–60, 63–70, 102–3;
contradictory nature of 38–9,
59–61, 102–3, 135–7, 160, 203,
245–6, 265–8; and cultural
anthropology 151–2, 156–60;
and the discourse of race 39,
69–70; and the Enlightenment
42, 49–51, 53–5, 68–9, 152; failure
of the struggle for 180, 261–5;
and the French Revolution 57–8,
68–9, 110; hostility to 63–4,
69–70, 74–5, 167–9, 238; as
oppression 261–2;
poststructuralist critique of 235,
258–9; as premised on existence
of a human essence 258–9; and
private property 59–61, 63–9,
98; redefinition of 261–5; as
separation 261–2, 264–5; and
social change 261, 264–5; as
socially constructed 39, 256,
258; social meaning of 38–9
Eskimos *see* Inuit
*Essay Concerning Human
Understanding* (Locke) 46
Essay on Man (Pope) 43, 75
Essays on the Inequality of the Races
(Gobineau) 83–4, 89, 168
Essentialism 247–8, 251 (*see also*
Anti-essentialism)
Ethnic cleansing 1, 10, 170
Ethnic group, as an alternative term
for race 125, 126, 174
Ethnicity 134, 174–7; as bridge
between race and culture 176–7;
creation of new ethnicities 217;
and culture 174–7; and
post-Cold War era 180, 260–1;
and race 174–7; as a Third
World phenomenon 213–15, 261
Ethnological Society (of London) 89,
96
Eugenics 99, 102, 112–14, 123, 157,
208

Eugenics Education Society 109
Euripedes 228
Euroasiatic type 125
Europe 119, 123, 173, 191, 228, 229, 231, 232, 238
European culture 240–7
European identity, the making of 228–9, 232, 238–9
Europeans 79, 81, 99, 111, 115, 125, 198, 238–9
Evolution 72, 90, 101, 158, 166; and society 87, 88–90, 99, 105, 106–7, 153, 159–60, 161, 166, 170
Eyre, Governor Edward John 97–8

Fabian, Johannes 81
Fabians, the 102, 105
Faces of Degeneration (Pick) 81, 82, 85, 109, 110
Facial angle 88
Facts, interpretation of 254–7
Failure of European revolutionary movements 240, 246
Falklands War 184
Fanon, Frantz 172, 238
Far right 9–10, 29, 196 (*see also* Fascism; Nazism)
Fascism 9–10, 13, 14, 31, 37, 124, 170, 238; Frankfurt school analysis of 240–1, 243–4; poststructuralist analysis of 241–2, 245–7
Fear of change 72, 85–6, 90, 102–3, 109, 262–4, 266
Fear of the masses 85, 90, 98, 104–14, 116–17, 238, 266
Feudalism 84; and the Enlightenment 55–7; difference between England and Europe 55–7 (*see also* premodernism)
Feuerbach, Ludwig 237
Final Solution, The 103, 241, 242
Fin de siècle 104, 106
First Man, the 215
First World War 123, 147
Fisher, Ronald 112, 113
Fitness: Darwinian concept of 91; in social Darwinist theory 91, 112–14
Flaubert, Gustav 106
Flight International 128
FLN (Algerian) 194

Folie et Deraison (Foucault) 221
Foreign Affairs 210
Foreigner, construction of the concept of 136–7, 140
Foreign Policy 210
Foucauld, Pierre de 194
Foucault, Michel 219, 221, 233–4, 238, 258, 262
Fox-Genovese, Elizabeth 180
France 9, 12, 114; and anti-Semitism 33; belief in science in nineteenth century 84; and Catholicism 196–7; contradictions of race relations policy 28–9; contrast of race relations policies in France and Britain 26, 28–9, 190–1; debate on Islam in 194–7; and immigration policy 27–8, 177, 197–8; impact of immigration on 26–9, 173; making of the nation 80–1, 138–40; perceptions of racial decline of 110–11; and race relations policy 26, 28–9; preference for European immigrants 28, 197; racism and collapse of postwar consensus in 33, 195–6; rewriting immigration history of 35; secularism in 196–7
Franco-Prussian War 85, 110
Frankfurt School 240–1, 243–4
French language 139
French national identity 80–1, 138–40, 144–5; and assimilation 193–4, 196–7; and Enlightenment discourse 133, 139, 193–4, 196, 198; and citizenship 130–3, 138–40, 141–3, 144–5, 190, 195–8; and the conflict between universalism and particularism 193; and the French Revolution 193, 194; impact of immigration on 173, 194–8; and Islam 194–8; and national decline 194, 195; and pluralism 193, 195–6; in post-Cold War era 194; and secularism 196–7; and social crisis 194
French Nationality Code 197
Frenchness 236 (*see also* French national identity)

French Revolution 57–9, 60, 74, 110, 133, 255, 256; backlash against 58–9, 72, 73–5, 83–4, 85, 109, 110, 154; as embodiment of Enlightenment ideology 57–8, 68–9, 133, 268; as expression of disorder 58, 109; mobilisation of the masses in 58, 68–9; and the National Convention 67–8; and national identity 194; and slavery 66–8

French West Indies 57
Freud, Sigmund 104, 107, 178
Front National (French) 209
Fryer, Peter 62, 81
Fuchs, Lawrence 180
Fukuyama, Francis 215
Functional anthropology 156
Functionalism 155–6, 160, 171
Furedi, Frank 14
Furnivall, J. S. 170–1, 172–3
Future of Science, The (Renan) 141

Galileo Galilei 178
Gall, Johann Franz 87
Galton, Francis 99, 113, 114
Galton Society (American) 57, 158
Gardner, Joy 38
Gasset, Jose Ortega y 106
Gates, Henry Louis 178
Geddes, Patrick 114
Geertz, Clifford 236
Gellner, Ernest 146
Germanic type 120
Germanness 230
Germany 9, 10, 31, 114, 115, 123, 151, 173, 190, 191, 240
Genetics 4–5, 126, 166
Gershwin, George and Ira 255
Gibbon, Lord 63–4
Giddens, Anthony 174, 175, 176
Gilroy, Paul 187, 191, 192
Girondins 66, 67
Giscard d'Estaing, Valéry 27, 195
Glazer, Nathan 174
Gobineau, Count Arthur 83–4, 89, 156, 162, 168, 229
Gobinistes 187
Goldberg, David 40–2, 68, 221, 231, 232, 241, 258
Gould, Stephen Jay 122
Goutte d'Or, la 33

Governor Eyre controversy *see* Eyre, Governor Edward John
Grand narratives 218
Great Chain of Being 43, 89, 91
Great Depression (1880s) 104
Great Society, the (US) 201, 204
Greg, William 87
Gumplowicz, Ludwig 86, 120, 121

Haddon, A. C. 125–6, 174
Haitian Revolution 67–8
Haldane, J. B. S. 113
Hall, Stuart 217, 220, 221, 264
Hampson, Norman 46
Handlin, Oscar 1
Hard Times (Dickens) 254
Hardy, Thomas 65
Harrington, Michael 201
Harvey, David 218–9
Hattersley, Roy 18
Headform 120, 152, 157, 254, 258
Headscarves affair *see* l'Affair foulard
Heartfield, James 245
Hegel, Georg 215, 268
Heidegger, Martin 237, 238, 244–5, 249
Henri-Lévy, Bernard 196
Herbert, Sir Thomas 43–4
Herder, Johann Gottfried von 78–9, 139, 144
Herrnstein, Richard *see* Murray, Charles, and Richard Herrnstein; *Bell Curve, The*
Hierarchy, explanations of 69–70, 74–5, 80, 82, 88, 89, 91, 93–4, 95, 96, 98, 99–100, 102, 106–9, 113, 116, 117, 119, 121, 160
Himmelfarb, Gertrude 95, 104–5
Hiroshima, atomic bombing of 211
Historical humanism 237
Historical specificity 78, 224, 248, 256–7, 267, 268; reconciling specificity and universalism 265, 267–68
Historicism 160
History 109, 127; as biology 86, 88–9, 90–1, 99–100, 159–60, 186; critique of universal conceptions of 253–6; distinction between historical and posthistorical worlds 215; national 139–40,

141–4, 180, 184–5, 186, 187; as
racial struggle 83–4, 117, 168;
the rewriting of 140, 192–3;
plural conceptions of 253–6;
teleological view of 87, 90, 127,
158–60, 186, 232
History of Jamaica (Long) 62
Hitler, Adolf 84, 124, 191, 243
Hobbes, Thomas 215
Hobhouse, Leonard 114, 116
Hobsbawm, Eric 42, 56, 116, 134,
137, 139–40, 147
Hobson, J. A. 114, 116
Hofstede, Geert 128
Hogben, Lancelot 2, 5
Holocaust, the 253; and impact on
perceptions of race 13–5, 33,
124, 211; as product of
civilisation 241–7; as product of
the Enlightenment 241–7; as
product of modernity 241–7
Homer-Dixon, Thomas Fraser 215
Honeyford, Ray 186
hooks, bell 261, 264–5
Hopkinson, Harry 21
Horkheimer, Max 240–1, 248
Hughes, H. Stuart 243, 246
Hulme, Peter 222
Human beings: continuity between
human and social world 87, 88,
89, 90–1; as creative beings
153–4, 237; as determined by
culture 78–9, 160–3, 164–6, 177,
185–7; as irrational beings 74–5,
154, 163; as rational beings 46–8,
153, 154, 237; as social beings
47–8, 52, 87, 237, 258-9, 266
Human consciousness 224
Human emancipation 42, 68–9, 237,
240, 241
Human essence 237, 247, 258–9
Humanism 89, 160–1, 236–7, 239–40;
as source of barbarism 238–9,
240–2
Human nature 87, 102, 106–7, 163,
164–6, 185–7, 237, 239, 247, 258
Human subjectivity, denial of 163,
164–6, 186, 247, 251
Humboldt, Alexander von 49
Humboldt, Wilhelm von 48
Hume, David 47, 48, 53, 56, 76, 237
Huntingdon, Samuel 210

Hunt, James 89, 96
Husserl, Edmund 221
Hutcheson, Francis 64
Hutus 214
Huxley, Aldous 107–8, 112, 113
Huxley, Julian 114, 124–6, 174
Huxley, Thomas 54–5, 89, 90, 96, 124

Idealism 230–7, 250–1
Idea of Poverty, The (Himmelfarb) 95,
104–5
Identity: ahistoricism of theories of
184, 224–6, 227–30; as choice
251–3; as created through
difference 78–9, 222–4, 227–8;
multiple 247, 251; as socially
created 247
Illiberal Education (D'Souza) 178
Imagined communities 252
Immigrants: and a contradictory
sense of belonging 177, 185–6,
195–6; national identity
measured against 34–6, 185,
195–7
Immigration 19, 23–4, 118–19; to
America 96; discussed through
the language of war 185; impact
of on postwar Europe 173;
Islamic 36; and national
decline 183, 185; rewriting
history of 34–6; role of in
contemporary discourse 34–6,
183–4, 185; as a social problem
19–20, 22, 25, 28, 30–1, 96, 126,
181, 185–6
Immigration controls: Australian
118; British 18–25, 189;
Canadian 118; economic
arguments for 23–5, 27–8;
French 27; link with race
relations laws 18, 24–5, 28–9;
racist nature of 21, 23, 24, 190
Immigration et 7e Plan (French) 27
Imperial ideal 211, 212
Imperialism 85, 90, 115–16, 117,
118–19, 123, 234–5, 238; as source
of popular legitimacy 115–16
Imperialist expansion 103, 114–15
Inalienable rights *see* Natural rights
Indeterminacy 248, 249–50
India 115, 118, 213
Indirect rule (in Africa) 171

Indonesia 170
Industrial Revolution 55, 109
Inequality 116, 242; *in capitalist society
as root of the idea of race* 69–70,
71, 82, 83–4, 98, 102–3, 160,
202–3, 265–7; *in
conservative/Romantic thought*
74–5, 83–4, 107; *and the culture
concept* 159–60, 167–9, 170, 171,
172, 202–3; *as essence of humanity*
168, 207–8; *historical specificity of*
256; *in liberal thought* 107–9,
117, 201–2, 207–9, 245–6; *as
natural* 88–9, 90–91, 93–5, 96,
98, 99–100, 107–14, 172, 203,
206–8, 245; *in the
pre-Enlightenment world* 43–5;
Rousseau's two sorts of 59–60, 71;
in poststructuralist discourse
258–9
Inferno, The (Dante) 106, 178
Inner voice, the 75–6, 77
Instinct 88, 106, 107, 108, 113, 161
Integration 24–5
Intellectual movements, relationship
with socioeconomic
developments 41–2
Intellectuals and the Masses, The
(Carey) 106, 113
International Affairs 210
International Air Transport
Association 128
International Institute of African
Languages and Cultures 171
Intuitionism 102
Inuit, the 151, 166
IQ 206–8, 254
Iran 243
Iraq 213, 243
Ireland 172, 224, 253
Isaacs, Jeffrey 262–3
Islam: demonisation of 36, 181,
188–9, 212, 213; in French
political discourse 193–8
Italian language 139
Italy 114, 138

J'Accuse (Zola) 144
Jacobins 57, 66, 67, 255
Jamaica 97, 185
Jamaica Committee 98
James, C. L. R. 67–8, 224

Japan 15, 115, 118–19, 123, 211
Jenkins, Roy 23, 169
Jews 2, 125, 144, 176, 45, 252
Jim Crow laws 17
Jingoism 116
Johnson, Lyndon B. 201, 204
Johnson, Paul 31, 37
Johnson, Samuel 134
Jones, Greta 102
Jones, Steve 4, 166
Joseph, Sir Keith 190, 202
Jospin, Leonid 209
Judeo-Christian civilisation 242 (*see
also* Christianity)
Jus soli, principle of 197

Kallen, Horace 173
Kantianism 145
Kant, Immanuel 47, 76, 77, 103,
132
Kaplan, David 213, 215
Katz, Michael 199, 201
Katznelson, Ira 18
Keneally, Thomas 260
Kennedy, John F. 169
Kennedy, Michael 66
Kenyan Asians 24
Keynes, John Maynard 114
Kidd, Benjamin 86
Kiernan, V. G. 98
Kilroy-Silk, Robert 187–8
Kipling, Rudyard 115, 211, 215
Kirk, Neville 250
Kirmess, C. H. 119
Knowles, Caroline 263
Knox, Robert 89, 90, 229, 258
Koran, the 188
Kroeber, Alfred 161–2, 164
Kuklick, Henrika 99

Labour Party (British) 205; attitude
to race 19–20, 21, 22, 23–4;
policies in government 19–20,
21, 24
Lacan, Jacques 219, 221
Lahontan, Baron 49
Laissez-faire policies, critique of
13–14, 112
Lamarckism 158–60, 161
Lamarck, Jean-Baptiste 158, 159
Language: and culture 171, 181;
national 78–9, 134, 139–40; and

race 141; as articulating social forms 250-1

Larkin, Philip 18-9

Laski, Harold 102, 112

Last Man, the 215

Laufer, Berthold 162

Laughlin, Harold 114

Lawrence, D. H. 113, 114

League of Nations 15

Lebon, Gustav 99, 106-7, 143, 144, 146, 157, 161, 162

Le Figaro 194

Legal definitions of race 3

Le Monde 241

Lenin, V. I., 16

Le Pen, Jean-Marie 192, 196

Levinas, Emmanual 234-5

Lévi-Strauss, Claude 150, 162, 163-9, 219, 221, 223, 240, 241, 250, 253-6, 258

Lewis, Oscar 201

Liberal hour, the 18, 19-25

Liberalism 102, 103; and ambivalence about equality 59-60, 63-4, 89-90, 93-4, 96-7, 102, 103, 107-9, 208-9, 245-6; and antihumanism 238-47; crisis of 103-5, 245-6; and democracy 114, 117; and fear of social change 85-6, 90; and humanism 237; and imperialism 116-17, 171; and nationalism 116-17, 135, 266; and race 96-7, 99-100, 101, 102, 116, 117, 125; and poverty 201-2; and social Darwinism 101-2; and the underclass 208-9; and the working class 85, 90, 104-5, 107-9, 112-14, 116-17

Lind, William 210

Linguistic races 141

Lion and the Unicorn, The (Orwell) 191

Livingstone, David 115

Lochak, Daniel 140

Locke, John 46, 47, 75, 76

London Corresponding Society 65

London Labour and the London Poor (Mayhew) 94-5, 200

Long, Edward 62

Long, Maurice 26

Lorrimer, Douglas 91-2, 98

Losing Ground (Murray) 205, 208, 209

Lower orders *see* Masses

Lowie, Robert 162, 163

Lugard, Lord 97

Lukács, Georg 237, 257, 267

Lyotard, Jean-François 262

MacDougal, William 114

Macmillan, Harold 14

Mafeking 116

Mafficking 116

Maistre, Joseph-Marie de 74, 237, 266

Man, critique of humanist concept of 238, 240, 242, 266

Manilowski, Bronislaw 155-6

Manning, Bernard 143-4

Mansfield, Lord 63

Marcuse, Herbert 218

Marginality 264

Marshall, Alfred 112, 114

Marshall, George C. 16

Marxism 219, 237, 251, 254; as a grand narrative 218

Marx, Karl 72, 90, 109, 154, 224, 228, 237, 246, 258; reconciling the universal and the particular 268

Mass democracy *see* Democracy

Massenet, Maurice 27

Masses, the 57-8, 67-8, 82, 93-5, 115-6, 119, 138; fear of 85-6, 90, 98, 104-14, 116-17, 238

Mass society 116, 241, 243-4

Masterman, C. F. 106

Mastery of nature as root of human barbarism 241

Mau Mau rebellion 212

Maurras, Charles 141

May 1968, revolts of 246

Mayhew, Henry 94-5, 97, 200

Mazzini, Giuseppe 116

Mead, Margaret 162

Meaning (in poststructuralist discourse) 249-51

Mediterranean: immigration from 96, 125, 157; type 125, 157

Melting pot 179

Melville, Herman 224

Mercer, Kobena 218, 251

Mercer, Shamira 263

Meyerson, Adam 180-1

Michelet, Jules 138, 139, 144, 147

Middle classes 93, 113; and the Enlightenment 55-7; and

Middle classes *cont.*
  eugenics 113–14 (*see also*
    Capitalist class; Élite, the)
Miles, Robert 3, 5, 54
Millar, John 64
Miller, Christopher 235–6
Mill, John Stuart 94, 134
Mind of Primitive Man, The (Boas)
  152, 157
Miscegenation 81, 83, 124, 157, 168;
  parallels with cultural mixing
  168–9
Mitterrand, François 194, 195
Mob, the 86, 106, 188; fear of 86, 90,
  98, 106–9,
Moby Dick (Melville) 224
'Model Eugenical Sterilisation Law'
  (US) 114
Modernism, relationship between
  elitism and 106
Modernity 40, 90; disillusionment
  with 152, 153, 156, 246; and
  race 41; postmodern critique of
  40–1, 241–7; as source of
  barbarism 241–7; two meanings
  of 41, 246–7
Mongolian type 120, 157
Mongrel race 168
Montesquieu, Charles de Secondat
  45, 62, 80, 266
Morel, Augustin Benedict 110, 111
Morris, James 118
Morris, Lydia 198–9
Morrison, Toni 183
Mosca, Gaetano 108–9
Mosley, Oswald 23
Mosse, George 40
Moynihan, Daniel 174, 204
Mulatto 124
Mulgan, Geoff 9
Multiculturalism 130, 145, 149–50,
  170–7, 180; ambiguity of 182; as
  basis of American identity
  179–80; as basis of British
  identity 191–3; conservative
  hostility to 186; conservative
  support for 190; and crisis of
  national identity 180–1, 183;
  and national decline 180–1;
  official support for 190; and
  Romanticism 150
Multiethnicity 170, 174, 180

Multiracial society 175, 176–7
Murray, Charles 205, 254; and
  Richard Herrnstein 202–3, 205–9
Murray, Gilbert 117
Muslims 10, 187–9 (*see also* Islam)

Nagasaki *see* Hiroshima, atomic
  bombing of
Nairn, Tom 30
Nana (Zola) 111
Nation, the 77; ambiguity of the
  revolutionary-democratic
  concept of 136–7; as a cultural
  community 77–9 133–40,
  141–4, 185–7; distinction between
  open and closed 136;
  nineteenth-century view of
  137–40, 141–4; as a political
  association 77, 131, 134;
  revolutionary-democratic
  concept of 133–7; Romantic
  view of 77–9, 130–3, 186–7 (*see
  also* National identity;
  Nationalism; Nation-state, the)
National Front (British) 191–2
National Front (French) *see* Front
  National
National identity: contrast between
  eighteenth- and nineteenth-
  century conceptions of 136–40;
  as embodiment of difference
  138–40, 141–4, 186, 195–7; and
  imperialism 115–6; nineteenth-
  century conceptions of 137–40
  141–4; problems of in post-Cold
  War era 34, 179–81, 183–4, 193,
  194, 195; remaking in opposition
  to immigration 34–6, 185–7,
  193–4, 196–8; remaking in
  opposition to the Third World
  36–7; use of pluralism as a
  language of 191–3, 195–7
Nationalism 85, 90, 116, 123, 137; and
  conflict with universalism 69–70,
  136; as a grand narrative 218
Nationality Commission (French)
  195, 197
Nation-state, the 137–40
Native cultures 171
Naturalisation (of social
  phenomena) 69–70, 71–3, 80–1,
  86–91, 93–6, 99–100, 106–11,

121–2, 127, 138, 150, 163, 202–3, 248, 258–9

Natural rights 38–9, 46–7, 66, 74, 258

Natural selection 90, 166

Natural Varieties of Man, On the (Blumenbach) 5, 87

Nature 126

Nature–nurture controversy 158

Nazis 114, 123, 242, 244–5

Nazism 242; in Britain 191–2; impact on concepts of race 10, 14, 15, 103, 123–7, 143, 174; impact on European radicals 240–6; as a product of civilisation 241–7; as a product of the Enlightenment 218, 240–7; as a product of modernity 241–7; as a product of the mass society 243

Negroes 53, 60, 62, 66, 87, 88, 92, 93, 98, 99, 124–5, 126, 157, 183, 203, 204, 224

Negro Family: The Case for National Action, The (Moynihan) 204

New Republic, The 205–6, 207, 208

New social movements, the 238

Newsweek 213

Newton, Issac 46

Nietzsche, Friedrich 104, 113, 178, 237, 238, 244, 250

Nixon, Richard Millhouse 200

Nordic type 125, 157

North Africans *see* Africans

Notting Hill riots 22–3

Noumenon (Kant) 76

Nouvelle Heloise, La (Rousseau) 75

Objectivity, poststructuralist critique of 232–6

Operation Restore Hope 209

Organicism 74–9, 78–9, 102, 156, 186

Orient, the 81, 83, 227, 228, 230, 231, 232, 233

Orientalism 227–33

Orientalism (Said) 223, 226, 227–30, 255

Origin of Species, The (Darwin) 90, 119, 158, 178

Origin of the Distinction of Ranks, The (Millar) 64

Origins of Totalitarianism, The (Arendt) 243–4

Orwell, George 191

Osborne, Cyril 22, 23

Othello (Shakespeare) 224

Other America, The (Harrington) 201

Other, the concept of the 220–4, 226, 227–30, 231–3, 238, 242; ahistorical nature of 222–6, 227–30; as source of racial difference 221, 238

Pagden, Anthony 44

Page, Robin 187

Paine, Thomas 58, 65, 70, 134, 258

Palestinian people, the 263–4

Pareto, Vilfredo 104, 107

Paris Commune 85, 110, 138

Pascal, Pierre 181

Patten, Chris 190

Patterns of Culture (Benedict) 162–3

Pauperism *see* Poverty

Pearson, Karl 14

People, The (Michelet) 139

Persians, The (Aeschylus) 228

Pessimism *see* Social pessimism

Pfaff, William 244

Phenomenology 219, 221

Phenomenon (Kant) 76

Philosophy of difference 217–19; as rationalisation of defeat 261, 262, 264–5, 268–9

Phrenology 87–8, 100, 101

Pick, Daniel 81, 82, 85, 109, 110

Plato 178

Pluralism 145, 169, 170–7; as acceptance of oppression 263–4; as basis of American identity 179–80; as basis of British identity 191–3; in colonial society 170–2; conservative hostility to 179–82, 185–6; conservative use of the language of 181–2, 186–7; in Western nations 172–7; as acceptable language of race 173; as language of antiracism 174, 176–7; and national decline 180–2, 185; in the post-Cold War era 179–82; and postmodernism 218–19; racists using the language of 196

Plurality of meaning 249–51
Policy Review 181
Political correctness 178
Politicisation of race 7, 24–5, 28–9,
    30–7
Politics of difference *see* Philosophy
    of difference
Polygenism 89, 96
Poor, the 93–5, 104–5, 198–201;
    racialisation of 70, 202–9
Pope, Alexander 43, 75
Popper, Karl 248–9
Population pressure 90–1
Porter G.R. 84
Porter, Roy 73
Positivism 86, 90, 95, 109, 147, 248,
    256, 257–8; breakdown of 103,
    104, 109, 112, 123, 148;
    poststructuralist hostility to 248;
    resemblance to poststructuralist
    methodology 258–9
Post-Cold War era 9–10, 11–13;
    debate about immigration in
    34–6, 183, 185–6; debate about
    Third World in 36–7, 209–16;
    problems of national identity in
    34, 179–82, 183–5, 193, 194, 195
Posthistorical world 215
Postindustrial society 218
Postmodern Condition, The (Lyotard)
    262
Postmodernism 218 (*see also*
    Poststructuralism)
Poststructuralism 164, 221;
    ahistoricism of 222–6, 227–30,
    242, 248; and antihumanism
    236–47, 250, 251, 258; and the
    celebration of oppression 264–5;
    and the concept of identity
    217–19, 247, 251–3; and the
    concept of the Other 220–4, 226,
    227–30; and the concept of
    respect 235; and the concept of
    space 263; and the concept of
    the social 247, 250, 251–2, 253;
    and the critique of
    Enlightenment discourse
    218–19, 220, 221–2, 227–8, 234–5,
    251; and the critique of equality
    235, 261–5; and the critique of
    essentialism 247–59; and the
    critique of modernity 40–2,

241–7; and the critique of
    objectivity 232–6; and the
    critique of positivism 248–9;
    and the critique of rationalism
    218, 240–2; and the critique of
    science 218, 220, 240–2; and the
    critique of totalising theory 218,
    220, 234–5, 253–7; and the
    critique of universalism 218–19,
    220, 253–7; and the critique of
    Western epistemology 220–4,
    226, 227–8; and the discourse of
    race 235–6, 258–9; idealism of
    230–5, 250–1, 252–3; and
    indeterminacy 248–51, 253,
    255–6; and pluralism 218–19;
    and relativism 232–6, 253–7;
    and representation 230–3; and
    the rejection of struggle 262–5;
    and the resemblance to
    naturalistic theories 258–9; and
    Romanticism 228–30, 232
Postwar consensus 10; ambiguous
    attitudes to race of 24–5, 173–4;
    nature of 10; immigration debate
    and the end of 34–6; impact of
    end on national identity 180–2,
    184; reasons for collapse of
    29–30; reasons for creation of
    14; racism and the end of 9–10,
    11–13, 30–7; social impact of the
    end of 9–10, 11–3, 34;
    underclass debate and the end
    of 31–3; and pluralism 169,
    173–4; the end of 36–7
Postwar radicalism 238, 240–7
Poverty 104, 109–10; culture of
    201–2; War on 201 (*see also*
    Poor, the)
Powell, Enoch 143, 181, 183–4, 185,
    186, 192, 193
Power distance 128
Power, poststructuralist concept of
    233–5, 262
Pravda 15–6
Pre-Enlightenment world *see*
    Premodernity
Premodernity 40, 43, 225
Premodern view of Africans 43
Pride and Prejudice (Austen) 70
Primitive races 81, 88, 89, 92, 99, 117,
    147

Pritchard, James 89, 96
Progress 71–3, 84–5, 100, 145, 147;
    critique of 218, 237, 241–2;
    difference between eighteenth-
    and nineteenth-century
    conceptions of 72, 87; fear of
    71–3, 147, 168–9, 237; perception
    of limits to 104–5, 110, 112, 147,
    151–4, 156; positivist conception
    of 87, 88, 89, 90; and race 101;
    as the root of barbarism 218,
    220, 241–2
Progress of the Nation (Porter) 84
Psychological crowd 107
Psychology 106–7, 164
Pym, Commander Bernard 98

Race: and biology 4–5, 80–91, 96,
    111, 112–14, 120–3, 15, 127, 157,
    158, 159–60, 161, 163, 168, 174,
    186–7, 206–8; and capitalism 6,
    69–70, 71–3, 102–3; centrality of
    to Western society 14–15, 37, 71,
    119–20, 121–2, 125; and class 81,
    91–5, 96–8, 99–100, 104–5,
    106–14, 121; comparison between
    impact of First and Second
    World Wars on concepts of 15;
    and the contradictory attitude to
    equality 69–70, 98, 102–3, 156–7,
    202–3; and contradictions of
    Western philosophy 265–9; the
    Cold War and changing concepts
    of 7, 15–17; and the collapse of
    the postwar consensus 30–7;
    and the concept of evolution
    158–60; contrast with
    pre-Enlightenment concepts of
    difference 42, 44–5; and the
    correlation between physical and
    mental characteristics 87–8, 96,
    110; and culture 130–3, 140–4,
    145–8, 151–63, 164–9, 172, 173–7,
    181, 182, 186–7, 196, 198, 202,
    203, 208–9; and degeneration
    71–3, 83–4, 110, 168;
    depoliticisation of 7, 10, 18,
    21–2, 28–9, 189–91; and elite
    theory 81–2, 93–4, 97, 99–100,
    105, 106–9, 116–17, 119; and the
    Enlightenment 6–7, 40–1, 42,
    51–5, 71–3, 80; and eugenics

112–14, 126; failure of
    anti-Nazism to destroy concept
    of 124; failure of the
    categorisation of 120–3, 152;
    and genetics 4–5; and
    imperialism 115–19; and IQ
    206–7; legal definitions of 3; and
    moral attributes 94–5, 96–7,
    106–7, 109–14; and non-
    Europeans 81, 83, 96–100, 111,
    115–16, 117–19; and pluralism
    170, 172, 173–7, 181–2, 186–7,
    196, 198; politicisation of 7,
    24–5, 28–9, 30–7; popular
    conceptions of 2; and
    poststructuralist theory 229–30,
    232; as the product of differences
    within European society 81–4,
    91–6, 99–100, 111, 126; as the
    product of humanism 238–9;
    and Romanticism 77–9, 82–4;
    and slavery 62–3, 69; social
    nature of the definition of 4–6,
    121, 122; and social pessimism
    73, 147–8; and science 15, 84,
    86–91, 100, 101, 106–7, 108–9,
    120–3, 125–7 (*see also* Science;
    Scientific racism); specificity
    of the idea of 224–5; and
    teleological conceptions of
    history 87, 88, 90–1, 99–100,
    147; transcending 268–9; and
    the underclass 31–3
Race relations 22, 23, 28, 189;
    British 3, 17, 18–25, 176–7,
    189–93; contrast between race
    relations policies in Britain and
    France 26, 28–9, 190–1; French
    26, 28–9
Race Relations Acts (British) 3, 18
Race relations legislation (French) 28
Race relations paradigm, the 2–3, 25,
    173
Races of Men, The (Knox) 89
Racial formalism *see* Scientific racism
Racialisation: ambiguity in the
    process of 37; of class
    differences 70, 81–2, 85–6,
    93–6, 99–100, 106–14; of
    immigration 35–6, 118–19,
    173–4; of the poor 70, 93–6,
    202–9; of social

Racialisation *cont.*
    discourse 33–4; of social groups
    252; of the Third World 209–16
Racial markers, plasticity of 120–1,
    152
Racial planning 112
Racial science *see* Scientific racism
Racial Struggle (Gumplowicz) 121
Racism 103; ahistoric understanding
    of 223–6, 229–30, 232; as an
    anti-British ideology 191–3; and
    the collapse of the postwar
    consensus 30–7; as a
    counterpart to humanism
    238–9; as natural 260–1;
    conservative rejection of 186; as
    a deliberate policy 253; as
    expressed through the language
    of pluralism 181–2, 196; as a
    German ideology 191–2; in
    Germany 9, 10, 31; and
    immigration policy 20–2, 23–4,
    34–6, 118–19, 189; as a mass
    force 116, 117, 119; and the
    post-Cold War era 9–10, 13; as
    undermining Western moral
    authority 15–17; and welfare
    policy 33
Radcliffe Brown, Andrew 156
Rattansi, Ali 247
Ravich, Diane 180
Raynal, Abbé 66
Reagan, Ronald 29, 178, 205, 215–16
Recapitulation theory 122
Rectoral Addresses – Facts and Thoughts
    (Heidegger) 245
Regression 72, 73
Relativism 78–9, 130, 142–3, 144–8,
    156, 182, 217–9, 232–6, 255–7;
    two kinds of 146–8 (*see also*
    Cultural relativism; Value
    relativism)
Renaissance, the 160, 220, 228, 237
Renan, Ernest 130–3, 134, 140, 144,
    147, 156, 186, 229
Reprimitivised man 214
Republican Party (US) 12, 179, 181
Residuum, the 95, 96
Retreat of Scientific Racism, The
    (Barkan) 121, 122, 123, 125, 157
Revolt of the Masses, The (Gasset) 106
Revolutions of 1848 85, 138

Rex, John 175
Rhodes, Cecil 98, 116
Ridley, Nicholas 192
Rights of Man 57, 65, 67, 68, 69, 134,
    266
Right to be different, the 261–2
Right to be the same, the 261
Ripley, William 4, 96, 119
Ritual, importance of for society
    74–5, 154–6
Robespierre, Maximilien 67
Rogers, George 22
Romanes, G. J. 159
Romanticism 72, 73–9, 82–4, 85, 130,
    151, 229, 232, 266; and the
    Enlightenment as contradictory
    aspects of Western philosophy
    265–9; and nationhood 76–9,
    131–3, 136–7
Roosevelt, Theodore 14, 114, 117, 119
Rorty, Richard 235
Rosebery, Lord 115
Rostock (Germay) 31
Rothermere, Lord 123
Rougon-Macquart novels (Zola) 106,
    110, 111
Rousseau, Jean-Jacques 47, 69, 74,
    76, 77, 78, 103, 109, 132, 133, 136,
    139, 142; contrast with Adam
    Smith 59–61; on equality
    49–51, 59–61, 258; on
    nationalism 69, 266; reconciling
    the universal and the particular
    267–8; on two sorts of
    inequality 59–60, 70, 71
Royal Commission on the British
    Population 20
Rubinstein, Richard 241–2
Ruling class *see* Capitalist class;
    Élite, the
Rushdie affair, the 187–9
Rushdie, Salman 181, 187, 230, 231
Russia 123, 211
Rwanda 170, 214

Sacred Cows (Weldon) 188
Said, Edward W 81, 220, 223–4, 226,
    227–33, 255, 263
Saint-Domingue 57, 58, 67–8
Salles, Eusebé de 82
Sans-culottes 58, 67, 68, 85
Sarajevo 170

Sartre, Jean-Paul 221, 238, 245, 253–4, 258
Satanic Verses, The 181, 187, 231 (*see also* Rushdie, Salman; Rushdie affair, the)
Saturday Review 93–4, 97
Saussure, Frederick 249, 250
Schelling, Friederich 74, 132
Schindler's Ark (Keneally) 260
Schindler's List (Spielberg) 260
Schlessinger, Arthur 179, 260–1
Science 86, 90, 106, 112, 153; and antiracism 15, 122–3, 125–7; belief in 84–5; as guarantor of social order 86; 'of Man' 87–8; as legitimator of political ideas 121–2, 242; poststructuralist critique of 218, 220; as the source of barbarism 218, 220, 241; subordination of to ideology 121–2, 242
Science 156–7
Scientific racism 84, 86–91, 96, 100, 106–9, 110, 111, 112–14, 119–23, 157–8, 159–60, 163, 166, 208, 242; demise of 122–7, 159–60; and social reform 101–2, 112–14, 158–9
Scramble for Africa 85, 224
Scruton, Roger 186
Second World War 12, 14, 15, 124, 191–2, 193, 211, 260
Semmel, Bernard 97
Shakespeare, William 224
Shame (Rushdie) 230
Sharpe, Granville 63
Shelley, Percy Bysshe 74
Sherman, Sir Alfred 186, 193
Sherrington, Charles 113
Signification 5, 224
Signified and signifier (in poststructuralist theory) 249–50
Sign, the (in poststructuralist theory) 249
Silverman, Maxim 35, 132–3, 136, 177, 193, 196
Sims, George 104
Sixties, the 23–5, 32, 33, 185
Skin colour 82, 91–4, 96–100, 111, 117–19, 254
Slave rebellions 67–8
Slavery 61–9; absence of racial arguments for 62–3; British debate about 63–6; debate about relationship of factory system to 92–4; French debate about 61, 62–3, 66–9; liberal ambivalence about 64, 68–9; impact on African-American culture 203–5; opponents of private property as most consistent opponents of 64–5, 68–9; and private property 63–5, 66–8; radical opposition to 64–6, 67–9
Smellie, William 88
Smelting pot 179
Smith, Adam 59, 64, 70, 75; contrast with Rousseau 59–61
Smith, M. G. 174–5
Social Contract, The (Rousseau) 49, 77
Social Darwinism 90–1, 101, 102
Social Darwinism and English Thought (Jones) 102
Social evolutionism 87–9, 90–1, 99–100, 103, 105, 106, 123, 127, 135, 147, 153, 156, 158–60, 170
Social fragmentation 180, 217–19; postmodern celebration of 218–19
Social pessimism 72–3, 85–6, 104–5, 109–14, 123, 130, 147, 151–2, 153–4, 156, 245–6, 261, 263–5
Social, poststructuralist concept of the 247, 250, 251–2, 253
Societal Cold War 36, 210
Société des Observateurs de l'Homme 51
Society: conservative/Romantic conception of 74–9, 186–7; and cultural anthropology 154–6, 162–3, 167–9; Durkheim's conception of 154–6; liberal conception of 75; pluralist view of 167–9, 170–7, 217–19; poststructuralist view of 251–2, 253; Rousseau's view of 267
Somalia 209–10, 213
Sonthonax, Légér Félicité 67
SOS Racisme 196
Southall, Adam 171–2
Soviet Union 16, 211
Spanish Civil War 170
Spearman, Charles 114
Species 80, 90–1

Spectator (British) 16–17, 24
Spencer, Herbert 90, 146
Spielberg, Stephen 260
Spirit of the Laws (Montesquieu) 45–6
Spivak, Gayatri Chakravorty 235
Spurzheim, Johann 88, 100
Standard of significance 256
Stanford University 178–9
Star Trek 171
State intervention 13–4, 102, 112–14, 137, 201, 202
State, making of the modern 137
Staying Power (Fryer) 62, 81
Stedman Jones, Gareth 250
Stepan, Nancy 87, 119–20, 121–2
Stephens, Leslie 102
Stillman, Edmund 244
Stocking, George 6, 52, 120, 147, 151, 154, 159–60
Stowe, Harriet Beecher 92
Street-folk 95
Structural anthropology 163
Structuralism 160, 219, 249
Subjectivity, denial of 163, 164–6, 186, 247, 251
Subspecies 125
Superorganic, the 161–2
Survival of the fittest 90, 91
Swann report (on British education) 176–7, 189–90

Taguieff, Pierre 198
Taine, Hippolyte 85–6, 110, 142–3
Tangle of pathology (Daniel Moynihan's thesis) 204–5
Tarcov, Nathan 47
Tebbit, Norman 34–5, 185, 189, 190, 192
Teich, Mikulas 73
Teleology 87, 88, 90–1, 99–100, 127, 147, 186
Tennyson, Alfred Lord 73, 84–5
Thatcher, Margaret 29, 184, 186, 189, 205
Theses on Feuerbach (Marx) 237, 258
Thierry, Augustin 80–1
Third Reich, the 103, 242
Third World, the 16; impact of Cold War on 211–12; liberation movements 246, 261; nationalism 123, 211, 212; perceptions of in the post-Cold War era 36–7, 209–10, 212–16; post-Cold War relationship with the West 209–10, 212–16; postwar relationship with the West 211–12; perception of as premodern 213–15; prewar relationship with the West 210–11; racialisation of 36–7, 117, 209–10, 213–16
Thompson, E. P. 251
Time 199
Times, The 24, 118
Tocqueville, Alexis de 61
Todorov, Tzvetan 54, 133, 136, 141, 143, 144, 168, 169, 242
Totalising theory 256–7; poststructuralist critique of 218, 220, 234–5, 244, 253–7 (*see also* Universalism)
Totalitarianism, theory of 240, 243–4; and racial theory 244
Totality 257, 267
Toussaint L'Ouverture, François Dominique 57, 67
Tradition, importance of for society 74–5, 78–9, 154–6, 186
Transcendental anatomy 89
Transracial adoption 149–50
Tribalism 213–14, 260
Tribes 171–2
Truman, Harry S. 17
Tutsis 214
Tylor, E. B. 142, 153, 266

Uganda 171–2
Uncle Tom's Cabin (Stowe) 92
Underclass, the 31–3, 198–209; as alien 32, 198–201; in Britain 205; contrast with Victorian discussion on residuum 200–1; and the culture of poverty 201–5; definition of 198–200; and liberals 208–9; as morally different 198–200, 204, 205, 208–9; as a natural phenomenon 202–3, 206–8; parallels with immigration debate 199
Unesco 15
United Nations 14, 15, 209
Universalism 42, 48–53, 68, 69, 132, 133, 134, 135, 142, 153, 237, 240, 267, 268; conflict between

particularism and 69, 75, 135–6, 265–9; hostility to 78–9, 83–4, 130, 139, 142–8, 160, 164–9, 238; postmodern critique of 218–19, 220–6, 234–6, 253–7; reconciling universalism and particularism 265, 267–8

Universal Rights of Man *see* Rights of Man

Utilitarianism 75, 266

Value relativism 78, 79, 144–8, 154–6, 167, 169, 182, 232–6, 255–7

Values, incommensurability of 78, 79, 144–8, 167, 233–6, 255–7, 266

Virey, Julien-Joseph 80

Volk 78

Volksgeist 78, 79, 144

Voltaire 47, 53, 54, 178

Wallace, Alfred Russell 101

Wallace, George 64

Wallas, Graham 114, 116

Wallman, Sandra 174, 176

Wall Street Journal 209–10

War on Poverty 201

Waste Land, The (Eliot) 106

Waugh, Auberon 24

Wealth of Nations, The (Smith) 59, 64, 75

Webb, Beatrice 105, 107, 116

Webbs, the 102

Weber, Eugen 81–2

Weber, Max 103

Weekes, Jeffrey 251

We Europeans (Huxley and Haddon) 125–6, 174

Weldon, Fay 188

Welfare: association with blacks 33, 204; and the underclass 31–3, 199, 202, 205

West, the 117, 123; claims for moral superiority of 36–7, 115, 209–10, 211; and Cold War relationship with the Third World 211–12; and post-Cold War relationship with the Third World 209–10, 212–16; and postwar sensitivity about race 15–17; prewar relationship with the Third World 210

West and its Others, discourse of 81, 220–6, 234–6; ahistoricism of 222–6; as implicit in Enlightenment categories 221–2

Western civilisation: concept of in Said's work 228–9; Stanford University course on 178; as Romantic fabrication 229

Western identity: poststructuralist theories of its construction 238–9; problems for in post-Cold War era 34–7, 179–81; remaking of in opposition to immigrants 34–6, 185, 195–7; remaking of in contrast to the Third World 36–7, 209–16

West Indian 143, 176, 186

'What is a Nation?' (Renan) 130–3, 140

What is History? (Carr) 254, 255–6

Whethams, W. E. D and C. D. 96

White Australia policy 118, 119

White Canada policy 118, 119

White consensus, the 123

White, Leslie 162, 163

White Man's Burden, the 37, 115, 211

Wordsworth, William 74

Working class 85, 86, 93–5, 96–100, 104, 107–9, 110–14, 115–16, 117, 119, 126, 137, 246

Wretched of the Earth, The (Fanon) 238

Wright, Ian 192

Yellow Peril, the 118

Yinger, Milton 175, 176

Young, Robert 230, 235, 239, 255, 256

Zeitlin, Irving 45, 46, 77

Zola, Emile 106, 110, 111, 144